skin for skin

Narrating Native Histories

Narrating Native Histories aims to foster a rethinking of the ethical, methodological, and conceptual frameworks within which we locate our work on Native histories and cultures. We seek to create a space for effective and ongoing conversations between North and South, Natives and non-Natives, academics and activists, throughout the Americas and the Pacific region. This series encourages analyses that contribute to an understanding of Native peoples' relationships with nation-states, including histories of expropriation and exclusion as well as projects for autonomy and sovereignty. We encourage collaborative work that recognizes Native intellectuals, cultural interpreters, and alternative knowledge producers, as well as projects that question the relationship between orality and literacy.

skin for skin

DEATH AND LIFE FOR INUIT AND INNU

GERALD M. SIDER

Duke University Press   Durham and London   2014

Designed by Heather Hensley
Typeset in Arno Pro by Copperline Book Services, Inc.

Library of Congress Cataloging-in-Publication Data
Sider, Gerald M.
Skin for skin : death and life for Inuit and Innu / Gerald M. Sider.
pages cm—(Narrating Native histories)
Includes bibliographical references and index.
ISBN 978-0-8223-5521-2 (cloth : alk. paper)
ISBN 978-0-8223-5536-6 (pbk. : alk. paper)
1. Naskapi Indians—Newfoundland and Labrador—Labrador—
Social conditions. 2. Inuit—Newfoundland and Labrador—
Labrador—Social conditions. 3. Naskapi Indians—Health and
hygiene—Newfoundland and Labrador—Labrador. 4. Inuit—Health
and hygiene—Newfoundland and Labrador—Labrador. I. Title.
II. Series: Narrating Native histories.
E78.L3S53 2014
362.84'97107182—dc23   2013026390

Cover art: Conte drawing of Sedna by the Labrador Inuit
(Nunatsiavummiut) artist Heather Igloliorte.

For Francine Egger-Sider
il miglior fabbro—the better maker

The Latin motto on the Hudson's Bay Company coat of arms is PRO PELLE CUTEM, which translates roughly as "a skin for a skin."

—Explanation posted on the Hudson's Bay Company's Internet site. The company traded for furs with the Native peoples of Canada from 1670 to the mid-twentieth century. This was their motto from the mid-1670s to 2002.

And the Lord said unto Satan, Hast thou considered my servant Job, that there is none like him in the earth, a perfect and an upright man . . . still he holds fast his integrity, although thou movest me against him, to destroy him without cause.

And Satan answered the Lord, and said, Skin for skin, yea, all that a man hath will he give for his life. But put forth thine hand now, [Satan continued] and touch his bone and his flesh, and he will curse thee to thy face. And the LORD said unto Satan, Behold, he is in thine hand; but save his life. So went Satan forth from the presence of the Lord, and smote Job.

—Job 2:3–7 King James Version

I have made it my study to examine the nature and character of the Indians and however repugnant it may be to our feelings, I am convinced that they must be ruled with a rod of iron to bring, and to keep them in a proper state of subordination.

—George Simpson, governor in chief of Rupert's Land and the Hudson's Bay Company in what is now Canada, 1821–1860, in 1825

CONTENTS

Preface xi

Acknowledgments xvii

ONE **Historical Violence** 1

TWO **Owning Death and Life** 25
Making "Indians" and "Eskimos" from Native Peoples

THREE **Living within and against**
Tradition, 1800–1920 59

FOUR **The Peoples without a Country** 107

FIVE **Mapping Dignity** 145

SIX **Life in a Concentration Village** 163

SEVEN **Today May Become Tomorrow** 209

EIGHT **Warriors of Wisdom** 235

Notes 251   References 271   Index 283

Gallery appears after page 154

Labrador is the northeasternmost part of mainland Canada—a stretch of rocky and rough land along the north Atlantic coast. It has long been the homeland of two Native peoples, the Inuit and the Innu, who are a branch of the Cree Indian peoples. Starting in the late 1960s and intensifying relentlessly since then, both Native peoples have been experiencing interwoven epidemics of substance abuse—mostly gasoline sniffing and alcohol—plus youth suicide, domestic violence, and high rates of children born damaged because their mothers drank alcohol while pregnant.

During the fall semester of 2001 I was living with my family in St. John's, Newfoundland, doing research on the declining Newfoundland fishery. Labrador is part of the Canadian province of Newfoundland and Labrador, and the Newfoundland media were then full of reports both about these epidemics and about the mostly ineffective measures that Newfoundland and Canada, who had shared responsibility, were taking in their attempts to help.

By 2001 I had been working on the historical anthropology of Newfoundland fishing villages for three decades. As a great many fishers from northern Newfoundland had been going, seasonally, to fish from the Labrador coasts, and had been doing this for over 150 years, I knew a bit about the history of Labrador.

What caught my attention in 2001 was the fact that the media were reporting a widespread consensus—among government officials, academics, consultants, and media pundits—that the epidemics of communal self- and collective destruction were provoked by the forced relocation of Native peoples into centralized communities that Native youth referred to as "concentration villages." These were, indeed, miserable places to have to live—poorly insulated or noninsulated houses with no running water, no toilets, no sinks, no showers, no sewerage, and all this in a sub-Arctic environment so that some people would wake up on a winter morning with the breakfast food in the cupboard frozen solid and find their children with skin infections because they could not wash effectively.

So to blame the tragedies that developed within Native communities on the forced relocation of Native people into such unlivable places that the government did not bother to improve for decades, despite their promises to do so, made undeniable sense. But there is a problem with stopping the attempt to understand at that point.

This problem, which I only dimly grasped at the start of the research, was that the suffering imposed by this forced relocation was not at all new, although the self-destruction largely was. Native peoples in Labrador had been subject to brutal abuse for several hundred years since contact, and what changed was their ability to deal with this abuse without turning on themselves and each other.

That question, that problem of what changed in Native peoples' abilities to deal with all the suffering imposed on them—what changed, and why, and what remedies might help address this issue—became the initial focus of the first several years of my research. My hunch that more was involved than relocation to, and continuing forced residence in, villages that were such difficult places to live was further supported when, in 2003, the Innu residents of one of the worst places moved to a new community, where the houses were well insulated, there were running water and sewerage, a community recreation center, and more, and the same problems very soon returned in full force. Beyond the hunches that began this research the work was far from easy or quick, for the relevant information was scattered among widely different sources, and these sources often contained little more than hints.

Moreover, I made an important mistake, which I did not realize until the midpoint of my work. I was quite unsettled by the emerging picture, as the data from different sources came together, revealing the frequency of imposed famines and forced relocations, devastating epidemics of introduced diseases, the murderous grind of constantly present diseases, including especially tuberculosis, and the relentless stress of coping with the loss of their resources. In this context my focus on how Native peoples coped, or tried to cope, with all this became too narrow. I did not adequately look at a wider range of issues, for I was finding it difficult both to look closely at these events and to look away from them.

In the spring of 2006, five years into this research, I gave a paper on it at Cornell University's anthropology department. In a wonderful turning, Professor Kurt Jorden—whom I had worked with when he was a doctoral student, studying with me—opened a rather serious critique of this paper, along with his even more forceful colleague, Professor Audra Simpson. They pointed out that I did not adequately take into account the strong and positive features of Labrador Native communities through all their centuries of suffering. That opened what became another five years of research, and I am grateful for the encouraging critique that started me on this work.

THE BOOK THAT IS presented here contains two histories, two "stories." These are not the stories of domination, imposed abuse, and suffering on the one hand, and the changing ways Native peoples responded to this on the other. Those questions organized the research but not at all what came from the research. Rather, this book is about the struggles between order and chaos. This includes the pressure to create order both from above, from those who sought to govern, to control, to use, to "save"—including missionaries, fur traders, and government officials—and those working for a different kind of orderliness from within Native communities, who have struggled to create some kind of order out of the chaos that comes with imposed order.

The second "story," as it might be called, is about this chaos. This includes the chaos of domination, and the chaos that has emerged within Native communities as people struggle within and against what has been done to them and supposedly "for" them.

It is important why I call these "stories," although they are not fictions. I do so as a tribute to what I have learned both from Robert Piglia and John Berger. Piglia, in discussing the logic of short stories, wrote:

> In one of his notebooks, Chekov recorded the following anecdote: "a man in Monte Carlo goes to the casino, wins a million, returns home, commits suicide." The classic form of the short story is condensed within the nucleus of that future, unwritten story. Contrary to the predictable and conventional (gamble–lose–commits suicide), the intrigue is presented as a paradox. The anecdote disconnects the story of the gambling and the story of the suicide. That rupture is the key to defining the double character of the story's form. First thesis: a . . .

story always tells two stories. . . . Each of the two stories is told in a different manner. Working with two stories means working with two different systems of causality. The same events enter simultaneously into two antagonistic . . . logics. The essential elements of the story . . . are employed in different ways in each of the two stories. The points where they intersect are the foundations of the story's construction. (2011, 63)

This may be a complicated way of making several useful points. What is happening can center on, or emerge from, the surprises, and it can help to focus on what the surprises may reveal. Further, it is helpful to not impose one logic, one perspective, one unified interpretation on the multiplicity of events that are happening, for what may be most important are the ruptures and the breaks, the way things do not fit together.

John Berger made a similar point very simply and very powerfully when he said, "If every event which occurred could be given a name, there would be no need for stories" ([1983] 2011). And in what follows the nameless—both for us and for the Native peoples—is often crucial.

What I have learned from Berger and Piglia turned into a bigger issue for this book than it might at first appear to be. It has led me to put aside, or to minimize, many of the central concepts of anthropology, including culture, social organization, and social structure. All of these concepts both suggest and seek to point toward a supposed wholeness or unity of social life, as when we say "a culture," or "a social organization" or, even more out of touch, we say "the Inuit" or "the Cherokee," and so forth. We could scarcely go very far if we started our discussion with, say, "the New Yorkers." What makes us think we could go much further starting from "the Inuit"? Or to press the point, "Inuit culture" as an abstraction from peoples spread from Alaska to Greenland, living from the coast or more from inland resources, or both, some now near mining camps or military bases and some more distant? This last point, putting aside such abstract and unifying concepts as culture and social organization, will likely make some readers uncomfortable, or even angry, for it rubs against the familiar. Wait until the book is read to see how this perspective unfolds.

I also put aside most of the standard methods of anthropological research. Almost all the data for what follows comes from public documents accessible to anyone at libraries and archives. I went to Labrador several times, partly to work in libraries in Happy Valley–Goose Bay, the administrative center of Labrador, and partly just to see several of the Native communities I was writing about. Seeing these communities meant just that—I mostly only walked around them, looking, bought food and some clothes at local stores. When I did talk to people, for some people approached me, I asked no questions whatsoever other than those that make social conversation, such as "Do you think it will rain today?"

To ask a research question, which anthropologists usually do, is to assume that you know what is important to ask about. I took my first graduate anthropology course in the spring of 1957, and for decades afterward I lived with the assumption that I knew what questions to ask and that I could almost fully explain the answers I heard. I now find both these assumptions more like obstacles than aids. Graduate students may still need to work that usual way, as Professor Linda Green has insisted, at least until they develop some practice at doing anthropology, but then it might well end.

So in my work in the field I just look and listen. Mostly what I listen for, as will be explained in detail in the book, are the silences, and I try, based on a long-term familiarity with the primary historical sources, to see the surprises.

This is, in sum, a different kind of anthropology. It has been a struggle to learn to work in this way, focusing not just on the silences and the surprises but also on the ways that the diversity of social life both does and does not fit together well, if it fits together at all. At best this perspective, which I will argue replicates how many people themselves see and seek to grasp their worlds, will lead to only partial explanations and incomplete understandings, both among the peoples this book is about and for us.

I am deeply grateful for all the people who have helped me learn to start working in this way.

A NOTE ON THE INDEX: One of the major analytical and political-strategic points of this work is to confront the uncertain boundaries between the usual categories and thus to expose, in useful ways, the chaos that domination inescapably imposes upon the everyday lives of vulnerable peoples. From this perspective, the very idea of an index—specific topics with specific page numbers—often, but not always, works against the formation of effective struggle, which must emerge from that chaos and uncertainty. I have tried to work against that—for example, by listing the mining company's pronouncements about "respecting" elders' ecological advice under the category "elder abuse," for much of it is well-paid mockery. So use the index lightly: read the book, and determine for yourselves what points you find helpful.

ACKNOWLEDGMENTS

I had the privilege, the pleasure, the pressure, and the special productivity of working, for a month or two almost every summer for twenty years, with the working group on the history of everyday life at the Max Planck Institute for History, in Goettingen, Germany. The two central members of this group, Alf Luedtke and Hans Medick, have shaped my sense both of the larger significance of everyday lives and methodological and theoretical ways of studying it. Two other very special German historians, Adelheid von Saldern and Ursula Nienhaus, have been crucial to my work. As I brought what I learned back, several of my doctoral students at the City University of New York, with their relentlessly quizzical engagement with my perspectives, helped shape my understanding of productive ways to work. I specially want to thank Avram Bornstein, August Carbonella, Kirk Dombrowski, Anthony Marcus, Unnur Dis Skaptadottir, and Elizabeth TenDyke. Peter Ikeler, then a graduate student in sociology, was my research assistant while this book was being written, and his combination of hard work and sharp insight became particularly helpful. My colleague Michael Blim, who also taught all these students, in addition both indirectly and directly shared his wisdom and his balanced vision with me.

As the manuscript developed and my ways of working changed, I was very significantly helped by Jane McMillan, with her long history of strategically brilliant and politically committed legal and political activism on behalf of northern Native people; by Carol Brice-Bennett, by far the most knowledgeable of historians of Labrador Inuit; by Gavin Smith, intellectual comrade and long-time inspiration; and by Linda Green, with her special combination of medical and anthropological knowledge and her focus on social justice. Kirk Dombrowski, who has also worked in Labrador, provided particularly useful intellectual and practical help.

In Newfoundland, which holds most of the archives for Labrador Native history, I received important guidance from Valerie Burton on the history of capitalism and gender, from Rex Clark on new ways to think with anthropology, and from Robert Sweeny on doing both history and Canadian history. And my working and personal life was made easier and better, in a very stressful project, by the hospitality and advice of Elizabeth Ann Malichewski and John and Mary and Doug Pippy; the Memorial University of Newfoundland [MUN] anthropology department, which gave me working space, supportive services, and much encouragement from the late Robert Paine, and then Sharon Roseman, Robin Whitaker, Wayne Fife, and John Kennedy; Jim Hiller of the history department; and the Queens College Faculty of Theology, which both put me up and put up with me.

Because so much of my understanding of the current problems and strengths of Inuit and Innu comes from a fundamental rethinking of northern Native history, this whole project is deeply indebted to several wonderful archives. The key archive for this project has been the Legislative Library of the Newfoundland and Labrador Legislature—the most useful library imaginable. Were I to design a magically effective scholars' library, it would be this, with wonderfully knowledgeable and helpful librarians, an accessible collection, and more: a very comfortable and friendly place in which to work. Special thanks here go to Kimberly Hammond, director, Andrew Fowler, in charge of the collection, Carolyn Morgan, archivist, who knew the entire collection, replaced by Andrea Hyde and Theresa Walsh, excellent reference librarians, and Trine Sciolden, with her deep experience and concern for women's issues.

Close behind this special archive is the Center for Newfoundland Studies of the Queen Elizabeth II Library, Memorial University of Newfoundland, esp. Jean Ritce, the wise director, and the Maritime History Archives, deeply known and well administered by Heather Wareham. The Newfoundland and Labrador Provincial Archives were particularly helpful, as was the small but focused library at the Labrador Institute, and the *Them Days* archive, in Goose Bay.

In New York the research library of the American Museum of Natural

History, at which Peter Whiteley helped me get a research appointment, has been a very productive place to work. Thanks to Tom Baione, director.

One of the special features of the Native situation in northern Canada is how close it is to the situation of Australian Aborigines—not only the same issues, but a deeply similar chronology. Here my colleagues in Australia Jeremy Beckett—a life-long source of inspiration—and Dianne Austin-Broos, Gillean Cowlishaw, and Gaynor MacDonald have been the source of multiple useful conceptual surprises.

I am particularly grateful to the Labrador Inuit (Nunatsiavummiut) artist Heather Igloliorte for allowing me to reproduce, both in the text and as the cover, her powerful painting of the spiritual story of Sedna. Her art and her vision deserve a wide audience.

Deborah Winslow, director of cultural anthropology, and Anna Kertula de Echeve, head of Arctic social science, both of the National Science Foundation, provided both grants that made this work possible. Although the funds from NSF were very important—air fare from New York to Labrador is much more expensive than from New York to western Europe—their advice and insights were at least equally important. And the Grants Office at the College of Staten Island, especially Anne Lutkenhouse, steered me through the process.

My editors at Duke University Press are the best I have dealt with: Valerie Millholland and Gisela Fosado, the production editor Liz Smith, and the careful copyeditor Jeremy Horsefield deserve more than thanks.

My sons, Byron Marshall, Hugh Sider, and Noah Sider, have shaped my vision of the world, joining my wife Francine Egger-Sider in loving relentless critique, with their critiques keeping me going and changing—the same thing, eh family?

And all of this brought together by a most special librarian, whom it was my good fortune to have married, a specialist in online searches, who thus brought New York closer to Northern Canada, and me closer to centered for this stressful project, dealing day after day after day with the mysteries and the in-your-face-realities of Native youth suicide, Native suffering, and Native confrontations with their destruction: Francine Egger-Sider. Thanks all.

This book is about two extraordinary peoples, the Inuit and the Innu (formerly called Indians) of Labrador, in far northeastern Canada. For the past five decades they have been particularly brutally treated by a domineering state. We cannot start a useful engagement with this current situation, as is often done, by romanticizing yesterday under the label "tradition." During the period of Native history called "traditional" both Inuit and Innu were also treated very badly, with very high mortality rates.

Before we can discuss Native peoples' extraordinary resilience in the midst of several centuries marked by high death rates, we have to start with some more general understanding of how Native history has been made, both by Innu and Inuit and by those who conquered and sought control. Making history, as I use the term here, is rooted in a past that is not quite past and a future that engages, continues, and contests this not-quite-past. In this sense making history is something everyone must do in their ordinary daily lives. As we shall see, history takes on a special dynamic when it happens in Native communities that have endured through much suffering.

Because the issue of suffering has been and is so close to the surface, this is not an easy place to begin, but it turns out to be a useful start on the pathways toward a different tomorrow.

THE DISASTERS WE WILL examine are socially produced, not natural catastrophes. Many so-called natural catastrophes, such as Hurricane Katrina and the floods that devastated New Orleans and the Gulf Coast in 2006, may be triggered by events that are rooted in the natural world, but they usually unfold in ways that are socially shaped. Here each catastrophe, start to finish, has been socially constructed. Disasters happen when only some survive, so in a small community no one is left without long-lasting open wounds. What it means to "survive" a disaster is not a yes or no matter.

On the surface we will be dealing with issues of both survival and failure to survive, or to completely survive, among small groups of marginal peoples. On the surface we are dealing with the few thousand Native people of Labrador, along the North Atlantic Ocean in far northeastern Canada. These Native peoples, both Inuit, formerly called Eskimo, and Innu, formerly called Indian, now have one of the highest youth suicide rates in the world, as well as very high rates of domestic violence, adult alcoholism, child substance abuse, and multiple other indicators of severe social stress. Altogether it is a messy combination of collective self-destruction, which may or may not be part of how survival now happens, and multiple kinds of destructive treatment by powerful others.

At first the problems were caused by Hudson's Bay Company (HBC) and the Moravian missionaries, and now the Canadian federal and Newfoundland provincial governments are more responsible. Especially since the 1970s, imposed destructive treatment has been combined with a substantial amount of nearly unstoppable self-destruction, and that combination is the issue this work addresses.

But we must put this self-destruction in a broader perspective, both socially and historically. The news department of the TV network CBS published on the Internet in November 2007 results of their investigations showing that over a year beginning in 2005 the average *weekly* suicide rate of U.S. Armed Forces veterans was 120 suicides per 100,000, double the national average for nonveterans. Veterans of the so-called war on terror—the butchery in Iraq and Afghanistan—were far more likely than other veterans to commit suicide.[1] Moreover, one-fourth of all the homeless people on the streets of New York City are reputed to be veterans. In this larger context we are dealing with something more than the problems of small groups of northern Native peoples. We are also confronting one of the key features of our "modern" world, something we might call, just to get us started, the production of overwhelmingly senseless chaos in the lives of vulnerable and disposable people—our soldiers, for a start. These are people who once, at least briefly, believed some of the lies that they were told, or that they learned to tell themselves, while they were being both used and used up.

In place of these rosy lies, usually about a future or a cause, the victims found a chaos that could not be reduced to reason, that could not be explained rationally, not by the victims, and not believably by those who imposed it. Furthermore, the victims live in a chaos that cannot be attributed simply to chance, accident, or the forces of nature, as was attempted with Hurricane Katrina's devastation of African American neighborhoods in New Orleans. The victims suffer in part because of their immersion in what seems to have been, or still is, senseless chaos that people have imposed on them: governments that spend billions bailing out banks to keep them alive while letting millions of homeowners and workers die social death; governments that pay billions for military contracts while sending soldiers to war in unarmored vehicles, so they come back, like the equipment they were sent out with, missing essential parts or capabilities—for the rest of their lives, for lives that will never again have rest. Natives, veterans, those betrayed by banks and dreams of home ownership—despite fundamental differences, all are victims of an endless and senseless violence that tries to hide itself under one name or another: normal, natural, ordinary, usual, necessary, proper, progress. There are thus more issues at stake here than just the well-being of the Native peoples of Labrador.

To call the violence imposed on people, as well as the consequences of this violence, *senseless* chaos, at least to start, is both to name a problem for the people we seek to understand and help and also to name a problem for ourselves. All my long life in social theory I have had the illusion that the problems before us could be understood and explained, that there was sense to be made. From this starting point it seemed we could help by joining with the victims to oppose what we understood to be the specific social causes of suffering. We could understand causes if only we worked hard enough, thought intensely enough, and began from something more intellectually serious than the seductive but empty platitudes of mid- and late twentieth-century social and historical "science."

The point here is different: it is to challenge the idea that we can completely explain what we see and hear, and that our success in developing and organizing a helpful intervention turns on that. There may be other ways to intervene than starting with a neat explanation, other routes to effective struggle for a better world, routes that are fully social but follow different kinds of maps.[2] Making sense of largely senseless chaos may do little more than utterly miss the main point. Here, by way of a few brief examples, I introduce the notion of partial and incomplete ways of "making sense" of suffering—for that perspective guides this work.

When children sniff gasoline, which, as they well know, both produces an unusually intense high and at the same time does severe neurological damage—as the kids themselves say, "This shit rots your brain in about two years"—we may well be dealing with something more, and more complex, than what can be reduced to a completed explanation. Sometimes it helps just to worry and wonder about it all. The following is an example that has caused me a lot of both.

Many Native children in northern Canada (and elsewhere of course), starting at eight or nine, sniff gasoline, which they steal. They do not, or very rarely, use alcohol, although that is around in ways that could be pilfered without too much difficulty. Perhaps alcohol, being expensive, would be more closely watched, and the punishment for taking it more severe. Adults, as much as they use alcohol, scarcely ever inhale gasoline. So there is a perhaps useful question before us: why do children use gasoline and adults alcohol? As difficult as it might be for youth to get alcohol, it would save adults a lot of money to use gasoline for substance-inducing change. But they don't.

Let me offer a speculation, not so much to answer the question but to suggest one way of thinking about the problem of addictions. Gas, people say, gets you very "high." It is, in common knowledge, the most intense high of any substance. A bit of alcohol also gets people "high," but this point is very quickly passed, if it occurs at all, in serious long-term drinkers. Mostly alcohol in that context suppresses some feelings and self-control, making people either more passive and socially relaxed or more violent, and then "putting people out"—making them fall asleep or pass out.

So we might well look at the difference between the use of gas and that of alcohol by saying that children still want to get high, to rise above their situation, and adults who have learned that this is scarcely possible want to just forget, to "get out" not just socially but away from their bottled-up feelings.

This attempted interpretation might just be nonsense, empty speculation.

But it has one useful virtue: it points us toward thinking about how people's actions are situated in the ongoing history of their lives—the pasts that they still carry with them, the futures they dream, desire, dread, deny. This interpretation leads, in sum, to what we will discuss as historical violence, not as a generalizing concept but as a way of getting our hands and our minds around the specifics of specific lives. The question about the different uses of alcohol and gasoline may or may not be answerable, but the question itself points us in useful directions. It is worth wondering and worrying about, even though or because it may not be an answerable question. Another still open question may take us further on that journey.[3]

The addictions in many Native communities are severe and getting worse, although they are still far from universal, even in the most intensely stressed communities. In 2007 I spent part of the summer in Labrador, on one of my research trips. A woman who has worked with Native peoples' health for a decade and a half, lovingly, sympathetically, and intensely, told me that since 2005 some parents had started placing gasoline-soaked tarpaulins or blankets over the cribs of their infants, because "it keeps the infants stoned quiet for four or five hours while the parents go out drinking." The shock of hearing this was like being hit in the pit of the stomach. These were their own infant children being sacrificed to an addiction. More may be at stake in this than the addictive pull of alcohol.

In the late mid-nineteenth century, across the rather narrow sea from Labrador, on the northwest coast of Greenland, Inuit people developed a truly intense addiction to coffee. Traders and administrators from Denmark, who had colonized Greenland and the Inuit there, were writing back to their homeland saying that the Native people were starving and freezing because they had such an intense craving for coffee that to get it they were trading sealskins they needed for their clothing and to build the kayaks they used to hunt food and fur (Marquardt 1999).[3]

Without denying that caffeine can engender some craving, probably not as intensely as does alcohol, this situation suggests that something even more profound than the addictive properties of alcohol as a substance is happening. This intense and destructive addiction to coffee might be rooted in something that has to do with what I will call *incoherent domination*, unspeakable domination, and the nearly uncontrollable cravings that emerge within and against this domination.

It suggests cravings that both join you to the foreign and alien world that came to assault you, merging you with the alien invader's powerful substance or allowing you to incorporate within you what they brought from afar, and simultaneously distance you from that same alien world that was imposed in your midst. Alcohol makes people uncontrollable in many ways; coffee in Greenland almost doomed the Inuit as trading "partners." These are cravings that join you to the substances of the dominant and simultaneously, in their effects, or in the effects of what you have to do to get access to these substances, break you apart from the "rational" demands domination imposes. The cravings, the addictions, also break people apart from each other, and ultimately from their prior selves. This is not a coherent package, in any sense of *coherent*: glued together, or cohering, in the middle, or coherent in the sense of easily and understandably speakable.

Neither is domination coherent, in either sense of *coherent*. That domination produces incoherence in its victims—being both chaotic and often unspeakable in its consequences—is a good part of how domination works, as we shall see. Because domination produces at least partly incoherent lives among its victims, it cannot itself be as orderly, routine, and predictable as it pretends to be and still maintain the control it seeks. Bureaucracies are both the reality and the fantasy of domination (see Lea [2008] for evidence of this in Native lives). The incoherence and the chaos of domination and the incoherence and chaos it produces in the lives of its victims, with and very much beyond the addictions, are separate issues and separate problems. We will consider both.[4]

But this perspective also does not lead to fully answerable questions. With women who drink so intensely while pregnant that it damages their children, we may be dealing with parents for whom the world seems so awful that at some level they do not want their children to grow up clearheaded, for it is widely known that children born with what professionals call "fetal alcohol spectrum disorder" (FASD)—and some locals call children born "hurt" or "damaged"—have trouble making connections in their minds by the time they are school-age. However well their teachers say they can think specific points, their teachers also often say these children cannot make connections. This might well be a temptation to a woman suffering from a childhood and a marriage marred by seemingly or actually inescapable domestic violence. Why would you want your baby to grow up clearly and fully understanding what lies in their future, particularly if you thought that their chances for a different future were small? Or this kind of child-damaging drinking could be encouraged by a number of other reasons that we cannot yet know or name.

There have recently been a lot of very simplistic interpretations of practices now called "the weapons of the weak" (for example, Scott 1985). We need to consider not just individualistic ways of making life a bit uncomfortable for the dominant but the potential of the weak to find those even weaker among themselves and make weapons that work on them, or work them over. A simplistic "weapons of the weak" perspective turns out to be an obstacle to understanding, in large part because it poses domination as a simple two-sided relationship between the dominant and a multitude of individuals in the category that is dominated—peasants, Blacks, Natives, whatever.

More generally, we should not be tempted to reduce complex issues to simple—and worse, complete—explanations. We should not try to invent what social scientists call "hypotheses to test" (we could also call them fancy-dress guesses about causes or connections). Let us put this temptation aside, even though it leads to well-paying research grants and high consultant fees, and immerse ourselves in what is happening. We must also do this without letting ourselves sink into mindless description, for simple description is always not just incomplete but inadequate, more incomplete and inadequate in more important ways than it pretends to be.

SEVERAL YEARS AGO A construction worker and my neighbor in the northlands, with whom I was quite friendly, said to me one late afternoon, in a moment of intense and shared closeness about the difficulties of building a good family life up there, "Gerry, I don't know what the fuck it all means. I don't know what the fuck is happening. I don't know why the fuck things are this way"—over and over again repeating and emphasizing his litany of confusion and sorrow. The worst and most alienating response I could have given to this open wound he was showing and sharing would be to say, "I know what is happening: have a look at pages 15 to 25 of my last paper, or my new book."

Moreover, such an answer to his sorrow and his unhappiness, to the impossibility of understanding, to the largely imposed incoherence of his situation, would not only have been foolish and arrogant; it would have been a lie.

What we need, here and now, is an admittedly partial understanding, in both senses of the word *partial*: limited and sided. It will be an understanding that at its best is very limited, grasping only a piece of the problem, and it will be an understanding that takes sides, for such disasters as we will address do not just happen, but are made, and hopefully can be at least partially unmade by taking sides with the victims. So this will be, at its best and if we can get there, an engaged work, formed with and not just about the needs and feelings and experience-rooted understandings of the people whose situations we "study." This is very far from a comfortable starting point, for it requires us to abandon our idea that our theories elevate us above the sufferings that our world has imposed upon the peoples we have made vulnerable both to our doings and to our theories.[5]

Part of the discomfort of this position is the muddiness of trying to write something more than a description of a major social problem without being able to offer much by way of understanding. What else, if not understanding, is the job of social science? Suppose, though, we say that while this has been the job of social science, we might do something else, perhaps something more and better, or at least less in the service of state power? For state power routinely uses what we produce, whether or not it hires us to produce it. The increasing collapse of the "welfare state" over the past few decades, in almost all the advanced industrial nations, should finally teach us, despite the remnants of our illusions, that the state does not any longer mean the vulnerable well, if it ever did. If we stop dancing in the big-house gardens of state and corporate-shaped science, what is the something else that we might try to do, closer to how the people we care about think and work, and whose problems we seek to helpfully address?

To start, our task will be to take hold of a piece of what is happening, without trying to completely understand, and figure out how to turn it around, or at least to bend it toward making less oppressed lives. It sounds like a modest task, until we see how profoundly it will change what we do, how we do it, and especially the tools with which we work. Then it becomes more significant. Neat explanations that describe "solutions" often, but not always, wind up serving the interests of state or of capital far more than the people they presume to help. And we have to wonder why the production of these "solutions" pays so well, at least by academic social science standards.

We start by naming the central problems and, in this context, the focus of this work.

The First Problem

The amount of suffering that has been imposed upon Native peoples staggers the imagination. In the Americas, in Africa, in Asia, and in Australia—everywhere the story is broadly similar. Moreover, everywhere the reactions that imposed suffering has produced among indigenous peoples are also similar: episodic confrontation with domination, along with attempts at evasion or collusion, all ordinarily put down with, or controlled by, overwhelming violence and abuse, and then, along with the confrontations and continuing abuse, substantial rates of alcohol and then drug abuse, domestic violence, suicide, and still more. And all these reactions, which are always more than just reactions, are soaked to the core by the horrendous mortality from the diseases and wars the invaders brought.

The expansion of Europe into the Americas, Africa, Asia, Australia, and the Pacific Islands was sickeningly brutal and violent in ways that are difficult to grasp, for the violence ordinarily went far beyond what was necessary to achieve the objectives of conquest and domination. But this onslaught remains rather easy to see, unless you believe the fantasy excuses and self-deceptions about civilizing the primitives or Christianizing the heathen, or the same thing put more abstractly: "progress" or "acculturation." It is the responses to, engagements with, and evasions of this domination that are far more complex, far more difficult to grasp.

In North America the colonizing onslaught was not a brief event in any one locale, starting on the East Coast and moving across the continent to the west, or in northern Canada starting also in Hudson's Bay and radiating outward. To the contrary, the onslaught has been a continuing event, everywhere, beginning in most places with the spread of new diseases and provoked warfare long before the arrival of many Europeans, and continuing not just to the present but, as its victims well know, to the coming tomorrow—continuing with ever-tightening, ordinarily seemingly senseless and openly destructive governmental control and massive economic and cultural intrusions.[6] All this, despite its overwhelming horror, is conceptually the easy part of the history to tell.

One of the many consequences of the continuing European colonizing onslaught is far more difficult to grasp and introduces the major problem for this hopefully helpful project. The amount of suffering that many—but very far from all—Native people have in recent decades come to impose upon themselves and each other, with alcoholism, with domestic violence, with suicide, with substance abuse, all with increasing intensity since the mid-twentieth century, staggers our ability to grasp and to help remedy. The point here is the opposite of "blaming the victims" for their troubles—it is trying to figure out how destructive domination from outside turns into something more, something that makes struggling against domination even more difficult.

While the two issues—destructive domination and collective self-destruction—are clearly connected, the connections are neither direct nor mechanical. Whatever those connections may or may not be, particularly as they shape the possibilities for healing and for remedy, the relation between domination and self-destruction becomes a central problem. The approach to this problem begins with the concept of historical violence.

Historical Violence

This book is about what I will call historical violence: the multiple ways in which several centuries of abuse, domination, exploitation, devastating epidemic and endemic diseases, and taking of Native lands and Native resources echo and ricochet like a steel bullet around the walls and openings of the present. The problems that Native peoples face are continually changing, as are the struggles against their oppression and their sorrows. These changes and the underlying continuities that stretch from the not quite past into the impending future form the core of what is called historical violence.

The problem before us, at least in its surface manifestation, seems clear. The Native peoples of Labrador, both Innu (reminder: formerly called and socially constructed as Indians) and Inuit (formerly treated as Eskimo), have one of the very highest youth suicide rates in the world. Suicide rates are difficult or close to impossible to measure in very small populations, because a few more or less in any one year changes the rate greatly. Suicides are also often underreported, for many reasons. Keeping all this in mind, the number of suicides among the Native peoples of northeastern Canada is proportionately extremely high. Moreover, there is a deepening epidemic of children sniffing gasoline, which gives intense highs and also does substantial neurological damage, and there is also widespread and severe adult alcoholism that permanently damages the brains of many newborn infants, in addition to all the consequences both for those who drink too intensely and for their families. All this is compounded by very high rates of domestic violence. When these epidemics of self-destruction started being major problems is crucial, for when has been taken to explain why. A simplistic connection between when and why has been an important cause of the failure of all existing programs to be of any help.

These problems of individual and collective self-destruction do not have a long history. They became severe in the late 1960s and early 1970s, when most Labrador Native peoples were relocated—the Innu primarily to two villages, the Inuit southward to north-central and central Labrador. The situation in their new villages was horrendous: government control over their lives was extreme, as was the lack of government provision for minimally adequate housing, for the availability of work (this for the Innu more than the Inuit), and for a social infrastructure. Worse, the governments of both Newfoundland and Canada lied about what Native people would get following relocation and never fulfilled their promises, despite decades of repeated reminders.

The places to which Native peoples were relocated, combined with the mid-twentieth-century withdrawal of the HBC from the fur trade and the Moravian missionaries from their mission-supply stations, made former ways of life increasingly impossible to continue. The villages into which Native peoples were forced, and increasingly confined, were the locales of very substantial, clearly imposed, and almost inescapable suffering. Later we will describe these places in some detail, for even though the problems have much longer roots than in the villages to which Native peoples were relocated, the conditions in these villages have also been deeply relevant.

The close association of this relocation with the onset of epidemics of self-destruction has led to the obvious but inadequate notion that relocation, one way or another, "caused" these epidemics. As these epidemics, which intensified further in the 1980s, caught Canadian national media attention in the mid-1990s, and as the stories and pictures of Native suffering were broadcast worldwide—including a video of one young boy, with a plastic bag full of gasoline in his hand, who screamed at the photographer "I want to die!"— the Canadian government came under serious pressure to "do something."

Two attempts to address the problems were directly based in the notion that relocation to these awful places was to blame. One attempt was to build a brand-new, materially very much better village for one Innu community, the worst of the relocation places, and to build new houses in the other major Innu relocation community. The second attempted remedy was to helicopter Innu "back to the bush" for limited periods of time, where they could "reconnect with their traditional life ways," and similarly to help Inuit revisit the locales from which they had been forced to leave.[7] None of these attempted remedies have been any help whatsoever in alleviating the epidemics.

The starting point for wondering about what else is happening beneath the epidemics, and especially why, is not the fact that relocation brought a very great deal of suffering, for indeed it did. We will start from the point that the imposed suffering is not at all new, although the self-destruction is. Beginning in 2001, I have gone through a large number of widely separate sets of data: health records from governments and medical missionaries, missionary journals and reports, travelers' and explorers' memoirs, government commissions of inquiry, police reports, judicial and legislative records, HBC records, and more. What these diverse records revealed, when combined into a chronology, is that the Native peoples of Labrador experienced a major assault on their well-being—epidemics, arranged famines to ensure compliance with fur-trade demands, forced relocations, the destruction of their resource base by the onslaught of Euro-Canadians, pervasive scanting of supply, all this and more, with a crisis every few years since the early nineteenth century, and all with significant mortality rates.

These episodic problems were in addition to major introduced endemic (constantly present) diseases, especially tuberculosis (TB) and venereal disease, which also had very substantial and socially devastating mortality rates. A great many all-too-young children watched their parents die and then had to figure out how themselves to be parents; a great many parents watched their children or each other waste and die from introduced diseases or imposed starvation and then had to figure out how to continue. And in the twentieth century, after Native peoples were forced to focus on commercial fur and skin trading to survive, there was an erosion and then a collapse of prices, which led both the HBC, the main traders to the Indians, and the Moravian missionaries, the main traders to the Eskimo, to abandon the trade, leaving the surviving Native peoples swinging in midair.

If introduced and imposed suffering is not at all new, why then is the suicide and substance abuse? With that question our work begins, and it starts with a focus on the concept of historical violence—how yesterday both does and does not become today for vulnerable people.

The answer will turn, in part but an important part, on the complexities of autonomy and dignity, as the basis for these kinds of relations was transformed after World War II and the increasing collapse of the fur and skin trades. To begin, people with nothing to do, no way of earning their living, do not have, or do not easily have, any autonomy. Autonomy turns out to be one aspect of relationships that simultaneously work toward other ends. But there is another aspect to autonomy: it is most realizable—literally, made real—when it is also a context for dignity. Dignity and autonomy for vulnerable peoples often emerge in the space people can make between imposed history and their lived histories. This space has been made in more productive ways than is widespread at present.

Partial Violence, Partial Coping

Put simply, historical violence is the unfolding of violence over several centuries. To pursue this straightforward beginning, we will focus on changing ways of using Native peoples and their skills and resources, and changing ways of discarding Native peoples, making them disposable, when what was wanted was obtained or used up.

To go further, the concept of historical violence also calls our attention to the changing ways Native people have been able, or unable, or most of all *partially* able to cope with the specific manifestations of violence they have confronted. They must confront this violence both with the memories and consequences of yesterday's violence and with what they know or fear, from their experiences, may soon be coming.

The most revealing point at stake here is embedded in the notion of *partial coping*. To be partial is to be incomplete, to have a partial solution to your problems, and also to be biased. A partial solution means that the solution, all in all, does not quite work. More likely, as the lessons of how famines unfold teach us, it works well enough for some, but not at all for others.[8] Native peoples' coping with the onslaught has been and still is partial because it is, unfortunately but often necessarily, selective. Some will survive, perhaps even thrive, at least for a while, and some will not at all, and when we and they look closely, this often turns out not to be random.

We have to try to grasp the implications for Native communities that the partial solutions to the problems created by imposed domination—and the only possible solutions for Native people, most of the time, were partial—meant that some among them would suffer much more than others. To try to "cope" with domination, as we all too innocently name it, means to be put in a position where you unavoidably consign or abandon some of your own to a much worse fate.

Our explanations of so-called coping have been horribly incomplete because most of our theoretical apparatus so far has homogenized Native peoples—made them seem, in important ways, internally undifferentiated.[9] We homogenized them—made their communities seem internally undifferentiated except for some political inequalities that were treated as part of a "shared" social structure and culture. Anthropological terms like *adaptation* or *coping* or *acculturation* or a generalizing *the*—"*the* culture of *the* x people"— were all ways of pretending that our hands are cleaner than they are. All these terms conceal from members of the dominant society a realization of what was done that has led to the increasing internal differentiation of Native societies. Partial coping, by contrast, calls our attention both to the incomplete-ness of coping and to the differentiation between those who do and do not, can and cannot, "cope"—those who do and do not, can and cannot, make it to tomorrow. Further, "partial coping" calls our attention to the characteris-tic, nearly universal fact that indigenous peoples' strategies for dealing with domination, whatever they may be, usually do not work, at least not in the long run. The continuation of domination over Native peoples depends on making sure of this.[10]

It does not aid understanding very much when anthropologists and gov-ernment bureaucrats continue to use the classic, now only partly discredited anthropological fantasy and talk about "the culture of the _____ Indians." This generalizing term conceals situations where some are surviving and some are not, which is particularly crucial when the distinction is not ran-dom. One might be tempted to say that we need to study *the* culture to see how it produces this distinction, but that is to assume that there is *a* culture, and that people simply have this as their own culture, rather than needing to set themselves very much against what others, or even they themselves, or, as we shall see, their elite, call "their" culture. Kirk Dombrowski, in his book on Native Americans in southern Alaska, revealingly titled *Against Culture* (2001), has very usefully described and analyzed three instances of a wide-spread internal conflict in Native societies about who "has" what is regarded as "their culture," and who in Native communities need to set themselves against, or partly against, what is asserted and claimed.

To use the notion of historical violence, of violence that continues through its changes over long periods of time, is to realize that the violence itself is also always partial, for the people it addresses still survive, still continue (at least some of them do) in some ways diminished and transformed, in other ways strengthened, but, like Job, still very much there—or better, here.

Socially constructed violence is not just incomplete but partial in the sense of biased in the attempted choice of its victims and survivors. Histori-cal violence is thus both partial violence and partial coping, and to study it and most of all to engage it—to get our minds on it and our hands around it—we must be partial also: not try to do it all, and take sides.

Nailing Tomorrow

I have long thought that the study of a significant social issue ought to be organized and judged by two main standards: First, what are the chances that it will productively surprise both us and the people studied? What are the chances that we will learn something we do not already know? The point is not just to add new details to old understandings, or add small modifications to current interpretive fads, but to develop studies that, like good art and good music, help us look at and listen to the world in new ways.

Second, we can judge the usefulness of a study by asking, to what extent has the project helped, or will it help, us to hear the silences? In my experience the most significant social knowledge is embedded in the silences of the social worlds we study. We can indeed learn to look for and listen to the silences, and when we do, they often introduce crucial surprises. Silences are active, and the more serious ones often have a material form. But we can never fully know them: that is why our work is always partial, always incomplete. Chapter 5 begins to explore and illustrate this point.

If we think with surprises, with what surprises us and our knowledge of the world, perhaps something different will happen. The notion of historical violence, as it is used here, is designed to surprise us with what it reveals, and also to orient our work toward the silences. To do this, we will have to use the concept of historical violence not just to engage what happened yesterday but also to think about tomorrow. That task, thinking about what may be coming tomorrow, can be started by using a related concept, structural violence. Structural violence is an introduction to historical violence.

A number of significant works have refamiliarized us with the issue of structural violence (e.g., Green 1999). Amartya Sen, who won the Nobel Prize in 1998 for his studies of who dies in famines and why, defines, in his foreword to Paul Farmer's *Pathologies of Power*, the concept of structural violence by calling our attention to "the social conditions that so often determine who will suffer abuse and who will be shielded from harm" (Farmer 2003, xiii).[11] At stake, as Farmer and Sen show, is nothing less than "the nature and distribution of extreme suffering." The concept of structural violence highlights how widespread forms of inequality are produced and used: gender, race, class, generation, differential citizenship, locality, and neighborhood. The concept also leads us to investigate how fundamental inequalities in access to power distribute different experiences of suffering—in particular, the kinds of suffering that shortens or terminates life, and the kinds of suffering that endures over long periods of time. Many social inequalities are what I call *terminal inequalities*—the kinds of inequalities from which people die soon or much sooner.

In my own previous work on the history of famine in Africa (Sider 1996), it became clear that people in a locality often know, rather clearly, who is—or what kinds of people are—at risk of starving in the *next* famine. Structural violence is ordinarily designed to deny a securely livable tomorrow—not just today—for its victims. One cannot understand the dynamics of socially produced inequalities—such as race, gender, and differential citizenship—any other way. Although they often are justified by reference to a fictive history, they are fundamentally about tomorrow: who will then get what, do what kinds of work, offer what kinds of deference. Beyond what is happening today, a denial of a livable tomorrow turns out to be crucial. It is the issue of tomorrow that the notion of historical violence, as used here, calls into our view and expands. Historical violence is violence that reaches from yesterday into tomorrow: it is history still very much in the making. And for healing, including especially collective self-healing, the issue is not just yesterday and today but always also tomorrow.

Let us start in the midst of one instance of historical violence, first to show what is at stake, and then to further develop new tools for thinking and acting.

There is a simple bit of home furnishing in the Canadian northlands called by many local Whites "the Indian coat-hanger"—a racist put-down of the poverty and the resourcefulness of hard-pressed Native peoples. It is a nail, or more precisely a row of quite large nails, put in the wall just past the entrance door of a home. When you come in, you can hang your coat on one of the nails. "Indian coat hangers" also can frequently be found on other walls inside the house, particularly where people change clothes, and particularly before the housing improvements in the past decade or so, which included building some closets.

In many, but very far from all, northern Native houses, these rows of large nails are surprisingly high up on the wall. If the woman of the house is asked why the nails are so high, she will occasionally say something like, "It's so when my husband (or boyfriend) smashes me against the wall, I don't hit my head on a nail."[12] Only a stranger to the village would ask; everyone but young children know what and why.

Now consider the situation of the eight- or ten-year-old child (the age when children start sniffing gasoline, although there may be no direct connection) coming home and dropping his or her coat on the floor, or on a chair, because they cannot reach the high nail hangers. Every time a child this age drops her or his coat, she or he may know why the nails are so high, or sort of know why, and he or she has the possibility of remembering what was seen or heard. And there also is, at least occasionally and perhaps particularly for the girls, as they grow into and through puberty, the provocation to wonder about their own future.

This is what I mean by historical violence, but in only the first of the important senses of the term. It is violence that situates itself between the yesterdays and the tomorrows of its present and future victims, as well as its present and future perpetrators.

There is another potentially useful sense of historical violence, revealed by asking: What was done to people to bring them to this situation, and how can they get out of it? In what ways, if any, will knowing how we got into this mess help us to get out of it? "We" is the more useful formulation; "they" allocates blame before we even begin.

There is a third sense of the term *historical violence* that is also crucial: the widespread tendency of people who were abused in childhood to become abusers themselves; in contrast but equally important, there are also those who were abused as children and because of this do not themselves become abusers. We are in the realm of the deeply connected issues of reproduction and transformation: how victim is transformed into victimizer, how victims often marry victimizers, and how they do not, or how they become part of the struggle against such practices. This is the issue of how yesterday becomes either a similar or a different tomorrow within families and communities. It is a particularly complex transition when the continuities are widespread, and domestic violence and substance abuse become what is called "normalized" because it seems "almost everyone" does it.

"Normalized" turns out to misunderstand or evade the crucial point of some people choosing or needing to do something they know is very wrong. For example, we do not want to say anything about Native men hitting, or hitting on, their wives and children that we would not also potentially say about Catholic priests or famous football coaches raping little boys, for there are likely to be some important similarities. At the core of these similarities, more than has been dealt with in studies of domestic violence, is the probability that a substantial proportion of the perpetrators know that what they are doing is wrong.

Historical violence calls into the foreground a history founded upon rupture, discontinuity, contradiction—upon breaks in all the heart-wrenching and also progressive senses of the word. That the perpetrators of the violence often know that what they are doing is wrong, and that this seems to be part of the what and why of what they do, is, from the perspective of the perpetrators, part of the break from what has been done to them. They are not, or not just, the victim: they have power, as much or more power as those who hurt them.

There is, in the midst of all this, a positive opening. The significance of the breaks, ruptures, and chaos within historical violence is that hope, as well as suffering, can be born in the spaces that chaos creates. As we shall see, both hope and suffering enter peoples' lives and peoples' histories in the discontinuities that shape and continually reshape historical violence, and our task is to join with the victims—and the victimized perpetrators—to find and nourish the hope.

IF A CHILD WHO has been abused grows up to become an abusive parent, or marries a person known to be abusive, how can we call this discontinuity? This question will require an answer that will have to be worked out over several chapters, but it turns out to also be an important opening for healing, for finding and using spaces that continually open up in the midst of change.

Let us say, only for a start, that violence usually introduces its own discontinuities, along with its repetitiveness and its demands for continual compliance. To the extent that violence produces dependency, which within families and so-called romantic relationships seems to be one of its characteristic goals, it necessarily also produces hostility. Dependency, as Freud insisted, is a hostile connection between people. For all the compliance in relations of dependency there is usually also a substantial separation and distance—the distance and the intimacy of hostility and perhaps also of hope for change. We will return to this issue when we start to consider the material and social bases for hope.[13]

We must, in the context of considering the particular relations of dependency that emerge within families, also consider the fact that the main institutions of community-wide domination—HBC for the Indians, the Moravian missions for the Eskimos, and, by the mid-twentieth century, the Canadian federal and Newfoundland and Labrador provincial governments, plus the resource-extracting mining, timber, and hydroelectric corporations—all centered their engagements with Native peoples on the production and intensification of dependence, a dependence that was always changing, always incomplete, always producing elusive subjects. Both substance abuse and the refusal to engage in substance abuse may each express the multiple ways individual Native people and their families evade domination and the open and hidden pressures, controls, and demands of the dominant.

Silent Violence

Concentration camp survivors from the holocaust, as is well known, rarely told their children very much about what they went through, but surprisingly, their grandchildren often know more, or admit to knowing more, than their parents, and they show in their lives some of the long-term effects of that horror. Continuity in some contexts seems to be embedded in silences: the kinds of silences that the French poet Paul Valery called "the active presence of absent things."[14] Thus, some of what we know becomes what we do not say, becomes what lives with us and within us as silence. Soldiers who years or decades after their war still wake up, from time to time, screaming in the middle of the night live both with and against their memories and their feelings. Moreover, their memories and feelings live within them, with a life and claims and demands of their own, for it is not easily predictable from the prior days' events what nights these veterans will wake up from their—or our imposed—nightmares calling out in pain. And many do not, or cannot, or will not talk about either what they lived through or what still lives within them. There is sometimes no point in openly knowing something if we can't do anything about it, or if we think we can't. Our silences are not just what we do not say to others; some are also what we do not or cannot say to ourselves.

This is not at all simply a moralizing perspective, where silences can be broken with sermons about right and wrong, although there are indeed rights and wrongs. Telling someone who is episodically violently abusive to his or her family that this is a bad or destructive way to act may be doing nothing more than telling the person something they already know and will not say. Part of the problem before us is how to write or talk about silences.

One approach to this problem is through another reach toward what might or might not be. I think that the silences embedded in such situations as domestic violence, as the continuing trauma of yesterday, are an expression of inconclusive struggle. To wonder how to write or talk about silences is to wonder about hard struggles that have led nowhere. The problems continue, despite the nameless struggles both within them and against them. This might well give our writing, our voice, a different form than usual.

"Let me warn you," said Harold Innis, Canada's foremost economic historian and author of *The Fur Trade in Canada* ([1955] 1999), "that any exposition . . . which explains the problems and their solutions with perfect clarity is certainly wrong." Yet grants are still awarded, and graduate students are still trained, by the criteria of pretended ability to explain with perfect clarity. Surprisingly, accepting Innis's point may make our work potentially more helpful.

For neither the Native peoples of Labrador nor we are helpless in the face of such suffering, including especially the suffering imposed upon the most vulnerable people, nor are we completely hampered by what cannot yet be known, written, or spoken. That is the beauty and power of worlds organized by struggle, even inconclusive struggles. As we have learned from the civil rights struggles in the American South, struggle itself not only dignifies but heals. The point is to produce struggles that have deep and effective roots, both among the people our work engages and within our engaged work. To write with and against the problems of violence embedded with silences is a journey that can only rarely if ever have a beginning, a middle, and an end, with a clear and unified narrative line running throughout. We should not pretend that we can write conclusively about inconclusive struggles: our struggle is not that different.

Rethinking Struggle: A Start

There is a widespread figure of speech heard throughout northeastern Canada and rural New England, especially among the White working class. When people are presented with routine friendly greeting questions such as "How'r you doing?" or "What's happening?" the response is sometimes "Same shit, different day," or even more poignantly, "sos," which means, to begin, "same old shit."

But of course sos is the worldwide, almost language-free, distress call: three long sounds or lights, three short, three long—originally from the telegraphic Morse code, and still often the clearest way to call for help across long distances or empty space. sos is not just "same old shit": along with the resignation, the acceptance, the cynicism, the quietly good-natured rebuttal to your hello question, implying "What did you expect?" there is, hovering well in the background, the notion of distress, the claim that more is wanted, more is needed, perhaps also help is needed. Even the more straightforward and superficially less complicated saying "same shit, different day" is not just resignation and cynical acceptance. It is said by people I know who struggle to do better and to have some fun on the way. People who say this almost routinely, in response to the routine greeting, also almost routinely take vacations, celebrate holidays, fix up their homes, and do what they can to hang on to or better their jobs. But this is often, as they and we so well know, a struggle against the odds, against "the system."

In the years I spent in the rural southern United States, embroiled in civil rights struggles, I never heard either of these phrases, not once. When you gave the routine greeting "How'r you doin'?" you called forth, invariably, the routine answer—so routine it often preceded the question (people would say it even before you asked)—"Doin' fine." We might pass this off as just a local cultural difference, but far more is at stake. In the midst of struggles for civil rights, even struggles that were lost, there was the pervasive sense, for two decades or more, that things were changing, that things were going to change. Even after change turned sour with the closure of all the textile mills in the late 1990s and their removal to Mexico and then China, there were still widespread memories of having made change happen in the face of very serious opposition, as well as with surprising support. The difference between the Rust Belt or resource-extraction "SOS" economies of the Northeast and a civil-rights-struggling "Doin' fine" in the nonwhite South is not—or, if you prefer, not just—"culture"; it is rooted in a clear-headed, realistic assessment of one's historical situation.

This introduces, briefly but no less significantly, a crucial point: people know, deeply, what is happening. They may not completely know why, or they may well know that "why" is not fully knowable, but they sure do know what. All that I have said about partial understandings, all that we must realize about the difficulties we have knowing why things are the way they are, must not subtract one microscopic drop from the point that people know, well and deeply, what is happening. The Euro-Canadian worker in rural Newfoundland who told me, decades ago, "We Newfs, we are all Niggers, we are all Indians, we are all Eskimos," knew. Along with the rest of us, he may not have known much of why, or what could be done to fix it, but he surely knew what his situation was in Canada.[15]

This living connection, this connection that people in difficult situations must live every day of their lives, this connection between knowing and not knowing, between knowing and silence, is where we too must begin our journey, our work. Hopefully this connection will also help shape our lives as scholar-activists, without the usual academic prop of thinking we can some day, in some way, know it all. Inescapable doubt is both a good and an unavoidable companion. There is no other way of getting close to the problems that lie before us, both far away and here.

Let me offer one last but absolutely crucial introductory point: do not mistake our focus on the problematic issues in Labrador Native communities for a characterization of the whole community. We are dealing with significant problems, and to begin we will focus on these problems. Before we can even incompletely understand, we must also know that there are other substantial parts of these communities, and other significant ways of living both within and against the histories of these communities, even since the 1960s and 1970s, when the epidemics of self-destruction began. To understand, even partially, we must also come to know those times and places and those people in these communities who, within and against all that has been done to the Native peoples of Labrador, within and against all the mess of so many lives, have managed to build good, productive, and caring lives. Most of all, to grasp what is happening, we must never divide these villages into productive and troubled, healthy and ill, good and bad, for if we do, we will miss all the surprises, all the contradictions that give and conceal meanings, that give shape and fractures to lives. And in particular, we will fail to see the material and social bases for hope and dignity in the midst of pervasive domination.

We will work through all of this bit by a small bit, so that the complexity of the issues we are trying to deal with does not become overwhelming. At the moments when it does feel overwhelming, perhaps that feeling within us—author, academic readers, concerned observers and activists, Native readers—will help us, in the end, realize a bit more about how the people we are thinking about feel themselves. People in difficult circumstances can be both articulate and clear-sighted at some moments and overwhelmed and confused at others. Don't ask for anything more than this for yourself, as you work through this book, because to want an easy and full understanding is to separate yourself from the people. Our search for a completed understanding may mostly just distance us even more than necessary.

Three Clarifications—and a Format

One: Throughout this work I will use the names, or labels, for Native peoples that were used at the time. In the early contact period in what is now southern Labrador, Native peoples were called "Esquimaux Indians"; later the names were split. In recent times Native peoples have taken, by their choice and with official and increasingly public assent, the names Inuit and Innu. To use these modern names throughout the history of colonial domination is to profoundly misunderstand both the intensity and the shape of domination. The names people are called matter quite a bit, not at all as descriptors of who they are but very much, as the term *savage* has shown, to shape how they will be treated. People who were called "savages" of course were not, but they were treated with true savagery. The name primarily specified not who they were but how the dominant society was going to regard and treat them. When talking about their history, to change their name or their labels at an earlier time to Inuit or Innu is not at all the mark of respect it claims to be, but an attempt to minimize or even erase the vileness and the violence of our own history. "Eskimo" and "Indian" turn out to name deeply consequential forms and processes of domination and response, which changed substantially but only partly for the better with the new names, Inuit and Innu. Using the names that were current at the time being written about is designed to help reveal these processes that sought to create what was named, as well as to keep us centered on what, and how much, is at stake.

Two: In contemporary Labrador politics it is a very sensitive issue whether or not the people who are called *Métis* are a "Native people" with the now significant rights associated with that status. The Métis (from the French word for "mixed") are primarily the descendants of colonial-era relations between Newfoundlanders or Euro-Canadians and people then called Eskimo. The issue of their Native status is not relevant to this research. This book primarily addresses the very high rates of substance abuse and suicide of Innu and Inuit children and youth, and the Métis do not share this high rate. Moreover, the Métis have had a very different relationship to the Newfoundland and Canadian governments from early settlement to the present, a different combination of productive activities, and very different ways of connecting to larger political and economic organizations and processes than Innu or Inuit. My use of the term *Native people(s)* thus refers to the primary topic of the research and writing, Innu and Inuit, and leaves Métis aside for most of the text, not because they are or are not Native people but because they are not the focus of the problem.

Three: I also need to clarify the use of the term Native or indigenous *people* and Native or indigenous *peoples*. This is a very explosive issue, particularly since several governments—starting with Brazil, and including Canada— came under some pressure in the late 1990s from the United Nations human rights and indigenous peoples' forums to stop abusing Native peoples. Brazil had offered to grant substantial legal rights and protections to Native *people*, which raised the fearful possibility that Native *individuals* would be granted something like the rights of citizens, as usual not well enforced, and Native *peoples* would lose even more collective rights—to their land, their resources, their own political processes, and their special collective identities. There was a powerful demonstration at a United Nations–sponsored meeting in which Native peoples from different regions of the world held up placards with one letter on each: "S." The testimony of the demonstrators made it clear just how much is at stake in the presence or absence of this one letter: nothing less than a significant amount of collective autonomy vis-à-vis the dominant, surrounding, individuating, and increasingly control-seeking state and society. Thus, in this book the operative term is Native or indigenous *peoples*; *people* is to be understood as used in a context where a generalization from a specific is being made.

AFTER THIS INTRODUCTORY engagement with the notion of historical violence, which the rest of the book will expand and deepen, the remaining chapters are organized as follows: Chapter 2 looks at the initial construction and organization of dependency for both Innu and Inuit, which is the process of making Indians and Eskimos from Native peoples. Chapters 3 and 4 examine how that dependence was used and the transformation of Native societies as Native people built their own lives in the midst of this invasion. Chapter 5 takes a closer look at the production of dignity, autonomy, and creative expressiveness in the midst of an exceptionally destructive domination. How this was once done may be relevant now. Chapters 6 and 7 address the ways that current forms of imposition on Native peoples, less directly domineering, have become even more destructive, transferring some of their murderous potential of destructive domination to Native peoples themselves, while at the same time opening new opportunities for some Native people to develop relatively prosperous, if in the long run not very secure, lives. The concluding chapter 8 centers both on a fable and on several "stories" about the lessons First Nations peoples have learned for dealing with recent and current manifestations of domination: ways of catching all-too-powerful manifestations of domination very much off guard.

TWO **Owning Death and Life**

Making "Indians" and "Eskimos" from Native Peoples

Questioning the Early Not-Yet-Past

For the issues that now confront the Native peoples of Labrador, history is not just what happened, nor how, nor even why. History in Labrador, as elsewhere, is primarily about pasts that are not past, pasts that still cause problems and, at the same time, are still used in trying to deal with present problems. There is nothing neat or simple about pasts that live openly, and at times confrontationally, in the present. This is often a special issue for Native peoples, who are often socially constructed in terms of what is, or is presumed to be, their history.

Using a perspective on histories that people don't just "have" but live both within and against, we need to address three issues: (1) the production of dependency among formerly autonomous Native peoples; (2) the uses to which this dependency was put, by people who could pull the strings more or less effectively; and (3) the transformations that took place as Native peoples struggled within and against this dependency.

At the center of all these issues is use—the ways that the HBC used, or tried to use, the dependence of the people they sought to shape into the Indians of the fur trade, and similarly, the ways that the Moravian missionaries shaped almost all the Inuit in this region into the largely Christianized Eskimo sealskin producers who were "gathered," at least seasonally, into or around the Moravians' northern coastal mission stations.

In all of this Native people were far from passive—they had their own strategies and their own goals. But both Native peoples, Innu and Inuit, had to deal with severe imposed constraints on their ability to develop and use effective strategies for their own purposes. The most pervasive limitation on Native action was continual dispossession and displacement. In its most basic features this worked the same way for both Native peoples in Labrador—those becoming Indians and those becoming Eskimos.

Considering how brutal the fur trade was, and the widespread belief that missionaries were mostly "good people," or people trying to do good, it is surprisingly difficult to say whether missionary or fur trader shaped more past and present suffering, despite the moments of satisfaction and sustenance each also brought. The Moravian missionaries probably were less openly brutal than HBC traders, and they did many positive things, but in the long run the suffering they caused was not that much different, especially not in its present consequences.

In both cases unavoidable Native dependence on traders and missionaries enabled imposed transformations of Native societies and cultures. In both cases this Native dependence was made inescapable by displacement. These displacements began at early contact and continue to the present, shaping and reshaping lives, shaping and reshaping deaths, all in ways that stretch, while changing, from early contact with Europeans very far into now.[1]

To grasp this long history, still living and still murderous, we will need a very broad and thoughtful understanding of displacement. This begins simply, as forced physical movement from one place to another. From that basic start we will also consider such processes as losing the possibility of adequately subsisting oneself through one's own activities. This was one consequence of physical displacement and use, but also a consequence of the invaders' appropriation or destruction of key resources, leaving Native people without the means to adequately sustain themselves, even if they were not yet forced to move. The increasing difficulty of meeting their own needs, of sustaining themselves, led to increasingly dangerous or unproductive extensions of procurement areas. As it became increasingly difficult to wrest a living from the land and the sea, it was possible to become increasingly displaced without yet moving. The scars of this kind of displacement could follow wherever you go, follow you into the future and sometimes be waiting for you when you got there, because Native people often "got there" with fewer people than started out.

To more fully grasp what displacement means and has meant, as well as the ways that displacement can happen while people stay in what was once "their place," we will need to consider something much more general, which happens in a variety of ways. It is something pointed to by the North American folk phrase "having the ground cut out from under you." This, in a related folk idiom, "leaves you hanging" in all the senses of that term, including out in space, ungrounded, hanging from the noose. "Getting high" can be trying to take control of what is being done to you when the ground is cut out from under you. But you can only get so far away, so high above your own suffering: what people do to rise above their abuse, their sorrow, or their tension often puts them back somewhere on, or in, the ground.

The major point here is to emphasize the fact that displacement, including being moved, or being unable to sustain a livable life, having the ground cut out from under you, is a complex matter, not easy to define or to understand. To aid in that task, we must return to displacement's brutal and brutalizing second-born twin: dependence.

Dependence of adults (children are always necessarily and productively dependent) has long been the most usual and the most useful consequence of displacement, for it makes Native people vulnerable to domination.[2] Domination sought to make Native peoples vulnerable first to the manipulations of traders and missionaries, then to the seasonal fishery from the Labrador coast, and more recently and even more pervasively to state and provincial governments. Yet dependence has never been total, and the partiality of the dependence and the vulnerability that came with it shaped a brutal history of what I will call *inconclusive domination*. This term names a core dynamic of Native history, for it points toward both their shackles and simultaneously their collective creative freedom.

What follows in this and subsequent chapters is not a general history of Innu and Inuit since early contact.[3] It is, instead, a history of the not-yet-past: the formation of displacement, dependence, vulnerability, and use, all in ways that still ricochet murderously off the walls of the present, chasing the present into the future.

THE OPENING SET OF questions on which so much Labrador history turns, the questions that deeply shape a new understanding of the contemporary problems in Native communities, are as follows: How did Native peoples who had lived for themselves in this region for so long so quickly become so dependent on the HBC and on the missionaries that HBC could starve them to death almost at will, for not doing or being unable to do just what HBC wanted? Similarly, why could Moravian missionaries bring almost all the Inuit in the region who survived the introduced diseases under their control? What enabled pressuring the Innu and Inuit to abandon their former religion (a different issue from also accepting Christianity) and the Inuit to separate themselves from those who did not convert, to change their kinship-residence-marriage practices, and to ignore their former spiritual-medical leaders? How could both Innu and Inuit be forced to move from one locale to another, as HBC trading posts and mission stations were closed and reopened elsewhere? How did HBC and the Moravians get such power and control over Native people?

It is important to note that these questions have not been adequately addressed in the historical or anthropological literature. While Indian dependency on HBC and Eskimo dependency on the mission stations have often been noted, the important question is, how was this rather intense dependency produced? This question about how it could be done turns out to help us all, including Native peoples, understand its consequences. The rapid collapse of Native autonomy is more than surprising; it is the foundational event that still very much shapes current issues.

Both the present forms of suffering and some of the major reasons why the programs designed to alleviate this suffering do not and cannot work are connected to the ways that dependency, formed in the early years of contact, continues to be produced and enforced, under new disguises, today. This continuity exists despite the fact that a succession of recent provincial (state) and national governments claim to have ended older systems of domination and abuse. They also claim to have a new "respect" and "concern" for Native peoples, and in recent decades these governments have increasingly provided what they regard as legal and legislative guarantees for Native rights. Yet the new and continuing forms of dependence and "concerned" control are, as we shall see, often more destructive than the openly brutal and disrespectful domination that came before.

Gaynor MacDonald (2008), an anthropologist who has worked with Australian Aborigines for decades, is one of several Australian anthropologists insightfully concerned with a similar set of problems among Aborigines. In Australia as in Labrador, problems within aboriginal communities have intensified dramatically from the late 1960s to the present.[4] The common elements in both cases are rooted in changing processes of state control, and these processes are far broader than Australia and Canada, impacting not just Native people but also other vulnerable peoples, such as undocumented workers, immigrants from disfavored places, women, and minorities.

In discussing the early formation of these specific instances of an enduring situation, we will start with the production of usefully dependent Indians and then shift to the more subtle, but in the long run just as destructive, dynamics of the production of the also usefully dependent people long known as Eskimos. Keep in mind that the peoples the colonizers wound up naming Indians and Eskimos were not "found" here at contact, but rather were made by conquest, displacement, and especially use. The history of early colonialism is the history of Native people becoming Indians and Eskimos.

In this becoming they did not lose, or give up, all their autonomy and their own claims upon the changing social and physical landscape. Far from it. Crucially, their ability to make and partly enforce their own claims in the midst of their vulnerability was rooted in the fundamental structures of domination. This will be discussed in the beginning of chapter 3, in the context of a discussion of the system of trade used by both HBC and the missionaries, called "truck." In the process of being made into Indians and Eskimos, one further important issue is how Native people were put in a position where they too had something significant to gain from becoming dependent, from becoming Indians and Eskimos.

Displacement and dependence are not abstract. They develop on specific landscapes that are, to begin, physically shaped and then, inescapably, socially constructed. A few preliminary words about the physical landscapes will set the stage for the relationships that made and remade peoples' lives on this land.

Landscapes of Struggle

Labrador, now a part of the Canadian province of Newfoundland and Labrador, began its post-contact history as "The Labrador," which some say is a modern rendition of a multilanguage fisher's phrase meaning the place of hard (*dur* in French, *duramente* in Portuguese) labor. The Labrador Atlantic Ocean coastline reaches from the Strait of Belle Isle, just north of the Gulf of the St. Lawrence River, where the river joins the Atlantic Ocean, northward to a place called Killiniq Island. Cape Chidley, only a few miles north of Killiniq Island and politically part of Québec, is the northeastern-most point on the North American continental coastline, where it then turns westward, making the southern shore of the ocean passage that is now called Hudson Strait. Across this brutally rough strait, forty to eighty miles north, is the southern shore of Baffin Island. Going west from Cape Chidley, about 450 miles, one comes to the eastern shore of Hudson's Bay, more than six hundred miles wide on average, and about six hundred miles from its northern opening to its southern shore, not counting the further extension of this bay southward, about another two hundred miles, into the much narrower James Bay.

The large mass of land between Hudson's Bay and the Atlantic Ocean, more than five hundred miles wide in the north to over a thousand miles wide from the southern end of the bay to the Atlantic, is called the Ungava Peninsula, or more recently, the Labrador Peninsula. To minimize confusion, I will use Ungava for the name of the peninsula and Labrador for the political entity on the eastern part of the Ungava Peninsula. From Cape Chidley in the north to the southern end of the Strait of Belle Isle in the south, Labrador is about seven hundred miles long,[5] if we ignore the complexities of the coast-line, which would greatly increase the distance.

It was only in 1927 that it was decided where on the Ungava Peninsula the political entity of Labrador would be. To make this decision, it was nec-essary to specify a boundary between Québec, a province of Canada, and Labrador, politically a part of the then independent British colony/country of Newfoundland.[6] Newfoundland confederated with Canada in 1949, tak-ing Labrador, which it by then "owned," with it. The province is now called Newfoundland and Labrador, although it is a far from equal relationship. Labrador, in fundamental ways and especially for the Innu and Inuit, is a colony of both Newfoundland and Canada.

Labrador, as the political boundaries were defined by a British court in 1927, in a quarrel between Québec and Newfoundland over which of them "owned" Labrador and where Labrador began and ended, is the eastern third of the Ungava Peninsula, from Killiniq Island in the north almost to the Gulf of St. Lawrence in the south. On the Atlantic Ocean coast the southern boundary of Labrador ends at the southern end of the narrow channel be-tween Labrador and Newfoundland, just north of the Gulf of St. Lawrence, the mouth of the St. Lawrence River. This channel, only eight miles wide at its northern end, is called the Strait of Belle Isle.

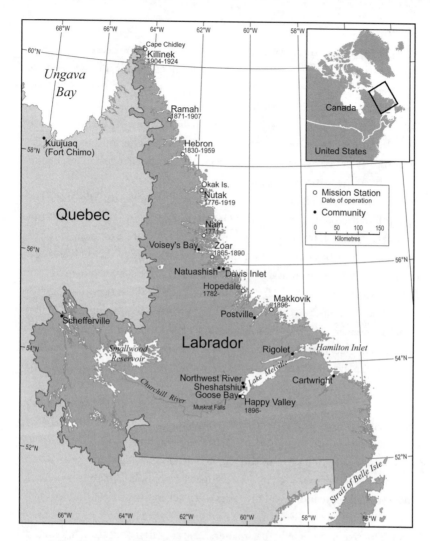

MAP 1. Labrador, with major Inuit and Innu communities.

This channel was the center of an early fishery, including very intense sixteenth-century whaling, from the early 1500s, if not before, through the next two or three centuries. It was also the center of major confrontations first between European fishers and Native peoples, who were also using these marine resources, and then between the peoples becoming Indian and Eskimo. Native peoples were both drawn into a confrontation with European whalers and fishers and then used against each other in ways that displaced and profoundly changed both.

The western boundary of Labrador, the map line between Labrador and Québec, is the height of land where the rivers divide, flowing eastward through Labrador into the Atlantic Ocean, or westward through Québec into Hudson's Bay.[7] The southern boundary of Labrador is a bit north of a different height of land where the rivers, instead of flowing east or west, turn southward through Québec into the St. Lawrence. The southern boundary was mostly drawn as a straight line, so it only approximately can be specified in terms of the features of the landscape.

The east-west height of land is an irregular line in the middle of the great plateau of the Labrador interior. The plateau receives about the most snowfall of any place in the world, as the moisture-laden air from the Atlantic and from Hudson's Bay crosses into the intense winter cold of the central Ungava Peninsula. When this massive snowpack melts in the summer, the river runs are extraordinary. Indeed, the whole landscape in the interior of Labrador is webbed with an uncountable number of rivers, streams, brooks, rivulets, and deep layers of living and dead moss, called muskeg, all punctuated by pockets of glacial boulders, major rock outcrops, and stretches of dry forest land. In the summer the frozen surface ground melts and much of the muskeg becomes water soaked.

The land becomes immensely difficult to traverse in the summer. The muskeg becomes spongy soft, and the vast clouds of mosquitos and biting flies, spawned in all this water, terrorize the people who must live there. It is also a hard land to live on in the winter, with intense cold and storms, temperatures that drop to −30 or −40 degrees Fahrenheit (which is −34 to −40 degrees Celsius), and ice on the lakes often seven to nine feet thick, difficult or impossible to cut through, from midwinter to spring thaw, to get access to fish. The rivers, especially the smaller ones, are often rock strewn, remnants of recent glaciation, with multiple rapids and difficult portages, making canoe travel more difficult than usual in Canada.

Southern Labrador is forest, mostly spruce and some birch, with alder in the wetter areas, giving way in the northern third of the interior to scrub, and then quickly into the caribou barrens of the north, with small pockets of trees in the more sheltered valleys, and the rest of the rocky, river-strewn land growing only moss and lichen. Strong winds keep much of the moss and lichen on the northern barrens free enough of snow cover to provide food for the caribou—the same animal as the reindeer of northern Norway, Finland, and Siberia, but in Labrador not domesticated.

The Labrador coastline is rocky, with cliffs and glacier-strewn boulders right down to the sea edge in most places, and with a multitude of islands, from tiny to large, along the length of the coast—fishing, sealing, and birding stations, or so these islands were. The northern half or two-thirds of the Labrador coast (in some years more, recently much less) is blocked with pack ice—sea ice driven against the coastline by wind, current, and tide, forming a solid mass in midwinter, safe to walk across to access sea resources, easily supporting dogsleds and now snowmobiles. It is treacherously almost impossible to cross, on top or in a small boat, during the several months when it is forming in the fall and breaking up in the spring.

John McLean, a chief factor (agent-trader) for the HBC, was sent to Fort Chimo, near the northern tip of the Labrador Peninsula, in 1837 to open a fur trade there, and over the next years to find a river route to the central Labrador Atlantic coast, which would facilitate supplying a string of trading posts or "forts" to be established in the interior. Although he had a long career serving HBC in the harsh northern interior of Canada, he thought this plan was particularly ill-conceived, partly due to the exceptional rigors of inland Labrador, which he described:

In so high a latitude as that of Ungava, the climate presents the extremes of heat and cold; the moderate temperature of spring and autumn is unknown, the rigour of winter being immediately succeeded by the intense heat of summer, and *vice versa.*

On the 12th of June, 1840, the thermometer was observed to rise from 10° below zero to 76° in the shade, the sky clear and the weather calm; this was, in fact, the first day of summer. For ten days previously the thermometer ranged from 15° below zero to 32° above, and the weather was as boisterous as in the month of January, snowing and blowing furiously all the time. The heat continued to increase, till the thermometer frequently exhibited from 85° to 100° in the shade....

The winter may be said to commence in October; by the end of this month the ground is covered with snow, and the rivers and smaller lakes are frozen over; the actions of the tide, however, and the strength of the current, often keep Ungava River open till the month of January. At this period I have neither seen, read, nor heard of any locality under heaven that can offer a more cheerless abode to civilized man than Ungava....

When the river sets fast, the beauties of the winter scene are disclosed—one continuous surface of glaring snow, with here and there a clump of dwarf pine, or the bald summits of barren hills, from which the violence of the winter storms sweep away even the tenacious lichens. The winter storms are the most violent I have ever experienced, sweeping everything before them; and often prove fatal to the Indians when overtaken by them in places where no shelter can be found. (McLean [1849] 1932, 248–249)

McLean, before his posting to northern Labrador, had crossed northern Canada from Hudson's Bay to the Rocky Mountains several times in all seasons: his point of comparison was very far from Europe. He had also some experience, almost a decade before, in overwintering in Ungava. The Atlantic coastal climate is usually much more moderate than the interior, for along the coast there is a spring and a fall, and the winter storms, while still severe, are not always this violent. McLean is describing a semilivable landscape in northern and interior Ungava. This is precisely the landscape to which Innu were driven by the violence and by the new and intensely deadly diseases of the coast, the landscape within which they became the Indians of the HBC's fur trade.

This was the landscape of Native peoples' displacement, and it is to this history that we now turn.

Arrivals

By the early 1500s, and very likely in the late 1400s, Basque fishers and whalers from the Atlantic coasts of France and Spain came out every year, from mid-spring to late fall, to work the waters of the southern coasts of what is now Labrador. In particular, they focused on the narrow Strait of Belle Isle between southernmost Labrador and the Northern Peninsula of Newfoundland. At its narrowest point, this strait is only eight miles wide, and it wonderfully concentrates the very large numbers of whales that once migrated through it seasonally. By 1520 the Basques had established a large and substantially built whale-processing center in a place now called Red Bay, on the Labrador coast just north of the strait, where they rendered oil from whale blubber, processed baleen (a specific kind of whalebone, the primary pre-plastic), and traded with the Inuit, who were also whaling, for even more of these valuable supplies than they could procure themselves (Barkham 1980; Taylor 1980; Tuck 1989; Auger 1991). The Basques were soon joined by Dutch, who mostly worked the coasts to the north of the strait, by the Portuguese, who concentrated on the exceptionally prolific cod fishery, and then by the English and the French, who, more dispersed along the Labrador coast, fished and whaled, and more intensively than others traded for furs.

For a hundred years or more Basque whalers predominated among these European intruders, and taken all together it was a surprisingly large and productive enterprise. Labrador sustained the major European fishery of the sixteenth century (Tuck 1989) and was a major source of European merchant wealth, worth "defending" intensely against those Natives who resented or resisted the invasive intrusion on their lands and their own food supplies, or who for quite a while effectively sought to use the intrusion to their own advantage.

Understanding the way that Native people, particularly the Inuit, sought to use this intrusion to their own advantage requires reworking the usual views of Inuit history and Inuit subsistence patterns. Far from being isolated primitives huddled in igloos and paddling tiny kayaks in search of an occasional seal or fish, the Inuit were long part of a northern world-trading system. The trade networks the Inuit joined stretched across the eastern Arctic through Norse Greenland and reached into Northern Europe and beyond to the Mediterranean. These networks had also included the pre-Inuit Arctic people, now known as the Thule-Dorset. Both Dorset and Inuit were suppliers of marine ivory from walrus and narwhale, with the Inuit in particular being substantial whalers in their own right and traders of whale and seal oil, as well as other northern products.

The Inuit, by the time the Basque whalers arrived in the late 1400s or the early 1500s, were familiar with iron, with trade with Europeans, and with the Viking propensity for (if not commitment to) wallowing in brutal violence—currently regarded as the primary basis for the Viking's expansionary success, which no longer can be seen as simply based on their cleverness with marine technology.

All the complexities of Inuit and pre-Inuit history, including some controversies over interpreting the data, can for purposes here be condensed to the following, to help understand the contradictory post-contact relations that developed between the Basque whalers and the Inuit.[8]

There were two major, different societies that peopled the high Arctic and the eastern sub-Arctic before the 1500s. The oldest, which lasted almost four thousand years when its earlier manifestations are included, is called the Dorset. It seems to have been a productive and secure way of life, with an effective coastal technology for procuring walrus, seals, and other forms of marine life, and the people used their effective production technology to develop a rich cultural life rooted in substantial communities with semi-subterranean houses. Sometime in the 1100s, for reasons that remain controversial, the Dorset declined and almost entirely disappeared from the eastern and high Arctic. Their place was subsequently taken by a people archaeologically known as Thule, or Thule-Inuit, who migrated across the northern continent from western Alaska in the period 1250–1350, soon filling the eastern Arctic, from northwestern Greenland back west to Baffin Island, and by the 1400s the Labrador coast at least as far south as the Strait of Belle Isle. These were the ancestors of the present Inuit people.[9]

What the controversies are about is fairly straightforward: Why did a people as successful as the Dorset disappear? When did the Thule-Inuit arrive (which now includes the questions of why they came and how long their migration from western Alaska took)? Did the Thule displace the Dorset, violently or technologically, for they were better whalers and probably more experienced warriors?

The standard view has been that the Thule arrived by the 1100s, in time to displace or absorb the Dorset—a view that has been popular, but one for which there is not much reliable evidence. The newer view, for which the evidence is not much more substantial, but which explains the facts much more effectively, is completely different.[10]

In this newer view the earlier eastern Arctic people, the Dorset, particularly in northwestern Greenland, were in active trade relations with the Norse farmers and hunters, from about 985 up to or through the 1100s. They were supplying the Norse with valuable goods, from marine ivory and rendered oil to furs and pelts, which the Greenland Norse in turn were using to pay their taxes to their homeland and also carrying in trade as far as the eastern Mediterranean.

The Mediterranean then was an incubator for many historically significant plagues, and it is argued (Maschner, Mason, and McGhee 2009) that the Norse brought back novel diseases to the Dorset, and the Dorset then spread the diseases among themselves, probably decimating their communities below the demographic level necessary for successful social reproduction.

After the decline and almost entire disappearance of the Dorset from the high Arctic and the eastern Arctic, the Thule Inuit, in the newer view, rapidly moved eastward, crossing the four thousand kilometers from Alaska to Greenland in only a few decades, and arriving in northern Greenland in the mid- to late 1300s. In this view they were driven out of western Alaska by the expansion of the Ming Dynasty in China, and then by the Mongol expansion, especially by Genghis Kahn, both of which cut off Thule access to iron and other necessities, which they had been obtaining via trade into Siberia.

The Thule thus went rapidly westward, seeking the iron they could get from the Norse and from the meteor fields of northern Greenland, both of which had been circulating, in small quantities at least, all across the high Arctic when this region was in Dorset hands.[11] The Thule Inuit became the new Norse trading partners, during the same period that the Norse in Greenland were increasingly doomed by a combination of climate change, plague, and louse-borne typhus.[12] Disease and the decline of agricultural productivity decimated the Norse, first diminishing their presence in Greenland and then finally driving them out.

Southern Greenland was settled in 985 by Norse under the leadership of Erik the Red, who had been expelled from both the Norse homeland and the Icelandic colonies for excessive violence. This was the beginning of a period of local and Northern Hemisphere warming, which made farming possible in southern Greenland and also kept this coast relatively ice-free. The Dorset and later the Inuit both settled in northern Greenland, where the pack ice against the shore from fall to late spring facilitated the hunt for marine mammals. Seals give birth to their young on this pack ice, making them particularly vulnerable to hunters. Norse and Dorset lived apart but interacted in many ways.

There is evidence for both trade and violence between Norse and Dorset almost from the start of Norse settlement, and then after 1250 or 1300, between Norse and Inuit. By 1300, however, the climate started to cool dramatically, first making farming by the Norse in southern Greenland and then even pasturing sheep and goats increasingly impossible. The Norse colony diminished rapidly, and between 1450 and 1500 it disappeared completely. The Norse abandonment of Greenland occurred at about the same time period that the Inuit of northern Greenland expanded across Baffin Island and on down the Labrador coast, into the North Shore of the Gulf of St. Lawrence, meeting Basque whalers and Jesuit priests, as well as a variety of explorers, traders, and slavers by the early 1500s, if not before.

It may well be that it was the decline of trading and raiding possibilities in Greenland, with the abandonment of the Norse settlements, that led the Inuit to expand down the Labrador coasts, which they did somewhat before the Basque whalers arrived, perhaps at first just to access richer whaling grounds and the thick forests of southern Labrador. The increasing cold may also have led the Inuit to abandon their communities in northern Greenland and migrate into southern Labrador. The major relevant point here is this: whatever the pressures leading the Inuit into Labrador, they were far from the isolated innocents subsequently constructed in western romantic fantasies. Nor were the peoples who became the colonists Indians.

When John Cabot sailed along the Labrador coast in 1497, the Innu were waiving pelts on poles to attract his attention. While much less is known about pre-contact history of the Innu, compared to the relatively rich Inuit archaeological record, it is clear that the Innu also had some very early dealings with Europeans, and by 1500 they too knew about European practices. For complex reasons Innu sided with Europeans against the assertiveness of the Inuit. This assertiveness, and the antagonistic separation of Innu and Inuit, requires some discussion.

The Inuit knew what iron was and wanted it when the Basques showed up, and they were far from naive about either terms of trade or what the Europeans wanted—the earliest recorded comments by explorers and fishers have the "esquimaux indians" showing up with packets of furs and whalebone. Nor were they naive about European propensity for, and routine reliance on, violence. They were also, and quite relevantly as we shall see, very successful whalers in their own right.

Indeed, the southward expansion of the Inuit into Labrador and northern Newfoundland was rooted in an effective production technology. It is not yet clear, from the archaeological evidence, to what extent the expanding Inuit absorbed or displaced prior Native peoples, both Dorset and Amerindian— that is, whether a good part of their technology spread to some of these peoples, making their material remains look Inuit, or if the Dorset on the Labrador coast mostly died out from Norse-introduced diseases, leaving only remnant populations.

J. Garth Taylor has two early articles that claim that the earliest fishers, whalers, and explorers called some people "Esquimaux" that later Europeans would call Indian (Taylor 1979, 1980). I see the issue somewhat differently: that the boundary between what became, in the early colonial period, Indians and Eskimos was not as clear-cut a separation as it subsequently became. This is not to deny that there were different languages and quite different practices. But just as the modern and episodically brutal separation of peoples in Europe—French, German, Polish, etc.—is an artifact of the long process of state formation and did not reflect the on-the-ground realities until more recently, so most likely was the situation between the peoples that became Indian and Eskimo. The brothers Grimm, linguists as well as folktale collectors, pointed out that in the early nineteenth century you could walk across Europe and between any two neighboring villages the language in use would be mutually intelligible. Arguments over whether a people or a community, in the earliest colonization, were Indian or Eskimo may miss the point. They could be both, and at the same time neither—under our current concepts of completely separate peoples. This is not the place to explore that possibility, but only to point out that we cannot take what became a later situation and impose it on an earlier set of social relations.

THE PEOPLE WHO BECAME the Indians not just of but for the colonists and the fur trade—as well as very much for themselves—inhabited the lands that became Labrador and eastern Québec since the retreat of the last glaciation and the subsequent reforestation: about eight thousand years before the present. A material culture emerged in the context of this inhabitation that in many of its basic features endured for about six thousand years. About two thousand years ago there was a transformation in Native material culture, which archaeologists have named for the type site where this difference was first observed: Point Revenge. Point Revenge changes were distinctive enough to serve as a marker of connections. Material remains similar to Point Revenge have been found from north central coastal and in a few places interior Labrador southward into the Gulf of St. Lawrence.

The people producing this material culture sustained an early and substantial onslaught both from European whalers, fishers, and traders and from a succession of early explorers who routinely sought to bring back as many captives—as slaves, as zoo-like objects, as future translators—as they could lure on board their ships or grab in forays inland. Their inland trips, up the bays and fjords, were also about trade, mapping, and "planting the flag." The devastating epidemic diseases they brought, which seem to have undermined Native peoples' abilities to sustain their own ways, were soon followed by another intrusion: Jesuit missionaries, who came to offer or impose new ways.

There is substantial evidence that the Jesuits were a very active part of processes that substantially diminished the status and well-being of Amerindian women: Karen Anderson's *Chain Her by One Foot: The Subjugation of Native Women in Seventeenth-Century New France* (1991) is excellent on this issue. Such increasing internal inequalities, very much including gender inequalities, make people much more vulnerable to external domination, for the emerging "elite" tend to become the allies of the dominant.[13] That is how it was in the colonial period, and that is how, in part, it is redeveloping today, with mining royalties and state subsidies offering very attractive, and sometimes necessary, inducements to Native elites.

More broadly and more significantly than the problem of Native elite cooperation with the dominant society—which produces gains as well as losses—is the general and very substantial increase in inequality in Native communities, and this turns out to be a major asset to the dominant society, which uses the increasing antagonistic differentiation within (and sometimes between) Native communities to facilitate appropriation of Native resources. It is a long history, despite substantial changes.

Grasping the Onslaught

In several places in the Americas very early European presence was far more intense than is popularly imagined. Almost everyone knows that Columbus arrived in the Caribbean in 1492; it is far less widely known that the following year he brought back between thirteen hundred and fifteen hundred colonists to the Caribbean island that he called Hispaniola, and that by 1497, five years after first contact, a very large proportion of the Native population— estimates are more than a third—had been exterminated by war, land seizures, and introduced diseases.[14] Southern Labrador has a similar story. The suddenness, scale, and severity of the earliest onslaught provide a different perspective on the encounter, one that makes the English, French, and Basques look as confrontationally disruptive as the Spanish in Mexico, who the English were fond of accusing of brutality they claimed they did not share.

Our knowledge of the changing early contact situation for Native people is built from several different kinds of data sources. Marine archaeology and history have been particularly helpful with the early European presence and also can be useful for the early history of Native peoples. Land-based archaeology, along with history and other kinds of documentary evidence, has helped to reveal the Native situation, but here much of what we know has to be inferential from very scarce data, as the archaeology is almost entirely coastal, and documentary evidence for the interior is exceedingly scarce until the mid-nineteenth century.

An overview, as well as a new understanding of the early history of Basque fishing and whaling, begins with Selma Barkham (1980, 1982), whose archival research discovered documents on the early whale fishery. By the 1530s the Basques were sending out a minimum of fifteen ships a year, with a total crew averaging about six hundred men. The center of the whale fishery was a place the Europeans called Red Bay, on the Labrador side of the northern end of the Strait of Belle Isle.

Three basic facts about Right and Bowhead whales, the focus of the hunt, shaped the social development of the whale fishery. First, both whales float when killed, making them easier to land and making it possible to hunt them from the small boats of the Inuit and the rowed boats carried over on the larger whaling ships. The harpoons, attached with lines to cloth or sealskin bags that dragged behind in the water, bled the whales to death. It was fairly easy to kill a large number of whales. From that point they just had to be towed ashore. Second, the Right whales migrated in very large numbers through the Strait of Belle Isle in early June, not long after the coastal ice broke up and either drifted off or melted. The Bowhead whales migrated through the straits in early October, not long before the winter storms made sailing even more dangerous for the unusually slow and cumbersome ships (even by contemporary standards) that were fitted out for the whaling trade. Third, these whales were both repositories of oil, which was boiled out of their blubber in large land-based vats and sold as lamp oil in Europe—the most valuable commodity of the trade. The whales also provided baleen or "whalebone," another valuable commodity and easier to transport. For the Inuit the whales were a very substantial source of food, as well as providing oil for lamps and heat and baleen for their own use or to trade with the Europeans.

The seasonality of the whale's appearance where they could be readily caught, combined with the severity of Labrador winters and the problems of travel to and from Labrador in the early spring and late fall, when the North Atlantic near Labrador was subject to very severe storms, meant that the Europeans wanted to leave behind, from one season to the next, the shore facilities necessary to process the blubber and to house the summer workers while most of the crew went back to Europe. At the end of the whaling season, the ships' captains would perhaps leave one or two men to overwinter and to guard the facilities. Leaving the shore facilities intact meant they could postpone the spring travel a bit and leave in the fall without taking the time to dismantle it all—and still have a good early and late whaling and fishing season. The Inuit's prior history helped them shape their own claims upon these largely abandoned shore facilities, facilities that were supporting an alien endeavor that was both taking and destroying a major food source. These facilities were a very rich source of iron, particularly when they were burnt in the winter to expose the iron nails in the wood, and when the small boats and other objects left behind for the winter could be taken.

The Inuit very quickly came under three sorts of pressures from the Europeans. First, the Europeans assaulted them directly, trying to drive them off, but also wanted to trade with them, especially for valuable furs and the Inuit's baleen, and this contradiction kept the violence against the Inuit from being totally murderous. Further limiting the deadliness of the early assaults upon them, the Inuit could disappear in the summer and return after the Europeans left—unless they decided to confront the Europeans with a massed assault, as they sometimes did. So direct assault by Europeans was not totally devastating, at least not at first. Second, the Europeans, by the late 1500s and increasingly throughout the 1600s, began to arm the people they called "Indians" and bribe them or use them for attacking "Eskimos" and driving them north. Third, the Europeans took a lot of whales—approximately twenty thousand in the half century from 1530 to 1580, by which time the whales in this region were largely gone. The whales migrated to northern Labrador and even further north, the Basques and, by the early 1600s, other European whalers, including especially the Dutch, following. The Inuit, deprived of one of their main sources of food, unarmed in the face of armed attack by Indians and Europeans, and subject to introduced diseases, began evacuating southern Labrador northward toward central, and then northern, Labrador. Yet even as the Inuit population shifted northward, they seem to have kept up an episodic and for the Europeans a menacing presence in and even beyond southern Labrador, all the way down into the Bay of St. Lawrence and the North Shore of the St. Lawrence River, until the late mid-1700s.

To understand the dynamics of Inuit becoming Eskimo, and their presence in and displacement from southern coastal Labrador, it is helpful to begin with the fact that both Eskimo and European were terrorized by each other, and both simultaneously wanted to use the other for a variety of reasons. Sieur Louis Fornel, an early French explorer and colonist, is particularly instructive about the tension between trade and terror that provided some space for the Inuit to do more than trade for iron and other items utterly on the terms set by Europeans.

I quote from his petition for a grant to operate a seal fishery and an attached trading station in central Labrador. This petition was the purpose of his narrative of his exploratory and land-claiming voyage.[15] Fornel traveled from Québec City down the northeast-flowing St. Lawrence River to its mouth, and then north up the coast of Labrador into the large bay that divides northern from southern Labrador, or he claimed he got that far. The bay is now called Hamilton Inlet; it was then known by a variety of names, including Esquimaux Bay, or for the French, Baye des Esquimaux, and, especially in its inland reaches, by variants of the Innu term Kessessakiou. The outer bay, in the early mid-1700s was inhabited by Inuit, perhaps not exclusively, and the inner bay by Innu, along with a few small trading operations and a scattering of settlers.

NARRATIVE OF VOYAGE BY SIEUR LOUIS FORNEL TO BAYE DES
ESQUIMAUX, 16 MAY TO 27 AUG. 1743 [EXCERPTS]

He starts:

> The narrative ... of the discovery made by me of Baie des Esquimaux ... [and a chart that gives] an exact knowledge of the Esquimaux coast, where no one, previously, had ventured to sail near the shore, for fear of these barbarians.

Fornel is, as his own document shows, inventing his primacy but not his fear:

> 4 JULY, 1743 ... we arrived opposite cape Charles [on the southern coast of Labrador]. After sailing for five or six leagues from said cape, we saw the entrance of bay St. Alexis.... Steering a north-quarter-north-west course, we sailed about five or six leagues along the Esquimaux coast, which is a very high and steep treeless cliff.... [We entered a bay we called] baye des Meniques.... We then put a [small] boat to sea, and many of our crew landed on a steep island at the summit of which they kindled a fire with peat. Having seen Esquimaux approaching in six canoes and three boats, our men jumped into the boat and came on board crying out to us to weigh anchor and to moor further from the shore so as to be out of reach of the arrows of the Esquimaux. Having shifted our anchorage, we then put our artillery in readiness and prepared our arms in order to be always on the defensive in case of an attack, and to avoid being taken by surprise during the night. Not venturing to board us, the said Esquimaux landed on a neighbouring island where they uttered cries, raising their oars and saying in their jargon, *Tout Camara Troquo balena, non Characo*, which means, No war, I am your comrade, let us trade whale.

Note that this is already a multilanguage (polyglot) trade jargon, mixing French and Basque, and the trade offering is from whales.

> As we had a speaking-trumpet on board, we took it to answer them in the same terms. Three Esquimaux then jumped into their canoes and came on aboard where they showed us great affection. I remarked that the presence of our small artillery and of our arms frightened them to such a degree that all their bodies

were trembling for fear of them and to such an extent that they naturally bled from the nose without striking themselves, which I found very queer. I had some gifts distributed to them, which seemed to please them, and in return they gave me whale fins, together with some of their seal clothing which is valueless, and which I accepted only to avoid appearing to refuse their gifts. They then embarked in their canoes. As they were leaving, I had a few rifle shots fired, which appeared to frighten them and caused them to cry *as if* asking for mercy. (emphasis added)

"As if . . ."? The aliens' need to have the last word in the language of terror suggests just how frightened they themselves were when they purposefully sought to terrorize the Natives with gunshots.

5 JULY, 1743 Having left Baye des Meniques,[16] we sailed about seven leagues along the Esquimaux coast. Then contrary winds having set in, we were compelled to seek shelter in another bay. . . . Before anchoring . . . we tried to tack about to leave this bay. And, at the same time, as the wind decreased, we saw nine canoes of Esquimaux and a boat which appeared to us to be paddled by only women and children. Fearing an attack, we had our arms in readiness, nine canoes of Esquimaux having reached the vessel. One of them gave us to understand that his name was *Captain* Hapé, and, seeing that we could not leave the bay on account of a contrary wind, he offered to show us an anchorage. (emphasis added)

Inuit at this time and in this region, perhaps as part of mobilizing themselves to deal with all the violence, had leaders, who were called, by themselves and by the Europeans, "Captain."

Having embarked in his canoe and proceeded ahead to indicate the course, he led us to the bottom of the bay to show us the anchorage. . . . As an acknowledgment of the good service he had rendered us, I gave him a few gifts, and some to the other *Indians* of his troop, who expressed great friendship for us and gave us whale fins. (emphasis added)

The colonists sometimes called people Indians that they otherwise knew as Eskimo, especially when they were having friendly relations with the Eskimo. At this point in Labrador colonial history, Eskimo names an enemy, Indian an ally.

6 JULY, 1743 The wind blowing from south-west, we sailed about four o'clock in the morning. As we were under sail, we saw three Esquimaux boats and a few

canoes of these barbarians, only one canoe of which could reach our vessel. . . . Having indicated our course to that Esquimaux, he offered to pilot us. Having taken the helm, he piloted us very well for more than two hours after leaving Hapé bay, and he piloted us for a distance of four leagues past steep bluffs to the entrance of another bay of one league width at its entrance by many leagues in depth, in which bay he gave us to understand that Captain Araby [a European] was anchored and that there lived Captain Amargo, another Esquimaux chief, which caused us to name this bay after him. Our Esquimaux pilot returned to shore and left us, seeing that we would not proceed to the bottom of the bay where he had intended to lead us. At the same time, we recognized the vessel of the said [European Captain] Araby, which was sailing to leave the bay. And having waited for him, to speak to him, he told us that, at night, he had been boarded by nine Esquimaux canoes and had seen twenty-two boats, but that the great number of these barbarians had prevented him from trading. . . . The said Araby added that the land of Amargo, the Esquimaux captain, was in this bay; that these barbarians were great numbers, and that he advised us not to proceed any further, as we would find opposition along the coast. I answered him that we were armed and could defend ourselves. Having then asked the said Araby what had become of the Indians whom it was known he had taken on board to serve as his guides, he answered that the fear of the Esquimaux had caused them to flee.

Fear of "the Eskimo" was used by early traders to scare off other Europeans, but there was some real basis to it, partly emerging as retaliation for the violence used against Native people.

Frightened by Araby's statement, our crew mutinied, saying that they were being led to slaughter, and wanted to return. . . . I threatened them, saying that I would send the cowards ashore and keep only those of good will. That, first, seemed to frighten, and to quiet them. However, as they persisted in their mutiny, I threatened them, saying that they would lose their wages, and be punished on the complaint I would make against them. That, finally, appeased them. Then, standing on our course, we sailed out of Amargo bay, and, after traveling four or five leagues, we saw, at one o'clock in the afternoon, smoke in another bay, the entrance of which is only one league and which widens gradually, and may have two leagues in depth, with islands and islets and deep water everywhere in its entrance. Having entered the said bay we fired a few gun shots, and were surprised by being answered from land by other gun shots, and we perceived that they were natives other than Esquimaux, because the latter do not use fire-arms. We steered our course towards the smoke, but a contrary wind forced us to anchor between the islands and land in ten fathoms of water. Having ordered other gun shots to be fired, they were answered. About eight o'clock in the evening, Indians came on board and told us that they had been taken on board of [European Captain] Araby's vessel. As many of these Indians spoke French [which they probably learned from the Jesuits, or the French fishers and traders], I asked them why they had remained. They told us that they were to pilot Captain Araby to Kessessakiou Bay [the interior of Esquimaux Bay], but that the said Araby, fearing the Esquimaux, had abandoned them and was returning. Having then asked them whether they knew the said bay, they answered that they did, and if we would take them on board with their wives and children, they would show us the way and pilot us there. I agreed to these terms, and meeting the Indians in that place caused us to name it baye des Sauvages. (Translated and reprinted in Great Britain, Privy Council 1927, 3280–3286)

At this point in the early mid-1700s, the more southern Eskimos were being killed or dying out from diseases brought by the Europeans, and the survivors were being pushed northward. Three decades later the Moravians were granted large tracts of land in northern coastal Labrador, now substantially peopled by Inuit, for mission and trading stations, which focused on Christianizing the Natives and simultaneously sought to support the mission through Native trade. The grants of land to Moravians were huge, usually well over 100,000 hectares (247,000 acres, or about 385 square miles) for each mission station. These very large holdings intentionally allowed the Moravians to exclude other traders and missionaries and to maintain exclusive and increasingly total control over the Native peoples whom they gathered around their stations well into the mid-twentieth century. That control was what the Moravians wanted, and that control was what the British government also wanted when they granted those very large tracts of land.

The Moravians established their first long-term mission/trading station in Nain, northern Labrador, in 1771 and began to supply the Inuit with guns in 1785, in part to get more trade goods from them, and in larger part to keep the Inuit from going south to trade. With both Indians and Eskimos armed, and with the Moravians dominating the Inuit and the Catholic missionaries and the HBC dominating the Innu, an increasingly deadly separation continued to develop.

The deadliness of the separation was very directly the result of the local equivalent of what is now called, often in the context of colonial, imperial, corporate, state, or drug-cartel expansion, low-intensity warfare. From the late 1700s to the early 1900s Inuit and Innu killed each other, as opportunity arose, in raids, in ambushes, in chance encounters—a murderous relationship punctuated by an occasional marriage, or more likely a sequential co-marriage, to a European or Métis trader.[17] There was much more to the deadliness of the separation than this. We start with the Indians and the issues of disease and starvation, which were core features of what became a new separation in areas of inhabitation and resource procurement.

The same reasons—disease, the need for external supply, and fear— that increasingly kept Innu in the interior also kept Inuit on the northern coast. Here the fantasy history is that the Inuit-becoming-Eskimos settled in Moravian missionary–built villages because of their attraction to Christianity. While there was one intense period of religious enthusiasm in the early nineteenth century, there is a lot more to the story of Inuit settlement with the domineering Moravians, and their subsequent religious enthusiasm, than a chance to be churched. The religious "enthusiasm" of the Eskimos, with widespread conversion to Christianity, occurred in 1804–1805; the need for the quantity of seals that could be caught in Moravian-supplied nets emerged during the same time period, and "Christians" had better access to these nets. This is not at all to say that the Inuit became Christian simply to get the necessary nets, but that there was more to their emotionally intense conversion to Christianity than belief without a material basis.

Their need for seal nets from the Moravians was inextricably intertwined with other needs and hopes and plans for tomorrow. Carol Brice-Bennett (1981) has insightfully argued that Eskimo women played a key role in the 1804 religious "enthusiasm," partly in the context of their declining status and family situation in these Moravian-dominated, commodity-producing communities. Moreover, as we shall see in subsequent chapters, the production of Eskimos from Inuit, and Indians from Innu, was always and enduringly partial, incomplete. Nonetheless, it was, for a while, significantly determinative.

In 1823, about fifty years after the Moravians arrived, the Eskimos at Okak, by then the largest settlement, had their last whale hunt—the end point in a long decline in the availability of coastal whales (Kleivan 1966). Over a hundred whaling boats from Holland alone were working their waters, and there was nothing left (Braat 1984). The Inuit increasingly turned full-scale to sealing for their spring and early summer food, and for the pelts that they traded to the Moravians' stores, run on an explicitly commercial basis, to get needed supplies. They were also soon going to be pressured to take up commercial cod fishing. It was, all in all, a strange emerging contradiction, for at the same time that the Inuit were becoming, in both image and practice, the Eskimos settled in Moravian communities, "the chances of maintaining a purely Eskimo life in these [subarctic] areas dwindle[d]" (Kleivan 1966, 50, quoting Kaj Birkett-Smith 1959). They were at the same time the Moravians' "primitive" Eskimos and modern producers for a transatlantic commerce. The Innu, pressed into the HBC's fur trade largely on imposed terms, lived the same contradiction.

As the Inuit were pushed north—with special intensity during the early 1700s, when the French were a major supplier of guns to the Indians, in return for their help securing French coastal trading and fishing posts against Inuit incursions—they found the northern Labrador coast already significantly depleted of its whales. The Dutch—who in the 1590s had the largest merchant fleet in Europe—had been whaling and trading off the coast of northern Labrador at least from 1614.

The Dutch were trading as well as whaling, and it was as usual a trade mixed with violence. Scholars of this trade have pointed out that the trade earned the Dutch as much revenue as did whaling[18] and included the Inuit supplying whale blubber, baleen, sealskins, walrus ivory, and the skins of bear, white fox, and martin. A Dutch explorer and whaler with the Latin name Carolus, who in 1620 made for that time an exceptionally accurate map of the Labrador coast, in 1634 wrote,

> The natives of this land on both sides of the [Davis] Strait are altogether heathens and wild cannibals. . . . All that they want to trade they tied to the oar which they paddle their canoes. They don't trust anybody and therefore can also not be trusted. Beware of walking on the shore unless one is well on guard with a good musket. They don't ask to be treated with a sword because one never gets so near to them. But they can hit you with their bows and arrows and their slingshots. However, when they see that one of them has been downed by a musket shot they run landward into the mountains where they live. (Carolus 1634, cited by Kupp and Hart 1976, 8)

After 1642, when a Dutch trading and whaling monopoly to the Davis Strait (separating the northern tip of Labrador from Baffin Island) ended, there was a major expansion of these activities by other Europeans, which persisted with varying intensity into the nineteenth century, but increasingly further offshore or amidst the middle-distance ice flows as the coastal whale stock became decimated.

Thus, when the Moravians came to establish their comparatively more peaceful missions and Labrador trading stations, starting in the 1770s, they gave the Inuit some relief from the violence, which, given their decimation by trade-born disease, they were probably increasingly unable to defend against. The Inuit also had opportunities for some trade relations outside of the unfavorable Moravian domination of the terms of trade. Inuit seem to have increasingly used these opportunities by the early 1800s, as the violence to the south of the Moravian missions diminished in the early nineteenth century. But at the same time that the Inuit could partly escape Moravian control, ecological changes were pulling them back into their situation as the Moravian's Eskimos.

DESPITE THE ROMANTIC, continually deceptive but widely appealing in Europe and urban North America "Nanook of the North" fantasies of seal hunting through blowholes—which did happen a bit, mostly for subsistence—since the beginning of the nineteenth century seals were needed in large quantities for three major reasons: to trade their skins and some meat to the mission stores, as a food supply for themselves, and as an increasingly necessary food for sled dogs. The primary technology for this increasingly intense seal hunt was very large nets, set to catch the seals migrating along the coast. The nets were owned and controlled by the missionaries, who loaned or rented them to the Inuit they favored from their church participation. The Moravians put a lien on the harvest: in return for the use of the nets, almost all the sealskins and a good part of the meat and blubber had to be brought to the Moravian stores to be traded on Moravian terms.

It was a complex situation. Without whales the Inuit needed both more seals and, increasingly, more caribou for food. Now that they had guns for their safety and for hunting, they could go into the interior during late winter and early spring to hunt caribou. Helge Kleivan, who, along with Carol Brice-Bennett, has done the best and most useful Labrador Inuit post-contact history, pointed out that large quantities of seal meat, which has an unusually high fat content, were crucial as sled-dog food to get the animals to make the long and arduous trip to the interior and to haul the harvest of caribou back to the coastal settlements. The dogs did not have the energy to do the work in the bitter cold if fed a diet of caribou meat (Kleivan 1966). To get this crucial supply of seal meat, the Inuit had to use the nets they rented from the Moravian missionaries, on the Moravians' religious and economic terms. The Inuit, in sum, had to be the Moravians' Eskimos, just as the Innu, confined to the forest almost year-round, except for quick trips to the coast, had to be HBC's Indians. That is the birth of what now passes for the "traditional" lifeways among the peoples who now have become Inuit and Innu.

DESPITE THEIR ATTEMPTS to isolate themselves from disease and to stabilize their food situation, Innu and Inuit were frequently stricken by epidemics that were often hunger fueled, until the mid-twentieth century, and by the mid- to late nineteenth century under severe pressure from endemic diseases, such as TB and syphilis, which were continually present rather than episodic, as are epidemic diseases. Both peoples were frequently forced to relocate to unfamiliar or unwelcome territory—the Innu from the constant shifting of HBC posts, and the Inuit from the regular failure and relocation of Moravian mission villages.

The Moravians, for all their long presence, were fairly dumb about the mechanics of Arctic and sub-Arctic survival—dumb in both senses: ignorant and mute, so they never learned. To try to isolate "their" Eskimos from any outside influence but their own, they put most of their mission stations in the far north, above the tree line, and then built large wooden churches and wooden-frame houses, which had to be heated with wood mostly hauled by "their" Eskimos from miles away. Not surprisingly, and at great cost to the Native people, most of these mission stations were unsustainable. The HBC frequently starved Indians to death, on purpose, when they felt that the Indians were not working hard enough, and they did not offer them any professional medical assistance until the mid-twentieth century, when their fur trade was collapsing. HBC was actively killing off a large portion of the labor force of their fur trade, in pursuit of a modern illusion that the best standard of how to run a business is cost efficiency. It was as short-term and destructive a practice then as now. Native people paid the price for the intruders' ignorant fantasies, as usual, and the price was quite high.

The Logic of Take
The Inuit, who before the arrival of the Basque whalers were substantially engaged in whaling as a major source of their food supply, particularly hunting the smaller coastal whales, traded and fought with the new European whalers and would not cede advantage to the Europeans. As the Inuit apparently became dissatisfied with European trade practices, they increasingly took to stealing, particularly metal, and to burning the whaling stations in the winter,

when almost all the European whalers and fishers returned to Europe, to re-cover nails and other iron. Additionally, they purchased by trade, built, or pilfered European-style boats, which enabled them to compete more effectively.

When two peoples trade and fight simultaneously, the relations between them become unstable, with an intensifying potential for major transformation. While in significant ways all relations of inequality are unstable, the contradictions between trading and fighting seem to have made the relations between Europeans and Inuit particularly volatile. The Innu were used to push the Inuit away by assault, at the least in the winter, when the Europeans' whaling stations were largely abandoned, making the Innu crucial for this task. When the Europeans were present, however, they often wanted the Inuit to come and trade.

The center of the early confrontation between Inuit and European was from the Strait of Belle Isle north toward Hamilton Inlet, then called Esquimaux Bay, the major bay that divides southern and northern Labrador. The Inuit were a serious challenge to the Europeans, quite capable of standing up for what they regarded as their due. Despite the serious inroads of disease and decimation by armed assault, the Inuit long remained capable of mass action: Captain Cartwright, one of the first English to settle, long-term, on the Labrador coast, wrote in his journal that he saw about five hundred Eskimos, in twenty-two boats, sail past his settlement in central Labrador one day in 1772 ([1792] 1980, vol. 1). This figure may have been a bit of an exaggeration, but by the late 1700s the people now being called "Eskimo," with access to lumber from the forests of southern Labrador and now with iron tools, were also using their own large boats, both their freight and passenger skin-covered craft called umiaks and those of European design, which they built or bought.

By the early to mid-1600s the seasonally present European fishers and whalers, incapable of defending or asserting their privileges by themselves or of protecting their buildings over the winter when they were not there, began to give the people they increasingly called "Indians" substantial numbers of guns, encouraging them to attack "Eskimos" and push them north. In the late 1500s and much of the 1600s the Native peoples of southern Labrador were mostly referred to as "Esquimaux Indians," with this term most often used to refer to people that subsequently were just called Eskimos. In the process of arming one cluster of people against the other the labels became "Indian" and "Eskimo." This change may signify that the European intruders were becoming clearer about North American peoples in their own minds, or, I think much more likely, the new and intensified violence was building new kinds of separation and antagonistic difference between Native peoples.

In any case, it seems likely that the Native peoples who became the post-contact Indians of the colonial expansion in the Strait of Belle Isle and southern Labrador were less experienced in dealing with the often violent, greedy, and arrogant intruders than were the Inuit, and probably somewhat more naive about various ways of acquiring what they wanted from the Europeans. The Innu were, at first, more willing than the Inuit to cooperate with, rather than confront, the expansionary designs of the whalers. But perhaps, as the long and intense hostility between Innu and Inuit makes somewhat likely, the Innu were reacting to the recent expansion of the Inuit into what had been their territory, as the Europeans provided the means to redress their own grievances.

But after disease had taken its enormous toll on both Algonquin-speaking Innu and the Athapascan-speaking populations just a bit farther inland—which seems to have started very soon after contact—confronting the European invaders became less possible, and there were few options other than becoming the agents of the Europeans in pushing away the Inuit.

Just at the point of contact it is not yet possible to tell how separate or interwoven were the peoples that became Indians and Eskimos. It is clear they were different, with different histories, but the extent to which these differences once were interwoven is unclear. After the early post-contact violence between Indian and Eskimo became regularized, difference clearly became a long-lasting antagonistic separation. The antagonism did not seem to diminish until well into the nineteenth century, when famines drove the northern Innu to the Moravian Eskimo settlements, seeking aid.

The increasingly deadly violence between peoples the Europeans armed and called Indians and the becoming-Eskimos led first to displacement and dislocation and then to dependency, and it did so for both peoples. The Inuit were pushed north, away from the trade relations upon which they depended, away from their primary source of whales, and away from the thick forests that provided both building materials and all the fuel for cooking and heating that was desired. The Inuit faced violence not just from Indians but also directly from the whalers and fishers that were increasingly working their way north on the Labrador coast, and the Innu were pushed into the interior by violence, disease, and a loss of access to what had been their resources.

The violence was severe and long-lasting; Sir Hugh Palliser, the naval governor of Newfoundland and Labrador, issued a proclamation in 1764 that he hoped would diminish the violence against Eskimos, in part to protect the fishery by diminishing Eskimo counterattacks:

> Whereas many and great Advantages would arise to His Majestys Trading Subjects if a Friendly Intercourse could be Establish'd with the Esquemeaux Indians, Inhabiting the Coast of Labradore and as all Attempts hitherto made for that Purpose have Prov'd Ineffectual owing in a great Measure to the Imprudent Treacherous or Cruel conduct of some People who have resorted to that Coast by Plundering and killing several of them from which they have Entertain'd an opinion of our Disposition and Intentions being the same with respect to them, as theirs are towards us that is to circumvent and Kill them: and whereas such Wicked Practices are most contrary to His Majesty's Sentiments of humanity Concilating their Affections and his Endeavours to Induce them to Trade with his Subjects. In Conformity to these His Majesty's Sentiments, I hereby Strictly forbid such Wicked Practices for the Future, and declare all such as are found offending herein shall be Punish'd with the Utmost Severity of the Law. (Great Britain, Privy Council 1927, 930)[19]

When the Inuit were pushed out of the place in central Labrador that Europeans called "Esquimaux Bay" (now Hamilton Inlet), they were living in semi-subterranean communal longhouses, not the more individualized tents and "igloos" that became their primary dwellings up north, at least until the Moravians started encouraging them to build frame houses, which were difficult both to heat with wood and to maintain. Pushed away from their resources and their longhouse communities in central Labrador that engaged these resources, they became the Eskimos "settled" within, and soon against, the Moravian missionary communities. At the same time, or slightly later, the Innu were pushed into the unlivable interior, where they became the abused Indian workers for HBC. This was, for both Innu and Inuit, a physical separation from each other, from the environment in which they lived, and more—a transformative displacement.

The separation of peoples called Indians and Eskimos was initially geographic. When the Europeans first arrived, both were living along the coast from mid-spring to mid-fall. The coast was a far more regular source of food from spring to fall than was the interior—sea birds and eggs, fish, seals, small whales, and a profusion of berries made possible by the moderations of an "oceanic" climate, compared to the severity of the "continental" climate of the interior. From about the late 1700s (it is very hard to date this with anything near precision) Indians were increasingly driven to settle in the interior year-round, coming out to the coast only for a few weeks in spring, and perhaps again in fall, to trade and to meet the missionizing Catholic priests. By the mid-1800s just about all Indians in Labrador lived in this pattern, increasingly also trading with the HBC, as that company moved into the interior of Labrador.

The interior of Labrador has several features that are relevant to food procurement. First, it has both vast and small herds of caribou, which migrate between summer and winter feeding grounds, and which can be caught, or missed, as their migration paths cross streams or lakes. The land is laced with a multitude of streams, lakes, and bogs and is very difficult for people to travel across save in winter, when it is frozen, and, when the ice is out, by boat along major rivers and chains of lakes. All summer long the land is infested with dense swarms of mosquitos and biting black flies. Contrary to the illusion that Native herbal knowledge allowed them to cope, late nineteenth-century explorers wrote that the Indians lived in terror of these insects.

A proper seasonal round, as it were, would consist of a winter in the interior, when the mosquitos and biting flies were dormant, hunting caribou for food and for their skins, which were used for clothing and shelter, and then a spring and summer along the coast, fishing, procuring water-fowl, sealing, and perhaps whaling. The mid-fall caribou hunt was the best, for the animals had not yet grown their winter coats. The spring hunt produced the thicker winter skins, which soon shed terribly. The coast, due to offshore winds, was far more insect-free than the interior, and on that ground alone a better place to live in spring and summer. And most of all, in the spring and summer the food on the coast was far more abundant and far more regularly available than in the interior.

By the early 1800s at the latest Innu were presented with a deadly choice: either come to the coast in the spring and run a much greater risk of contracting one of the new and often fatal diseases that scoured the coast (measles, influenza, smallpox, TB, and a scourge of others), plus run the risk of a deadly encounter with the Inuit or settlers, or stay in the interior and run the risk of starvation, particularly in the spring. The same violence that Palliser protested against the Eskimo (quoted above) must have also occurred against the Innu who stayed too long on the coast. As the Europeans were less concerned about Indian retaliation, they paid less attention to this. Or perhaps by 1764, when Palliser tried to interdict violence against Eskimos, the Innu were mostly gone from the coast.

Knowledge of Labrador Innu history from the early 1700s to the early mid-1800s is scarce, fragmentary, and mostly inferential. Since there has been scarcely any archaeology in the interior of Labrador, and since the Jesuit priests stayed mostly on the coast until much later, letting the Indians come and visit them, it is not easy to reconstruct more than some general outlines of the interior until the 1830s. HBC, which did record many aspects of their dealings with Indians, did not maintain posts in the interior of Labrador until well into the nineteenth century. Once the Innu disappeared from the kinds of records that were made along the coast, it is difficult to reconstruct their history for this period in any depth. A few features of this history are clear.

In the interior forests food procurement was not easy, except for catching the herds of caribou on their spring and fall migrations. Fall was the most important hunt for obtaining clothing as well as tent materials. Spring was often a hard season to survive. Thick lake ice in the spring was difficult or impossible to penetrate; northern lake fish are not very nourishing, and the small food animals, such as Arctic hares and porcupines, are subject to major demographic cycles and offer not much caloric return over the energy it takes to procure them. The other source of food, when people stayed all or most of the year in the interior, was to go trapping for HBC, particularly for the desirable fall and early winter pelts. The horrendous problem here was that the commercially most valuable furs had the same seasonality of availability as the caribou but were found in completely different and distant places from the caribou migration routes, especially from where the caribou swam across lakes and streams, and so could be harvested with spears or other locally made weapons. One could trap furs or hunt food, but usually not both, because of the distance between the locales for each. To get the few caribou moving in small groups or singly in the forests, Indians needed guns; hunts were necessarily collective.

Caribou could not provide an annual source of food, except in good years, for the Innu on the northern barrens.[20] The Europeans called the northern Innu Nascopie (with a multitude of spellings, including more frequently Naskapi),[21] as opposed to the Innu living in the more southern forests, called Montagnais, who were the very same people. As HBC had a much harder time getting the Nascopie to work for them and with them, HBC and others treated them as if they were two separate and different people, inventing the "fact" that they looked different and acted different, although they intermarried and moved back and forth. Without a spring and summer residence on the coast, the Innu called Montagnais Indians were increasingly driven to work for the HBC, for the forests did not provide enough food year-round.

When the Montagnais, and more occasionally the Nascopie, brought furs to the trading posts, they got food supplies, such as flour, tea, sugar, and lard, but not much of these, and rarely also adequate supplies of ammunition, so they could hunt the smaller clusters of caribou that were in the forests. While the Montagnais Innu continued to make brief trips to the coast, to trade and to church with coast-bound priests, they were increasingly confined, year-round, to an unlivable interior. The Nascopie Innu seem to have come to the coast, in the nineteenth and early twentieth centuries, only when famine drove them to seek aid from the Moravians.

There are a lot of superficial histories, taking a "blame the victim" form, that claim that HBC lured the Natives into trapping with alcohol and baubles, which they were unable to resist. HBC itself, in various post records and correspondence, claimed that alcohol was what brought the Indians to the trading posts. This might be partially true, but it erases a few key points in Innu history. There is substantial evidence that drinking was very much under control until the 1960s, and what harnessed Natives to HBC was the introduced violence and diseases that put all Native people in an increasingly vulnerable and dependent position, rooted in an artificial, almost annual fixity in the interior forests that intensified the need for externally supplied food and guns. The annual presence of the Innu in the interior was subsequently treated as both timeless and natural for "Indians."

Eskimos, similarly, have been supposed to only have lived in the far northern coasts, hunting seals in blowholes with harpoons, rather than the whales that were their mainstay. Whales were, in the largely treeless coastal north, a substitute for wood: their bones provided building materials, their blubber heating fuel; thus, when the whales were gone in adequate numbers by the early 1800s, Moravian nets for catching seals became as indispensable to the Eskimos as HBC flour, lard, sugar, and tea was to the inland Indians. Without realizing the novelty of these residence patterns and simultaneously the changing possibilities for Native self-sustaining food production, the dependence on HBC and the Moravians cannot possibly be understood.

In both cases the harness that the Europeans sought to impose did not fit at all well. Native people retained a substantial amount of autonomy from both HBC and the Moravians, even under severe pressure. This is a crucial point, because the governments of Canada and the province of Newfoundland and Labrador, along with what these governments are pleased to misleadingly call "economic development," have now severely eroded Inuit and Innu ability to claim some substantial autonomy.

How these governments, with the aid of corporations, managed to further erode Native autonomy is very relevant to how some autonomy might now be reclaimed—well beyond the government-orchestrated and largely government-controlled fantasies and programs of "sovereignty" and Native "self-government." To see how some substantial autonomy for Native peoples might now be reclaimed (and why it is important), we must first see how it once was developed and maintained in the context of an earlier colonial domination. This task requires us to begin with how and why an earlier aboriginal autonomy was lost. This is a three-part history: how the pre-contact autonomy was lost, how a significant autonomy was reclaimed and rebuilt in the context of HBC and Moravian control, and then (in chapters 6 and 7) how this autonomy-within-control was broken and replaced by government programs in recent decades. The earlier parts of this history return our attention to displacement, and in later chapters to its more contemporary successor, forced relocation.

The history of displacement is also the formation of what is now called "traditional ways of life" for Innu and Inuit. Despite its glorification and romanticization—for reasons that have some merit—the historical periods in Native lives that get called "traditional" were very difficult to survive. Recognizing the difficulties of survival is crucial to appreciate how it was done. In different ways the current practices are even more difficult to survive.

At the same time, the capacity of both Innu and Inuit to resist earlier attempts at domination and control—the part of tradition well worth celebrating—may provide important lessons for the current situation, particularly when we put aside the romanticization of tradition and see what Native people faced in their everyday lives and what they did in this context.

THREE **Living within and against Tradition, 1800–1920**

Truck, Tradition, Tomorrow

The 1825 quote from George Simpson that I used as an epigraph for this book went further, stressing the role of credit in this explicitly brutal and controlling form of trade and governance. Simpson was the governor in chief of Rupert's Land, which became almost the whole of Canada, and of HBC from 1821 to 1860.

> I have made it my study to examine the nature and character of the Indians and however repugnant it may be to our feelings, I am convinced that they must be ruled with a rod of iron to bring, and to keep them in a proper state of subordination, and the most certain way to affect this is by letting them feel their dependence upon us. In the woods and northern barren grounds [which included Labrador] this measure ought to be pursued rigidly next year if they do not improve and no credit, not so much as a load of ammunition, given them until they exhibit an inclination to renew their habits of industry. (Merk [1931] 1968, 179)

The credit system was not just credit but also something called "truck." Both together were used by HBC in their dealings primarily with Indians, and similarly by the Moravian missionaries with Eskimos. As hard as this pressed on them, and as much as truck and credit were explicitly designed to control them, Native peoples found ways within this relationship to build and assert a great deal of autonomy.

ONE OF THE most peculiar aspects of the current situation is the widespread glorification of what is called "traditional society" among both Native peoples and outsiders. This glorification of a significantly fictional yesterday includes government officials, who use their concept of traditional society to organize programs that seek to heal the damage done to Native people. Until recently I could never understand how a period—the nineteenth century, plus a bit on either end—filled with so much suffering in the form of recurrent epidemics, famines, and forced relocations, could be so romanticized. It turns out there were reasons working within, against, and to make separations from the problems.

Against this romanticization there is the fact that the control that both HBC and the Moravians sought to maintain over Indians and Eskimos brought epidemics of novel diseases, starvation, major famines, and other forms of devastation, one disaster after another, every three to six years, each with substantial mortality.

Yet the current epidemics of youth suicide, child and adult substance abuse, domestic violence, and substantial numbers of infants born with FASD were much less prevalent during the earlier "traditional" period. They came into prominence in the late 1960s and early 1970s and intensified in the 1980s (Maureen Bakie, MD, 2007, personal communication) with current forms of domination and abuse, after both HBC and Moravian missionaries disappeared as an active presence in Native village life. Further, in the midst of all the imposed suffering associated with the earlier traditional period, there were crucial and surprising positive dimensions to Native social lives that are much less present, or present in a very different way, now. This turns out to matter greatly.[1]

Thus, at the core of my work now are the following questions: What happened to Native peoples' ability to deal with suffering without self-destruction? And, to the extent that it is possible to address such questions, why? Native peoples have unfortunately had a lot of experience with imposed suffering, long before the government-forced relocations in the 1960s and 1970s that are associated with the beginning of the current epidemics of self-destruction, and relocation is unfortunately not itself novel. Romanticizing tradition is an obstacle to understanding this crucial new development in the consequences of imposed suffering: it hides the specifics of what actually has happened, which is not just about the changes in what is done to Native peoples, but about the changing ways in which they deal with these impositions.

It was easy for me to blame the government and outsiders for wanting to diminish the suffering they caused in the nineteenth and early to mid-twentieth centuries by romanticizing what they called tradition. But I needed to come to terms with why Native people would have a similar attitude toward the past, without blaming them for accepting the dominant society's fantasy history. The question then became, what was there about this "traditional" period that would lead Native peoples to talk about it now with some substantial pleasure? This is a question that is most usefully approached by seeing how so-called traditional society was organized, rather than by more romanticization about "love of (or respect for) nature" or "respect for elders." Both surely existed, but neither of these values can explain their own existence. One cannot usefully explain culture by culture.

THE PERIOD CALLED traditional starts in the late 1700s for the Inuit and in the early 1800s for the Innu, and in both cases it went into a slow and conclusive decline in the first half of the twentieth century.[2] During traditional times, "Eskimos" hunted seals with nets they obtained from the missionaries (on an imposed share arrangement, just like southern U.S. sharecroppers), and "Indians" trapped with iron and steel traps they obtained, also on credit at very unfavorable terms, from HBC. There was very little in what is called traditional society that was actually pre-trade, pre-contact Native practice. Further, the actual practices during the "traditional" period changed almost continually, so there was no one set of practices that could almost exclusively be called traditional. One stable aspect of the situation was that the commercial production of both furs and sealskins in the sub-Arctic forests and coastlines was hard and often deadly dangerous work.

The strategy used here to understand "traditional life" is to look closely at how commercial trade was organized, with a special emphasis on credit, and how this organization permeated everyday life. By the early nineteenth century this credit-based trade had become crucial to the continuing existence of both Indians and Eskimos, and it would stay one of the central supports of their lives for more than a century. There was no way to live where and how they were living without devoting most of their time and energy to the trade and making their living with what they got from this commercial trade. Moreover, it was impossible to separate what they were doing in the context of the trade, or what was being done to them, from ordinary everyday life. For the Indians this was obvious—they were denied crucial long-term seasonal access to the coast and its resources and forced to survive on the much more limited resources of the interior, which were difficult to get in adequate quantities year-round.

For the Eskimos it is important to remember that they were whalers before the European whalers decimated the stock, and whales were a major source of both food and oil for cooking and heating. From central to southern Labrador, before they were driven north, they also had easy access to unlimited quantities of wood for cooking, heating, and building. Much of northern Labrador is above the tree line, save for pockets of trees in sheltered valleys. The Europeans so intensely destroyed and drove away the coastal whales that by the early mid-nineteenth century several Eskimo communities had experienced their last whale hunt, replaced primarily by the trapping of large quantities of seals with nets rented from the Moravians (Kleivan 1966; Brice-Bennett 1981, 1990; Hiller 1968).

The most revealing aspects of the organization of this necessary trade, for both the Innu-becoming-Indians with HBC and the Inuit-becoming-Eskimos with the missionaries, are found in two of its main features, truck and credit.

Truck is a term in economic and world history that is only distantly related to its current reference to a wheeled transport vehicle. An older and broader sense of the term once pointed to a crucial feature in the colonial expansion of Europe, as well as to the economic organization of some widespread early forms of capital. In this earlier context, *truck* had two main meanings.

First, in Jacob Price's useful summary (1990, 360–373), *truck* meant the involuntary acceptance of shop goods as payment of wages, which early businesses with large labor pools, such as mining, did to help lower their labor costs, since they usually set the prices of the shop goods provided. England repeatedly sought to outlaw this form of payment, culminating in the Truck Act of 1831 (Hilton 1958), for the abuses it permitted, the troubles with workers it caused, and the fact that it allowed the employer to capture all the profit from the workers' wages, by excluding other businesses. But the Truck Act focused only on the payment of wages, and only on Britain—in Canada it persisted, in a different form. The difference, for which a brief explanation will be helpful for understanding Native peoples' situation, was that in eastern Canada truck was used as the form of payment not primarily for wages but for commercially valuable goods delivered to the store or trading post (or fort, as HBC revealingly called many of these places). It sounds like a small difference until we see its very substantial effect on Native autonomy.

Native people, Innu and Inuit, were given production supplies, usually on credit, against the future delivery of skins and pelts. If these forest and coast products were "worth more" than the credit previously given—in the trading posts' calculations of both prices—then the Native producers were given more supplies when they delivered the goods. If worth less, the debt was carried on the books.

The trade ordinarily included advances for the supplies necessary for both production and consumption—the traps and food supplies that HBC gave "their" Indians; the seal nets, tools, and clothing that the Moravians gave to "their" Eskimos. These were credit advances against the "harvest." If the harvest was worth more than the advances, in the reckonings of the trading post manager or, particularly for the Moravians, if need was absolute, further consumption supplies were given at the time of delivery. This form of payment for delivery of goods, as well as its association with both production and consumption supplies given on credit to make possible Native production of furs, sealskins, and other goods, is the second, usually colonial, reference of the term *truck*.

This second reference of the word *truck* is to a set of practices that were never outlawed, but instead became the predominant form of trade with all the Native peoples in eastern Canada—to pay the Native producers for their commercially valuable products with shop goods, not cash. One might ask, "What good was money in the far northern forests and coasts?" but this misses several points. One is that the people who ran the trading post, or the store, chose not only how much the Indians and Eskimos got in return but, much more significantly, a substantial part of *what* they got in return for the goods they brought in. If they paid in money and accepted money for goods, they could have extorted as much, for they still controlled the prices, but they would have had less control over what Native people got in return, for Native people could possibly have taken their money elsewhere to get desired supplies.

We have already noted that the Indians who trapped for HBC could not trap for furs and hunt for food at the same time: the locales of availability of the valuable beaver and fox pelts were far from the places where caribou, the main food source, could be most readily obtained, and both had the same prime seasonal availability. All the literature that cites and discusses HBC post records for eastern Canada notes that Indians were frequently pleading for ammunition for their guns, which had become necessary to hunt the much more widely dispersed food animals, including caribou, near where they were trapping. The same literature also notes that HBC, to force their Indian suppliers to spend more time trapping than hunting, almost always scanted the ammunition they supplied in return for furs, giving instead meager and often inadequate basic foodstuffs (flour, sugar or molasses, lard, tea, etc.) even though it was clear that Native peoples were frequently dying of famine as a result of this widespread policy (McLean 1932, especially W. S. Wallace's introduction; Merk [1931] 1968; Great Britain, Parliament, Select Committee 1857). The Moravians, in the nineteenth century, had to make an artificial separation between their trading posts and their missionaries, because the open and increasing Eskimo resentment of the trading practices (Brice-Bennett 1981) was interfering with attempts to convince Native people to become what the Moravians called Christians. Truck was, in sum, control: destructive and resented, but seemingly necessary to those who organized the trade.[3]

Credit was a particularly complex and important feature of the whole organization of the trade, well worth a further book, or at least an article, in its own right.[4] What is relevant here can be briefly summed up.

To give credit to people who do not have the kind of property that creditors can usefully take in the event of a default is, as Jacob Price notes, a particularly risky business. Price claims that HBC could give credit to what HBC regarded as propertyless Indians because the trading posts were so far apart that the Indians could not easily take advances from one post and deliver their goods to another, and there was a similar situation with the Moravians' Eskimos.[5] I am sure that distance between or access to other traders was some part of the situation that confined Native people to their regular supplier, but to this I would add that HBC made it a widespread policy of only advancing "necessary" (if barely adequate) food supplies and some ammunition to its "best"—most productive and most regular—trappers, scanting others even more and leaving them to their relationships within their communities and to what of their own resources they could muster. The need to support others among their kin and community was very likely part of the trap that chained those who got better credit and more supplies to either HBC or the Moravians, who clearly favored their "best" converts for access to production supplies. Native peoples' commitments to one another also ensured their commitments to the trade.

The Moravians, for their part, as soon as they had a productively useful number of Christianized Eskimos in any of their mission stations, tended to focus their credit advances on their Eskimo converts. One of the key credit advances the Moravians gave were the very large seal nets that were "rented" to Eskimos in return for a major share of the crop, usually about two-thirds, that could be made with the nets. These nets became, as we shall see later in this chapter, increasingly necessary for the Eskimos for just their own purposes. The Moravians knew this; it was an extra pressure for Inuit to become Christian Eskimos, and the Moravians were well rewarded for their concern for Native souls by a much larger quantity of valuable sealskins and seal oil.

The system of truck and credit, which was the center of the trade throughout the whole of the so-called traditional times, was thus a system that facilitated a very intense domination and control of Native peoples. It also, however, facilitated a very substantial autonomy on the part of Native peoples, and how it did both is crucial both to our understanding of traditional Indian and Eskimo societies and to a new understanding of the current situation.

WE CAN NOW RETURN to our basic question: Against this domination and control, or more precisely both within and against this domination and control, what did Native people find that was good and positive about this time period, worth remembering with some satisfaction and pleasure, and perhaps also worth now reconstructing, of course on a new basis, as a route to a better future?

It is clear that HBC and the Moravians controlled the overall organization of the production of furs and pelts and the other commercially valuable goods and supportive services demanded from Native peoples. What was produced, with what tools and technologies, the intensity of production, the returns Native people got from their work—all this was largely, if never entirely, in the hands of the dominant outsiders.

But—and this is crucial—the way the actual work of producing the goods was organized and done remained almost completely in the hands of the Native producers, both Innu and Inuit. Who worked with whom, doing what, specifically where, and who in the community sustained the workers, and how, and with what—all this belonged in large part to the Native people themselves. Even though domination intruded into and reshaped daily life—

the Moravians sought to change kinship, marriage, and residence patterns among "their" converts; HBC's murderous scanting of supplies had the same effect—Native peoples retained a great deal of autonomy and control over all the work of production and in consequence over much of everyday life. Native people, in sum, were, at the same time, both the Eskimo of that presence and existence in a dominating world and still also the Inuit, in and for themselves; both the Indians of the fur trade and still, both for and among themselves, the irreducible Innu.

The control that both Innu and Inuit had over their own work and much of their everyday lives had one further crucial feature. That was found in their unavoidable need to plan and organize not just for their todays but for tomorrow. The need to continually figure out exactly where to hunt and trap, for what, with whom, and which of the several possible techniques to use, and, for those who stayed at home (often women, children, and the elderly), how to support and sustain those who were out trapping and hunting was a constant issue in Native lives. In addition, those who were not hunting faced the questions of how, and with what social relations, to do the work of preparing the pelts and skins, reducing the blubber to oil, making clothing, procuring local foods and fuel, and more. All this gave Native people a very forceful and major role in constructing each everyday and each ordinary tomorrow.

In addition, the very aspects of each everyday that came with domination—frequent forced relocations and epidemics of novel, devastating diseases, each with high death rates, each changing the productive base of Native communities, a base that for each community was rooted in communal knowledge, skills, and the kinship-alliance-labor pools, plus relations with other Native communities—meant that planning for a very different tomorrow was both necessary and, in its difficulties and uncertainties, so complex a process that it had to be collective: a social, not an individual, act, an act that depended on, and in the process remade, Native peoples' own social relations.

The organization of the trade for both Innu and Inuit thus produced at one and the same time both their domination and their autonomy, each shaping both today and tomorrow, and the Native peoples retaining, while the trade lasted, a very substantial communal, and communal-making, autonomy. It is precisely the material and social basis for this autonomy that has now been largely eroded, leaving for many, but clearly not for all, drugs and violence and an individualizing centering on oneself as a poor and destructive substitute for this former materially rooted autonomy and collective self-expression.

The Many Deaths of Tradition

At the same moment tradition was forming it was also dying. First were the frequent and imposed deaths of Native people caught in the clutches of the trade. There is a fable that goes back to the end of the Roman Empire, which was retold, in various forms, throughout early modern European history, most likely as a protest against the intensifying squeeze on rural and town producers, which by the 1600s had degraded relations within families and peasant communities (Medick 1981). It is the story about a goose who laid golden eggs, time after time, and the out-of-control greed of the farmer who killed the goose to try—in vain, in both senses of that term—to get his hands on the source.[6] That same fable tells the story of HBC in Labrador and, to only a slightly less extent, that of the Moravian mission stations there. We start with HBC.

The deaths they caused were often intentional, for they scanted ammunition to try to force "their" Indians to do more trapping, fully knowing that famine struck hard as a result. They also, increasingly knowing what they were doing, brought a variety of deadly diseases from Europe, including especially smallpox, measles, influenza, and the baby-killer whooping cough, in addition to introducing alcohol explicitly to try to bind Native peoples to the trading posts. But disease importation and especially its consequences did not matter to HBC, for it was not until the mid-twentieth century, when the fur trade was almost over, that HBC brought any professional medical services to any of its trading posts.

Georg Henriksen, a historical anthropologist, spent a year and a half from 1966 to 1968 living and traveling with the Mashua Innu—the Naskapi (or Nascopie)—in their seasonal coastal village, through the forest, and out on the northern barrens, as this way of life was coming to an end. Discussing the heritage of the Naskapi, he wrote that in the 1850s an HBC post wanted to pressure them to trap martin rather than hunt caribou and so withheld ammunition. "During the next two winters," Henriksen wrote, "approximately 200 Innu starved to death" (1973, 4).[7]

We should play close attention to the phrase "during the next two winters." If two hundred people had starved to death in the first winter, this would have been a horrible and massive tragedy, for this must have been a very large percentage of the Innu that traded with, and lived within reach of, this HBC post. If it happened in one year, it might be argued that this was a mistake, a miscalculation by HBC. The fact that the deaths stretched over two years showed that it was, instead, likely to be policy, part of the "rod of iron" that George Simpson claimed was crucial.

Simpson became the governor of Rupert's Land in 1821, HBC's territory east of the Rockies and above the St. Lawrence River Valley and Great Lakes northern watershed. He was knighted in 1841 and remained the guiding figure in the company until 1861, with a continuing reputation for "hardness" put into unbending practice, even by contemporary business standards. So two hundred Indians, more or less, who traded with one post, starved to death over two winters. The HBC online site that gives its own version of its history brags that when Simpson died his estate was worth "well over £ 100,000 sterling." This is about two thousand times the annual wages of a skilled workman in the 1860s, equivalent to over $100 million in current U.S. or Canadian currency. Then as now, there as elsewhere, there is a lot of money to be made from fatally impoverishing already hard-pressed Native peoples.[8]

There are now two tasks before us. The first is to indicate the enormity of the suffering imposed on Native people openly by HBC and more indirectly by the Moravians, who also both wanted and needed to keep "their" Eskimos dependent on them. The second, more difficult task is to appreciate the possibility that Native societies, while being devastated by mortality, were also being strengthened by their growing opposition to, and distancing from, those who dominated them. This is easier to see for the Eskimo, primarily thanks to the historical researches of Carol Brice-Bennett, than for the Indians working for HBC, where the historical data relevant to this issue are more indirect.[9]

With these tasks before us—grasping the enormity of the devastation and the complexities of the consequences—we turn to a brief review of the data. One further orienting perspective helps this review.

There is, in Western economic history, a simplistic fantasy by economists that is called "the iron law of wages." In the mid-nineteenth century an economist, Ferdinand Lassalle, put forth two propositions in his "iron and cruel law." First, wages must meet basic subsistence costs; otherwise, workers would not be able to come back tomorrow and the economy, lacking workers, would collapse. Secondly, Lassalle proposed that the competition for jobs among an increasing population of workers would, in the long run, drive wages down to this subsistence level.[10] Let's put aside the second issue, which is not relevant here, and focus on the primary feature of what has been called the "iron law of wages"—that workers have to be paid enough to come back tomorrow, or in more abstract terms, that the return that workers get from their labor has to support their social reproduction, or, in other words, if workers and their children all starve to death, those who employed them would also be doomed.

Would that this were so; the whole history both of colonialism and of inequality within the so-called advanced industrial societies would be very different. Start simply: if a worker dies and another rushes in to take his/her place, why would the employer care? If workers die like flies, and there are a lot more flies waiting in the, or on their, wings, so long as the replacements arrive with low training costs the employer is free to not care. Get a bit more complex: if active, hard-run workers require, on average, 2,200 calories of food a day and only get 2,000 or somewhat less, they do not instantly die. Life expectancy shortens, infant mortality rises as the consequences of family undernourishment become focused, diseases proliferate, and often ways are found to transfer the bulk of the burden of malnourishment away from the elite in the community of workers to the less favored, which often means intensified withdrawal of sustenance from some combination of the elderly, young girls, and, in various places, married women before the birth of their first child, mothers nursing daughters—we all know the drill, and who it hollows out first and deepest.

HBC's high-handed treatment of Native people was probably less destruc-tive to their business on the central forests and plains of Canada, where the Native population density was much greater than on the Ungava Peninsula and replacement workers were easier to find and engage. What they could "get away with" in central Canada (or Rupert's Land, as it was then called) destroyed both Native people and their business model when it was used in the more sparsely populated Ungava Peninsula. They seem to have tried to compensate for their destructive practices in Ungava by moving their trading posts frequently, looking for more productive sources, but it scarcely worked to save their business there. They kept on killing the geese that laid golden eggs: folk wisdom turns out to be wisdom.

The point here is very simple and very stark: there was no "iron law of wages" for Native producers. What happened to them was their problem. The Moravians noted the death of converts and seemed to regret these deaths a bit when they were not celebrating the little souls of dead children resting with God.[11] HBC scarcely ever left its pervasive cost-accounting stan-dard. The Moravians worried a bit about having a similar standard, for it seemed "un-Christian," but they also resisted modifying it. This all-pervasive cost-accounting standard got George Simpson, the head of HBC in Canada, knighted; it got the Moravians almost all the Eskimo souls in Labrador saved for Jesus at enough material profit to help support some mission stations in Africa and the Caribbean for many years; it got Dick Cheney the vice presidency of the United States, Mitt Romney the Republican flag, and General Motors a huge bailout at taxpayers' expense, while they don't pay a penny of taxes on their profits. Why change this wonderfully effective standard just because a bunch of Indians and Eskimos die? Yet more is at stake than criticizing the deplorable standards that have organized the accumulation of capital, wealth, political power, and access to Native labor and resources.

Beyond all this we must understand the crucial fact that Native social organization in the traditional period was formed with earnings from the trade below the iron law of wages. Native social organizations and Native cultures took their shape, in this traditional period, in a context where Native people often could not get the resources, including the freedom from disease contagion, to sustain their own social reproduction. They related to one another, necessarily, in ways that were inadequate for making it to tomorrow. They lived their todays and their yesterdays—for we all live our yesterdays within our todays—in ways that made it more or less clear that tomorrow was even more uncertain than usual. Could there have been a famine or an epidemic every few years without such an impact? Helge Kleivan (1966, appendix) illustrates the enduring impact. Discussing the spread of epidemics among Moravians' Eskimos, she quotes from a Moravian journal entry: "Hopedale 1916–17 'To isolate an infectious case among the Esk. is almost an impossibility. . . . Friends and acquaintances will visit the sick and will not obey the rules of isolation. They are saturated with fatalism, too, and this tends largely to make them very careless. . . . . Before the summer ended practically every Esk. family had one or more member sick. 13 died.'" That is, or was, a central fact of Native societies in the "traditional" period: that however much they were in control of each today, from organizing among themselves the work of production to organizing the daily lives that made production possible, their own social relations, their own material goods, their own technical knowledge, their own social relations were not adequate to ensure tomorrow. What this meant in detail we cannot know, for the self-serving fantasies that shaped the record keeping of HBC and the Moravians are not very useful, and oral history on this issue has not been done.

This situation, where one's own resources and social relations are not quite adequate to secure a tomorrow, is unfortunately widespread, indeed characteristic now of places like Haiti and large areas of Central America and Africa, so that it is possible to develop some sense of how such situations unfold and then refold back upon people (Farmer 2003; Sen 1981; Sider 1989).

In some ways this situation, which bound people together in the effort to survive and split them apart with the unavoidable doom of some, but not all, is similar to that produced now by substance abuse. Drinking alcohol regularly, sniffing gasoline, taking crystal meth—doing any of these together with other people, as is usually done, both produces a deep sociability and simultaneously makes one witness the destruction of social relations with others, including with one's own children, just as in traditional society one was helpless to protect one's children from whooping cough, measles, influenza, and especially famine—all the diseases and imposed constraints that came with the same trade that helped to sustain social life, while at the same time destroying it. In this sense, and perhaps only in this sense, this simultaneous production and destruction of sociability through drug and substance abuse is a continuation of one central feature of traditional society—the worst and most brutal feature—into the present.

And there are more continuities than this. We might usefully appreciate the fact that "doing" drugs and alcohol is, among other things, an expression of one's autonomy, and it produces the social connections with others rooted in this autonomy. The starting point here is that people who engage in what the dominant society calls "substance abuse" usually know full well that it is "wrong," know that it is not approved, know that it is illegal, know that it is destructive, whatever. So to do it is to express one's freedom and autonomy from such strictures, such control, such dominant statements about yes and no—even though it is also the case that the users themselves know it is destructive to themselves and others. They are, at least for the moment and beyond the compulsions and satisfactions of addictions, making their own lives as they choose, even though . . . , even though . . .

This current mixture of autonomy and conscious self-destruction is only one of the many possible reasons why people do what they do, but it is an important reason. Not because it is a "correct" or good interpretation, but because it calls our attention to a long history of autonomy, disaster, and the complex pathways of collective self-assertion. Along with continuities we should pay attention to differences.

In the midst of all the dying, traditional society was continually reborn among the people themselves. It was reborn from the autonomy of work processes and the daily lives of people whose relations to one another sustained the producers of commercially valuable goods: the women who made the clothes, prepared the skins for sale or use, had the babies, participated in the quarrels and antagonisms; the elders who conveyed both crucial and useless knowledge; all this and more. In the midst of largely imposed disasters, riven with premature deaths, Native people lived autonomous lives. Now people still die prematurely in substantial numbers—from suicide, from substance abuse, from the accidents and diseases that befall substance abusers—and in the midst of these disasters current societies are also reborn, but in a different way, and the difference will turn out to matter greatly.

Current society is continually reborn in the midst of these many deaths in part because it serves the needs of corporations and the state for a "legal" entity—the "Native government"—to sign over access to its communal resources, and to accept, in its "sovereignty," levels of industrial pollution and destructive forestry and mining and hydroelectricity production that would not be permitted outside Native lands (Dombrowski 2001, 2010). Now Native societies are reborn, only in part but continually, from the financial resources that are poured into them, from the programs that are run through them and on them, from the welfare payments made instead of job creation, from Native elites and their arrangements with external states, corporations, and nongovernmental organizations—in sum, through everything but the activities and the productive work of ordinary Native people who, during the so-called traditional time period, were themselves responsible for the continual rebirth of their society. At the most fundamental level of the social reproduction of Native communities it is literally a breathtaking difference from the way things were before. Ordinary Native people are left, as far as the dominant society is concerned, with one major, and largely despised, role: ill and needy Native peoples constitute one of the largest sources of non-Native middle-class and secure working-class jobs in Labrador. Dealing with ill, injured, and need-swamped Native people is a major industry in Labrador for Whites, including academics, professional helpers, and service workers.

I must emphasize that this is not an endorsement of Widdowson and Howard's *Disrobing the Aboriginal Industry* (2008). Their book focuses on the work dealing with Native problems in order to critique both the opportunism of many such workers and, it seems to me, to demean Native peoples for their multiple problems.[12] To the contrary, I am using the difficulties and destructiveness of domination to show the resourcefulness of Native societies seeking to cope with this, and to critique how the dominant society both exploits Native peoples' productivity and simultaneously exploits the suffering caused by their appropriation from Native resources and Native productivity.

The Innu Become Indians, but Not Completely

In the region that became the United States colonists primarily wanted Native American lands, and however much they took, it was never enough. Further north, in the spruce and alder forests that became northeastern Canada, the hunger for land taken from Native peoples was not as great, at least until the recent demands for hydroelectric dams and reservoirs, oil, timber, and minerals that are sited on Native lands. Agriculture was much less possible north of the St. Lawrence River valley, and colonial settlement less desirable there. What was wanted were furs, and this required Native producers who were more experienced at that task than the new arrivals and especially had the social relations that could organize the substantial amounts of labor needed to procure, prepare, transport, and trade the furs. For we are not talking about a few skins here and there, but a major industry, one that was a substantial component of the shaping of Canada.[13]

Bruce Trigger (1990, introduction), the primary historical anthropologist of the Huron of the St. Lawrence River valley and northern highlands, has noted that this meant that until the fur trade was no longer economically significant, approximately the late mid-nineteenth century, the Canadians did not assault the Native people as violently as was done in the United States after it ceased being a colony of Great Britain. But we need to realize that northern Native mortality and the amount of violence and destruction northern Native peoples were subject to were at least as severe, if less direct, as in the future United States. Examining why and how this was so requires us to say a few words about two surprisingly interwoven features of the early colonial landscape: beavers and disease. Let's look at beavers first.

Beavers build their lodges—sometimes a combination of house and dam, sometimes two nearby structures—usually across slower-moving portions or narrow passages of smaller creeks and streams. Beaver dams are very effective: as the slower sections of creeks run across flatter terrain, these dams often back up and spread out the watercourse quite dramatically. That means that anyone who has even a slight familiarity with the landscape can find beaver quite readily, and even those with little or no familiarity with the terrain can recognize beaver ponds, partly by placement and partly by the beaver-cut saplings at the pond's margins. Newcomers in unfamiliar terrain have the problem of sustaining themselves, not finding whatever beaver may be there.

The ease of finding beaver and, once found, of trapping them had a very substantial impact on relations between Native peoples, and this often adversarial relationship was an important factor driving surviving Native people into the arms of the colonists: their trade relations, armaments, viruses, and bacteria.

Once Native people started hunting beaver commercially, even if they had access to a relatively large trapping region with a lot of beaver, it rarely took twenty years for the supply of beaver to be reduced below commercial levels. But the survival of a great many northern Native communities and peoples—or if not survival then at the least a substantial portion of their well-being—usually came to depend on their continuing effectiveness in the beaver trade. And once a Native people in this situation ran out of beaver, they had very few options.

These options were not exclusive: a Native community without their own beaver could pursue different combinations. They could get into transport, carrying European or their own trade goods into the interior and bringing back pelts; they could assault and drive away Native peoples beyond the existing trade networks and take over their territory; they could conquer and subdue a more distant people and force them to procure pelts on imposed terms; or they themselves could either run away or stay and, with their numbers reduced by disease and violence, become small-scale providers of goods and services for the expanding colonial political economy. Quite far north there was an alternative product, white or silver fox, but they were much more scarce and their range much more restricted. Beaver were for long the center of the trade, and there was often a lot of violence as one Indian group sought to muscle others out of direct connections to the long-distance trade networks. At stake was one of the key items in the trade: muskets. With muskets one's area of trade and control could expand; without muskets everything contracted.

Trade was survival for most Native peoples in the northern forests and on the central grasslands; the exception in the region that is our focus are the Naskapi of the northeastern corner of the Ungava Peninsula.[14] Until the mid-twentieth century the Naskapi were erroneously identified as a separate people from the Montagnais of central and southern Labrador primarily because, living in the caribou barrens, with access to herds of caribou that, while having extreme demographic cycles, usually numbered in the hundreds of thousands, they did not so quickly and so pervasively become dependent on trading with the HBC.[15] All the rest of the Native peoples in the region did.[16]

With trade came access to both guns and disease. The Europeans who directly or indirectly engaged in or profited from the beaver and pelt trade knew about as well as did the Native peoples the problem of the quick reduction in commercially viable numbers of beaver, as well as what Native options were for doing something about it. One early way the Europeans addressed this issue was to supply guns—muskets at first—to the Native peoples with whom they traded, to help them expand their control over other Native peoples.

In 1648–1650 the Iroquois slaughtered the Huron, who were settled just north of the North Shore of the St. Lawrence River and westward to the lands above Lake Ontario, from north of Montreal to the west. It was a genocidal holocaust: the Huron were destroyed as a separate people, with some of the survivors joining the Iroquois and some fleeing westward, as far as Wisconsin, pursued and still assaulted there by the Iroquois. There were two main factors in Huron vulnerability to this assault. The first was the fact that since the French explorers had entered their region in the early 1600s, along with sailors, settlers, and traders, the Huron population had been substantially reduced by disease. Further, the Iroquois had just acquired four hundred muskets, provided to them by the Dutch at and beyond Albany. Since two Iroquois leaders had been killed by musket fire by Champlain in 1610, the Iroquois had well-developed ideas about what muskets could do. It is revealing that this genocide was the culmination of what some historians, following colonial practice, have called the "Beaver Wars" (Trigger 1976).

The price that Native peoples paid for their access to guns was not just providing pelts and military assistance subduing or breaking other Native peoples, but exposure to very high rates of disease mortality. The Iroquois, as seems to have been usual for the larger and more powerful confederacies, dealt with their own reduction in numbers from disease and war by continually "adopting"—incorporating—captives, the conquered, or those fleeing from other Native nations. The smaller or more vulnerable peoples did not as effectively have this option, although there was a substantial amount of merging and combining, along with splitting and separating. The numerically smaller and more vulnerable Native peoples could not as effectively provide a refuge to other Native peoples fleeing impossible circumstances (Sider [1986] 2003b, chapters 10 and 11).

The Huron were one of the larger and more dynamic Native groups near the northern shores of the St. Lawrence River, and they were allied with many smaller groups, including the Montagnais. The Huron lived in a region where it was possible to grow corn, beans, and some less preservable vegetables such as squash. They probably based part of their relations to other Native communities in the region, particularly those further north and northeast, on the supply of dried corn and beans, for dried corn was, as frequently noted by the Jesuits, the primary food for traveling, including especially journeys to and along the trapping routes. The corn was pounded and often boiled, making metal pots, which very much speeded up the cooking process (compared to stone boiling), a much desired item of trade, for they significantly facilitated travel along the trap lines. Metal pots and kettles were a trade item that the European fur traders were only too glad to provide, for they helped Native peoples work long-distant trap lines.

The Montagnais, allied to the Huron, lived in the Laurentian hills to the north and east of the Huron and further east and inland along the North Shore of the St. Lawrence River, as well as, especially in the early colonial period, at or near the Jesuit missionary settlement at Mingan, where the Mingan and Manitou Rivers entered the St. Lawrence River. These rivers were major travel and trading routes into the central interior of the Ungava Peninsula and were heavily used as trapping routes into the interior by the Montagnais in Labrador from the eighteenth through the twentieth centuries.

Huron history ricocheted well into the Ungava Peninsula, because the Montagnais Innu enter into the colonial period records as allies of the Huron against the Iroquois, and their lives were changed when the Iroquois butchered the Huron to secure their own relations with the Europeans. The Native historical tradition that the Montagnais were pushed up into Atlantic coastal Labrador, and then into the central Ungava Peninsula first by Iroquois and then by European violence, as well as by epidemics of new diseases, seems more than just probable.

The situation of the Native peoples of this region—the North Shore of the St. Lawrence, the Atlantic Coast from the Gulf of St. Lawrence north to central Labrador, and the fluid boundaries of what we might call, for Euro-Canadian traders and missionary priests, the reachable interior—was shaped by the beaver trade and Native warfare. The Native situation was also shaped by the contradictions of early French colonial culture, as these values, attitudes, and practices worked both with and against the plots and plans of the French Jesuit and Recollect priests. The French were the dominant European presence and power in this region from the early 1600s until the loss of Québec City in the middle of the Seven Years' War—in 1759—and the subsequent loss of the Labrador coast at the end of the war, in 1763, with those arrangements finalized in 1765. The French treatment of Native peoples and the contradictions embedded in this treatment were thus formative.

One part of these contradictions is revealed by the name that the French imposed upon the people they called the Huron. This name is derived by combining the early modern French word *huré*—rough hair, unkempt, ruffian, a rough and uncivilized person, animal-like, and other derogatives—with the French suffix *on*, which is a diminutive. The name *Huron* was first used to refer to French peasants in 1358, who went into rebellion against the nobility shortly after the Black Plague subsided, while the French king was in English captivity. The peasants were rather easily and very brutally put down, hence the diminutive. The Native peoples called both savage and Huron are, in this sense, almost the same as those peasants for the early French colonists and their mainland sponsors: potentially dangerous villains, perhaps a bit more dangerous than the peasants, who "don't know their place," who must and can be kept down and suppressed if and when they assert themselves.[17]

Another part of the contradictions underlying French treatment of Native peoples is revealed by the Jesuits, who, while sharing an elitist contempt for the people regarded as poor savages, also sought, with quite some personal toil and stress, to regard them well enough to seek to save their souls. But the Jesuits never quite understood, or only rarely admitted some understanding of, one of the major reasons Native people turned to this imported religion. In the early to mid-1600s the Jesuits described themselves as most frequently successful at converting—or superficially converting—Huron who were dying from one European-introduced disease or another. Native people in that horrendous situation turned to the Jesuits for what the Jesuits thought was eternal relief. Perhaps Native people were just seeking help from the same people who brought them their new and strange forms of suffering and death. As a Jesuit saw it, "The kingdom of God is being greatly advanced in these countries. We have here a nation from without, taking refuge with us both on account of the Hiroquios, their enemies, and of the epidemic, which is still causing great mortality among them; nearly all of them are baptized before death. I have baptized some of them, and it is no small task for our Fathers, morning and evening, to instruct and visit these poor sick people, who seem to have escaped cruel death from their enemies only to die the glorious death of the elect" (Letter of Father Francoise du Peron, SJ, to Father Joseph Imbert du Peron, *Jesuit Relations* XV, 161). One can sense a bit of sad irony in the final phrase, along with the self-satisfaction that supposedly justifies it all, for the Jesuit priest is also one of the elect.

As is widely known, every once in a while Native peoples struck back against the explorers, colonists, and missionaries in large-scale assaults. These were not often very successful, certainly not in the long run, although the threat of major assault may have brought some dignity and some gains to Native peoples. What is much less widely known is how individuals and small groups of Native peoples tried to retaliate against the Europeans, both for their introduced diseases and for the intruders' ineffective "medical" or religious countermeasures. These attempts to strike back at the people who brought such suffering often seem surprisingly inconclusive. While the Huron at one point killed seven priests, more usually their retaliation just evaporated—in ways that indicate a complex underlay, with a deeply ambivalent and conflicting range of ideas about how to respond. Consider one early Jesuit priest's example:

> I left three Rivers on the 4th of September, and reached the Huron country on the day of Saint Michael [September 29], at twelve o'clock at night. The journey is one of 300 leagues by water, through many very long and dangerous rapids.... Consequently no others except savages can undertake the journey.... I fortunately embarked with the Huron captain, who showed me every courtesy along the way. Reverend Father Lallemant, our superior, and Father Lemoyne, who departed before I did, did not fare so well. The former was almost strangled by one of the island savages [this is an Algonquin nation that is encountered upon the way], who tried several times to put a bow string around his neck,—"to avenge," he said, "the death of one of his little children," who had been bled by one of our men who had gone up a day or two before the Father. I encountered this same savage near the island, who, when he first saw me, said he must do the same to me, and for a long time tried to persuade our Hurons that they ought not to bring Frenchmen into their country, that it was we who made them all die; my Capt. pacified him as well as he could. Notwithstanding all this talk, one of his comrades came to see me morning and evening, to have me help him pray to God in his Algonquin language; I did so.
>
> As for father Lemoyne, he was obliged to part from his savages, as he had no longer any provisions. Accordingly, they left him on the bank of the river with one of our [Huron?] men, whose hunting, which was very successful, furnished him with food for two weeks. Then he embarked in one of the canoes of our band. The master of this canoe, two days later, wished to leave him upon a rock, and I had to give him my blanket to satisfy him. (Letter of Father Francoise Peron, sj, to Father Joseph Imbert du Peron, *Jesuit Relations* xv, 151)

Whatever caused such small-scale attempts at remedial justice by Native people to often be so inconclusive[18]—and a wide range of factors are all possible—my sense is that the Innu retreat into the forest interior of Labrador was partly impelled not only by a need to escape both disease and violence but perhaps also by a desire to live life more on their own terms. As we have sought to show in the first two sections of this chapter, that both was and was not possible. That difficult contradiction does not make living on your own terms any less desirable.

Trade, disease, assault, guns, missionaries—all of these created a strongly sprung, inescapable trap. There was one escape route for the Montagnais/Naskapi: the land in the central and northern Ungava Peninsula was such a difficult place to live and had, comparatively, so few commercially valuable furs that the Iroquois, who were willing to pursue some surviving Huron as far west as Wisconsin, did not bother to pursue the Montagnais/Naskapi into the closer territories of central and northern Labrador.

But the diseases all did. As described by the Jesuits from the early mid-1600s on, these included diseases that now would be recognized as varieties of influenza, smallpox, and measles. Together they both decimated the Huron and spread far beyond what the Jesuits saw.

THE EARLY COLONIAL HISTORY of the Innu people in the interior of Labrador, from the 1500s to the late 1700s and early 1800s, is currently not possible to undertake in any detail, for the necessary data have yet to emerge. It is difficult to tell when the Innu moved for most of the year into the interior, and whether that was a relatively long or a brief and sudden process. They were firmly in the interior in the early mid-1800s, but for determining how long this was the case, all we have are probabilities and bits of evidence.

In the early 1600s the Innu lived near and were allies of the Huron. As the surviving Huron were driven westward, the Innu moved east, settling for part of the year at Mingan, on the St. Lawrence River, about halfway between Québec City and the Atlantic Ocean. Mingan was a Jesuit mission settlement, and the Jesuits there came from the same European disease reservoir as did the Jesuits who worked among the Huron. Innu were also on the coasts of Labrador at the Strait of Belle Isle and were trading there with Basque whalers from the early 1500s, and then with the Dutch and French. On both grounds—their closeness to the Huron and their contact with missionary priests and French, Dutch, and Basque fishers—it is more than probable that they were severely impacted by the new diseases. These diseases, primarily epidemics of smallpox, measles, and influenza, were the other trinity that Europeans brought, along with something that led to often fatal dysentery. Later, intensifying in the nineteenth century, this second pantheon became more populated: these life-taking and, for the survivors, life-shaping diseases were joined by the always present TB and syphilis, endemic rather than epidemic. Much later, with increasing intensity from the 1980s, the epidemic diseases finally declined with vaccinations and more effective medical care, but in their place was the very significant intensification of new health crises—diabetes, renal failure, alcoholism, and especially suicide.

To understand the crucial, long-term, life-shaping consequences of these diseases, we need to distinguish between epidemic and endemic disease. Epidemics spread literally like wildfire, killing victims and maiming survivors, and moving on until their next return. Endemic diseases stay constantly present in the population, killing far more slowly, often maiming far more.

A horrible point: an epidemic that kills too quickly does not give the virus or bacteria much of a chance to spread, so when there is no effective treatment, the quicker it kills the better—although sometimes it is just plain worse. *Ring around the rosie / pocket full of posies / ashes, ashes, we all fall down.* In one probably fictional but still suggestive interpretation of this children's rhyme, the rose-colored ring was the first sign of the bubonic plague; the pocket full of posies signified the flower that was supposed to protect those who carried it from the plague; the ashes were the burnt corpses, supposed to constrain the spread of the disease. But despite posies and ashes, a great many survivors of one moment all fell down the next. Quick deaths are often not quick enough, or the disease is carried by fleas and lice, which do not die so quickly if at all. But sometimes quick-moving epidemics have limited destructiveness. Endemic—constantly present—diseases, while less dramatic, are at least equally horrible. Doing their damage more slowly, they can sometimes spread and devastate more widely than epidemics.[19] But they are very much less noticeable in the historical record, for the deaths do not cluster as dramatically. We will see how the epidemics devastated Indians and Eskimos, for these epidemics at least occasionally attracted comments. The endemic diseases, including routine starvation (as opposed to famine crises), probably caused as much chaos and loss (Kleivan 1966, appendix; Father O'Brien Papers). This point is particularly important to help us think about situations where the more or less well people are helpless to effectively care for the ill, as well as the long-lasting consequences from times when this situation becomes either suddenly widespread or continually recurrent.

While we do not know when the Innu started moving into the interior, it is clear that one of the major causes for this move was to escape exposure to disease. There were a range of other issues in the late 1700s and into the early 1800s, when the Innu were forced to abandon the coast and its more regular and secure food supply for the rigors of the interior. Inland for most of the year, they made brief trips to the coast to trade, to meet the priests (who rarely went far inland), and to get food.

In the 1760s the French almost entirely left the Labrador coast, thus ending the Innu's access to guns until they started working for HBC in the interior, sixty to eighty years later. In 1785 the Moravians, who had founded the first of their mission settlements for the Inuit in 1772, started supplying the Inuit with guns, which put further pressure on the Innu to move away from the coast, as the Inuit retaliated for earlier Innu violence. And when the French fishers and whalers departed, the French fur traders closed almost all their posts and also went, taking with them a more supportive relationship to Indian fur trappers than HBC ever had or ever would have (Great Britain, Privy Council 1927, 6:3128).

In 1763, at the end of the French and Indian War, the French handed over the region that is now Labrador to the English. Four years later General Murray, in his report on this transition in the region, wrote that the French fur traders, who had been dealing with Natives on credit—supplies for future delivery of pelts—were committed to Native survival, not from caring but from the logic of the trade. "It was to the interest of the Lessee [those who held a license to trade] that the Indians should not perish from want or privation, as the native had no property from which he could obtain repayment of his advances" (Great Britain, Privy Council 1927, 6:3112).

HBC, as it came to dominate the trade on the Ungava Peninsula from the early 1800s to the mid-1900s, provided much less credit, showed no concern when Natives with whom they dealt died, and even actively used starvation, including fatal starvation, to harness the Natives to the fur trade. After TB became endemic in the early nineteenth century, with high mortality rates, HBC paid no attention and did not have a single doctor in the whole Hudson's Bay region until 1960. HBC had little concern for doing anything for Native peoples other than getting furs from them: in 1822 George Simpson wrote to his patron in England, Andrew Colville, expressing his "strong objection to establishing schools for Indian children in Rupert's Land [all of the HBC territories]; they will serve merely to fill the pockets and bellies of hungry missionaries, they will rear the natives in habits of indolence, and an enlightened Indian is good for nothing" (Merk [1931] 1968, lviii).

As the Innu were being pressed to settle in the interior, primarily by disease, violence, and the appropriation of their coastal resources by Europeans, there seem to have been several ecological disasters in the interior region. In 1785 and 1814—on compelling but not conclusive evidence—there were major forest fires in the interior, with the cloud of smoke and ashes visible hundreds of miles away (Hind 1863, 1:250).[20]

While fires in dense forests produce the new low growth that allows foraging animals to proliferate, restoring their numbers after several years, after such fires the surviving people who live from these animals face a period of real dearth. The ground was being prepared and peopled for the entrance of HBC into Labrador, mostly in the early to mid-nineteenth century. Innu were being driven into the central forests, and the animals, on which the Innu depended for food, were being driven away or dying in the conflagrations. It is instructive to realize that when HBC minimized supplying substantial foodstuffs to their European-origin workers in their posts, in the 1820s, to lower costs, and told their workers to live more off the land, this meant the workers turned to an intensely protein diet, for vegetables other than potatoes, turnips, and local berries in the fall were in very scarce supply. The Innu diet was also primarily protein—meat, fowl, and fish—and when the protein supply declined, they were in serious trouble. When HBC moved into Labrador, trading basic foodstuffs—flour, tea, lard, molasses—plus blankets, canvas for tents, pots and kettles, ammunition and guns (in a very limited and controlling way), and, of course, metal traps, all in return for furs, they were offering goods that were dearly needed by the Innu, and even by the Inuit at the margins of Moravian engagement. HBC's northernmost Ungava trading post, Fort Chimo, was visited by Naskapi, Montagnais, and Inuit after it was reestablished in 1831.

HBC and its supplies may have been dearly needed by the Innu, but the Innu got proportionately very little for their furs. At one point in his 1824–1825 correspondence to London, Simpson lays out the costs and returns that he estimated for a set of three new trading posts. The figures he gives are as follows:

8000 beaver and small furs in 150 packs at £60 per pack.	£9000
wages of four clerks and 44 men at £30 per annum each	£1440
outfit [goods given to trappers in trade]: 150 pieces goods	
at £8 sterling each	£1200
contingencies	£1000
total costs	£3640
probable gain	£5360
	(Merk 1968, 70)

Note that the value of the goods given to the Natives in return for the furs they procured was approximately 13 percent of the sale value of the furs, and this proportion was indeed fairly standard among several sets of figures for various posts that I checked. This paucity of return, above and beyond all the other forms of domination and control, including especially the scarcity of ammunition, was a substantial part of the squeeze that turned Innu into Indians.

There is no need to review here the specific history of HBC in Labrador. The relevant first point of this history can be made by noting that HBC's operations in Labrador were far less profitable than elsewhere and that however much they squeezed their Indian suppliers, their posts continually opened and rapidly closed. Ungava was an expensive place to supply the interior, for most rivers were not good for transport, being strewn with rocks and rapids. Moreover, the harvest of fur was not large. The problem was compounded by imposed famine and the death of the producers either directly or by being weakened by hunger and stress for the next epidemic or the circulating endemic diseases. Would that the current conservative and supposedly liberal governments in Canada, England, France, Germany, and the United States could learn the inevitable long-term consequences from this squeeze on the primary producers. The whole history of HBC, as well as the writings of the domesticated historians who celebrate its macho history, makes the point that the lesson is unlearnable by its perpetrators and its celebrants, although it lives all too openly and destructively in the everyday life of its victims.

John McLean was one of the smartest and most observant of HBC's post managers. He was constantly denied promotion and then forced to resign by Simpson, who would suffer no competition to his arrogant belief that his "rod of iron" would produce positive results, were it only enforced sternly enough. McLean was posted to Fort Chimo, in the northern Ungava Peninsula, because two Moravian missionaries, in 1811, wrote back to England that the lands were plentiful. Once there, McLean quickly urged HBC to go elsewhere, saying the trade there was too difficult, too costly, and too unproductive to be worth pursuing. Simpson and his successors persisted in the belief that if only the Indians were pressured hard enough, including being starved and drugged with alcohol into submission, they could produce enough furs to matter. McLean was right; it did not happen. But on the route to that perpetually recurring disaster, some significant features of the Innu's Indian culture developed.

Here I would call attention to two features of this culture that carry from the past into the present and the impending future. The first is a well-developed Innu resourcefulness, rooted in communal insights into how the larger system on which they have been chained works, as it has changed from the nineteenth century into the present. While the Inuit have recently been pressured and bribed by their own leaders into signing a land claims agreement that is at its best a fundamental betrayal of their rights and their needs—Inuit leaders promised and delivered $5,000 to each adult if the land claims agreement won the election—the Innu long refused to sign a similar compact of perfumed self-destruction.

Innu resourcefulness is one component of the nineteenth-century "traditional" period that persists, with substantial productive effects, into the present. This sense of their situation was very hard-won: Indians recently again becoming Innu were treated with far more brutality, well into the present, and have lived and still live even harsher lives, than the Eskimo as they once again become Inuit. The second component of Innu living their history, their not-yet-past, is far more destructive.

The extraordinarily vicious and brutal squeeze that HBC put on Native peoples in Labrador, combined with the inescapable need of the Innu to deal with HBC on HBC's terms—somewhat less in the north, until the collapse of the caribou herd in the late nineteenth century—created long-lasting problems. The Innu, as HBC's Indians, had to pay with their own skins to deliver skins to HBC, as HBC's motto bragged, which, while it may have suited HBC just fine, took a larger toll on the Innu than just the high mortality rate. The HBC motto was emblazoned on the company flag above its trading posts: *pro pelle cutum*, skin for skin. It had very specific consequences among both HBC's Indians and now among their descendants, the Innu people.

The price the Innu paid for their need to be in the trade, a price that has persisted into the present, is simply and brutally this: *a people squeezed so hard are often not able to meet the demands of their own values about their own relationships.* People who want, deeply and intensely, to take care of their children, their family, their kin, and others in the community are put in a situation where they must watch their children, their family, and others starve and die from famine or, weakened by famine, succumb to disease. Or they themselves die, leaving their children and their elderly parents with the ground cut out from under them. This is a break between ought and is, between one's feelings and commitments to family, friends, and community and what one can actually do. What HBC, and only to a slightly less extent the Moravians, did was to create a fundamental rupture in the intimate and positive relations in Native families and communities.[21]

To my mind this is one component of the current epidemic of alcoholism and abandonment of responsibilities found in Native communities. It becomes more than abandonment: the high domestic violence rates are an aggressive assault on intimacy, an anger at people who present you with needs you cannot meet and feelings you cannot recognize or, if recognized, you cannot do much about. They just make you feel inadequate, weak, and empty, and they deserve what they get for doing this to you. And all this is in addition to the current profound mistreatment and abandonment of caring by the provincial and federal governments, which is a substantial part of the current problems.

To counter the present government and popular romanticization of and fantasies about "tradition," it is crucial to raise the issue of what tradition was, and how its unromantic parts may reside within the present.

This interpretation may be at least partly wrong, for it is indeed a reach. But it may be helpful to think about and explore, to see whether putting people in a position where they can do something about each other's needs and feelings might bring broader changes. The most important aspect of this interpretation of the consequences of yesterday is the strategies it suggests for making a more livable today.

THE INUIT HAVE A different history that reaches toward a similar present situation. The differences and similarities between Innu and Inuit present a substantial analytical problem. For reasons we will address in chapter 6, the relocation communities that the Innu were forced into have been garbage strewn, marked until recently by broken glass and burnt houses. The government built both communities and houses for the Innu that are very difficult places for living. The Inuit communities, even the large sections that house relocatees, by contrast are better built and more orderly places, with clean streets and mostly tended houses. Yet the substance abuse and youth suicide rates are nearly identical, as are the incidents of domestic violence. History and domination each have their own deep logic, different surface appearances to the contrary. The Inuit were also often in the same situation where they were unable to care for their own, where they had the same rupture between is and ought, but this one fact does not account for the differences or the similarities.

The Inuit Become Eskimo, but Not Completely

To understand the interweaving of autonomy and disaster among the Eskimo at the Moravian mission posts, we need to begin from the point that their increasing "confinement" to the mission stations was explicitly designed to constrain their autonomy. This was done partly to "protect" the Eskimo from the violence of the Europeans and Americans fishing from the Labrador coast, and perhaps more—to protect those folks from the Eskimo's revenge and their assaults from other motivations, including plunder, or retaliatory plunder for their plundered whale stocks.

The early and direct opposition to Inuit autonomy is nicely expressed by a proclamation of Governor M. Shuldham, naval governor of Newfoundland, in 1772, one year after the Moravians established their first mission station in Labrador, at Nain:

> Whereas I am informed that the Esquimaux savages inhabiting that part of the coast of Labrador where the Unitas Fratrum [the official name of the Moravians] and its society have formed a settlement for the furtherance of the Gospel among the heathen, *have lately strolled from the said settlement to the southward*, and with a view of trading with the shipping which touch upon that coast. And whereas many barbarous murthers have been committed on both sides by the English upon the savages and the savages upon the English, occasioned by disputes and misunderstandings in bartering their traffick; for putting a stop thereto for the future I do hereby desire and require that the said the Unitas Fratrum to use every fair and gentle means in their power to prevent the said Esquimaux savages from going to the southward, without first obtaining their permission in writing for so doing, and till such times as other settlements be formed and extended down along the coast. (Jenness 1965, 9; emphasis added)

I love that phrase "have lately strolled from the said settlement to the southward," for it conveys, in the one word "strolled," both the autonomy and the self-possession of the Inuit at this point of early contact. Gathering and if possible confining the Inuit to the Moravian communities sought to undermine this autonomy and self-possession, but it did not quite work. One of the reasons that the Inuit continued to go south was to get guns from trading with visiting schooners and the independent traders—mostly fishermen along the southern coast who wanted to do a bit of trade to supplement their earnings from the catch. So the Moravians started providing guns to the Inuit by late 1785, which enabled the Inuit to defend themselves against the armed Indians—whose supply of guns had been markedly diminished when the French, as part of the surrender negotiations in 1763, abandoned the Labrador coast at the end of the Seven Years' War. Simultaneously, the guns enabled the Eskimos, no longer as terrified by Indians who held the inland hunting regions, to go inland in the fall or early spring to hunt caribou.

Going inland to hunt caribou was a deeply contradictory practice, both supporting and undermining Inuit autonomy. On the one hand, it provided a substantial subsistence base. But to go inland after caribou required large quantities of seal meat for dog food. Helge Kleiven (1966), in an insightful analysis of Eskimo history, has shown that the sled dogs could not do the exceptionally hard work of the long trip inland and hauling the meat and skins out without being fed seal meat, for caribou meat did not contain enough fat to give the dogs the energy for this work. To get the quantity of seals necessary for the trip inland, the Inuit had to get seal nets from the Moravians, which they started to do in 1805, but to get these nets, they had to rent them on Moravian terms. Autonomy and dependence came deeply interwoven. In this sense the Inuit were in a similar situation as the Innu, with an autonomy that was both encouraged and simultaneously undermined.

The Moravians' hand was further strengthened in 1773, one year after Governor Shuldham's proclamation, as Great Britain transferred control of the whole Labrador coastline to Québec, and Québec paid no attention to what was happening north of Hamilton Inlet (Jenness 1965, 9), where the Moravians had their missions and, increasingly, "their" Eskimos. In the time period when the Moravians were establishing and consolidating their control, they could do, or try to do, just about whatever they wanted.

There is one widely known feature of the organization of missionary communities in Labrador whose social implications are never discussed, although it is worth some attention. Many of the missionaries were married, and their wives came with them from Germany and worked in Labrador as missionary-teachers, quasi-nurses, or in various supportive roles. Other missionaries married each other in Labrador. When any of these couples had children, the children at about eight years old were sent back to Germany to be "educated," while both parents stayed in Labrador. They could send and receive mail to and from their children once a year, with the supply boat. Most never saw their children again until the children were in their twenties, when the missionaries returned to Germany or retired. It is likely that the Inuit had some substantial reactions to people sending their own children away—as children, forever—for in these small communities the Inuit had to know both the parents and the children. Whatever these reactions were, it seems that the Moravians taught more lessons about the ways of the dominant Europeans than their Bible lessons.

One of the major pressures keeping the Eskimos at the mission stations was the fearful mortality rates of the more independent Inuit in southern and central Labrador. Central Labrador was the region around what by then was called Hamilton Inlet, formerly Eskimo Bay, and southern Labrador the region south of that great fjord, down to and a bit past the Strait of Belle Isle. Diamond Jenness, an anthropologist whose work was used to help form mid-twentieth-century Canadian government policy toward Eskimos (and Indians),[22] published a book that, in 1965, surveyed the problems of Canadian and provincial administration of Eskimo affairs. In a section entitled "Extinction of the Eskimos in Southern Labrador," he states, "The estimated 400 [Inuit] whom Jens Haven met in Château Bay [near the Strait of Belle Isle] in 1765 may well have been the sole survivors [of a very much larger population of Inuit that once lived in Mingan, six hundred miles southwest of the straits in the Gulf of St. Lawrence]. For eight years later [in 1773] Lieut. Curtis calculated at no more than 270 the total Eskimo population between the straight of Belle Isle and the District of Nain [in northern Labrador]" (Jenness 1965, 10).

In the 1770s Captain Cartwright, who had established a fishing and fur-trading station on the southern Labrador coast, just south of Hamilton Inlet, took five Inuit to England with him to visit. Four of them contracted smallpox and died, while the remaining survivor contracted smallpox and lived to return to her Labrador community, where just about everyone soon died of the disease. When Cartwright subsequently visited her community, all that was found were bones on the ground, without enough survivors to bury the dead, or with some survivors, sick or well, having fled—perhaps to other Inuit encampments. The Inuit, who had formerly lived, fishing and whaling in southern Labrador, especially at the Strait of Belle Isle and Eskimo Inlet, were now increasingly confined by disease and the impossibility of maintaining themselves to northern Labrador, where, in the community of Okak, then the largest mission community, they had their last whale hunt in 1824. The Moravians were a very strange substitute for the whales and the landscape that had once sustained the Inuit.

At the center of the tensions that emerged between the Moravians and the Eskimos settled at their mission stations was the contradiction between running a trading post that generated a substantial profit and the missionaries' attempt to Christianize the Inuit by offering love and concern. E. J. Hutton (1912), in his history of the Moravians, put the matter wonderfully well:

For two simple reasons, however, this trade with the Eskimos caused the SFG [the Society for the Furtherance of the Gospel, in London, that supplied and organized the finances of the Moravian missions] much anxiety. . . . If a layman took charge, the trade was mismanaged [meaning the Inuit were, by their and the prevailing standards, underpaid]; and if a missionary took charge the Eskimos ceased to love him. Each system had its defects; and, therefore, the brethren changed from one to the other. First (1771–1861) the missionaries had full control; then (1861–1876) the trade was placed under a general manager, with a layman at the head of each store; then (1876–1898) the missionaries resumed control; then (1898–1906) a layman was appointed as general manager while a missionary managed each store; and finally, in 1906, the law was laid down that trade and mission should be kept strictly apart. For the former the SFG was responsible; for the latter the mission board; and that is the system still [in 1912] in force.

Hutton subsequently continues:

The other cause of trouble was the brethren's kindness. For some years there existed in the minds of the natives a remarkable delusion, spread first by certain schooner men, that while the SFG claimed to be a trading concerned, it was, in reality, a charity; each article . . . [imported by boat] therefore, belongs by right to the natives; no missionary had any right to charge any price whatsoever; and all those who sold goods at the stores were mere robbers and swindlers. At last the danger became so serious that the mission secretary (1888) was sent on a visitation; and yet so he explained the facts of the case, there was still so much suspicion left in fact, next year, at Hebron [a major mission community] the people even blockaded the schoolhouse and held the missionaries prisoners. By slow degrees the truth prevailed; the missionaries regained the people's confidence; and the people excused their evil conduct by saying that if they had been more efficiently taught they would not have sinned so deeply." (Jenness 1965, 18; citing Hutton 1912, 30, 39)

A very fine answer: the Inuit are saying that had the missionaries done their job of "educating" Eskimos better, they would not have encountered such troubles! This is far from just a joke, or teasing their interlocutors: the Inuit clearly knew who to blame for the Eskimo's situation.

The contradiction between the social relations appropriate for Christianizing by the missionaries and the social relations that enabled the trading operations both to support the mission and to turn a profit above that was never solved by the Moravians. The failure to quiet these tensions, however, was a major source of Inuit autonomy—a major factor keeping the Inuit from more completely becoming the Moravian's Eskimos.

Carol Brice-Bennett's 1981 master's thesis on the relations between Inuit and Moravians, from the 1804 religious "enthusiasm" to 1860, is by far the best general history of the Inuit in the nineteenth century. She has pointed out that throughout the first half of the nineteenth century the tensions between Inuit and Moravians increased substantially, and that the Inuit by midcentury were very forcefully and successfully asserting their rights and their own needs against the missionaries. But living where they did, with the oceans so pervasively plundered by Europeans, Canadians, and Americans, they still needed the missionaries. Before the Europeans arrived the Inuit lived this far and even farther north, but the whole northern resource base in marine mammals was substantially depleted by the early nineteenth century. The small coastal whales were gone, as well as the walruses and polar bears, and even the bird populations had been reduced by the intense harvesting of eggs and nesting birds.

Brice-Bennett has convincingly argued that one of the substantial pressures for the widespread acceptance of Christianity by the Inuit, in 1804—after decades of resistance—was the worsening situation of Inuit women. With the increasing hardship of life in the north, the irregularity of the food supply in the locales where the Moravians put their settlements, and the increasing and unsolvable pressures on Inuit, the women were increasingly the victims of communal and family stress. In this context they turned to the missionaries for support and sustenance—including food that the missionaries supplied.

As Brice-Bennett (2007, personal communication) has pointed out, increasing tension was rooted in the history of settlement location. In their exploratory travels the missionaries looked for places where Inuit were gathered in substantial numbers to locate their mission stations. These exploratory travels were by boat, so they took place in the summer when the coastal waters were largely ice-free. The first mission station location that the Moravians chose was at Nain, where relatively large numbers of Inuit gathered for the summer. Nain was, indeed, a good place for summer sustenance. But the Moravians wanted and pressured Eskimos to stay in the mission community from Christmas to Easter, the high points of the ritual calendar, which the Moravians with some good reasons thought would become an important part of the conversion process. But Nain was not at all a good location for Inuit to access winter foods—they were being increasingly pressured to winter, and later to live year-round, where it was particularly hard to live in the winter, and this pressure continued through the founding of other mission stations.

As the whales gave out, the Moravians encouraged the shift to seals, by supplying large nets. This enabled their Eskimo to intercept large quantities of seals while the seals were on their shore-hugging seasonal migrations, using these near-shore anchored long nets. The Eskimo turned over to the Moravians the bulk of the sealskins and the oil rendered from seal blubber, both of which had substantial commercial value. This same harvest also fed the missionaries with seal meat, and what was left fed and clothed the Eskimo. But along with HBC, the Moravians were incapable of understanding the basis for their own continuity. In the nineteenth century they "sold"— under the pretense that they owned—some of the Inuit's best sealing locations to Euro-Canadian commercial sealers.

The second major way that the Moravians tried to make summer-subsistence places livable in winter was to pressure and encourage their Eskimos to get into cod fishing, salting and drying large quantities of cod. The missionaries took—partly by purchase—a large quantity of the catch, some of which they sold for export, some of which they sold back to "their" Eskimo, at inflated prices, during hunger times, a bit of which they handed out to the destitute, and some of which they used themselves.

It was, altogether, a lot of pressure, both in the realm of the radically changing productive economy and in the social relations that organized this production, largely but not entirely "from above." Partly the pressures were also in the domain of the missionaries' attempts to Christianize on their terms: to shun Inuit still following "old ways," to humiliate former religious leaders and their followers who would not convert, and to get people to regularly attend church and not "sin." The missionaries offered some inducements that were much appreciated: they imported musical instruments, which Inuit enjoyed using, and they taught reading and writing, which were also desired. But this was all in the context of a chaotic swirl of stress and transformation, compounded by high mortality from recurrent disease among hunger-weakened people and the high rate of accidents by people pushed, or pushing themselves, to their limits to do the work of subsistence and commercial production. From, or with, this pressure Brice-Bennett (1981) has shown a growing anger by the Inuit toward the missionaries, which by the mid- to late nineteenth century episodically took direct and confrontational expression, including, for example, locking the missionaries in the trade house, robbing the trade stores, and other assaults upon mission property and ways.

There was also a significant and insightful dismay among the Inuit about their worsening situation. This dismay reveals a range of very deep and long-lasting tensions in Inuit relations with Euro-Canadians, then and now. Consider the following example.

In 1926, in a folklore journal, the popular anthropologist Franz Boas published a brief note on two Inuit "riddles." One seems to be teasing or mocking Boas while also becoming serious, the other seems more a parable than a riddle, with a deeply poignant message. Boas is a very strange anthropologist by several current standards. Justly famous for his critique of racism and for extensive fieldwork (but fieldwork that exploited and appropriated from his field assistants), he had almost no sense of history or of the larger social context of the Native peoples he studied.[23] In fact, he avoided both history and context, for anthropology in the early twentieth century worked by ignoring the present and imagining "pure" Native ways that supposedly once existed. It is useful to reintroduce both history and social context when we look at what Boas called "riddles."

Boas wrote that he "found recently among a few notes obtained about 1896 from an Eskimo from Hamilton Inlet, Labrador, the following two riddles which had escaped my memory":

[1] *Oqiriyoq; oqagungnangituk. suna? nauyap miqoa.*
It is light; it does not speak. What is it? A gull's feather.
[2] *Oqapiluayoq. qaqqungatunit isik quilayoq; tutunik ungumedliyoq. suna una?*
ukusik tiktitoq. sorosit ainiarase.
It is grumbling. Beyond the mountain smoke is rising; it chases away the caribou. What is that? A boiling kettle. Children, take care! (Boas 1926, 486)[24]

In the 1890s only a few Inuit remained, or survived, in Hamilton Inlet. By this time most had been driven north to or beyond the Moravian mission settlements. Some, who had all of the Moravians they could take, moved back to Hamilton Inlet, joining the few who had survived there. Hamilton Inlet, formerly called Eskimo Bay, is a very special place on the Labrador coast. It is the major water route into the interior, first through the bay, which stretches about 150 miles inland, and then via two of the more navigable rivers in Labrador—one going almost westward, now named the Churchill River, and the other, the Naskapi River, going more toward the northern interior. The Naskapi River starts inland from the northwest end of Grand Lake, with the lake reaching a further fifty miles northwest from the inland end of Hamilton Inlet. As water travel until very recently was the only way of covering long distances in a reasonable time—by small boat when the ice was out, or on top of the open and relatively flat ice and snow by sled or snowshoe—Hamilton Inlet was long the major center for access to trap lines and trapping territories in the interior of Labrador, and it was along this important inland route that by the 1890s the Euro-Canadian settlers were decisively muscling Innu and Inuit trappers from the best and most productive trapping territories, bringing their skins to one of several trading posts—HBC and a few independent traders—on the shores of the inlet. Hamilton Inlet, in sum, was the locale confronting Inuit and Innu with their continuing loss from an intensifying appropriation of what was once theirs. And the intensity of this loss cannot be underestimated: in 1891 the Canadian government severely restricted Indian salmon fishing on many Labrador rivers, so the fish would be more available to tourists.

We start with the first so-called riddle: "It is light; it does not speak. What is it? A gull's feather." "Light" here refers to color, not luminescence, as the first answer, "a gull's feather," makes clear. The question, put more in European concepts, would be, "What is white (or White) and does not speak?" In that context think about this: Columbus, in his journal entry for the very first day he landed and encountered Native peoples, wrote, "Our Lord willing, at the time of my departure I will bring back six of them to Your Highnesses, that they may learn to speak." The translation here is exact: he did not say "talk our language," although having worked the Mediterranean and most likely sailed with multilingual crews, he knew the difference between "speak" and "talk our language."[25]

This invocation of speaking as a measure of connections and a rough equality is particularly widespread and poignant among dominated and abused peoples, who themselves make the point explicitly, would we only listen. The following example is an excerpt from Elizabeth Traube's presentation and translation of a poem-plaint from the Native people of Timor, decades before the Indonesians had only their most recent and best-known ethnocidal butchery of the Pacific Island Native people of Timor. She listens; her work is exemplary for this. The Timorese are speaking to the Indonesians who dominate them:

When there is hunger, it overcomes you
When there is thirst, it possesses you
Maybe it is the rifle that you carry on your shoulder
Maybe it is the gunbelt that you gird around your waist

Because it is you who is stupid

It is you who is ignorant

We two might simply converse

We two might simply talk together

But you come with the sharp thing

You come with the pointed thing . . .

You come to chase me like a deer

You come to pursue me like a pig . . .

As if I had no speech . . .

If we two do not speak together, we do not speak together because of this . . .

If we two are not kin, we are not kin because of this. (Traube 1986)

So there are two further possibilities contained in this question, what is white/White and does not speak? The starting possibility is that this Inuit, in a stroke of brilliance, is taunting Boas about his thickness—his insensitivity to what is actually happening—which later anthropologists would celebrate as "thick description." If Boas wants to believe that it is simply a gull's feather that is w/White and doesn't speak, he and his followers can go for it.

There is a further and sadder possibility. The Inuit in Hamilton Inlet in the late 1800s knew the situation of Eskimos living among the Moravians in some detail—they either had left these settlements or hosted those Eskimos traveling south from the mission settlements to trade on more favorable terms or to visit. The Moravians knew Inuktitut, the Inuit language. It is possible that the Inuit telling this lesson to Boas was also making a distinction between people who could talk but not speak—who did not speak with the Inuit but talked to their Eskimos. Hopefully, like gulls, they will fly away, splashing the rocks as they go. This interpretation is a stretch, but we should think that something more than a gull's feather might be at stake in this question: "What is White and does not speak?"

The second so-called riddle shows that all this is not simply a joke at Boas's expense, not simply pricking the balloon of Boas's historically shallow seriousness. The second "riddle"—or parable, more of a teaching tool than the simple play of a riddle—is also a call to recognize the difficulties and dangers of Inuit lives: "It is grumbling. Beyond the mountain smoke is rising; it chases away the caribou. What is that? A boiling kettle. Children, take care!" This one is painful to contemplate when it is put in the context of Inuit and Innu history.

Pots that could boil water were a key item for fur traders to supply to Innu and Inuit—and Whites as well—for they permitted far quicker cooking than the stone-boiling method that the Innu had been using, as well as the utilization of a far larger range of foods than were customary for the Inuit. Meat can be cooked over an open fire, or even eaten raw. But some of the key staples for inland journeys were such lightweight and nutritionally dense foods as dried corn, dried peas, and flour—transported foods that when boiled in local water became bulk nutrition, or at least seminutrition. Kettles, more for tea than for cooking, were more of a luxury than were pots for poor and hard-pressed travelers. You can boil water in a pot easier than you can cook in a kettle. We can speculate that kettles were more used by Euro-Canadians on the interior trap lines than by Innu or Inuit, for by the late nineteenth century the Euro-Canadians went up the easiest rivers to travel to the best territories for the shortest trap lines. The Inuit men usually went further inland, often by sled and snowshoe, leaving their families at the coast. The Innu primarily traveled as whole communities, also quite far inland as Euro-Canadians took over the best and most accessible trap lines. In both cases Native inland long-distance travel pressed against carrying extra weight: the essentials were difficult enough to pack and portage, and the distances were great. And for the Innu and Inuit the hunts for caribou and for their meat and their skins were crucial to their well-being, as was commercial trapping for the Innu: they had to travel. It cannot be the case that kettles were only a Euro-Canadian luxury, for the HBC post records note them as a desired trade item with Indians. There is a distinct possibility that on the inland trapping journeys they were more in use by those with the easier travel. From the grumbling kettle to the grumbling HBC post trader, who gave more to the Euro-Canadians than to Native peoples, from the smoke beyond the mountains to the smoke and the vapor of the boiling kettles in the interior that once was Native territories, until the Euro-Canadian settlers muscled them aside—all this leads to the far less speculative ending: "Children, take care." Boiling water can indeed seriously injure children, as the parable specifies (but is a danger to adults also). Were we Boas, or followers of his ahistorical anthropology, we could stop there and not think about what else is happening beyond the mountains that makes children especially need to take care for their near or distant future.

All that we need to do here is not argue for this or that interpretation, not defend this or that speculation, but just make the point that the Inuit knew they were being dominated by people who could or would not speak with them, and that their children were in serious danger—because tomorrow was likely to be even worse than today. We will return to the point of the dangers children face in chapters 6, 7, and 8.

And indeed the end of the nineteenth century was the beginning of the rush to catastrophe. This was a period of several decades, from the last two decades or so of the 1800s through the first decade and a half of the 1900s, that laid the groundwork for the utter devastation that the so-called Spanish Flu wreaked in Labrador—killing at least a third, perhaps half, of all the Native people alive in the winter of 1918–1919, when it struck. The core of Inuit history that is relevant here is this increasing rush toward the flu's devastation. For the Inuit there is far more evidence for the development of this catastrophe than for the Innu, but as we will see in the way the catastrophe developed among the Inuit, it is exceedingly unlikely that the Innu escaped a similar fate, for the Innu came to the coast to trade, on their annual trading visits, about the time the plague struck along the coast, and Innu band composition was quite fluid, with people often changing residence. We now look at the Inuit, put on the road to catastrophe, with the realization that this may well have been a similar history for the Innu.

Pathways to the White Plague

The Spanish Flu was one of the deadliest pandemics ever to strike the world, killing between fifty and one hundred million people from mid-1917 to the end of 1920, with the winter of 1917–1918 being the deadliest period. It was the most serious epidemic since the bubonic plague of 1347–1350—the Black Plague—that killed over a third of the population of Europe, and in some places over half, plus countless millions in Asia and Africa. The Spanish Flu pandemic came in the midst of World War I, when most of the countries in Europe and North America had censorship that sought to conceal both how many people were dying and the ensuing problems. Spain was neutral in that war and had no censorship, so the disease was most widely reported there, even though it spread there from France and Central Europe. The publicity of it in Spain gave it the name "Spanish Flu."

It came to northern Labrador on a Moravian supply ship, which had met the mail boat from St. John's, Newfoundland, in southern Labrador. St John's, although hard-hit by the disease and knowing it was highly contagious, had placed no restrictions on boats sailing out to the isolated communities. In these communities the death toll was much higher, from lack of medical facilities, from the harshness of the climate in the northern winter as one went farther north, and from the difficulty for the survivors and those not fatally ill of provisioning themselves and keeping from freezing. So that while the disease killed 1 percent of the population in the Newfoundland capital city, St. John's, the effects, particularly for the Inuit, were much worse in northern Newfoundland and devastating in Labrador, where the plague killed, as is usually said, one-third of the then living population, and in many places much more. It may have been equally hard, or even harder, on the Innu. That is difficult to know, partly from a lack of data, and partly because the Innu death toll from the simultaneous epidemics of smallpox and measles makes it difficult to sort out just what was happening, beyond the point that substantial numbers of Innu were also dying.

In Hebron, the most northern major Moravian village, eighty-six of the one hundred residents died, and in Okak, the largest Inuit community, it killed every adult male.[26] The disease seems to develop its deadly consequences by hyper-engaging the immune system, so that those with the strongest immune systems—adults, usually—die, whereas children and the weak elderly survive, at least until they freeze or starve.[27]

The "Black Death"—called black perhaps because the victims' skin darkened due to extensive bleeding just below the skin[28]—reappeared in 1348. This was only one, but the most deadly, of several prior occurrences. In the years around 1348 it devastated both China and Europe, and elsewhere as well. China had been torn asunder by the Mongol conquests, which impoverished vast sections of the populace and massively undermined agrarian productivity. European peoples were weakened by crop failures from decades of unusual cold, with consequences supposedly magnified in the context of population increase (as is widely but more speculatively claimed); by the start of the destructive Hundred Years' War, a decade before this plague started; by recurrent famines in the prior decades; and—I think—very much by the rack-renting of the peasantry that accompanied and financed the building of the great cathedrals across Europe.[29] Canterbury, Chartres, Notre Dame, Rheims, and almost a dozen others were all built on the backs of, and the rents extracted from, the peasantry in the twelfth and thirteenth centuries. The grandeur of these cathedrals is so impressive, and the destructiveness of inequality so taken for granted or ignored in so-called European civilization, that people scarcely wonder what these cathedrals cost in surplus extracted from mostly low-level agrarian producers, and whose lives paid that price. As I see it, the rents extracted from the population to finance these cathedrals paved the pathway to the Black Plague.

For the Black Plague did not just travel down the Silk Road from China to Europe, as is usually stated, like hitchhiking viruses that grew inside rats, fleas, and other small mammals. The disease traveled along pathways that had been cleared and carpeted by privation and the kinds of suffering that undermine production of necessary goods. This point is crucial to understanding what I will call the 1918 White Plague in Labrador: "White" not just because it was sent there by a Euro-Canadian elite in St. John's that did not care to constrain northern shipping from its infected city, and not just because in the sub-Arctic snows and winter ice storms it is hard for the non-ill, mostly the young and the old, to take care of themselves and those in need, but because of the sequence of imposed and introduced events, primarily by HBC and the Moravians, that prepared the human soil for the disease to grow so quickly and so strongly among Native peoples—far worse than among the Euro-Canadian inhabitants of Labrador.

It will help to understand how the pandemic developed in Labrador if I give a bit of a chronological history.[30] It might help to partly explain why it took the toll it did, and what some of the consequences of this appalling devastation have been. Keep in mind that St. John's, the Newfoundland capital city, had a quite widespread incidence of people coming down with the Spanish Flu—the hospitals were overflowing—but only about a 1 percent mortality rate, while Labrador was devastated. Part of the usual explanation for this is that St. John's had a good supply of doctors, nurses, and hospital facilities, whereas Labrador did not. While this is true, the simplicity and innocence of this explanation are undermined by the fact that both Euro-Canadians in Labrador and the Métis, with whom they were intermixed, had vastly lower death rates in this pandemic, although almost all lived in small, usually quite isolated fishing and trapping communities in climates just a bit less severe than the areas where the Innu and Inuit lived, and also for the most part with limited medical access. They were hard-pressed, but not as deprived of basic sustenance as were Eskimos and Indians. While other explanations are possible, it seems that the long history of suffering—diseases and famines and the stress of forced relocation—had a significant role in the vastly higher mortality rates among Indians and Eskimos.[31]

In the famine of 1836–1837 many Inuit ate their sealskin boots and tents and then died. At Okak in 1837 only 20 dogs out of 360 survived the famine. "Starvation [of Eskimos] due to scarcity of seals occurred in 1837, 1846, 1851, 1856, and 1871" (Jenness 1965, 28, citing Gosling 1910). In 1851 the missionaries distributed seventy thousand dried fish at Okak, and yet many people starved to death, particularly those somewhat distant from the station (Jenness 1965,

29). In 1843–1844 famine in the interior forced the Naskapi to the coast, where the Moravians offered a bit of help to them (Leacock and Rothschild 1994, 58). Between 1855 and 1860 recurrent famine again forced the Innu out of the northern caribou barrens to seek help from the Moravians at the coast. They certainly were not going to get this help from HBC. McLean, who was earlier in charge of HBC posts in the Ungava Peninsula, wrote,

> In intercourse with us the Nascopies evince a very different disposition from the other branches of the Cree family, being selfish and inhospitable in the extreme; exacting rigid payment for the smallest portion of food. Yet I do not know that we have any right to blame a practice in them which they have undoubtedly learned from us. What do they obtain from us without payment? Nothing— not a shot of powder—not a ball—not a flint. But whatever may be said of their conduct towards the whites, no people can exercise the laws of hospitality with greater generosity, or show less selfishness, towards each other, then the Nascopies. (McLean 1932, 264)

The similarities in the dating of Inuit and Innu famine indicate that the general situation of dearth was widespread: climatic and animal-demographic fluctuations exacerbated the policies and practices of domination. Jenness notes that the disappearance of the caribou (which occurred at both ends of the nineteenth century) deprived the Inuit of warm clothes and the Innu in the interior of both clothes and food. He also notes that by 1910 the walrus and the polar bear, decimated by being hunted with guns, had retreated north of Cape Chidley, the northernmost point in Labrador.

In 1857 Newfoundland-based cod fishers started working the waters of Labrador around the Moravian mission communities in northern Labrador. Jenness notes that in the same year an American boat started trading rum to the Inuit, and by 1861 the fishing boats were taking some of the Inuit's best fishing locales at Nain: "Six Newfoundland vessels fished off Hopedale in 1863, 25 touched at that settlement in 1866, 108 in 1868, and in 1870 more than 500 vessels passed the place on their way north. . . . In 1900 the [total Labrador] Newfoundland fishing fleet . . . counted between 1,500 and 1,800 vessels, operated by crews that numbered from 15,000 to 20,000 men, women and children" (1965, 24). These fishers were a mixture of blessing and scourge— only partly from the quantities of rum that they used to attract and lubricate the trade.[32] On the one hand, they offered an alternative trading possibility to the missions; on the other hand, they pressed hard on an Inuit resource and on locales for procuring and preserving that resource.

The year 1857 was also the onset of increasingly difficult times for the Innu. In that year Great Britain held a parliamentary inquiry into the operations of HBC in Rupert's Land. This inquest was motivated primarily by the impending end of parliament's earlier grant to HBC of a monopoly on the Indian trade, to see if renewing this monopoly served larger British interests, particularly as a bulwark against the northward expansionary claims of the United States. Secondarily, in the eyes of this inquest, they were investigating several reports, in the form of letters to Parliament of people in the northern lands, of intense brutalization of Native peoples by HBC, both willfully starving Native peoples and paying no attention to the multiple health crises.

Parliament had received several substantial letters from people in Canada alleging very serious mistreatment of Native people. George Simpson, the same director of HBC who invoked the rod of iron policy quoted in an epigraph, dismissed every allegation of mistreatment in the most cursory manner possible, simply saying he had never heard of any such thing. The inquest accepted without question his dismissals. We recount just one section of that inquest to give a flavor of the proceedings:

PARLIAMENTARY QUESTION, QUOTING FROM A PASSAGE IN A LETTER: "starvation is, I learned, committed . . . among your old friends the Nascopies, numbers of whom met their death from want last winter; whole camps of them were found dead without one survivor to tell the tale of their sufferings; others sustained life in a way the most revolting—by using as food the dead bodies of their companions;" . . . quoting from another letter . . . "at Fort Nascopie [an HBC trading post] the Indians were dying in dozens by starvation; and among others your old friend, Paytabais. . . ." A third [letter] . . . "a great number of Indians starved to death last winter; and says it was . . . 's fault in not giving them enough of ammunition." Do any facts like that come within your knowledge?

SIR GEORGE SIMPSON: No; that is an exaggerated statement.

QUESTION: in your thirty seven years experience in that territory you have never heard of any transactions like that, and any deaths like that?

SIR GEORGE SIMPSON: Never, except in Mr. Kennedy's letter. (Great Britain, Select Committee on the Hudson's Bay Company 1857)

HBC was doing, the inquest decided, such a fine job protecting larger British interests, along with earning quite large sums of wealth for the elite owners of HBC, that the inquest accepted without question HBC's perfunctory denials of mistreatment, and by renewing their monopoly control of the trade, they gave HBC a carte blanche to do to the Native peoples whatever it wanted or felt it was advantageous to their profits to do.

In addition to whatever HBC was or was not doing to or for the Indians of this region, disease took its own toll. Henry Youle Hind, explorer and naturalist, explored the interior of Labrador by getting himself and some companions canoed up the river network that flowed into the St. Lawrence at Mingan, a Catholic mission center and a trading post. In his 1863 description of this journey he described the situation at Mingan:

> Five hundred Montagnais had pitched their tents at Mingan, a fortnight before we arrived, there to dispose of their furs, the product of the proceeding winter's hunt, and to join in the religious ceremonies of the Roman Catholic church. . . . They had assembled from all parts of their wintering grounds between the St John's River and the Straits of Belle Isle—some coming in canoes, others in boats purchased from the American fishermen on the coast, others on foot. A large number had already procured their supplies and started for . . . [the interior and] different parts of the coast, in consequence of an epidemic which had already carried off ten victims. . . . [A] few still lingered in their birch-bark lodges, some of them being ill and unable to move. The poor creatures seem to be attacked with influenza, which rapidly prostrated them. . . . There is no doubt many would recover if properly fed and clothed." (Hind 1863, 112–114)

Hind ascribed part of the blame for the lack of food on the decline of food-source animals: "In many parts of the Peninsula the wild animals which formerly abounded have almost disappeared, and consequently the means of subsistence of the Native races have been withdrawn. Rabbits were once quite common on the mainland as far east and north as the Atlantic coast of the Labrador Peninsula. The porcupine was everywhere abundant on the Gulf coast, and reindeer [caribou] 'covered the country.' The destruction of mosses, lichens, and forests by fires has been the most potent cause in converting Labrador into a desert" (1863, 111).

By the last quarter of the nineteenth century the pressures had culminated into what we might well regard as a general health collapse among both the Inuit and the Innu. Jenness (1961) listed only some of the better known and more widely reported epidemics—interspersed with changing relations to external influences and missionary domination that may or may not have been contributing factors to a decline in well-being sufficient to encourage health crises.

In 1871 the coast was blocked with ice until July, ruining the cod fishery.

Credit at the Moravian trading stores ballooned, creating what the Moravians regarded as a fiscal problem. In response, in 1874 the Moravians restricted credit, which had enough of an impact on Eskimo well-being that they protested strongly. This was the end of a period of relative prosperity, in which the Inuit, on the basis of their trade with the fishers, bought large wooden fishing and trading boats and kept far more sled dogs: "between 1861 and 1876 their dogs had increased from 222 to 716, and their wooden boats, . . . nearly all bartered from Newfoundlanders, from 117 to 237" (Jenness 1961, 26). But Jenness noted that in 1880–1882 "whooping cough and measles caused the death of large numbers [of Eskimos]," and in 1885, measles struck again.

In the winters of 1892–1893 and 1893–1894, there was widespread death of Innu from famine and diseases. Low, a geologist working in northern Labrador, noted that the famine of 1892–1893 reduced the number of Indians trading at Fort Chimo, the HBC trading post, from 350 to less than 200 (1896, 41). He went on to note for the following years that "in consequence of both the shift of HBC to the coast and famines in the interior, the number of Indians trading with the interior posts has declined from 735 to about 300."

Hesketh Prichard, who explored the Labrador interior in 1911, blamed the fluctuations in the migration routes of the caribou: "Both for the Montagnais of the more wooded south and the Nascaupees of the Barren Ground, the caribou forms the main support of life. . . . The path of the migration changes from year to year, and in some seasons the tribes fail to meet with the deer at all. . . . Such a year was 1893, when many of the people died, only half their number surviving to the spring. It is no exaggeration to say that the Nascaupees depend for their very existence upon the caribou" (1911, 193).

This is the period when the caribou herd collapsed to a small fraction of its former size, with substantial famine among the Naskapi, and a further pressure on the Inuit, who were going inland in the fall to hunt caribou.

In 1894 typhoid struck the Eskimos very hard:

In 1893 a colony of Eskimos [from Labrador], consisting of 57 men, women, and children, were taken [by a schooner] to the Chicago exposition [to be put on display]. . . . The survivors were returned to Newfoundland, in an absolutely destitute condition, at the expense of the colony. They brought [typhoid fever] with them, . . . to which a very large number of Eskimos, from Hopedale to Hebron, fell victims. At Nain, out of a population of three hundred and fifty Eskimos, ninety died during one winter, their dead and frozen bodies awaiting burial at one time the following spring. (Kleivan 1966)

In 1898 the same promoter was allowed, by the government of Newfoundland, to bring a number of Eskimos to Europe, and they brought syphilis back to Labrador. It's hard to imagine that the Newfoundland government would do this again, would grant the same promoter permission to take a number of Eskimos to display in Europe, but they did, and from this second permission, if from nothing else, we can get a sense of the depth—or lack thereof—of Newfoundland's concern for the well-being of the Native peoples of Labrador.

By 1901 the Moravian missions had reached the limits of the credit they felt able to extend, and there was the growing realization that the debts of their Eskimo to them were unpayable. What they did was wipe the slate clean—forgive all debts—and start fresh. But this fresh start was a much more severe start, for three main reasons. First, they gave much less credit, which made it significantly more difficult to get by in times of dearth; second, they bought more fish and seals from the Eskimo than they exported, saving a portion of their take to sell back to the Eskimo in times of need; and third, they seem to have given less aid to the vulnerably dependent. This was the squeeze: to put the missions on a more "sound" financial footing; but when the price of shop goods, including basic foodstuffs, warm clothes, and production supplies, rose significantly with the onset of World War I, in 1914 (Jenness 1965, 31), the squeeze on Native people moved, as it were, from the chest to the throat.

1904 The midsummer epidemic of influenza brought by the fishing fleet carried off 65 persons at Okak, 19 of them children.... [33]

1911 At Okak and Nain, again in 1911, some 500 Eskimos died of influenza [quoting the medical missionary] (Grenfell 1934, 11)

In the early twentieth century the situation of the Native peoples in the Ungava Peninsula was seriously worsened by Canadian bans on Native fishing and hunting in order to encourage tourism. In 1912 the anthropologist Frank Speck writes to Edward Sapir, chief ethnologist of Geological Survey of Canada, saying there is great suffering among Montagnais of the St. Lawrence River valley because they were banned from fishing for salmon on rivers, to make the rivers available for lease to sportsmen (Townsend 1910, 116). In 1912 Speck, among the Montagnais at Lac St. Jean, and Armand Tessier, regional Indian agent, ask for exemption for Indians from the ban on killing beaver, which deprived them of needed food and cash income. Both of these requests were denied—a preview of the Canadian governments' recent and current restrictions on Innu hunting, as the Canadian federal and provincial governments still seek to keep the surviving Innu as their Indians. "The Naskapi continued their nomadic existence as caribou hunters in the interior of northern Labrador until approximately 1916, when the great caribou herds passing through Indian House Lake changed their migration route. This caused hunger and near starvation for the expectant Indians. The Indians then moved to the coast to seek help from the stores operated by the Hudson's Bay Company" (Henriksen 1973, citing Strong 1929).

In 1918 flu or smallpox struck the Naskapi: "The Barren Ground people are said to have been unfortunate since the epidemic of 1918 because all the old men died at that time. In 1918 the Barren Ground people had moved to Voisey's bay, on the coast, going back into the interior on occasional hunting trips" (Strong 1929, 47). "Unfortunate" is a stunningly mild term for such a loss, and it is also surprising that there is no mention of women.

> During the summer of 1918 the Barren Ground people were in two camps, one at Voisey's Bay where they were cutting wood, the other on Upatik Bay. Here the smallpox and measles epidemic of that year reached them, killing 40 at Voisey's Bay and others at Upatik. Between Hopedale and Nain the epidemic was smallpox and measles. To the north the influenza wiped out the Eskimos at Okak and decimated those at Hebron. . . . About 350 Eskimos died at Hebron and Okak. The latter, formerly a prosperous settlement, was practically depopulated when I visited it in 1928. The influenza reached south to Nain but had little effect there due, presumably, to the fact that the southern stations were already suffering from an epidemic of smallpox, which was brought north by patients from the hospital at Indian Harbour. . . . About 40 persons died altogether at Nain and Hopedale. It was this disease [smallpox] plus the measles, which reached the Barren Ground and Davis Inlet Indians. (Strong 1929, 47)

This too was the White Plague, which seems to have been the Spanish Flu on the coast and measles, smallpox, and perhaps other varieties of influenza in the interior, all together decimating peoples weakened by decades of stress and domination. This mixture of simultaneous epidemics underscores the point I have been trying to make: it was more complex a situation than the simple arrival of the Spanish Flu. The Native peoples had been put in a situation where they were intensely and fatally susceptible to whatever disease came along.

The foundation of these recurrent famines was the Native peoples being forced to live in nonviable areas and having their resources appropriated from them, in addition to HBC and Moravian credit policies. Even though caribou have their own demographic cycles, famines are ecological crises, and most of the time ecology is a social construct.

I want to finish by quoting extracts from the wonderfully detailed Eskimo chronology of Helga Kleivan (1966, appendix) for the two years or so preceding the Spanish Flu, and for the flu itself in the winter of 1918–1919. Were there space enough, I would also extract from the decade before: 1904–1905 was also a disastrous winter. Her full chronology, drawn from and quoting Moravian records, starts in 1773 and continues to 1955; it is crucial for anyone interested in Inuit history to read the entire chronology, and her book as well, for she carries the story developed by James Hiller and Carol Brice-Bennett forward.

> Nain 1916–1917 "a severe form of rheumatism was widespread among our people, and many heads of families . . . during the whole of the winter . . . were unable to do anything towards the support of their families."
>
> Okak 1916–17 "On Sept 27th 1916 the first cases of measles occurred" . . . and the illness spread rapidly. "Some of the older folk, too, made fun of our precautionary measures and maintained there was no escaping from anything which God had sent us. . . . In . . . October . . . 29 adults and children died. . . . A large number . . . only recovered very slowly . . . and were unable . . . to dry their fish. . . . The statistics for the year 1916–17: 4 births, while 44 persons died, chiefly due to measles."
>
> Hopedale 1916–17 before the summer ended practically every Esk. family had one or more member sick. 13 died. . . .
>
> Hebron 1916–17 "everybody who had not had the measles in the 'eighties' of the last century was attacked. . . . One young man and one woman died of consumption [TB] . . . Many men lay a large part of the winter because of rheumatism."

Then came the catastrophe year: 1918–1919. The Spanish Flu was not the only killer: there was an autumn epidemic of measles in Nain (and other diseases in other mission stations) that also "wrought awful havoc in our congregation. 13 children and 10 adults have died . . . chickenpox has been very light in the case of the children . . . but . . . our . . . old people are being carried off by it."

The Spanish Flu decimated Okak. "The total deaths from the epidemic number 207, out of a congregation of 263; the total deaths for the whole year amount to 215. The entire male population has been wiped out." Kleivan notes that the Okak mission station was abandoned the next year, with the survivors moved into Hopedale and Nain: "Hebron, 1918–19 'Out of a population of 220 at Hebron only 70 remain . . . in the course of about nine days nearly two thirds of the Hebron congregation were corpses.'" Kleivan notes that if we put aside the outlier camps, out of one hundred people at the mission station itself only fourteen survived.

In her comment column Kleivan notes the following horrendous situation, the consequences of which remain until now: "In Okak and at several of the sealing places the dogs played havoc with the corpses. At Sillutalik (Cut Throat) 36 persons died, but only 18 remained to be buried. The only visible remains of the others were a few bare skulls and a few shankbones lying around the houses" (1966, 178–181).

On that horrendous note we can end this chapter—theirs and mine—of Inuit and Innu history. This has been a long chapter to read, and a hard chapter to write—for emotional as well as material reasons. But at stake is putting aside the simplistic glorification of "tradition." There were, as we have only begun to indicate, aspects of it that were good and productive, alongside a brutal and relentless destruction. Without seeing "tradition" for what it was, the present seems to be built on air and on simple current policy mistakes. Would that it were so.

The point we must keep before us is that for all the ensuing difficulties and the current disaster of the present situation, in some fundamental ways the survivors of this nightmare did more than just survive, and the next two chapters seek to show how this was done, in the face of continuing adversity.

FOUR

The Peoples without a Country

Two major changes reshaping the lives and situations of Innu and Inuit occurred between the Spanish Flu pandemic and the 1960s, when the Newfoundland government began its emphasis on confining Innu people in slum-built concentration villages and relocating many Inuit to their own, socially and negatively marked neighborhoods in more central Inuit villages. These two post–Spanish Flu developments were first the 1926 sale of the Moravian mission stores to HBC and their subsequent closure in 1942 as HBC retreated from northern Labrador. Then second, in 1949 Newfoundland gave up its separate country status and confederated with Canada, taking Labrador, which it governed, into Canada with it. This was done in ways that erased, or tried to erase, the aboriginal status and the Native rights of both Innu and Inuit peoples, making them officially just ordinary citizens. Both peoples then had no special needs or rights that were constitutionally recognized, even though Native peoples elsewhere in Canada had substantial constitutional protections and benefits.

This situation was compounded by the Moravian missionaries' departure from their northern mission communities. Without Native status they had no lands that belonged to them. Their territories were then what in Canada are called Crown Lands, open to anyone if they follow identical government regulations: for example, regulations governing sport fishing and hunting seasons, and open to commercial logging, hydroelectric dams, whatever.

It will help us to grasp the consequences of the retreat of HBC and the Moravians and confederation with Canada if we also address issues of memory and endurance—the endurance of memories of trauma, and the endurance of people who live with and against their memories of trauma and the ways trauma denies hope. For both these two developments brought very substantial new traumas and recalled prior ones.

Living against the memory of trauma is even more difficult than it may at first seem. People can be hurt so profoundly, their hopes for something better so consistently denied, that afterward hope itself can hurt. The full impact of the denial of hope for a more livable future, as well as its partial reconstitution on new grounds, will be further addressed in chapters 5, 6, and 7. We start with the issue of living with memories, of peoples living today and tomorrow with and against their memories of trauma and the remnants of hope.

As we get closer to the present, we must often take a long route to get there. The issue before us is not what but why, and the why of the present is very far from an answerable question. The partial answers we reach toward are not derivable just from what happened, certainly not in any simple or linear way. To reduce why to what happened is to assume that a description explains its own existence. Here, instead, it is necessary to reach far into the beyond.

Be patient as we reach into the yesterdays of the Native peoples of Labrador. Part of what is needed is to explore new ways of talking about the past, or the not-quite-past, as it becomes entangled with tomorrow.

The Future of Memories

W. E. B. Du Bois, one of the most sensitive and perceptive analysts of race issues within the United States, wrote two books with what at first seem strange titles—titles hinting at a complexity that defined his books. This complexity was scarcely addressed by specific passages in the book, but only in the book as a whole. John Berger, poet, artist, and storyteller, clarified what was at issue in such titles, whose focus encompasses the whole, when he wrote, "If everything had a name there would be no need for stories." It took a book full of Du Bois's stories and ideas to give the title of the book substance, and to turn the openness of the titles into their very special meaning. In recovering some of their meaning we can learn something useful about Native lives in Labrador.

The titles in question are *Dusk of Dawn: An Essay toward an Autobiography of a Race Concept* (1940) and the earlier *Darkwater: Voices from within the Veil* (1920). *Dusk of Dawn* is the more complex and the more far-reaching book. Note that the title is not *"Dusk before Dawn,"* referencing a simple path from slavery to emancipation, from darkness to enlightenment. Du Bois was a man who knew full well the setbacks of the Jim Crow segregation laws in the early twentieth century and the fluorescence of lynching and the murderous and property-destroying riots against African Americans in the first half of the twentieth century, which intensified with, and were inescapably violent against, the victories that followed the emancipation of slaves. The dusk of dawn is the night *within* the arriving day. It is also, in the most subtle and powerful way, the liberation of America as a whole by the liberation of Black folks, the dusk that calls forth the impending dawn.

This realization, that the Black struggle for justice will liberate everyone, is crucial to the collected essays in his earlier book, *Darkwater: Voices from within the Veil*—voices that expose the lies and the unredeemable violence just barely underneath the surface of "democracy" and "civilization." "Darkwater" is, in Du Bois's usage, just one word, not the usual two, as African Americans, in the context of a pervasive racism, have been in some fundamental ways one people, with one condition, rich and poor, compliant with domination or oppositional—a lesson the Inuit and Innu elite have yet to learn.[1]

And the wonderful subtitle of *Darkwater* suggests its own lessons: *Voices from within the Veil*. Du Bois was a genius for understanding inequality and domination from the bottom up. To be within the veil of suffering is to be within the silences and all that power seeks to hide from view. What happens is not beneath or behind the veil; it is part of the veil.

That is the work of this and the next three chapters. These chapters show both the shaping of the current world and the semihidden or open struggles against it, taking us from the Spanish Flu to the present; taking us to the dusk within the dawn, along with the glowing reality of the current dawn; taking us from both the suffering only partly left behind and the still open wounds to the still living hopes of the present, and especially to the social relations that carry both wounds and hopes, and all that lies between.

THE WHOLE SITUATION in Labrador, from the Spanish Flu (and probably before) to the present, echoes the much more widespread situation of war veterans with posttraumatic stress disorder (PTSD)—veterans who continually mix and merge what was done to them with what they were led to do to others. For both veterans and the Innu and Inuit the "post" in PTSD is a fundamental evasion of the seriousness of the problem: the memories that cannot be just memories, but still must be lived; traumas that are carried within victims and perpetrators alike, continually recreated, a living presence in these lives, often for decades if not lifelong. Those who put young people and Native people in that situation always want to pretend that the trauma was yesterday, that it is history and now things should be better if only the victims "got over it." It may help us to help those who need it, and for them to help themselves, if we stopped calling it "posttraumatic stress disorder" and started calling it "continuing trauma stress"—dropping the "disorder" label also, because the chaos in their lives is not their responsibility. Their continuing response to what we had them do, and to what was done to them, may in fact be healthier than if they just said something like, ho hum, a whole bunch of people next to me died really horrible deaths, I killed a whole bunch of people in really grisly ways, and meanwhile I had one of my legs blown off and I'm almost deaf. Do we really want to call the continuing intense upset about this a "disorder" of the person who has those feelings? Not unless the term *disorder* means that we can no longer order their lives for them.

There are only two points to all this. First, the very way we talk about the long-term consequences of suffering usually lays blame on the victim and puts us in the role of concerned and decent helpers, which may be a further offense. Second, perhaps all this will help us to understand the people who say to us, by their actions, "Screw you, I want to drink and fight and maybe kill myself." The victims may be saying that you did all this to me, now I can at least do it to myself. For Native peoples the pathways to the present are more tangled than for military veterans, but not by much.

THE ATTEMPTED SILENCING of the living and their continually recreated memories of domination, abuse, unmet needs, and a profound lack of caring or understanding is one of the core lies of power, crucial to the continuation of control and especially to the intimacy of both state and family domination and control: *"I'm sorry, I will never do it again, I love you, I promise."* This attempted and always incomplete suppression of memory, of current reality, and especially of what is very likely to soon happen again, is the central lie of both intimate and political violence,[2] as men lie to the women they hit, women to the children they abuse, and as governments apologize for letting residential schools rape and beat and humiliate their children and then turn around and continue to hurt Native people in new and continuing ways. These official lies are also in their way a marriage—a bad marriage between past and future that becomes difficult to escape because there is nowhere else to go. There are few kin, friends, or neighbors who are not in similar marriages, who do not suffer as you do, or lie to you, or just do not see you or your situation as it is, who fail to see what you and your situation have become, which deeply interferes with your own ability to see your own situation.[3]

We more than live with our memories and our memory-driven anticipations. As Freud realized, we are our memories, memories that are also anticipations that are almost always both there and not quite there. To distance them by calling it all posttraumatic is to make it more difficult to transcend them. You don't heal festering wounds by saying, "You got that yesterday," nor by offering to "reconnect" people to the time in their lives when they got wounded. Recently established government programs do just this. At substantial expense they helicopter Innu people back into "the bush" for a few months so that they can "reconnect" with their traditions, and then the program planners wonder why so many people after a week or two claim to be ill and ask to be helicoptered back to town. Lived and living history is not clinical psychology.

The Naskapi Nation's own history of their relations with HBC and the Newfoundland government makes explicit, in a sorrow-full way, the living pain of memories that are made more painful by repetition of the kinds of events that started the memories. In the following quote from the Naskapi Nation's public (online) presentation of their history, they are discussing a long history of forced relocations, starting with what was done by HBC in the nineteenth century and continuing into the present, when they were finally consulted by the Newfoundland government about what they wanted. It was clearly written by someone else, but the Naskapi Nation put it up on their online site as theirs.

> Perhaps because it was the first such process in which they had been involved, the Naskapis placed considerable faith in the consultation undertaken by Indian and Northern Affairs. It is a source of considerable bitterness even today that, in the minds of many Naskapis, not all of the promises or reassurances that were

made were lived up to. Two examples are most commonly cited: the insistence of [the government's Department of] Indian and Northern Affairs' representatives that the Naskapis live in row houses that, in the event, proved not to be adequately soundproofed [although the Naskapi were promised they would be] and that had a variety of other faults; and the fact that the brochure prepared by Indian and Northern Affairs [to convince them to move to these government-built houses] showed a fully landscaped site with trees and bushes, whereas no landscaping was done, and no trees or bushes were ever planted.

Incidents like those may seem very minor to persons with long experience of large and impersonal institutions such as government departments, but they happened to the Naskapis when they were in a very formative stage of their relations with Indian and Northern Affairs and when they had still not forgotten their callous treatment by the Hudson's Bay Company. It should not come as a surprise, therefore, that these matters are still spoken of frequently today and that they maintain very considerable importance and significance for many Naskapi. (http://www.naskapi.ca/en/History, accessed December 2011)

In addition to all the memories of suffering from forms of imposed treatment that endure and whose continuities can be named, as the Naskapi Nation noted, there are all the continuities that are just there, that can be described but probably never effectively named. They live all the more pervasively in the present because they cannot be fully named, cannot be bounded and contained by a name, cannot be called forth by their name and set aside. Without names they are hard to address; they just remain there, sometimes everywhere, sometimes nowhere. Consider the following example.

In 2007 I was in Labrador, working on the history that went into this and the previous chapter. I went into the office of an Inuit government official, simply to introduce myself and inform about my work. She was about forty-five years old, fluent in English and Inuktitut. I told her I was researching a health history of the Inuit and the Innu from colonial times to the present. She became very assertive, rightly so, telling me I had no right to come into the community for purposes of research, without asking permission from the Inuit government. I was not allowed to do this. I told her that I was only using printed and public records, mostly government reports, HBC and Moravian published documents, and local writings in libraries and public archives, and that I was asking no one in the community any questions relating to the research, none at all. This last point, as I have indicated in chapter 1, is crucial to how I work: I think asking research questions is a very major obstacle to doing serious research, for among other problems it assumes that the questioner knows what is important to talk about—a very limiting assumption. I told her that I came to her office just to introduce myself, not to ask her any questions, and I told her that at that present time the focus of my research was on the 1918–1919 Spanish Flu pandemic and its consequences.

She stared at me, completely silently, for more than several minutes, which made me increasingly tense, and then she softly said that her grandmother was a little girl, about eight years old, in [naming an Inuit village that was quite hard-hit] and watched the sled dogs eat the corpses of her parents. After saying this, she was again silent for quite a while, just looking at me. After a while I said I was truly sorry that her family had to suffer so, thanked her for talking to me, and left.

Of all the things we might say about this horrendous incident, I think what is particularly significant is the lack of anyone to help this little girl in the midst of her suffering: not just anyone in her Inuit community, for most of the adults were dead or incapacitated, but also anyone from "outside"—a missionary, a trader, a Newfoundland or Canadian government official; there was no one who would or could help that little girl in her frightful miseries, although "outsiders" had been pressing on them for more than a century. This lack of help at times of suffering and need is a lesson that has long endured among Native people and has become worse with the government-sponsored relocations that force people to spend the bulk of their year in miserable villages, while the government does nothing, for decades, to address repeated complaints and requests for help. It is a continuing history, and the consequences of earlier traumas also continue into and beyond now.

Unlike HBC and the missionaries, who did not make any promises (except about heaven, Jesus, and starvation if trapping was unsuccessful), the governments of Canada and Newfoundland make and break promises routinely, lying to Native people about what they will get and what will be done to help them. After making commitments, the governments routinely do nothing, or often worse than nothing, and turn a very deaf ear to repeated Native requests to do what they promised to do—making sure that Native people know they are helpless to get what they were told they would get.

This is a special, local version of a much larger and more widespread issue: the capacity to act toward relatively helpless and vulnerable peoples with utter impunity—for those in power to do almost whatever they want to do to or with them, laws and promises to the contrary notwithstanding. We want to call what we have done *yesterday*, as we do with lynching African Americans, but it is alive today in paramilitaries, in Guantanamo, in the routine and long-well-organized, state-financed, and internationally negotiated practices that the historically illiterate media name "extraordinary" rendition, and of course in Canada, with housing, education, low-level flying, and the so-called land claims process, which is the current name for land and resource grabs and often also the deeply encouraged formation of collusive Native elites.

IMPUNITY WORKS IN UNUSUAL ways in Labrador. Impunity is the ability to do something very wrong, even by local laws and local standards of acceptable action, and get away with it, unpunished. In fact, the knowledge that you will not be punished is crucial to assaults made with impunity. Thus, for example, with the lynching of African Americans in the United States, throughout the first half of the twentieth century, none of the perpetrators or the crowds that came to celebrate the event were ever masked, nor did they take any steps at all to conceal their identity during their acts of major felonies: kidnap, torture, rape, murder, and more.[4] The lack of masks, of concealed identities, underlined the fact that they were literally reveling in the state's grant of impunity to act as felons committing capital crimes without worrying about ever being punished. Similarly, in Central America, throughout the last half of the twentieth century and into the present, so-called paramilitaries butcher/rape/murder peasants, villagers, rainforest defenders, union organizers, and townspeople, knowing that the state will not call them into account. That is what impunity is, just to begin.

Two points can be made about all this that are relevant to understanding Labrador. First, short of armed or mass resistance to those who act with impunity, which unfortunately many times is or seems impossible to the victims, there is nowhere for the victims, their families, and their communities to turn for help but to the same state that granted the impunity. That contradiction is the central mechanism of the victims' trap, both the bait and the bone-crushing jaws of the trap. Impunity further undermines the state's pretense of legitimacy, for those who are similar to the victims and who, for the moment, survive. The claim to the legitimacy of state power is scarcely taken seriously except by sociologists, political scientists, and the elite,[5] but it defines the situation of the abused who, beyond themselves, have nowhere else to turn, particularly when effective opposition—opposition that changes domination—cannot be mobilized from within the group.[6]

Second, and of particular concern both in Labrador and for other Native peoples where the situation is often similar, such as Australia and India, in Labrador the state did and does not grant impunity to groups outside itself: to groups such as paramilitaries, Ku Klux Klans, White Citizens' Councils, fundamentalist Hindu mobs, whatever.[7] In Labrador both the Newfoundland and the Canadian governments give *themselves* the impunity to do or not do what they will to Native peoples, without even the pretense of a cover, without having other people do the dirty work, without even letting others "get away" with what the state either wants done or wants not to stop, in ways that enable the state to pretend that its hands are clean. The governments to which Native peoples appealed for relief from their suffering were worse than deaf—they had no ears at all. Lacking ears, they also had absolutely no sense of balance.[8]

By granting impunity to themselves, rather than to others, states put Native people in an even more difficult position than is usual with impunity. The Canadian state partly conceals the violence that always accompanies impunity, that is always what impunity is about. The violence in Canada, as now in the United States, is hidden first behind "policy" and bureaucracy and then by creating circumstances that make it likely that a significant proportion of Native people would assault themselves and each other, in large part as a consequence of the way they are treated.

So, as we shall see, Newfoundland could take a vast region of the best Innu hunting territories and flood it for a hydroelectric project without even bothering to tell the Innu that it was happening, or how much of their land would be flooded, much less offer any compensation, much less even ask or get permission. That was several decades ago, and Newfoundland still hasn't even bothered to adequately answer Native complaints or concerns. When the state grants itself the impunity to do as it wishes to Native peoples, it is even harder for the victims to fight or appeal to the state or other groups in the dominant society than in contexts where it gives this impunity to paramilitaries or lynching parties.[9]

There are always serious consequences from the hopelessness of appeals to an absolutely unconcerned structure of domination and exploitation. Native peoples are too few to matter, so long as it does not attract the sustained critical attention of the media, and the attention span of the media is usually more like three days than three years. The lack of hope for effective redress seems to turn the victims of state impunity inward to become the authors of both their own dignity and their own suffering. Both will have surprising consequences.

To introduce the issues now before us, we start with the point that all the unmet—and worse, unrecognized—needs, all the broken promises, all the dependencies created and then not cared for or about, and all the pain suffered by youth like the young girl in the Spanish Flu epidemic, utterly defenseless with the loss of her parents to control the starving sled dogs, did not just happen and then become yesterday. It all very much lives on in what we simplify as "memory" but is more effectively thought about as lives lived both in, and incompletely against, an intense, sometimes shattering, sometimes sustaining not-past.

IT IS DIFFICULT to even suggest what the survivors of a pandemic like the Spanish Flu continue to carry with them from such an appalling situation. It is more complex than the analogy of PTSD suggests, although PTSD is a useful start for thinking about the issues. What makes the situation in Labrador more complex is the way that the Spanish Flu, killing people by overly intensifying the immune system, struck adults the hardest, leaving little children and the quite elderly as the major survivors. In the harsh sub-Arctic winter the survivors had great difficulty getting food, fuel, and even water: they were, by and large, helpless in this new context. It was not so much what they did or what was done to them that devastated the survivors; it was what they could not do, what no one came to do for them.

In that sense they were somewhat like holocaust victims in concentration camps: no one could help them very effectively, if at all, and they were not able to help themselves in the face of destructive assault. A great many, perhaps most, of the inmates who survived the camps were not even able to be proud of surviving, as many survivors wrote or said afterward, because of all they saw around them, because of all that happened to them, and because of all that they did, or more often could not do, as part of surviving. "We who have come back, we know: the best of us did not return"—so wrote Viktor Frankl (1959), a Jewish survivor of two German concentration camps.

One of the classic points that are made in the literature about concentration camp survivors is that the children of the survivors hardly know—directly and consciously—what their parents went through. It is the grandchildren, perhaps owing to the greater distance, that lets them engage, who know more explicitly, but who also express in their actions and emotions some of the long-lasting consequences of such horrors, even more than do the children of the direct victims, who grew up with, and in, that more immediate context.

All this is to explain that in discussing the decades following this pandemic we need to consider not just the chronologies of what happened when, but also how all this unfolded within the communities that endured into unforgetting futures. There are scarcely any data for this task. Native historians may one day produce it, should they find it important. All we can do is what Walter Benjamin and Theodore Adorno called gesture in that direction.[10]

More specifically, we need to raise and center issues that we cannot yet fully grasp: show how to get our minds and our hands on these issues in ways that enable Native people to encourage healing change in their own communities—their task more than ours—while we seek to force changes in what our society still does to recreate the problems, what our governments do to reinvigorate the memories by not even trying to remedy today the injuries we caused yesterday. This is not what some call truth and reconciliation, but a pathway toward truths and remedies, or to give it its full name, justice.

JUSTICE CANNOT BE SERVED by making a descriptive anthropology out of this still lived history. A. P. Low, who was stationed at the HBC post, Fort Chimo, in northern Labrador, wrote about Native suffering in the 1890s: "A curious custom was noted in the interior, on the arrival of various families at the [HBC] posts in the spring—instead of joyous greetings the women clasp one another and indulge in a period of silent weeping, after which they cheer up and exchange gossip" (1896, 48).

A curious custom indeed that women should so "indulge" themselves, before reverting to what women do—gossip. For all its chauvinism, for all its classic anthropology that I have termed "the quaint customs of the fuzzy-wuzzies," for all the usual historical and contextual illiteracy, and for all the distance-making and "we are superior" nonsense this quote evokes, it raises one crucial point that we must deal with in this and the next chapter.[11] We have to grasp that in the midst of all this suffering, all this abusive treatment, a great many Native people have managed to do what Low calls, trivializing what is at stake, "cheer up"—that is, turn toward the future, toward living good, productive, and caring lives. That victory they shape within and against their suffering is crucial. It is crucial because of the context from which it springs: hope embodied and made real in actually existing social relations, not fantasy. We will return to a discussion of hope in chapter 5, and again in the second part of chapter 8.

The Take and Give of Traditional Native Lives

In the early mid- to mid-twentieth century, the Innu and Inuit peoples of Labrador began to be detached from the clutches of HBC and the Moravians, with both actual and attempted control transferred to the government of Newfoundland.

The firestorm that reshaped Indian and Eskimo lives, hurting them badly but setting them firmly on the path back to a reassertion of their Innu and Inuit identities, started smoldering before the 1918 epidemics and blew open with the 1949 incorporation of Labrador into Canada.

In 1905 Mina Hubbard was traveling across the interior of Labrador to finish, as it were, the journeys of her late husband, who died trying to do this, in part because he would not follow the routes suggested by the Innu. She reported that the caribou herd in the interior was in serious decline (Hubbard 1909), making the Indians more dependent on store food and tent canvas from the HBC trading posts.

A year later the Indians complained to HBC that settlers were increasingly invading their trapping territories, seriously diminishing the amount of furs they could trap to trade for necessary supplies. As a result, the more northern of the inland Indians increasingly needed to move to, or toward, Davis Inlet and North West River, to be nearer the coastal HBC trading posts (Brice-Bennett 1986, 39). Much is at stake in the loss of their trapping territories, which became a problem in the nineteenth century and seriously intensified throughout the first half of the twentieth, including the fact that documenting the losses is crucial to current Innu land claims for their historically prior use of inland territories. A lot of prime lands were lost: several times in the early mid-twentieth century HBC post managers wrote that the White trappers were doing very well while the Indians did not get enough furs to trade for food and were starving (e.g., Harry Andrews, North West River, August 18, 1927, Father O'Brien [henceforth FOB] Papers).[12]

In part the move to the coast—to Davis Inlet and North West River—was to trade with the HBC posts that were supplied directly by ocean-crossing boats, rather than by inland canoe and sled freighting. These coastal posts had more and a broader range of goods and paid a bit more for furs.

Even more important, starting in 1921 a priest, Father Edmund O'Brien, came to North West River, and then also to Davis Inlet every summer, arriving after the ice went out in May or June and staying until freeze-up in early winter. Father O'Brien was an absolutely crucial link between the Innu, the Newfoundland government, and HBC. Without him—and the Indian commitment to his Catholicism—there were multiple years when they would have starved in much larger numbers. Indian dependence on Father O'Brien was shaped and secured by a declining ability to survive by commercial trapping and caribou hunting, and increasingly for the Inuit after 1926, with a major and unmanageable intensification of commercial trapping that was forced by HBC's takeover of the Moravians' trading posts, which made the Eskimos more dependent on mission welfare, as they could not secure their minimum needs by trade with HBC. This situation for both Innu and Inuit was, to a substantial extent, socially constructed and not due to ecological changes.

Most years from the mid-1920s on, the Innu could no longer procure enough furs to feed and supply themselves—at the level of production and consumption supplies that they were allocated for their furs. Even in years when most White trappers had bountiful harvests, the manager at North West River noted that a substantial proportion of the Indian people there suffered greatly, from a variety of causes, including having to go further into the interior, and to less productive regions, with the increasing loss of their best territories to the encroaching Euro-Canadian trappers. All this had a wide range of consequences. The post manager at North West River, by then a major Indian settlement, wrote,

> The Indians appear to have had a hard time last fall, at least one crowd, as old Bob's wife has died, Sennapest's wife also and three children from the same crowd who were all together, and Peter Jacks wife is also quite sick; Chimun Poons canoe upset on the way inland last fall late, and his wife almost pegged out from the exposure, but is now over it, they lost everything they had, rifles, Guns food etc. as it was in a strong rapids, and this meant that the others had to help them out. Napistish Shooshem also got in the water after ice, and caught a chill, and is very sick, I think he is probably TB and this makes it worse.
>
> They did not have a great deal of fur, but fortunately the prices are high, and this gave them enough to carry on with till spring. There are some of the older women now at the rapids in one camp with Susapish's crippled boy and one or two other children they're going to stay out here for the spring until the rest come out in June, they are Susapish's widow, Sinnish's widow, and Poon's widow, this means I will have to keep them going with a little food, but I have made the men promise that they will pay for it when they come out in the spring; I imagine that these old people are quite a hindrance to the others, and this is probably why they are staying here this spring?

Several of them told me to tell you that they are keeping a Mink for you, and will be pleased to see you again in the summer.

The Whites have had another good year trapping, again chiefly with foxes. (Letter from Jack Kemp to Father O'Brien, North West River, February 22, 1936, FOB Papers)[13]

The ranger's report for the Inuit at Hebron, April 8, 1942 (FOB Papers)— an exceptionally good year—made a similar point: most of the Inuit were stressed and destitute, while a small proportion of Native people could do well, good years or bad. Those who could not do well were destitute before the next trapping season started and needed to be supplied with relief in the form of goods, primarily flour, lard, and tea—a diet that maintained life but not anything resembling health. Indeed, HBC post managers who distributed relief wrote that it was only supposed to keep Indians alive (for a particularly good example, see June 28, 1947, letter to O'Brien from Davis Inlet, FOB Papers).

For the Indians who were destitute Father O'Brien wrote, or later telegraphed, what was needed to the government in St. John's, Newfoundland, followed by a list of trappers or families and how much each would or did get in the form of relief supplies. These supplies were disbursed by HBC, with government reimbursement for their costs. There is a lot of indirect, and some direct, evidence that HBC disbursed these supplies not simply by who needed what but by who, by their standards and their fur-production desires, deserved to be supported.

At about the same time the Inuit were also under increasing pressure, with increasing deprivation for many. In 1924 the Moravians, trying to keep up their mission finances, stopped giving credit to Inuit at their stores, which was devastating to those who did not have a good trapping season, as credit funded both consumption and production supplies (Brice-Bennett 2003, 94–95). This strategy did not work, because while it lowered costs, at the same time it diminished productivity.[14] HBC took over the Moravians' trading posts in 1926 and ran them on even harsher credit terms than did the Moravians in their final years of trading—to no avail. HBC closed all its northern Labrador trading posts in 1942 and left, leaving the Indians and the Eskimos to the mercies and the bureaucracies of the Newfoundland government. Newfoundland had gone bankrupt in the Great Depression, and in 1933 Great Britain turned Newfoundland and its Labrador territory back into a colony under direct British administration.

For the sixteen years (1926–1942) that HBC ran the former Moravian trading posts the distribution of supplies was scant and harsh. Between 1942 and 1949, when Newfoundland and Labrador became part of Canada, the distribution of supplies to Native people along the coast seems to have been done more in terms of need. The Newfoundland Rangers (an early and local version of the Royal Canadian Mounted Police [RCMP] or "Mounties") took over this task. But it was not done more humanely by the rangers right away, for at first it was done by an arrogant and oppressive ranger, with what has been reported as extreme brutality, ignorance, and unconcern. Father O'Brien played an important role in getting that situation changed, underscoring the dependence of the Indians on his mediation. With his complaints, that ranger was removed from the relief process, and the situation went back to the "normal" squeeze, which in some ways was worse, because it was quieter and, as it were, familiar, and so attracted less complaints and oppositional attention, although in the long run the less flamboyant forms of oppression were probably at least as destructive, for they were much longer lasting.

The central point here is that the Innu needed Father O'Brien; he became crucial to their survival. Why and how this happened illuminates several more general and long-lasting issues, as illustrated by the following quote from the published ethnographic journals of William Duncan Strong, who (much to his own dismay) left the Field Museum of Chicago and spent the winter of 1927–1928 among the northern Innu.[15] He describes situations but does not make any connections between them. I think the association between the increasing hunger of the Innu and their susceptibility to disease is a more than plausible connection (see Carmichael 1983). Strong's longer comments on the run-up to 1918 provide the basis for what happened next.

> About 1916, the caribou migration, which had been slackening for some years, stopped almost entirely and no deer at all came to Indian House Lake [a major interior gathering place for the northern Innu, and for a while the site of an HBC trading post]. . . . The Barren Ground people [i.e., the Naskapi] were forced to come to the coast . . . as they had done in 1843 and between 1855 and 1860. During the summer of 1918 Barren Ground people were in two camps, one at Voisey's Bay where they were cutting wood, the other at Upatik Bay. Here the smallpox and measles epidemics of that year reached them, killing about 40 persons at Voisey's Bay and others at Upatik. Between Hopedale and Nain the epidemic of 1918 was of smallpox and measles. To the north the influenza [the Spanish Flu] wiped out the Eskimos. . . . About 350 . . . died at He-

bron and Okak. . . . The Davis Inlet people [the so-called Naskapi] were in the interior at this time hunting, but failing to get sufficient game, they were forced to come to Davis Inlet for supplies where they contracted the disease [which was] rampant on the coast and several died. The epidemic seems to have hit older people the hardest, and as a result there were no people of really advanced years among either the Davis Inlet or Barren Ground bands at the time of my stay with them [1928]. (Leacock and Rothschild 1994, 57)

After the epidemics, Okak was closed as a community, and fifty-nine survivors were relocated to Nain and Hopedale. In these communities new arrivals and former residents were increasingly moved into frame houses, which substantially increased the need for fuel and diminished the nearby, easily available woods that were used for heating and cooking. As efforts to get wood increased, it seems that productivity declined (Brice-Bennett 1986).

In Father O'Brien's first visit to Davis Inlet, in 1924, he referred to the Indians as "a lowly and unbefriended people"—for indeed they were having very hard times and, having no influential "friends" or allies, were particularly vulnerable. During this first visit Father O'Brien appointed an Indian "chief," so he could have someone who supposedly could speak for, and to, the community, and with whom he could coordinate his annual visit and his relief activities (Henriksen 1973, 13).

The Eskimo's situation continued to decline after the 1918 pandemic. Until 1926, when the Eskimo situation in several communities changed drastically, Brice-Bennett has shown that the Eskimos pursued two different fisheries (1986, 5). They did commercial and subsistence cod fishing in the summer, and seal netting both in the fall, which was the most productive time for seals, and again in the mid- to late spring. In the winter, between the two seal hunts, they went inland after furs and caribou, using the seal meat to sustain themselves and the sled dogs for the travel and the work. Between the end of fur trapping, often in February, and the start of the second seal hunt, in May, could be a time of hunger if the furs were not plentiful enough to purchase food, but for most of the year this seasonal organization of production "worked," at least until 1926.

That year was like a hurricane that blew the structures of social life away, with damage that was soon revealed, along with many further long-term consequences. The Moravians, not financially secured by their 1924 restrictions on credit, abandoned their trading business and sold a twenty-one-year lease to HBC to run the stores in all its mission communities. HBC insisted on a monopoly for this trade, which the Moravians could give owing to the vast size of their original land grants. While this monopoly was never completely secure—a bit of trade could occasionally be done with a fishing schooner or an independent trader—it was secured enough to give HBC substantial control. Brice-Bennett has shown that one of the first things that HBC did, when it got control of the stores, was to lower credit advances (1986, 7), which left the Inuit with not enough supplies to keep them out on the trapping grounds, but required regular trips back to the post to trade for more supplies. This was compounded in the 1930s, as she explained, by the collapsing prices for fish and seal products, including the introduction of rubber boots, in 1933, which broke the market for sealskin boots (1986, 7, citing the Moravian Periodical Accounts, Nain, 1936, 7:103).

They used this control in ways that were so increasingly destructive that it not only hurt the Inuit but also contributed to destroying their own business operations, even in posts that were managed by decent and reasonably caring managers. The destructiveness was explained in a ranger report in early 1942, just before HBC decided to close almost all their northern trading operations, five years before their lease expired:

> One must not forget, the Hudson's Bay Company is and always has been, primarily, a fur trading company and nothing else; they are not interested in the welfare of the Eskimo, they are not interested in any form of the fishing industry, neither cod, seal, seal oil, or any other kind; consequently when the fur season is over the Eskimo may fend for themselves as best they may. The mission has been here a great number of years, they taught the Eskimo all they know about the white man's civilization, and then when they [the Eskimos] went beyond their control they stepped out. The Hudson's Bay Company that agreed to contract to operate a fur trading post here to the exclusion of all other free traders . . . seems to be rather dictatorial in its use. The company usually imports its supplies during October, it is usually enough to last during and until the end of the trapping season, about April 1; this year is no exception; at present at the Hebron Post there is none of the following: butter, molasses, sugar, yeast, baking items and other items not so badly needed. At the Nutak post there is a shortage of flour. Any relief orders issues now at Hebron may only be for flour and tea. The same situation has been going on for years.
>
> Nothing has been done for years to relieve the existing situation. Whether anything will be done in the future remains to be seen. Again due to the fur industry, the natives are usually short of seals, both for dog food and clothing

and skin boots; the shortage always happens in the middle of the winter trapping season; because as soon as the trapping season opens the natives have to try to earn something through trapping, forgetting all about sealing, which years ago comprised their main means of livelihood; consequently when March comes along, quite some natives are unable to travel inland due to not having dog food; which again cuts into their earnings. Also around Easter, though it is toward the last of the trapping season, the natives have to come to the post for their Easter festivals, thus again reducing their earnings a great deal. There seems to be only one solution to this problem.

Under existing circumstances the Eskimo is not nor ever will be independent or self-sufficient. His earnings are taken from him as soon or even before they are earned with no prospect of any further advances to tide them over until he can make another windfall. He is being taught to depend on only the fur season for his livelihood, disregarding all other means and forms of work; although they are interested in fishing to a certain extent, they are not encouraged to prosecute it. Immediately the fur trapping season opens, they are encouraged to get fur, fur, and more fur if possible, forgetting all about the coming winter when seals will be needed both for dog food to continue the trapping and also for skin boots, and seal fat to help supply light and warmth for them. (Ranger Reports, May 1942, FOB Papers)

After this wonderfully clear-headed analysis the report continues by trying to figure out how the Inuit, still being made into Eskimos, might better be controlled. It is a chilling continuation, for despite some good ideas, and clearly a heightened level of concern for Inuit well-being, the issue is framed in terms of total control, only better intentioned and better organized—*almost exactly the present situation*—from the perspective of the Canadian and Newfoundland governments and the mining corporations. Seven decades later, and despite Inuit self-government formed through land claims and Native rights and mining agreements, the Inuit, as well as the Innu, live within and against agreements and arrangements that are, underneath the rhetoric of respect for "Inuit culture," still brutally, if a bit more subtly, controlling. The ranger's report continues, introducing the point that better control would solve all the problems created by prior impositions and controls: "The solution would seem to depend upon having someone or something here with direct control of the Eskimo having no interference from anybody, except from the directors of any organization having control. The produce of any kind from the Eskimo, could be marketed whether it be fur, fish, seals

fat, skin boots, curios or anything; the Eskimo should be paid a fair and reasonable price for it, and all goods brought in for trade should be sold at a
fair and reasonable price. His earnings as well as expenditures could then be
controlled" (Ranger Reports, May 1942, FOB Papers).

As we shall see in chapters 6 and 7, this intensifying control, no matter how
well intentioned, undermined the productive autonomy that is the foundation of social life and has left Native peoples mostly with destructive forms of
autonomy that provide illusions of self-assertion. It will be useful to unravel
these two concepts, "productive autonomy" and "illusions of self-assertion."

Productive autonomy is not simply autonomy in production, even though
—as we have discussed in chapter 3—in the nineteenth and early twentieth
centuries the autonomous actions of Native peoples were crucial to their
commercial and subsistence production. Productive autonomy has one of its
main roots in what we have discussed as the autonomy of Native peoples in
organizing their own processes of production, and their own support of the
producers, within and against the imposed pressures to get them to produce.
But productive autonomy has another major root: their ability to produce
their tomorrows with, for, and at times against one another—to produce and
reproduce themselves as a people through their own activities, their own
relations to one another. As hard as things were for them, by design, they
were people in substantial control of their own lives, not just individually
but as a people.

That is the productive autonomy that is at stake now: the ability to produce your collective selves, your collective tomorrows. It is never, of course,
complete, nor is it ever completely lost. When kids who sniff gasoline say,
"You know this shit rots your brain in two years," they are also producing
their own tomorrows, but producing and destroying at the same time. Perhaps they have been put in a situation where the only reachable productive
autonomy is one that is doubled: productive and simultaneously destructive.
And an utterly destructive illusory autonomy is also the profoundly tragic
emptiness of domestic violence, especially for the people—mostly men—
who do it: an emptiness that shapes its repetitive wrongs.

What has happened when this productive autonomy was increasingly
undermined? It was fragmented by the collapse of partly autonomous work
in the production of furs and skins, and by governments' manipulation of
need, dependency, and vulnerability. And autonomy was undermined more
for men than for women.[16] All this leads us to issues embedded in illusions of
self-assertion, which seem to have substituted for autonomy.

Here we must be as forcefully clear as possible, to prevent hasty and shallow interpretations of the points being made. There are, for all significant social developments, scarcely ever any linear progressions, any simple one-directional developments, any single causes, or single sort of outcomes. Other than in trivial ways, social life is not like a train moving down a track, but more like pigeons and flies jostling for access to a lone horse pie, with hawks and insect-feeding birds circling overhead, before the rains wash the pie away. In this more complex context there are significant linear sequences—a hawk does dive and catch a pigeon—but linear sequences in social history occur within a much more multistranded situation. People, or governments, who associate themselves and their identity with the hawks and the equally predatory eagles do see situations more in terms of linear narratives, but they delude both themselves and each other, while thinking they also delude the pigeons, who above all have to eat, hawks or no hawks.

As productive autonomy—and much else—was lost, substance abuse, domestic violence, and suicide increased, as did the number of children born with FASD, from their mothers using alcohol when pregnant to both shape and deny their future. But very much else was also happening. Beating on your family, or drinking to the point where you can't care for them or yourself, can very much be an assertion of one's autonomy, one's capacity to defy authority, or the authorities, one's freedom to make and remake one's relations with others. Doing so may *produce* one's social world, but it is a dead end; it cannot *reproduce* it for long, which is why it is best understood as an illusion of autonomy, embedded in a situation where some people have other, more hopeful ways of moving, or trying to move, into the future.[17]

We will look only briefly at episodes in the erosion of productive autonomy, and only to illustrate one key point: the relentless, inescapably recurrent pressures on Indians and Eskimos that, as it were, "softened them up" for what followed during and after the collapse of the Native fur-trading economies. What followed was not just relocation and confinement, but also an utter denial of Native rights. We will soon arrive at that point. First, we need to at least briefly look at the softening, as prisoners are softened in the prelude to their interrogation—even those who manage, as did many Innu and Inuit, to maintain their dignity in the process.

In 1926, when HBC took over the Moravian trading posts, they almost immediately restricted credit from what had become customary, forcing the Inuit further inland to try to trap more fox. That set up an oppressive contradiction in their lives as Eskimos: to purchase food and supplies, they had to get more and more fox, but they had less and less seals to sustain this endeavor. At the same time the Innu, still needing to survive as Indians, were under equal pressure, driven by the simultaneous scarcity of available furs and of caribou. In 1926 the HBC post manager at Davis Inlet, John Keats, wrote to Father O'Brien, "Enclosed please find $2.00 given to me by Senna Best Rich [an Innu] for the church. He asked me if you would send him a cross and a set of prayer beads. They wish to be remembered to you and have told me to tell you that they could not go over [to see you at the coast] this year owning to sickness and a poor spring hunt" (July 2, 1926, FOB Papers).

There are multiple connections emerging here that were becoming, or had already become, routine: the connection between a poor hunt—hunger—and both sickness and an inability for many in the group to travel either down to the coast or back into the interior. What in this context, a context that the letter writer gave, is one to make of the request for a cross and prayer beads? Many things, for the request is irreducibly multiplex. What the request included is suggested by a letter to Father O'Brien written in the fall of the same year from the HBC post at North West River, saying in adjacent sentences that the Indians "are depending on your visit next summer. There has been a lot of sickness among them" (October 10, 1926, FOB Papers).

One year later the HBC post manager at Hebron wrote to Father O'Brien,

> I am sorry to hear the state of your Indian friends at North West River. Isn't it possible . . . to find something for these people to do during the summertime, so that they may be able to leave for their hunting grounds [in the fall] better equipped with provisions, etc. . . . We can not hide from ourselves the fact that in that locality furs are fastly diminishing, as the White man keeps pressing inward, and the time is not far hence, when our Indian, equipped for hunting as he is today, will not in an average year find sufficient furs to keep him alive. (Harry Andrews, Hebron, August 18, 1927, FOB Papers)

It was, in an oft-repeated forecast of future developments, completely unthinkable either to restrict the appropriation of Innu trapping territories by "White trappers" or for HBC to equip the Indians for more efficient trapping. Kindness in this context consists of "finding something" else for the Indians, which of course did not happen, as their situation worsened even further. The future developments consisted of trying to force Native people to live, or barely survive, in contexts that strongly favored both Euro-Canadians and the Canadian and Newfoundland governments—for example, by overwhelming both Native people and the caribou with low-level supersonic flying, as their air space was rented to NATO for air force training, or simply taking their lands for mines and hydroelectricity, and more.

Harry Andrews, author of the quote just above, continues, in the same letter, to note that while the Indian gets no protection whatsoever, and very scant addressing of their needs, they are the source of substantial revenue not just for the trading posts but for the Newfoundland government: "These poor old Indians, do not receive many blessings through being under the 'protecting care' of our legislature—for which they have to pay so heavily in duties on merchandise. As they are in no way a bother or drag to the Gov't. I can not see any reason why they would not at least hand them back the greatest part of what's taken from them . . . who are so sorely pressed to wrench from nature their means of livelihood" (Harry Andrews, Hebron, August 18, 1927, FOB Papers).

In that same year, the winter of 1927–1928, the ethnologist William Duncan Strong noted that porcupine, a major source of food in the interior, were very scarce, as were other small game, and that this, combined with a scarcity of caribou, "quickly reduce[s] the Indians to the point of starvation" (Leacock and Rothschild 1994, 7). The experience of starvation among the northern Innu in 1927–1928 was compounded by their active memories of earlier famines, for they told Strong about several of them: "Some forty years ago a Naskapi [northern Innu] band came out of the country near Upatik bay and went to Davis Inlet. The storekeeper there (a new man) would give them no food and all nineteen in the band starved to death except two women and one small boy . . . who found a deer killed by wolves, made a trout net from the skin. . . . and managed to live until they met other Naskapi" (Leacock and Rothschild 1994, 134).

To this they add two more stories. The first was of a trader at White Whale River who would give no cartridges, because they had nothing to trade, so one man starved. Others found a deer, and managed to survive, but "about two years later starvation drove them to the coast" (Leacock and Rothschild 1994).

In 1928 the letters to Father O'Brien about Indian starvation became almost routine, noting that only government relief is keeping them alive. But government relief was primarily in the form of flour, tea, and lard, not a diet that could possibly sustain health. And by 1930 Father O'Brien was also supplying used clothes, donated in St. John's and shipped to be given, or perhaps sold (the data on distribution are scant and unclear), to Indians.

And by the 1930s, as Brice-Bennett has shown, the price for cod fish had fallen so low that it scarcely paid for the salt to cure the fish; the price for seal skins collapsed; Native people were further scanted on both nets and twine to make nets, and they had to give the bulk of the seal meat they did get to the sled dogs, subsisting themselves even more on flour, lard, and tea (Brice-Bennett 1986, 8).

HBC post managers knew that their tight credit policies were starving the Natives. In 1933 the post manager at Nain wrote to Father O'Brien, "Every effort is being made to keep the natives on a 'pay-as-you-go' basis, but it is hard to maintain and very trying on the nerves" (Doug White to Father O'Brien, January 18, 1933, FOB Papers).

Father O'Brien had a very complex relationship to HBC. Several post managers were writing him in these tones, strongly suggesting that HBC policies and practices were hurting Native people deeply. Other post managers simply wrote that Native people were starving and many were sick. Nonetheless, Father O'Brien, for whom HBC had helped to build a church and a house at Davis Inlet, gave a talk to the Rotary Club in St. John's, the capital of Newfoundland and Labrador, praising HBC, and it was reported at length in St. John's major newspaper, the *Telegram*.

On October 17, 1932, he received a letter from the director of the main Canadian office of HBC, in Winnepeg, Manitoba, noting that "there is no need for me to tell you how much we appreciated your kind words concerning the work of the Company on the Labrador Coast. . . . I'm sure that it will have far-reaching effects, not only in Newfoundland but in Canada and England" (FOB Papers).

The next year, August 2, 1933, this same Winnipeg office wrote to Father O'Brien, complaining that the medical missionary, Dr. Patton of the International Grenfell Association, wanted to take over relief distribution on the Labrador coast, and asking for his help in keeping this from happening. The Grenfell medical missionaries had been by far the major source of medical aid in coastal Labrador, primarily for Euro-Canadians but with some attention to Innu and Inuit. Perhaps the Grenfell medical people realized that continual semistarvation was a medical problem; HBC made clear they saw it as a problem of cost and control, for in the same letter HBC stated that "if the government will contract with us to relieve all the sick and destitute for a fixed sum we could do it at less than half of what it has been costing them in previous years and having control of relief, we could make the people fully 50% more productive than they are at present."

HBC is here trying to make a transition in its domination of the fur trade, from control over credit to control over relief, for control over credit was not increasing productivity. And HBC is persisting in its fantasy that people already half-starved into at least partial submission can be made more productive if only they were starved more, squeezed harder. Cut the goose that lays the golden eggs deeper, and we will finally and completely get our hands on the source: in this manner power writes the invitations to its doomed but still destructive marriage of arrogance and ignorance.

The situation of the Innu and the Inuit did indeed get worse, even though HBC was not given further control of relief. Native people once again, as they did in the midst of the nineteenth century, openly rebelled against their treatment: "The Hebron natives had been very much out of order, and had broken into the store in late November and taken various articles of merchandise. They had gone so far as to tackle Massie [the post manager] and Dora [his wife?] in the store demanding various things and when refused had helped themselves" (Letter from Doug White, Nain, February 24, 1934, FOB Papers).

While the police came and took the "ringleader" of this event away, HBC knew that "trouble was brewing" among the Inuit. At the same time there are multiple letters, year after year, that Indians are starving and dying. In 1938 HBC stopped providing seal nets to the Eskimos, and their conditions deteriorated further. While HBC was intensifying their squeeze on Eskimos, they were joined by at least some Moravian missionaries: "I have known people who . . . have applied [to missionaries] for medicine for sick relatives and have been refused same because they were not in a position to pay for it. In one case the post manager advanced 50 cents from his own pocket to a man who had been refused by the missionary medicine for his sick child, so that such could be obtained" (Ranger Report, November 11, 1939, FOB Papers).

But in the same document, by the same person, there is an attempt to justify "manhandling those Eskimos" because missionaries do it also "when all other treatment has failed" and also bragging that he has the size and strength to do so. This Ranger Report then concludes with a series of "official" statements, from family relatives of people who recently died, which seem to have been required in a postmortem inquest, in each case stating that the deceased did not starve to death, even though several said there was no, or almost no, food in the house when the relative died, and they were just drinking water.

Just as the White trappers were encroaching on the Innu trapping grounds, using their general social dominance to deny Native access, so similarly, in a variety of ways and sometimes with the collusion of the Moravian missionaries, who "sold" Inuit sealing places to Euro-Canadians, the Inuit were losing some of the more productive locales in northern Labrador for shore-anchoring sealing nets to catch the migrating seals. Helge Kleivan notes that in 1928, when the HBC post at Nain supplied nets to the Inuit and gave them access to their old sealing spots, they caught 2,500 seals. She continues, noting that ten years later it was profoundly different:

> The fact that the sealing places have been given up has added to the general distress. . . . A new set of ideas holds sway. It may be said: "Surely the Eskimos can maintain the sealing places themselves." . . . They cannot do so. The Company will not, in Nain, provide nets or fit out sealing-teams, although they have done so on other stations. And so the Eskimo sinks deeper into poverty year by year, accumulating debts that he can never hope to repay; and there is no doubt that shortsighted policy lies at the root of the evil. (Kleivan 1966, 132, citing Periodical Accounts, June 1939, 133)

These quotes broaden the general context for this deteriorating situation: we are dealing not just with the fur trade but with merchant- and missionary-shaped colonialism, manhandling what British colonialism usually called uppity Natives and getting away with it through state power, not personal strength. Since the Inuit or the Innu could have collectively killed their tormentors—the Inuit did it to the Vikings, who were even more directly brutal than this modern manifestation—being put in a situation where this could not be done to people who "manhandled" them was very likely to be both personally and collectively debilitating.

Still, 1942 was an unusually good year for both the Indians and Eskimos, and for HBC as well:

> Approximately 135 fox pelts were brought to the post [Hebron] during the month; this number earned the natives approximately $2000, of this amount the natives bought; clothing, and most of them are now well fitted regarding same; food, some of them bought enough food for the spring; some of them still have cash on hand, due principally to shortages of supplies at the Hudson's Bay Company store. Native have bought practically everything there and the store has now a rather lost look about it. (Ranger's Report for the month of March 1942, Hebron, FOB Papers)

This extraordinarily good season for furs was widespread in northern and central Labrador, but it still had very mixed consequences for the Inuit, and similarly for the Innu.

The Ranger's Report from Nutak that month (FOB Papers) is similar, with the Inuit earning $2,100 for the months of January, February, and March,

> but the HBC post was mostly empty of supplies and the natives there and at Hebron were short of clothing and other necessities that were very badly needed including food. . . . [There were] severe living conditions for the past few years and [they] were short of clothing etc. Future prospects, from present outlook, are not very promising; it seems there will be no industry of any kind during the summer; the HBC Co. will not be buying trout, nor outfitting for the cod fishing industry which throws natives right back on the government.

The report continues from Hebron, April 8, 1942 (Ranger's Report, FOB Papers):

> For the past winter the trapping of foxes had been good, some of the natives getting as high as 40 foxes; total number in this district approximately 535 for which natives were paid approximately $7000; this seems to be a large amount for a population of 300 persons, including man woman and child; this amount was earned by 15% of the population, balance of persons being women children and those [who earned] nothing during this season; though this amount was earned one would be willing to wager that by the latter part of May they will all be soliciting relief due principally to the lack of necessities of life suffered by the natives for the past few years, when their earnings has been very small; also due to the exorbitant prices charged for dry goods, food and other sundries; also due to the native habit of squandering money on any little thing or any geegaw that meets their eye. They simply cannot save or look ahead; they must be applying the old axiom "live well today for tomorrow you may die."

Indeed they may. Are they being blamed for what we can see was at least in one perspective a very realistic assessment of their situation?

The correspondence to Father O'Brien made it clear that by the mid-1930s the fur trade with the Natives was generally a losing proposition, but HBC agents noted that one very good year would clear the books of the accumulated losses. That very good year was 1942, and HBC knew how unusual it was, because at the end of the fur trading season, and five years short of the end of the trading lease they had purchased from the Moravians, HBC closed all its northern trading posts, starting a few miles north of Hamilton Inlet, leaving open only a few that dealt primarily with Euro-Canadian trappers. The Innu and the Inuit were left without a place to sell what they produced or to purchase the supplies on which they had become irreplaceably dependent.

The Newfoundland government took over the HBC posts, placing the Innu and Inuit in the hands of the Department of Natural Resources—a chilling portent of how the Native peoples would be subsumed.

In 1942 the militarization of Labrador began. In the context of organizing its airborne supply lines for the European "theater" of World War II, the United States began to build a very large airbase in Goose Bay, Labrador, at the inner end of Hamilton Inlet, about twenty-five miles from North West River. While Inuit were hired for construction work on the base, which brought them a solid and useful income for several years, for some reason Innu, even though they lived much closer, were kept from employment there. The head of the Newfoundland Ranger Detachment at North West River wrote to Father O'Brien on November 30, 1943,

> TRAPPERS who have returned from HAMILTON RIVER have reported that there is a very poor sign of Fur to date. While they did not state how the Indians were doing I took it for granted that they too may return with small catches....
>
> I am very much opposed to having these Indians work at Base Construction and if they do it will be at their own volition.

While this sounds like the Innu could if they would, in fact the next year Father O'Brien wrote to John Puddester, commissioner for Public Health and Welfare, saying there has been "an unprecedented scarcity of fur and no further work for the Indians on the base" (O'Brien to Puddester, October 23, 1943, FOB Papers).

This is our introduction to modernity for the Innu in Labrador. Even though there is wage work readily available, the Innu are not going to be allowed access to it. They are going to be kept as Indians, in the Euro-Canadian political organization of the labor market, and so far as the governments can make this happen. *And in the most peculiar twist of fate, at the same time that the Newfoundland and Canadian governments will work to keep them as Indians they will also seek to erase them as Indians—and erase the Inuit as Inuit as well*—penciling Natives out of existence by claiming that the only people who live in Labrador are ordinary citizens of Canada, plus a few temporary foreign workers and visitors. The history that developed toward and after the Spanish Flu, the history of so-called traditional life, comes to an end with denying Native peoples their Native status, and all the consequences that developed along with that.

We should keep in mind, now that we have worked our way through this harsh history, that what it depicts is precisely one characteristic of the "traditional" society to which the Canadian and Newfoundland governments now want to "reconnect" Native peoples to help heal them of their woes. The next chapter introduces other, far more positive components that have lived alongside, but not replaced, all that we have just seen, but first we need to look at the process of penciling Native peoples out of their Native status.

Getting the Pencil

When Newfoundland confederated with Canada, on April Fool's Day, 1949 (at the last minute it was moved a day earlier), there had been long and intense negotiations over the so-called terms of union. One of the problematic features in these negotiations was what would happen to the Native peoples—Indians and Eskimos—of Labrador. (The existence of the Mi'kmaw people in southern Newfoundland was scarcely recognized.) Canada had constitutionally mandated and specific responsibilities for Indians and Eskimos, which included health, welfare, and education. Newfoundland did not want to admit that there were Native peoples in Labrador, most likely because they and their rights would be an obstacle to "development."

Newfoundland got away with a form of social murder: ethnocide. As genocide is the mass murder of people, ethnocide is the mass murder of *a* people in their existence as a somewhat separate and distinct people. Newfoundland "penciled out" of the terms of its union with Canada any recognition that there were Native people or peoples in Labrador, claiming that since they could vote they were just ordinary citizens. At the same time they got Canada to agree to pay for the bulk of the costs of Native health and welfare—which Newfoundland, not Canada, would administer. Native peoples paid, and still pay, an extraordinary price for this destructive manipulation.

NO ONE WHO LIVED in Europe during the feudal period in European history called their social world "feudal." That term was invented in France after the French Revolution—after what came to be called feudalism as the predominant social form was finished, and most of its remnants in Western Europe had been destroyed by revolution and economic transformations. But the name stuck as a general term for several different social formations, for it summed up in one word a whole history of social and cultural domination that shaped an entire society, from religious organization to everyday life.

Similarly, no one, at least on public record at the time, said, "Let's pencil the Native peoples of Labrador out of the Articles of Confederation"—the agreements negotiated between Newfoundland and Canada that set the terms of union. These were the terms by which Newfoundland would give up its dominion-colony status[18] and join Canada as its tenth province. But the Natives were "penciled out" of the terms of union, with severe, society-shaping consequences that gave the phrase, coined after the fact, its enduring and widely used meaning.[19] This act, as well as the forms of domination and control that it encouraged, along with what it permitted governments to ignore, has shaped much of the daily life, political organization, and social relations for the Native peoples of Labrador since. Among other intrusions it permitted, Newfoundland was able to simply take vast tracks of Native lands for hydroelectric development and to lease the airspace over Native territory to NATO to practice treetop supersonic flying, with thousands of flights occurring each month.

But just like in the feudal period of European history, when there was always a substantial portion of the population that was not organized under, or who managed to evade, feudal commitments, so with the Native peoples of Labrador: some managed, or all managed some of the time, to make their lives in ways that transcended power's control and its fantasies about who it could pencil out of what. Nonetheless, being penciled out of their Native status caused massive harm.

The reshaping of Native peoples' status when Newfoundland joined Canada was done in ways that flouted the Canadian constitution and the routine practices of Canada, which elsewhere in Canada reserved dealings with, and programs for, Native peoples to the federal government. This special arrangement in Labrador was made possible by the very active collusion of Canada with Newfoundland's attempts to deny Native peoples their indigenous rights. Newfoundland benefitted greatly from this; Québec and Canada even more so. Native peoples still continue to lose greatly, even though this policy has been reversed and some Native rights and land claims recognized.

Joey Smallwood, the prime minister of Newfoundland after confederation with Canada, and through the developing relations with Canada following confederation, had very large dreams for the economic development of Labrador, and Native rights would have gotten seriously in the way of his dreams and plans. Nothing better illustrates this than his flooding of a huge area in the interior of Labrador to make a hydroelectric project, which was done without even telling the Native people of Labrador that it was going to happen, so that some Native trappers left their interior cabins and trap lines in the early spring to come back late next fall and find to their surprise that they were under water. Altogether the arrangements between Newfoundland and Canada ensured that the Native peoples of Labrador were treated even worse than were Native peoples in the rest of Canada—and keep in mind that Canada is now paying substantial reparations to Native peoples for what it allowed to happen in the residential and religious schools into which Native children were forced. In Labrador the issue of reparations for being penciled out is unfortunately not yet on the table, and reparations for brutalization by residential schooling just at the very beginning of being considered.

There are further changes in the relationship of other First Nations peoples in Canada to the Canadian government that may become relevant in Labrador. The consequences of these changes have just begun to unfold as of mid-2012. At this point I can just point toward what is happening.

In 1982 Canada "repatriated" its constitution from Great Britain—freed itself from the last vestiges of colonial control—and subsequently affirmed Native peoples' existing treaty rights. After court cases that pursued these rights, this eventually had several generally positive implications for Native peoples with treaties. Labrador Native peoples, lacking treaties, were not included, although they were included in the land claims processes and through this achieved some substantial gains and some not yet fully realized major losses.

In 2006 Canada acted on the increasing pressure to acknowledge a wide range of abuses in the "residential Indian Schools" to which Indian and some Inuit children were confined for the bulk of their childhood and youth. These abuses included beatings, rape, punishment for speaking Native languages, and long-term separation from parents and community. Parents were prevented from doing anything about this, by force of law and police, and survivors of the residential schools talked, in the hearings of the Truth and Reconciliation Commission (www.trc.ca/), about hating their parents either because they did not intervene—when they could not—or because their parents, having grown up in a residential school, had little idea how to be a parent. The hearings in Halifax, Nova Scotia, are particularly poignant on this issue.

After the Truth and Reconciliation Commission was set up, by 2010 hearings were being held, and a variety of remedial actions were being undertaken, including cash payments to former residential school inmates. Labrador Native peoples, Inuit, Innu, and Métis, were excluded from all remedial activities as the Canadian government held that their schools were not established or run by the government but by religious organizations or by Newfoundland. In 2011 the Newfoundland Supreme Court held that the

Native peoples of Labrador were indeed entitled to have their history in residential schools addressed, with remedies.[20] There were about four thousand plaintiffs in this class action suit.

The point here is the continuing exclusions of Labrador Innu and Inuit—and also Métis—peoples from protection or redress for the wrongs that were and continue to be done. Little by little, and always late, a few of these wrongs are officially recognized. Labrador Native people are, so far unavoidably, dealing with unrecognized and untreated stress trauma: their history that we are discussing is the lived history of their everyday lives.

SINCE THE MID-TWENTIETH CENTURY, Newfoundland has had a complex and mostly destructive relationship with Labrador Native peoples, by itself and in collusion with Canada.[21] How this relationship developed from the early twentieth century turns out to be relevant to what is happening now.

Until the mid-twentieth century the primary interest in Labrador of the Newfoundland government, and the fish-merchant and supply firms this government largely represented, was as a site for a seasonal cod fishery and seal hunts. Even though Newfoundland was supplying relief rations to Innu and Inuit as a consequence of HBC and Moravian trade policies, they paid scarcely any attention to governing or regulating the inland fur trade or the coastal seal fishery. They did keep, or try to keep, Native peoples from fishing salmon on most rivers, to encourage the tourist sportfishing trade, and for similar reasons, plus some issues of herd protection, they constrained the hunting of caribou.

For all of this Newfoundland wanted and needed access to and control over the coast, and little more. In 1922, Newfoundland—then an independent dominion of Great Britain—asked the Privy Council of the British Parliament to determine where on the Ungava Peninsula (or, as it is sometimes called in twentieth-century documents, the Labrador Peninsula) was the boundary between Newfoundland's Labrador and Canada. At stake were the claims to Labrador by the adjacent Canadian province of Québec. As the Privy Council was taking the case, Newfoundland turned around and asked Québec if the province wanted to purchase all of Labrador from Newfoundland, minus a three-mile wide coastal strip, for $15 million. Newfoundland was broke and did not then much care about whether or not it "owned" Labrador. Québec turned down this bargain-basement offer, certain it would win the case for even less.

But in 1927, when the decision was given, the British Privy Council gave it all to the British dominion. Newfoundland got a Labrador where "the coast," which was its original claim, was defined as reaching back to the height of land—several hundred miles in southern Labrador—where the rivers flowed eastward into the Atlantic Ocean. Québec got only the former HBC territory, once called Rupert's Land, where the rivers flowed westward into Hudson's and James Bays, plus the St. Lawrence River valley.

By 1934 Newfoundland was all too visibly bankrupt, and Great Britain, afraid that it would default on all the bonds and bank stocks held by British and Canadian banks and elites, took over the government of the dominion, with the Newfoundland Parliament voting to give up its independent status and again become a directly governed colony. From 1934 to 1947 Newfoundland was ruled by a "Commission of Government," with Great Britain sending out three commissioners to run the island of Newfoundland and its Labrador. The commissioners showed a bit more concern for Labrador than had Newfoundland—at times by choice, at times by necessity. The Commission of Government created a national police and rural administrative unit, called the Newfoundland Rangers, and posted nine of them year-round in Labrador—the first time the Newfoundland government had a year-round presence there (Tompkins 1988). Previously magistrates visited communities briefly by ship in the summer, hearing cases and providing a slight touch of law and regulation to the coast. Otherwise, what happened happened.[22]

When Newfoundland took over the HBC trading posts in 1942, it ran them as part of a government bureaucracy: somewhat more responsive to Native needs when it distributed relief rations, but very slow to change, to address new needs, or to help create new kinds of production. Little of this changed in 1949, when Newfoundland joined Canada.

A period of transformation began in 1949, similar to that in 1918–1926, when the fundamental structures of Native life were broken and over the next decade or more rebuilt very differently. In this second transformation the surface changes were often less dramatically visible, but the deeper consequences were even more destructive in the long term. The lead-up to these transformations happened in Newfoundland and Canada, not in Labrador.

After World War II, Great Britain, with its own financial troubles, wanted to shed its responsibility for the particularly poor and unproductive colony of Newfoundland, and so in 1947 it organized a referendum on Newfoundland and Labrador's future, in which the populace was offered three choices: a return to independent dominion status, joining Canada, or staying a colony of Great Britain. This last option was not pressed forward, and one popular option, joining the United States—popular due to the wages and benefits that flowed from U.S. base construction in Newfoundland during the war— was not permitted on the ballot. In the second round of balloting confederation with Canada won, and what was called the "terms of union" had to be negotiated. In fact, the negotiations for some of these terms began even before the referendum.

In Canada Native peoples, both Indians and Eskimos (as they were called when they got the rights), had constitutionally guaranteed rights. Great Britain, in 1867, granted Canada status as a dominion, unifying what was called Upper and Lower Canada.[23] Britain then purchased Rupert's Land, the territory granted to HBC, for inclusion in Canada. This territory was, in most of its regions, primarily peopled by Natives, and the British North America Act, which created the dominion of Canada, constitutionally guaranteed at least some rights for Indian peoples as a responsibility of the Canadian federal government. Eskimos were left in the hands, and to the presumed tender mercies, of the provinces, for they did not yet have the same constitutional protections as did Indian peoples. That changed in 1939, when Québec went to the Canadian Supreme Court with the question "Are Eskimos Indians within the meaning of the British North American Act?" (Canada Supreme Court Reports 1939, S.C.R. 104). At this point not only were the Eskimos in the hands of the provinces, with the largest number in Québec, but the provinces had to pay the costs. The court answered yes, and from that point on Eskimos were supposedly somewhat protected by Canadian constitutional rights. Providing these on-paper rights and benefits was the financial responsibility of the federal government. Tester and Kulchyski (1994) show how murderously, and for how long, Canada interpreted this constitutional responsibility.

As Labrador was not part of Canada in 1939, but a region of Newfoundland, neither the Indians nor the Eskimos there had any protection, and the terms of union when Newfoundland joined Canada crossed Native rights out of the agreement, to maintain the situation where the Native peoples of Labrador and Newfoundland had no special rights whatsoever. This was a fiction that turned out to be hard to maintain in the long run, because at the same time that Newfoundland and Canada penciled Native rights—and more, their political existence as Native peoples—out of the terms of union, Newfoundland wanted and needed Canada to pay a substantial portion, if not all, of the costs of Native welfare and education, and as these costs rose, so did Newfoundland's claims upon Canada. Native peoples in Labrador were in the deeply contradictory position of both being and not being Native peoples. Newfoundland claimed they were ordinary citizens, because they could theoretically vote, and to make them Natives, or to give them Native rights, would be a setback to the process of assimilation—an argument that Canada bought—while Newfoundland at the same time claimed that Canada needed to pay the bill for Native education, health, and welfare, as well as other administrative costs.

As with other fundamental contradictions, this one gave both Newfoundland and Canada a relatively free hand (or hands, actually) to squeeze Native peoples as it suited them—or at least to try, and to succeed in areas such as relocation and what was called education in ways that were truly devastating. It was not a completely free ride for these governments; Native peoples both fought back and managed, rather intensely if at times not productively, to evade the clutches of state and state-favored corporations.

Edward Tompkins, whose research clarified this process of denying Native rights and its immediate consequences, introduced the situation in the negotiations for the terms of union by contrasting Newfoundland's claims with the underlying issues. We begin with Newfoundland: "The question of responsibility for the provision of public services to the Eskimo and Indian populations has been discussed by representatives of our two governments since we entered Union, and settlement should be effected without further delay. For many reasons we feel that we are in a preferential position to administer the services, but, on the other hand, we feel that the responsibility for payment of these services should be carried by the Federal Government." Tompkins comments,

> This 1952 comment from a Provincial to a Federal minister . . . manages to perform two complex functions. First, it ignores the fact that Federal responsibility for providing services to the native population of Newfoundland and Labrador, upon Newfoundland's joining the Canadian Confederation, had been recognized and extensively discussed since 1946. Second, it highlights the problems caused by the non-inclusion of the province's native population under the terms of the Indian Act, which gave the Federal Government exclusive jurisdiction of Canada's Indians and Eskimos. (Tompkins 1988, 1, citing National Archives of Canada RG 85, vol. 2079, file 1006-5 [2], December 20, 1952)

It is breathtaking what Newfoundland got away with, as this was put into practice. They could do as they wished with the Native peoples, give what they wanted and take whatever they would, and pass the bill to Canada. This was the "legal" framework for the forced relocation of Native peoples, for stuffing them into unsanitary and unfit houses, when they got houses at all, and for an education system that was appallingly oppressive. Parents were forced to stay in the relocation village to keep their children in school, when schools were built in the relocatees' villages, missing the opportunity to go trapping or hunting for food. The schooling was almost entirely useless, for the curriculum was the same as in the capital city, St. John's. The major effect of this "education" system was to make sure that the parents were reduced to living on welfare, rather than leaving the village for the winter hunting and trapping season, or the fall and spring sealing season, for it did not seem to matter if the children actually went to school, or stayed in school for the day, so long as they were in the village and available to go to school. As late as 2005, in one Innu village, out of a high school class of thirty or more, about six children stayed in the school all day. But if the parents took them and went out in the woods to teach them hunting and trapping skills, the police and "the authorities" intervened.

The betrayal of Native rights that Newfoundland managed to establish was wide ranging and is clarified by reviewing what Canada was supposed to be responsible for—even though Canada ordinarily scanted these responsibilities with Native peoples elsewhere. Even scantily administered and enforced rights were much better than nothing. The responsibilities were, as Tompkins noted, very much needed in Labrador:

> In June 1947 an extensive document was sent [by Canada] to the members of the Newfoundland Delegation, which, among other things outlined the nature of Federal involvement with native peoples. Under classes of subject in which the Federal Parliament exercised exclusive jurisdiction, "Indians and lands reserved for Indians" was listed. . . . This included control of their education, the administration of their lands [the fact that there were native lands in Labrador would not be recognized for another five decades], the community funds and estates and the general supervision of their welfare . . . including hospitals for Indian health services. . . . In Annex W of this document the size of the native population and general health conditions . . . [in Labrador were noted] especially the prevalence of tuberculosis. (Tompkins 1988, 12–13)

The draft agreement for the terms of union included the phrase "assistance for Indians and Eskimos, as provided under the Indian Act as amended from time to time." "*This clause was then pencilled out and this was the last reference to Indians and Eskimos in the Terms of Union"* (Tompkins 1988, 17; emphasis added).

At the same time that this was happening, Father O'Brien was also penciled out of his exceptionally helpful connection to the Labrador Innu:

Vicariat Apostolique du Labrador, Blanc Sablon, Quebec
Quebec, May 7, 1947, to Father O'Brien

Dear Father,

For a long time, I had the desire to come in contact with you . . . but I could not realize that great desire of mine.

As you know, I have been put in charge of the missions on Labrador Coast; the Supreme Authority of the Soverain Pontif has put on my shoulders the burdens of all the souls in that district. I had nothing to do with that nomination but I have to do all what I can to fulfill the mandate I received.

I know you have been at North West River for a good many years [forgetting or omitting or not knowing about Davis Inlet] and that you have been doing a great work among the Indians and Eskimos coming there every summer. I know that you loved them as your children and that it was a great sacrifice to leave them into other hands. I want to thank you for all the good you have done there. Should I tell you that, if you want to go see them during the summer, I will be just pleased to give you jurisdiction to hear confessions and preach as you want. . . .

I am planning a short trip to Newfoundland and, if I can, I will be glad to go to see you in your parish [on the Island of Newfoundland].

[signed] Lionel Scheffer o. mis. [Oblate Mission]
Vicar Apostolic of Labrador

However hard this penciling out must have been on Father O'Brien, it was in many ways very much harder on the Innu, for the priest that was sent in his place did not come close to filling his shoes, much as he spent his time stomping around Indian communities in his rubber boots, dragging children to school by their ears.

THE NEXT CHAPTER was originally the concluding section of the present one. But it is important to emphasize the extent to which Native people were capable of maintaining and expressing their dignity both for themselves and, even more importantly, with and for each other, against all we have just seen.

To do this, I have made the topic of Native peoples producing their collective dignity an entire chapter. This focus on the social construction of dignity is a particularly important point to make for the Innu, who have seemed, and in some ways were, even more battered by domination than were the Inuit. And I think it also makes a very important point to end this chapter, as some other chapters are ended, in midair. This is to emphasize that the wounds we have depicted are still very much open. The dusk remains within the dawn; the veil within which Native voices speak is still re-created by governments, corporations, and within Native communities by themselves. Du Bois, with whom we started this chapter, turns out not at all to have been a rhetorical flourish, but the seedbed from which the flowers of hurt, as Baudelaire called them, and the flowers of hope both bloom.[24]

FIVE **Mapping Dignity**

In the midst of all the pressure on Native peoples while they were dealing with HBC and the Moravian missions, in the midst of all the chaos and loss, Native people still managed to live lives of dignity, still managed to construct and continually reconstruct social relations of mutual respect and shared concern. None of this was only based on "ideas," or "values," or what anthropologists would call "culture." Rather, it was also deeply rooted in both the silent and the material social relations of daily life.

These social relations are not "silent" because they are not talked about, or because people do not talk to each other very much if at all when they are in these relations. That kind of silence sometimes occurs, as we shall see, and it does so in ways that can be quite significant. But the social relations where people created mutual dignity and mutual respect are here called silent because it is not possible, or useful, to single any of them out as a separate named entity, a special, specific kind of event or relationship. They are how life was, and in part still is, lived. They are unspoken because they were, and in important ways still are, everywhere.

Some examples will make this all less complicated, by showing how respect and dignity become integral parts of a Native community constructing itself and its collective endurance. This will also set the stage for showing, in chapter 6, how the state and corporations could so profoundly break into Native communities, robbing them of much of their frameworks for mutual respect and the relationships that made dignity with and for each other.

GEORG HENRIKSEN LIVED with the Naskapi between 1966 and 1968, including traveling with the hunters for their winter trips out on the northern caribou barrens and staying with them in Davis Inlet, their summer coastal trading post settlement (Henriksen 1973). At this point in their history, the Naskapi were engaging in both "subsistence" caribou hunting in the winter and commercial cod fishing from Davis Inlet in the summer, although they were under increasing pressure to settle almost year-round in Davis Inlet.

The trip of 150 miles or so inland from Davis Inlet to the caribou barrens was risky. The temperature could drop to −40 degrees Celsius, which is also −40 degrees Fahrenheit. The travelers needed to find a sheltered valley with trees to put up their tents and to get fuel, and driving snow in a storm could make that quite difficult. When the snow was hard packed and with a team of several strong dogs, one could make the trip of 150 miles in about a week or sometimes much less, but with soft snow or bad weather or people needing to pull and push their sleds owing to deep snow or lack of an adequate dog team, the trip could easily take two weeks, and there was a serious risk of running out of food for the hunters, their families if they came along with the hunters, and the dogs. Once the hunters got to the caribou barrens, the caribou might not be there. It was altogether an uncertain situation, but when it worked well, there were a lot of caribou—for the herds often numbered in multiple thousands—and life was fulfilling and good.

Deciding where to go to hunt and with whom was a very complex business. Henriksen has an excellent and detailed description for a situation where hunters go together into the interior to try to kill and cache a supply of caribou and then go back to the coast to bring their wives and families with them for the winter, with the cache of food providing some security. At the point where the following quote from Henriksen begins, the married— i.e., in this context, full adult—hunters are trying to organize their own trek inland:

As head of a household, a hunter throws himself into the feverish political activities that take place in Davis Inlet a week or two before the great trek inland
in the fall, trying to determine who will go with who, where, and when. Endless
visiting may take place; a man may enter the same tent more than 10 times in
the course of a few hours in the evening. . . . Most men are reluctant to commit
themselves [although a few do]. Moses advised me [Henriksen] how I should
behave. . . . "I say nothing. Nothing to anybody. One day I go off, and then I go
off with anybody."

Moses is not the only hunter who "says nothing." Once when I [Henriksen]
returned to his tent after a round of visiting, Bill came over. We sat a long time
without a word being uttered. After he left, Moses . . . asked if Bill had said anything when I was in his tent.

The best hunters all seek to draw a following so as to secure a prestige-giving
audience. The effect of this strategy is that the thirty-three households split into
smaller groups when hunting in the interior. . . . The difficulty that Moses and
Bill had in communicating with each other reflected the difficulty they had . . .
where one had to be the leader and the other the follower. Moses was the old
and experienced hunter, while Bill was young and ambitious and certainly the
next most capable hunter in the camp. Both want the other to go on the trip so
as to maximize the possibility of a successful hunt, yet both aspired towards the
leadership of the hunt. (1973, 55–56, 59–60)

It is not helpful to focus on why they wanted to have one leader in this system, or why they did not talk over a strategy for that year's hunt and come to
a consensus. A range of answers to this question which move us further along
can be suggested. Perhaps it happens because the competition for leadership
pushes many to work as hard and think as intensely as they can, with many
small groups that often go out, each on their own search, each bringing back
their harvest to share; or perhaps with caribou herd movements being often
so unpredictable, and the consequences of missing the herds so momentous,
consensus would not be possible. In some ways, particularly when overall
herd numbers are down as they cyclically are, it would be like trying to reach
a consensus about what number on a roulette wheel to bet on. Someone
guesses as best as can be done, with experience, with listening and watching
everything, and with omens, which are only divine pointers. As Heraklites
noted, the Oracle at Delphi neither conceals nor reveals but indicates. Those
who guess take responsibility for the decision, making the decision as in-

tensely thought as possible for an individual, but an individual with a sense of a group's knowledge built from multiple visits, multiple indirectly suggested possibilities, and perhaps helpful subtle pointers.

The focus here is not the contest for individual leadership but the silence. This silence runs very much deeper than two men sitting together and not saying anything. It is framed, in the material context of provisioning their lives, by the need to sit together, one by one, one after one, in one tent after another, and the importance of social relations shaped and reshaped by not saying anything, or nothing much. This silence is how people stay together as a whole and simultaneously separate from each other with a minimum of hurt feelings. The seeming and claimed spontaneity ("One day I go off, and then I go off with anybody") of who follows whom out to the hunt can be the public justification for private choice: how the heightened prestige of some is merged with the dignity of all. This will change in crucial ways after the Inuit and the Innu are forced into concentration villages.

An Inuit illustration takes us a bit further, and in a slightly different direction. In 1993 Carol Brice-Bennett began to do representative life histories of three generations of Inuit men. For a spokesperson for the elder generation she chose Paulus Maggo, born in 1910, who lived in Nain, and whom Carol had known for twenty years, since she started living and researching in Nain. Her original research for life histories was a project for the Royal Commission on Aboriginal Peoples. Carol then took the recorded and translated interviews with Paulus Maggo and put the transcript of the interviews into chronological order—with Maggo's approval of this presentation of his text. It produced an extraordinary book: *Remembering the Years of My Life: Journeys of a Labrador Inuit Hunter*, recounted by Paulus Maggo and edited, with an introduction, by Carol Brice-Bennett (1999). Maggo is here discussing how he grew up:

> My father taught me the most when I first started going along with him to hunt or to set up camp. I watched what and how he did everything. I went hunting with other people, mostly with Martin Martin, and learned from them as well before I really went on my own after my dad died. When you're with experienced hunters you can learn a lot from them just by watching. There is no need for words because their actions can teach you a great deal. For instance, you can learn to predict that something can be expected by looking at what they are doing at any given time. Their mood may reveal a trace of concern or their pace may quicken. They may start picking up snow knives, axes, harpoons, and the

like and stick them all up in the snow which can indicate their expectation of a snowfall. They may pile heavier items on top of things, which could suggest their anticipation of stormy or windy conditions, and so on. A lot of belongings have been lost by being buried under snow or blown away in the wind. . . . Traveling in the country was not difficult in fine weather but it could be a problem during a storm, if you were unfamiliar with the surroundings of or unsure of your direction. . . . We were always aware of where we were going and where we had come from. (Brice-Bennett 1999, 77)

The elders must have known they were being watched, must have known that this was active teaching, because a very large number of Paulus Maggo's descriptions of hunting or traveling are about paying close attention to the landscape on the way out, to enable finding the way back; about observing the weather as it changes, and what that portends; about observing the traces of animals and their behavior while they are being tracked and after they are actually spotted; and about observing the other members of the traveling or hunting group: the first sense of an impending storm, Paulus Maggo noted, may come from another person's limp. A hunting trip, particularly in the rigors of a sub-Arctic climate, with so much at stake in whether or not food is found, is necessarily and intensely a trip of paying attention and listening, not just to the land but to each other.

Watchfulness—a clear realization of what is happening—is crucial. So the issue before us now is the double silence of the relationship of young Paulus Maggo to his elders. First there is a silence in the lack of questions and explicit answers, which teaches the need to take it all in. Snow knives and other tools stood upright in the snow at the end of the day when travelers stop "means" it is likely to storm. What indicates the likelihood of storms? Look *all* around, listen to the winds, keep track of the shifting snow drifts and how they change the look of the land, note how the weather changes are felt in your body and the bodies of your companions, pay attention to the changing behavior of the dogs. Not saying something like "See that cloud over there? . . . " but teaching in silence orients the attention to totalities, not arbitrary particulars. It also makes a framework for the dignity of the young and inexperienced boy, who does not have to ask the questions that announce ignorance, and simultaneously for the elders who, as all knew, were so respectfully closely watched, and who could not possibly always be right, for some storms come with very little warning, and some animals traverse the landscape in very unusual ways.

The second silence is about the teaching relationship itself—when it is and is not happening, and where, and why. Teaching is not often a separate activity. It usually remains an unspoken and thus fluid relationship. It is how life is lived, not in this or that exemplary moment where I teach you, or where you teach me, but in our living together, in our living that both brings and makes us together, as whole persons with our future based on my aging out and your aging in. Those transitions are crucial to what is happening.

Paulus Maggo describes a bittersweet situation when he was a bit older than in the previous example. After the death of his father, he had been hunting with and following an older man. One stormy day, distant from their usual places, he asked the older man which direction they should go, and the older man said he didn't know, that he would follow Paulus (Brice-Bennett 1999, 83). The totalizing relationship of learning and teaching turns out to be the future for both the teacher and the taught.

When both were in a difficult situation, the older man, who said that he would follow Paulus, which he did then and afterward, was putting his and their future in the hands of Paulus, in what he had once taught, and what Paulus, in his own learning and with that help, had become (Brice-Bennett 1999, 77–87). This is more than teaching. It is rooted in undifferentiated, nonspecific, completely generalized claims on one another. It is necessarily, at that time in Inuit and Innu history, the production of we.[1]

WHILE THESE EXAMPLES from both the Naskapi and the Inuit are drawn most specifically from men's social relations, it is clear from unfortunately more fragmentary evidence that women have similar social relations. Paulus Maggo mentions that a young boy's early kills, including birds that youths kill with stones, need to be gifted to the woman who helped his mother give birth to him, and there are many examples of women doing technically very difficult things, from delivering babies, keeping them as healthy as possible, to making sealskin boots and parkas that are completely waterproof, to making a new casing out of skins for the brass base of a shotgun shell, so their husbands can reload their cartridges, and fixing this skin casing to the brass base with animal tallow. One can sense in women's tasks and skills an equally complex and crucial skill set, as well as a pervasive set of relations between both women and women that sustained these skills and between men and women that put these skills to use.[2]

THIS WHOLE DISCUSSION of silence turns out to be about more than silences. It is about how people construct both their own and each other's futures in an uncertain and changing world; it is, as the examples show, about bringing tomorrow within today, about seeking as best as possible to secure an uncertain tomorrow in a lived today.

There is one further example that helps to explain the issues before us. It does so by showing how an intense focusing of an encyclopedic knowledge can emerge from kinds of relationships that we can only dimly, only incompletely, sense or perceive.

Eleanor Burke Leacock did field research among the Montagnais-Naskapi in Labrador in 1950 (published primarily as Leacock 1954). There she worked with an Innu elder-hunter, Mathieu Medikabo, who was sixty years old at the time. In the course of their discussions, and to help Eleanor, who at that time had no map of the interior of Labrador, he drew one for her. In 1969, in her article in David Damas's very useful edited book on the anthropology of band societies (Damas 1969), Leacock published this hand-drawn map by Mathieu Medikabo, followed by a modern (aerial survey) version of the same features in the same region (see maps 2 and 3).

The closeness of the two maps—the accuracy of the map drawn from experiential knowledge—is conceptually overwhelming. Keep in mind that what Medikabo accurately drew is the basic river and lake system of almost the whole southeastern Ungava Peninsula, plus the north shore of the whole St. Lawrence River valley for several hundred miles—altogether an area of several thousand square miles, all roadless except for stretches of the St. Lawrence River coast.[3] The map was drawn with no other aids than what he knew, what he knew that mattered.

It is helpful to think about how this could be done. To begin, it is inconceivable that he traveled every river he drew, paddled or snowshoed across or around every lake he placed so well. What can be seen in the map is a lifetime of talking with others, listening intensely, listening to how others help reshape and build on the knowledge each offers to the others. We are seeing in this map—in the ability to know and then to produce such a document—a life deeply intertwined with other lives, so deeply intertwined in mutual listening and collective thinking that we can witness here, as more subtly elsewhere, the individual manifestation of a collective mind. In passing, we can also see this as a critique of our ways—a critique, for example, of the utter simplicity and egocentric narrowness of Descartes's formulation "I think, therefore I am." No, buddy (as people say in the far north), the better

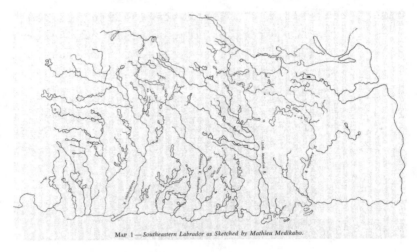

MAP 1 — *Southeastern Labrador as Sketched by Mathieu Medikabo.*

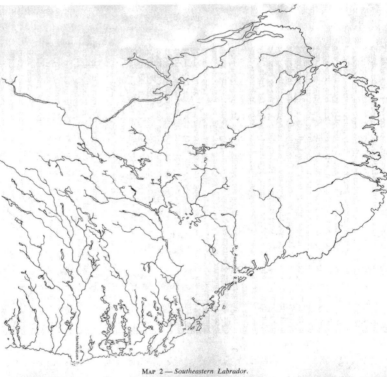

MAP 2 — *Southeastern Labrador.*

MAPS 2 AND 3. The interior of Labrador, drawn for the researcher Eleanor Burke Leacock by the Innu elder-hunter Mathieu Medikabo in 1950, and a modern (aerial survey) of the same features in the same region (published in Damas 1969).

formulation among the Native peoples we have so arrogantly been trying to use and then to erase is, "We think, therefore we are."

WE HAVE BEEN DISCUSSING not just silence but what is technically called "social reproduction": the problem of making and reaching tomorrow as it emerges within, and sometimes necessarily against, today. And what I find so deeply moving, so worthy of respect for the Innu and the Inuit, is how they managed to build this life that reaches toward tomorrow while the social context for their current lives became increasingly oppressive. While Native peoples were sustaining their relations to one another that helped reach tomorrow, their current situation moved increasingly out of their hands. The destructive and enclosing forces of state and corporations brought chaos, ruptures, and fractures, and most of all blame to Native peoples for the consequences of this imposed destruction.

All the listening and looking in Native communities, the worlds they built of caring and concern—and antagonisms—in their socially constructed silences, had deep social roots, but the roots were fragile. The specific forms of silences that once shaped these communities have partly given way to new kinds of silences with new kinds of meanings. The assaults that made that happen and how this new situation developed, with what consequences and against what resistance, are now the subjects before us.

This is far from an easy question, for as we have seen, the Inuit and the Innu are people who have suffered a long history of assaults. What is different about the recent decades, making the assaults deadly in very new ways, turns out to be something we can only suggest. From this point on the bulk of the work of getting our hands on this new and developing situation passes from the author to the reader, from the already-almost-yesterday's activist to a new generation. Such transitions happen quickly. The following two chapters, about the situation since the late 1960s, and then especially the conclusion only seek to draw a helpful map, suggesting routes across the terrain of recent decades.

ONE. Mental Health Awareness Week. Nunatsiavut Inuit community building in the central Labrador administrative town, Happy Valley–Goose Bay. May 2010. Photo by the author.

TWO. Youth at the edge of Nain playing jumping between ice floes. Across the bay, looking northeast, the caribou barrens begin. May 2010. Photo by the author.

THREE. A main street in Nain. No roads connect this community to anywhere outside, but this is a very good and very expensive pickup truck. May 2010. Photo by the author.

FOUR. Nain Husky Centre—a community recreation building, primarily for ice hockey, which the girls and women mostly can watch. The surprise here is that "Husky" was a quite derogatory White term for the people they then called Eskimo. May 2010. Photo by the author.

FIVE. Nanuk Road. A street in Nain, in part evoking—particularly for outsiders—the utterly fictional, romanticized movie by Robert Flaherty. Nanuk is also an Inuktitut word for polar bear. The assertion of local culture within, against, and apart from the dominant society keeps a core that remains irreducibly ambiguous and ambivalent, as this photo and the Nain Husky Centre illustrate. May 2010. Photo by the author.

SIX. The plank path to the newly built section of Nain. May 2010. Photo by the author.

SEVEN. The northern edge of the Nain airport, their primary connection to the outside world for much of the year, save a few months in the summer, when the supply boat from Newfoundland or Happy Valley can dock. May 2010. Photo by the author.

EIGHT. The Sheshatshiu Innu government offices, with the new grate over the front door, since the building was broken into and ransacked by community residents. There has been a substantial amount of anger in the community over the gulf between felt needs and perceived concerns of the Innu political elite. May 2010. Photo by the author.

NINE. The new school built in Sheshatshiu by the Canadian and Newfoundland governments. It is a beautiful and very expensive building, with vastly more funds than thought about a relevant curriculum poured into this building and then, for the most part, quickly out of the community. Ordinary Innu for the most part derive only a little, and only temporary, useful benefits from this and other grand projects. May 2010. Photo by the author.

TEN. The youth treatment center at the edge of Sheshatshiu. For an adolescent or child in trouble this is not likely to be an inviting or a welcoming sign. Most of the clients in this building are referred by those who have the power to do so. May 2010. Photo by the author.

ELEVEN. New houses in Sheshatshiu. These are very much better and more livable houses than the ones they replaced. As usual in building Native housing, no effort was made by the planners or builders to landscape the neighborhood. The plan was to build houses, and that is what they did. May 2010. Photo by the author.

TWELVE. The cemetery at the Catholic church in Sheshatshiu. The pain is stunningly visible. May 2010. Photo by the author.

THIRTEEN. A memorial built on the road between Sheshatshiu and Happy Valley–Goose Bay. Happy Valley is where people go to "escape," to shop, to find some entertainment. The memorial to death on the road suggests—urges—the poignancy of the connections between Sheshatshiu and the supposedly "outside" world. May 2010. Photo by the author.

SIX Life in a Concentration Village

When parents deny a child food, clothing, and shelter it's considered abuse.
Yet when governments do it, it's called fiscal responsibility.
—Newfoundland and Labrador Strategic
Social Plan (1996), vol. 1, *What the People Said*

From Expendable to Disposable

Starting in the 1950s, and intensifying greatly in the 1960s, there was a provincial government program to centralize coastal populations all across the island of Newfoundland. The Newfoundland fishery, the mainstay of that economy, was shifting from a small-boat, near-shore enterprise organized by kin and neighbors from small villages strung all around the long Newfoundland coastline to a larger-boat, middle-distance fishery and then to an openocean, deep-sea trawler fishery prosecuted from major island ports. The coastal villages of the inshore fishery began to cost far more to service than they produced in revenue for the state or for capital. Newfoundland, in its imposed centralization program, forced the population out of these villages and into a jobless life in what the government called "regional growth centers." Not publicly, but explicitly in private, the government knew it was throwing away the social lives and working careers of the middle-aged population. The planners did seem to firmly believe that the better educational possibilities, along with good road access that the small villages did not usually have, would give the younger generation access to better-paying production-line jobs in fish plants and various other primary processing facilities. Centralization would be the modernization of "traditional" Newfoundland, as the political elite, in its historically narrow view, defined modernity.[1]

What is called "traditional," in Newfoundland and Labrador, was of course always fully modern, fully current with its times. "Tradition," to be more precise, was always produced by imposed demands for an ultra-low-cost supply of goods and labor, so that what became called traditional would be more accurately named "impoverished." Moreover, the production of traditional communities and societies, partly through imposed poverty and partly through peoples' creativity and resourcefulness, made communities and societies with supposedly "backward" or old-fashioned ways and social relations that could be pointed toward to justify further exploitation and control by "the civilized" and "the modern."[2]

When they were no longer wanted, no longer usable, their social and cultural differences from the dominant society took on a new dynamic, often becoming the justification for these communities to be hung out to wilt and dry. The same process of divergent development—here tradition, there modernity—that led to their political and economic marginalization and social death enabled their resurrection as romanticized objects of "culture."

Primitive people of course don't own the mines on their lands; corporations do, and the Natives should be grateful for the royalties and the few jobs they get, unfortunately along with the pollution that comes with progress. In the Arctic construction camp where I worked in the 1960s, building an airfield on Inuit lands taken without either permission or compensation, "Eskimos" were hired to clean the toilets, while at the same time "Inuit Art" was becoming a very high priced commodity in galleries in the United States, Canada, and Europe.

A little-known but intense example, drawn from African history, makes this point about the production of "primitives" in a forceful way and helps to illuminate it as a quite general process, with Labrador one of many instances.

In 1590, a half century before the Atlantic slave trade in West Africa intensified explosively, Timbuktu was a major world city, about as large and as dynamic as Amsterdam—which was then the major city in western Europe. Timbuktu was located on the interior end of the great bend in the Niger River, the major transport river of West Africa. Above Timbuktu were rapids that were impassible for freight boats. Timbuktu was the point of transshipment between the very large camel caravans bringing trade goods back and forth across the Sahara—with up to three thousand camels in a caravan—

and the river transport into the downriver forest kingdoms. The currency of exchange was imported silver. The first major "western" university was not in Cambridge but in Timbuktu.

When the first European "explorers" got to Timbuktu in the mid-nineteenth century, after the slave trade's rack and ruin of West Africa, and especially the regional wars in good part provoked by the slave trade, they did not find the fabled city but a small town of mostly mud houses. The currency of exchange by then was primarily cowrie shells, introduced by the Europeans as part of their control over the slave trade (Sider 1996), and it was this new "primitiveness" of these African communities that made them available to, and useful for, colonialism and anthropology, along with becoming part of the retrospective justification for slavery and for missionaries' cultural assault.

That is the crucial lesson of "modernity." The centuries-long history of modernity manufactures, in pursuing its own ends, "primitives." It always has and still does, despite its claims to the precise contrary. Modernity, development, progress, colonialism, imperialism, neoliberalism—whatever name you call it, it is rooted in constructing more "primitive," "less developed," "historically backward," and, just underneath all these labels, usually more dependent and impoverished social forms. What domination in its various names has created is then used as a justification for displacement, destruction, and appropriation—in sum, taking. And this taking substantially finances domination becoming modern (or, in the current elitist self-amusement, postmodern) and developed.

The social construction of Eskimos and Indians from Inuit and Innu is a deeply analogous instance of this general process. The issue here, in this simultaneous social construction of fully contemporary yesterday and today, is much more than just the production of Indians and Eskimos within a colonial political and cultural economy. An almost equally destructive development is the internal divisions within Native communities that emerge with this process of unequal development.

These internal divisions in Native communities include the imposed distinction between "Naskapi" and "Montagnais," which named little more than different styles of domination and survival, and the more recently imposed distinction between Québec and Labrador Innu, with destructive laws about which Innu can hunt what and where, and also the destructive distinction in Inuit communities, reinforced by housing built in neighborhood ghettos, between relocatees and longer-term residents—in all cases with life-shaping, life-diminishing consequences. The centralization of supposedly "primitive" peoples who no longer could continue in a "modern" world created even further divisive and destructive situations within Innu and Inuit communities.

While the Newfoundland government was centralizing and, in its terms, modernizing the Euro-Canadian fishing populations of Newfoundland, it started to centralize and "modernize" the Indian and Inuit populations of Labrador. Newfoundland started to encourage its own village population to voluntarily centralize in the mid-1950s, but it did not start increasingly squeezing Newfoundland villagers, by withdrawing crucial services such as mail delivery, until the mid-1960s. In Labrador the force came earlier. The Inuit community of Nutak was closed in 1952; the Hebron Inuit were forced out of their community in 1959; the Innu, whose pressure to centralize started before, were given few if any other options than centralization by the 1960s, into what the youth explicitly called "concentration villages." The similarity of time period of the Newfoundland and Labrador centralization programs masks a fundamental difference—a very substantial and subtle difference between an expendable generation in Newfoundland and disposable Native populations in Labrador. The distinction between expendable and disposable is only subtle if you are not one of the victims. An expendable population is a population that is being used to serve the purposes of a dominant sector of the society. It did not matter to the British how many million Irish died in the potato famine, so long as the British could keep exporting Irish potatoes to England—and this export scarcely diminished, even at the height of the famine. When HBC used Native peoples to procure furs, it did not matter to them how many starved and died in the process, as long as enough fur trappers remained to produce the furs.

Similarly, it did not matter to the Newfoundland government that they were destroying the working lives, dignity, and social relations of a generation of adult fisher-folk, so long as their children were available at low wages to staff a new industrial labor force as part of the planned transformation of Newfoundland.[3] Expendable populations remain useful populations in one capacity or another, and the issue for the dominant sectors of the society is not what price these folks pay for being useful, so long as some remain useful, or replacements can be made available. Indeed, from the perspective of those who use them, often the worse expendables are treated the more compliant to the demands of use the survivors may be. Those who have little choice learn to keep going, until they can make a different kind of choice.[4]

The benefits of making a people expendable is one of the major lessons of the production of "illegal aliens" in the United States and their participation in the most dangerous, oppressive, and low-paid sectors of the labor force. In Southeast Alaska, for example, one of the most dangerous, injury-prone jobs is climbing up very tall trees, with a chain saw dangling from a harness around your shoulder, to top the trees before they are cut for timber, so good wood does not split in the fall of the tree. Lumber companies recently shifted from using Native people to using "illegal Mexicans" for this task. Despite all the talk about how Native people were "naturally" good in the woods, undocumented workers turned out to be much less costly when injured or killed.[5]

Disposable people, different from expendable people, are people who are no longer wanted for any use, or whose usefulness depends on their disappearance, or on the kinds of compliance that can be gotten from those who have been taught that they probably will never have anything in the way of a viable future, that almost all of them are of no future use at all. The centralization of the Inuit and Innu peoples of Labrador was built around their increasing transition from an expendable to a disposable population, along with promises that they would once again be useful.

The brutality of becoming disposable is hidden, particularly for those responsible, behind a simultaneous glorification of the victims' "lost traditions" or "traditional culture." The anthropologist Julian Pitt Rivers (1963, personal communication) pointed out that no one in the French urbanized elite was wearing peasant blouses or singing peasant songs when the peasants were beating down the city gates; it was only after the peasantry had been destroyed as a viable political force that what passed for their culture became available for appropriation and celebration.

The world is now increasingly full of disposable peoples. Indeed, that is one of the most significant transitions over the past several decades—far more significant than the often vacuous talk about contemporary forms of "globalization." There are vast regions of Africa, Asia, and Latin America, as well as large sectors of the African American population in the United States, along with many other folks, where nobody with the power to shape social and economic situations seems to care what happens to such people. As far as those who hold the power to shape large portions of what happens are concerned, it does not matter whether these disposable people live, die, or kill each other, so long as they don't die of contagious causes that might spread, or causes that might provoke expanding rebellions and the "terrorism" of poor peoples' engagement with the "technology" (not, as the elite of imperial societies put it, the "terrorism") of our tanks, bombs, and drone airplanes.

Even worse than not mattering to the dominant, the well-being of the elite and the middling sections of the dominant societies would be enhanced if these disposable folks simply disappeared, or quietly killed each other—in noncontagious, nondisruptive ways, of course. And the disposable people now include not just Native peoples, undocumented "aliens," and darker-skin "minorities." The category is expanding to include large sections of the Greek, Italian, Spanish, Portuguese, and Irish working classes, along with the bottom half of the so-called middle classes and the increasing vast numbers of long-term unemployed and homeless U.S. citizens, who turn out to be not as "citizen" as a large bank or a major corporation.

But—and this is crucial—disposable people do not simply disappear, even though they may suffer and die in large numbers and increasing percentages. They struggle, necessarily and inescapably, not just to survive but to continue. Otherwise, their suffering and their death rate would increase exponentially. But oppressed peoples sometimes struggle in ways that seem, or are, individually and collectively self-destructive. The problem before us, from an engaged and partisan perspective, is the same problem as that faced by the people themselves: what are the possibilities and the limits of struggle for people who have become disposable? What, in the eyes of the disposable, are the pathways, if any, to tomorrow?

To understand this even a bit, we need to look more closely at what we are calling disposable. It is more complex than it may at first seem, and when we look at the actual situations of the Native peoples of Labrador in the last third of the twentieth century, and now as well, we will see that these complexities matter to how people struggle to live today and reach toward tomorrow.

To begin, we need to put aside what I call a light-switch view of social and personal worlds—where people, and specific kinds of persons, like lightbulbs at the end of an electric wire, are either on or off, either alive and working or dead. Being disposable, to the contrary, is rooted in a *continuing* situation. In the context of Labrador—and other places as well—I define being disposable as being put in a situation where what you can earn or produce through your labors, combined with what you are given by the state, community, your kin, and others, is less than what you need to make it to tomorrow. This is not at all a matter of insufficient income, but of the whole material and social apparatus of a viable life—clean water, livable housing, minimal violence. The whole point is that the specifics of what you don't have, what is not given, are irrelevant. The whole point is that what you have and can get is never quite enough.

EXPENDABLE PEOPLE ARE also severely scanted—we saw that with the "traditional" Indians and Eskimos. However, they had good years and bad years: the crisis episodes were terrible, and routinely recurrent, but they were still, at least in the nineteenth century, episodes. As Native people increasingly were transformed from expendable to disposable, from the late nineteenth century on into the twenty-first, the scanting became less episodic, more routine. A house without running water or adequate insulation does not have good years and bad years.

When the promises by the state to fix it, change it, make it better, are denied year after year, decade after decade, for two generations of Innu, more than forty years, people learn. They learn where they stand in the larger world and who will not care when they are laid down.

When people do not have what they need to reach, or reach toward, tomorrow, they don't just all die. Life expectancy declines, infant and maternal mortality rates rise, and of special significance for what then happens, they often take their lives in their own hands. Local forms of inequality intensify among the victimized population, as the people suffering the costs of this inadequacy seek or need to make sure that it is not shared equally. A starving family in the woods—a family sent out with inadequate supplies—needs to make sure the children die first, because if the parents go, they all do. *Sic transit gloria mundi.*[6]

Amartya Sen, in his stunning and Nobel Prize–winning studies of famine and famine mortality, puts this situation in stark clarity, but without at all exploring its internal dynamics. In a wide range of famines that he studied the death rate was approximately double the decline in available foods. An 8 percent decline in food stocks in situations that get called "famine" ordinarily leads to about a 16 percent increase in deaths (Sen 1981). This proportion remains the same both in the violently unequal societies we call colonial and in societies whose elites were pleased to describe themselves as socialist or communist: dearth of the kind that leads to death rarely gets shared equally, sometimes from bare necessity. This is just an introduction to the logic of what I call terminal inequalities—life-ending inequalities. But there is much more to the logic of inadequacy and the resulting inequalities than the fact that serious scarcity is only rarely shared.

One relevant point that helps us grasp this situation more completely, get both our minds and our hands on it, is the fact that systematic inadequacy, a continuing lack in what it takes to make it to tomorrow (or more, to make tomorrow), often transfers control over the people in this situation to outsiders—usually the same outsiders that massively contributed to making the people they now increasingly control disposable.[7] Tomorrow does not just arrive; it has to be made, and some of those who are trying to participate in making tomorrow do not have the vulnerable peoples' best interests in either their hearts or their plans.

This situation, as it has developed and is developing in Labrador for both the Innu and Inuit peoples, has some very special and revealing features. Once the fur and sealskin trades ended, Native people, as individuals, became disposable. No one had any use for most of them in any sector of the productive economy, not until quite recently. A few jobs here and there as guides or in other slots in the tourist industry, a bit of work at the bottom end of mining, timber, or construction, and some craft production, all more for Inuit than Innu, and all completely replaceable, and that was the sum of it. But after several Canadian court cases in the 1990s, which established that Native *peoples* had rights that could not be simply ignored or erased, the Innu and the Inuit, as peoples with both rights and resources, became both useful and necessary.[8] They were thus in a deeply contradictory position, as disposable people and useful peoples, and this contradiction has transformed their situation, most importantly by being the basis for an intensifying inequality between those in a position to manage and negotiate their collective utility as a people, as a political entity with rights to resources, and those many who have little if any say in how they are used as a people, and nothing to do that earns them wages or respect.

Unmanageable Inequality

The semisovereignty that Native political entities have been granted or allowed by the dominant state is always less than what they claimed, or actual justice would provide. But it usually allows Native peoples to permit the kinds of resource extraction—mining and timber cutting—that would be forbidden on lands controlled by the dominant state, for the ecological destructiveness or health consequences of such practices. Native political elites have something very valuable to give away, or to sell, often far below value, in addition to their resources: they have the right to consent to methods of production that would not be allowed on non-Native lands (Dombrowski [2001, 2010] is very informative on this). The consequences of this situation are both immensely complex and, in broad outline, easy to imagine. These consequences include substantial royalties—substantial only in terms of what Native people are accustomed to getting, not what the resources and permissions are actually worth, or paid for elsewhere. The allocation of these royalties and other payments and fees often intensifies the inequalities in Native communities that are already present. And the pollution and environmental destruction that usually accompany resource extraction contribute to the disposability of ordinary Native people.

Further reshaping their situation as disposable people is the fact that when people are treated with a flamboyant contempt, making their ill treatment too publicly obvious, it can lead to a very public and embarrassing press. Colin Sampson, and the group he worked with—Survival for Tribal Peoples—published a very fine pamphlet, *Canada's Tibet: The Killing of the Innu* (1999), which had a wide impact, especially when it was picked up by Canadian, and then some European, media.[9] The response of the Canadian government to this situation was to develop multiple "programs" for, or on, Native people. These programs have clearly benefitted the very high priced Euro-Canadian consultants and construction firms and those few local Native people who have been hired to work in, or consult to, these programs— often on the recommendation of the Native political elite. Although it was publicly advertised that the funds were for Indians and Inuit, it is not clear that these programs, which did fix up some of the material circumstances of Native lives, had any significant effect on the social problems, which was their announced intent. They may have kept the situation from getting even worse—that is impossible to tell—but they did not make it much if any better for the ordinary people in Native communities.

All this—the resource extraction and the "programs"—has created a situation where there has been a growing gulf between the Native leadership, necessarily allied with the state and capital while often struggling against this domination, and the ordinary people of Native communities who, despite all the "programs," "remedies," and "interventions" of state, capital, and their own governments, remain in the general situation of disposable people.

IT IS USEFUL TO note that the current "Native leadership positions" were not at all Native when they emerged in the mid-twentieth century. They were introduced by Father O'Brien and the Moravians. O'Brien wanted or needed a "chief"; the Moravians encouraged Eskimo church officers—deacons and such. Native leadership and political hierarchies were further developed by the Newfoundland and Canadian governments, mostly in the 1950s, to have an apparatus in Native societies to deal with the soon-to-be-imposed relocation and centralization programs.

The leadership that unfolded in the context of Newfoundland and Canada's encouraged development of Native political organization, to be the intermediaries to their communities, often incorporated personnel from earlier developments, with significant continuities. One important continuity was the practice of dealing with powerful outsiders. These "intermediaries" had a lot of practice dealing with power, which could be helpful to their communities as well as to the state. Native people were far from passive recipients of such manipulations. They used their changing political organization for their own ends, along with or against the ends to which they were harnessed. But the experience dealing with external pressures and inducements, along with the significantly increasing funds that get funneled through Native political organization, especially in recent decades, meant that Native leaders became key sources of patronage and access. They could thus form coteries, with client-supporters, that held on to power and their own self-interest, as community needs intensified and developed in different directions from the interests of the political elite. A politically based inequality has been created in Native communities. This became economic inequality as well, as government programs and wage employment opportunities came to be largely funneled through the political elites to their clients, kin, and followers (see Dombrowski [2001] for a well-developed comparative instance).

There is a further development in all this. The recent land claims process, to be discussed in chapter 7, which gave Native communities specific rights, has been organized by the state to severely limit the capacity of local Native political elites to act effectively on behalf of their own people. The fundamental point here must be kept firmly in mind: it is not that the Native political elites are venal, corrupt, or simply self-interested—some are, while many are not—but that the state and capital, which ordinarily have a well-developed ability to try to assure their own self-interest, have together structured a situation through the land claims, rights-granting process that quite effectively limits what Native political elites can accomplish, and for whom. The developing problem for Native peoples and leaders is how to best and most effectively act within and against the nearly inescapable and totalizing self-interest of the state and capital. In this difficult context it is hard to tell what does and does not make sense for the Native elite to do, or to try to do.

As an example of this problem of what to do and how to respond, in 2001 a Labrador Native social worker told me that a government program took several Native youths from a community across a river impassable to all but steel-reinforced government patrol boats, to try and dry them out from substance abuse with counseling and control. After a while the government asked an elder from the community to come and talk to the youths. His response was, "Pay me—$500 a day. That's what you pay the psychologists you bring in to talk to our children, that's what you pay me." When I first heard this story, I was dismayed that an elder would ask for money to talk to the youth of his own community. Now I realize I was wrong—that he had a better insight into these "programs" than I then had, for they far more effectively have served the consultants and corporations than ordinary Native people.

This chapter and the following one address two "moments" of this situation. The first, in this chapter, is the imposition, particularly by centralization, of modern forms of domination over increasingly disposable Native people, and the forms of resistance and struggle that Native people engaged from the early 1960s to the mid-1990s. The following chapter addresses the situation, from about the mid-1990s to the present, where the Innu and the Inuit became necessary to state and capital, as holders of rights to lands and resources, along with other entitlements. The Innu and the Inuit have responded very differently to this new situation, and the different gains and losses following from these differences in strategy can be quite instructive for future actions.

Honey-Bucket History

In the late 1960s most of the Innu were forced to live year-round in one of two coastal villages, with much smaller Innu populations in a few other locales. We start with the two main Innu villages. The northern village, the government-built community it named Davis Inlet, housed a bit less than half the Labrador Innu from 1967 to 2003 and became a media spectacle from the intensity of the disaster that the Canadian federal and Newfoundland provincial governments created for the people who were forced to live there. We begin with the given name of this new community, which as usual is domination's mask for its moral arrogance and cowardice.

Davis Inlet was the name for a sea channel between a medium-sized near-shore island and the northern Labrador mainland. Davis Inlet was also the name of an HBC trading post that was located on the island. The Innu began to settle on the mainland side of Davis Inlet in the 1920s. There was then a serious scarcity of caribou, and in this locale they could access the HBC trading post on the nearby island to trade fur for basic foodstuffs and some ammunition. This mainland community at Davis Inlet became a summer settlement, with fall and winter spent hunting and trapping inland (*Wikipedia*, "Davis

Inlet," June 30, 2012). In 1948 the Newfoundland government relocated this community over two hundred miles farther north, to the Inuit settlement of Nutak, to try to make the Innu into commercial fishers. They were taken up in the hold of a steamer, promised houses and jobs, dumped into tents, and essentially left to figure out how to survive in the context of being told what to do. The Innu stayed less than two years and left, doing what they could to reclaim their own lives.

In 1967 the government closed Davis Inlet and, with pressure from the missionary priest, forced or induced the residents to move to a newly built community on the island, to which the government gave the same name, Davis Inlet. The new village built on the island could be reached by ocean-going freight boats and naval patrol boats for at least a good part of the year. Government claimed that the mainland community, which was more expensive to supply and for their functionaries to access, lacked room to hold an expanding Native population. The island community had much easier access for the parade of Euro-Canadian officials, Royal Canadian Mounted Police, teachers, social workers, a judge, some program officers, and the supplies necessary for these folks and for the Innu, who by this time had to purchase much of their food and their clothes from the store.

The channel between the island and the mainland was completely impassable for the small boats of the Innu for several months in the fall, when the sea ice was forming, and in the spring, when it was breaking up. While they could cross in midwinter, on hard ice, and in midsummer on open water, Native people living on the island were prevented from getting to the mainland when the winter hunting and trapping seasons began and peaked. As most of the writing about the notorious new community built on the island has not engaged the point that people were seasonally confined there, I prefer to call the resettlement village Davis Island, not Davis Inlet, by way of a reminder.

Davis Island village was built on almost solid rock and had no available source of water adequate to build a piped water system to the houses. While such a system was constantly promised to the Innu, the expensive surveys that were done before the community was built should have made it clear that this was impossible, for in fact it was. The houses thus had no sinks with running water, no showers, and no toilets for the whole thirty-seven years of settlement. What served for a toilet was a device that was once widespread in midcentury Arctic construction camps, built to house workers on very short term projects: the "honey bucket"—a five-gallon metal or plastic pail, with a plastic bag inside. As there was also no sewerage or septic tank system

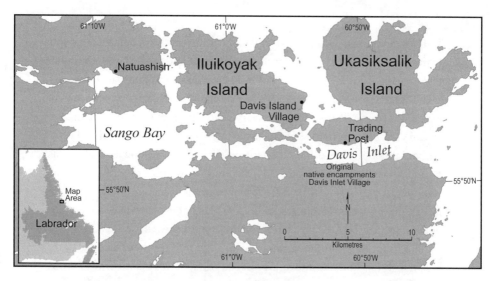

MAP 4. Davis Inlet Village, 1924–1968; Davis Island Village, 1968–2003; and the new
village of Natuashish, inhabited in 2003 when Davis Island Village was abandoned.

in Davis Island, the honey buckets tended to get emptied just outside the
house, rather than carried to the town dump, particularly when people had a
few drinks or were tired or angry, or during the recurrent storms.

Thirty-seven years of living in a village—far different from living in
a frequently moved forest hunting camp—without running water, and in
government-built houses that were at best very difficult to heat adequately
and at worst had windows broken by upset children or angry adults. When
people could not get to the woods to hunt or trap, there was little to do but
sit in these houses and drink. In Davis Island the houses for teachers, government officials, police, and the priest had running water and good heating
systems. There was enough of a good water source for that.

It is hard to know how to name the ideas of the government's people who
created and maintained this situation—houses with no running water and
no sewerage—and perhaps giving these views, this dominant culture, a name
misses the point. It does not seem totally purposive, in the sense of the term
that would imply something like "let's stick it to them." Nor can it be dismissed as a mistake, for there were expensive consulting studies about where
to put the new Native communities, which noted that water was not readily
available and the hard rock base would make septic systems difficult and
expensive. When it was tried to bring some water to the community without
deeply burying the pipes, the pipes froze and burst, which could also have
been easily foreseen.

If we pursue the issue of what was on the minds of the people who did this to the Innu, we do not get very far at all before we bog down in basic contradictions. By the 1950s the percentage of Innu (and Inuit) with TB was shockingly high—about 9 percent of the surveyed population (actually probably more), which was ten times the national rate. It was decided, in the usual "blame the victim" perspective, that what the governments of Newfoundland and Canada and their advisors called "the tent syndrome" was responsible. This was claimed even though then the Davis Inlet Innu, most of whom still lived year-round in tents, were known to have the lowest rates of TB of any Native people in Labrador—by far (Ryan 1988). This changed after they were moved into houses on the island, to help cure "the tent syndrome" that was causing TB.

The Innu were induced with promises and forced with regulations to relocate to the island and move into houses that, it was claimed, would not only diminish their as yet nonexistent TB epidemic but "settle them," ending their "migratory ways." It would also, their mission priest insisted, make them more available for schooling (in the capital city's curriculum) and for modern ways (Ryan 1988). If this doesn't make sense to us—or far more importantly, if the required capital city educational curriculum did not make sense to them—that may be a central part of why it had such a devastating impact.

To understand the depth of this problem within the dominant society, how and why it did what it did at Davis Inlet and Davis Island, it is useful to know that the second major Innu resettlement community, the community now called Sheshatshiu, then called Sheshatshit, was built across the narrow river channel from the Euro-Canadian community North West River, where every house has water and sewerage. Even though Sheshatshiu is on the same kind of land as North West River, with the same possibilities, the Native houses there, housing several hundred Innu, also went without water and sewerage for almost four decades. So doing this to Native people was not at all just based on the local ecological situation in Davis Island. As both communities were built by the provincial government, with Canadian funds, it was something that was done to "Indians," even when it could easily have been different. And it is still done: the Canadian press, from mid-December 2011 to February 2012, is full of stories of northern Indian communities still denied water, sewerage, appropriate schools, and insulated houses and how the current conservative government is, at best, offering to "study" this situation. While the liberal opposition makes some noise about this, when they were in power they also did nothing but actively maintain this situation.

Maybe it was thought, by those who did it, that Indians have been using the forest for water and toilets since time immemorial, so why spend the money to change that now? Water and sewerage are very different issues for a people continually on the move than for people who live in one fixed house, surrounded by many other houses, for decades. But at the end of this concern it turns out to be neither necessary nor relevant to wonder what was in the minds of those responsible for creating and maintaining this situation, and especially also for lying to the Innu people about its immanent remedy, decade after decade. It is sufficient to think of it the way it was likely to be seen by many of the people who lived with it for two or three generations: that's how they treat us; that's who they think we are; and, in the worst, the most destructive, of the extensions from this treatment, that's who we are.

People who do standard field work, with questionnaires and clipboards, will ask what makes me suggest, or speculate about, the impact of this on the Innu, since I did not, would not, ask. I did see the honey buckets emptied just outside the house. Decades ago, in the early 1960s, I worked driving a rock wagon in an Arctic construction camp on Baffin Island, far north of Labrador, where the workers' barracks, but not managements', were given honey buckets. That's how we—the laborers—saw the situation; you guess how relevant this might be. I wish, quite strongly, that we had the sense to confront the company by emptying these buckets out the window. So I have a hunch I know some of what it means when the Innu do it in a village where the priest, the imported teachers, the imported social workers, and the police all have houses with water and toilets. I don't want, or need, to pretend I know it all. I can live with this as a hunch, as I lived with the honey buckets: you decide whether or not you want to try following down this pathway of thoughts—hopefully after you try a honey bucket, and see how you deal with it when, month after month, it is full to the brim, forty pounds of sewage in a five-gallon bucket, and raining hard. This is participant life, as opposed to anthropology's sometimes more distancing and often illusory field work method called "participant observation."

But there is a much more important point at stake here, which goes far deeper and broader than the detritus from almost four decades of homes with honey buckets and no easy place to even wash your hands. That far more important point is that we are dealing with peoples, both Innu and Inuit, utterly without rights while this was being done to them—people who were mostly no longer useful and so could not make effective claims. Newfoundland, with the connivance of Canada, called them "citizens." This was such a deceptive response to reality that it is not worth serious consideration, except hopefully as a basis now for a court case, along the lines of the cases and settlement reparations against the residential schools that First Nations children were forced into—schools that beat and raped Native children so intensely, for so long, and forcibly kept children away from their parents, their language, their ceremonies, the ways of their community, all "for their own good," as the governments expressed what they were pleased to think of as the justifying intent of those schools. It is a surprise worth considering that anthropology, for all its interest in strange and peculiar cultures and practices, did not discover and prominently discuss what the dominant society was doing to vast numbers of Native children in these residential schools. Humpty Dumpty did not sit on the wall, but behind it.

Naming and Fixing

In the early years of Davis Island many Innu bought snowmobiles for access to their caribou hunting territories, about 150 kilometers or more into the interior, after the ice formed on Davis Inlet channel. The snowmobiles made it possible to get to the interior quickly, and to quickly follow herd movements. Caribou provided most of the winter food and also the skins for boots and parkas, which needed to be frequently replaced. These early snowmobiles were known to break easily. The government store on Davis Island, which took the place of the HBC trading post, did not stock snowmobile parts, although it sold the snowmobiles to the Innu. The store would order them, mostly to arrive on the freight boat next summer, so that if your snowmobile broke you were very likely to lose a whole hunting season. Without access to subsistence food and winter clothing material, and with an increasingly constricted market for furs and pelts, people became inescapably dependent on their welfare checks, for which they qualified by living where the government dictated. And the government, for its own reasons, wanted them in town. The same situation, in general, held the Inuit in dependence to the government stores and the government that made the policy for these stores.

There are two initial questions: why did northern Innu people, the people once known as Naskapi, and still known by that name when they were resettled at Davis Island, agree to move to this place, and once there, why did they stay? In part they agreed to move there because of all the promises that were made about what they would be given, how "education" would help their children, and because the priest, upon whom they had been so dependent for their survival, wanted them to do so. One of the reasons they stayed was that their welfare payments, which by the 1960s were essential for living, would only be paid if they lived in that community and, increasingly, if their children were "available" to attend school. If the parents took the children out of the resettlement community, the welfare payments stopped, and with no viable market for furs or pelts, these payments were crucial. If people without children left the community, the welfare payments stopped because they had "no fixed address." There were other reasons, other methods, why and how the government, in alliance with priests and missionaries, "settled" Innu and Inuit. But the relevant point here is that it was done, largely inescapably.

The English word *fixing* has multiple meanings. One meaning is to mend something that is broken. The Newfoundland and Canadian governments very rarely spoke that language. Another meaning, probably deeply related as domination sees it, is to fix, hold, secure, stabilize things and people in one spot, keeping them from moving. Now the government is talking. Half this talk consists of dictates to Native people, telling them where they should stay. The other half is the government talking to itself: this kind of fixity in place is supposed to make people more controllable; of course it does not, as even a superficial acquaintance with the history of the vulnerable, almost everywhere, shows. The out-of-control practices of the victims of the governments' policies of concentration and confinement in relocation communities have their downsides, along with their semieffective defiance of the attempts to control. The downsides are the epidemics of collective self-destruction among some of the ordinary people and opportunism among some of the Native political elite.

To help understand the current epidemics of collective self-destruction, which make people into the authors of their own and each other's misery, rather than just letting the governments do it to them, we need to look a bit further into what the Newfoundland and Canadian governments were doing to Innu and Inuit peoples on the context of "resettlement." Keep in mind that if you are going to suffer, inescapably, it may help avoid having this done to you, or become a critique of those who do it to you, if you do it to yourself or to each other.

IN THE LATE 1960s the Montagnais, as the more southern Innu were then still called, were settled, year-round, in a village across the channel from the Euro-Canadian community of North West River, about twenty-five miles from Happy Valley–Goose Bay, at the start of Grand Lake, an arm of Lake

Melville–Hamilton Inlet. With the connivance of their missionary priest the Indians were pressured to leave the predominantly Euro-Canadian village of North West River and form a new village on the other side of the river. This new village, from its founding as a separate community in 1935 until about 2001, when the name began to be changed, was officially and publically known by the extraordinary name "Sheshatshit." This was the name on maps, on all government documents, and in popular discourse by English-speaking Labradorians. Anthropological linguists were deeply implicated in developing a let's-pretend, supposedly traditional, deeply illogical rationalization for this name, whose obscenity—the name is exactly "She Shat Shit"—lies far more in its imposition by Euro-Canadians on a Native community, and what was done to make this name real, than in its words.

José Mailhot, perhaps the major linguist working on Labrador Innu dialects, offers to "explain" the name, in the opening of her book *The People of Sheshatshit*:

> Sheshatshit, a contraction of *Tshishe-shatshit*, is a very old place name. . . . While the name takes many forms in the early documents, it is most often written "Kessessakiou." In all likelihood the Innu of 300 years ago pronounced it *ki shay sa kew*. . . . This . . . is an old form of the more recent *Tshishe-shatshu*. . . . [The locative is transcribed] Tshishe-shatshit. . . . The first syllable should be pronounced shay, as a short vowel without a dipthong. The second should be pronounced sha, much like the first syllable in "shallow." The third should be pronounced jeet. Thus the word is written *Sheshatshit* but pronounced *shay sha jeet*, with stress on the last syllable. (1997, 1–2)

Even though Mailhot is a truly excellent linguist and her book contains much that is insightful, so radiant is the innocence of cultural anthropology and cultural pluralism that there has not been a word of wonderment, much less concern, from her or from those who have seen or heard the name, or used and cited Mailhot's book, quite widely used in northern Native studies, about how a word in the Innu language pronounced something like *Kessessakiou* or *shay sha jeet* got turned into Sheshatshit—and put in that way on all government documents, reports, maps, road signs, etc. The consequences included, just to begin, making a village to fit the name.

The original Innu settlement was on the north side of an inlet separating Grand Lake from Lake Melville, the inner portion of Hamilton Inlet. There was a trading post here in the late eighteenth century, taken over by HBC in 1837 and turned into a regional headquarters for HBC operations. As this village on the north side became increasingly White or Métis, with the opening of a regional Grenfell mission hospital and orphanage in the early twentieth century, in 1935 Native people who camped seasonally near the Hudson's Bay post were moved, by their priest and by the racism of the White community, across to the south side of the river to a new community, which supposedly was an old Innu camping ground, as of course was also the north side of the river, near the HBC trading post. The Whites living in North West River wanted "Indians" out of "their" community and, with the assistance of the priest, got them to move across the river, or channel as it is called. It was this Innu community on the south side, settled primarily by Innu in tents and built up in the 1960s, that became known as Sheshatshit. The Euro-Canadian settlement across the channel, where no Innu now live, is named North West River. Nice name—in the culture of the dominant.

THE PROBLEMS BEFORE both the Native peoples of Labrador and those of us trying to usefully see what has been and is happening are far broader than the combined domination/humiliation of Innu peoples. The insults routinely confronting African Americans, Native peoples, Moslems, undocumented workers, and others in the United States, Canada, and Europe (and the equivalent in India, China, Japan, Saudi Arabia, etc.) alert us to the point that domination ordinarily comes packaged with humiliation: that is central to how it works. But inside and underneath this package of force and "culture" is something much more complex.

One of the more startling features of Native peoples' situation in Labrador, until quite recent changes, is the intense contrast between the appearance of the Innu and the Inuit villages, as well as the lack of correlation between appearance and some key realities. Specifically, Innu villages were, in general and until quite recently, desperately hard-looking places: garbage strewn about, broken windows, rutted dirt roads, and more. Inuit villages, by contrast, were generally neat and quite clean, with well-maintained roads and houses that for the most part were solid, if too thin walled. Yet the suicide, substance abuse, and domestic violence rates are about the same. This is by way of a caution: the process of forcing Inuit into concentration villages was seemingly a bit less brutal than what was done to the Innu, and the villages were seemingly more livable places, but as Carol Brice-Bennett (1994, 2000) and others have shown, the transition was enough of a shock, was associated with enough long-term suffering, to leave disaster in its wake. How villages with such different external appearances could have such similar deep consequences is a crucial question, and a portion of the answer may have to do with the route of Native people into these villages.

At stake are even broader issues than mistreating people who are becoming increasingly disposable. What happened in Labrador is not at all a singular instance—something that could be done "under the radar" to small populations of Native people hidden in the middle of a place few know or care about. The most general issue before us is modernization, the major excuse for the concentration of Labrador's Native people, and the changes imposed in the name of modernization and its ruler: development.[10] These changes have included displacing, in World Bank estimates, 10 million people a year worldwide just in the context of development, almost always to less than they had before—to harder lives in harder places.[11] It is within the imposition of so-called modernization and development that what has happened and is happening in Labrador must be understood—and what has been happening in Labrador helps us see modernization and development as both the creation of and simultaneously a fantasized solution to the problem of disposable peoples. They or their children will now supposedly become useful in a more modern economy. At the same time, they have been put in a position where it seems as if they are doing themselves in, relieving the dominant society from the burden of facing up to what it has done and is doing to them.

Modernity, Management, Silence

3 When I kept silent,
   my bones wasted away
   through my groaning all day long.
4 For day and night
   your hand was heavy on me;
   my strength was sapped
   as in the heat of summer.
—PSALM 32:3–4, NEW INTERNATIONAL VERSION

Silence is often very far from quietness, and very far from just not speaking. Silence in the face of suffering, as this psalm makes very clear, can contribute not just to the perpetuation of suffering but to its intensity. Some of so-called social sciences' concepts impose, rather than explain or lessen, silences.

There is a surprisingly popular notion, put forward by the French cultural historian Michel Foucault (who seems to have done no actual field engagements with the populations he discusses), that is called "governmentality." This notion essentially argues that power makes its subjects governable by shaping collusion, cooperation, obedience, and so on, on the one hand and resistance, evasion, defiance, and so on, on the other. Power thus ultimately shapes its subjects' sense of self and situation, creating within the subjects of domination what Foucault calls "governmentality." It is fairly clear that domination has helped very substantially to shape the peoples who have been known as Indians, Eskimos, Aborigines, and others. But it is a very serious mistake to think that this contributory shaping has made its victims governable, beyond making them victims and necessary participants in the fur and skin trades. Since those trades have ended, it has been a rather different story.

Let's turn this self-aggrandizing fantasy of domination upside down. As I have argued throughout this work, domination produces far more chaos in the lives of its subjects than order; so domination is always in trouble. Its trouble is that it needs some substantial order "beneath it," as it were, to effectively and efficiently govern. So it creates, in Native communities, Native governments—political organizations that are supposed to be agents and intermediaries, plus visible symbols, of the necessary order. The sham of "democracy"—voting in a deeply manipulated process, both there and here—provides the justification both for assuming that the supposed order is legitimate and for requiring the populace to follow the dictates of "their government."

It does not usually work very well, but domination keeps trying, keeps believing in its own beliefs and practices. Governmentality, in sum, is the fantasy of power and has little to do with the realities of lives lived within and against its clutches. At least this is the case in the Native communities of Labrador, and I think also in many other similar places: not just Native communities but, for example, the destroyed former industrial towns and cities.

However we want to conceptualize "governmentality," there has been an extremely intense struggle, particularly instigated by the state, to manage and control the Native population. At the same time, the state seeks to push Native peoples aside, out of the mainstream of what is happening, and usually also down. One of the strongest manifestations of this contradiction has been emerging in the land claims process, where the Canadian and Newfoundland governments offer to "give" Native peoples a few rights to an exceptionally restricted territory "in return" for Native people renouncing a very large range of all their other potential rights. But, as it seems to some Native peoples, a few rights are significantly better than none, especially as "development" tears across their land.

The Canadian government was very explicit about the "deal" it was offering and still seeks to force Native peoples into:

In 1973 the Government of Canada announced it was prepared to negotiate comprehensive land claims settlements with native people in Canada who could demonstrate aboriginal use and occupancy of specific areas of the land, from time immemorial. This policy was directed toward native people who had never entered into a treaty relationship with the crown, and whose interest in the land were never abrogated or superseded by law. The basis of the 1973 federal policy was that all aboriginal title or claims to land were to be exchanged in return for the specific rights and benefits of a land claim settlement.[12]

Much more is at stake here than a simple trade, with the government offering to "give," or more specifically return, to Native peoples a handful of their own beans in return for everything else that Native peoples might well own, if and when the courts decided that Native peoples were actually entitled to at least some justice. The Canadian and provincial governments, probably quite worried about what the courts might award, are seeking to head off that possibility by offering this "trade." But the terms of the trade will be intensely controlled by the governments, which in the ensuing negotiations are very specific about what rights Native peoples will and will not be allowed, on the lands that are returned to them. In this modern guise the issue is ultimately still control.

And state control, however framed and however enforced, increasingly does not work. That point, *increasingly*, is at the core of the issues before us, the most difficult aspect of the situation to grasp, to try to get our hands and our minds around. In some respects the problem will be very simple; in some respects it will remain intractable. The Newfoundland and Canadian governments both try, especially in the past few decades, to do more to remedy and control the situation, and yet they do not manage to do what is needed. This contradiction was posed with exceptional clarity by Peter Sarsfield, a medical doctor, twenty-five years after confederation, when the epidemics of collective self-destruction were both intensifying and adding to the existing health crises of TB, influenza, and a wide range of untreated, often officially unrecognized, medical problems. He was asked, in the fall of 1976, to do a survey for the Canadian government of health conditions on the Labrador coast, with special reference to the health of Native peoples. He wrote,

My qualifications include a medical degree from Dalhousie University, Halifax, Nova Scotia, 1973, and three years of work as a general practitioner with Grenfell in Labrador. For over a year I was the traveling doctor for the coast, from Black Tickle [in southern Labrador] to Nain, and I am familiar with most of the people of the communities as well as the nursing stations, health problems, and facilities available. Following my time as traveling doctor, I was assistant to the director of northern medical services at Northwest River Hospital, being either officially or functionally in charge of transportation, drug purchasing, consultant visits, referrals, much of the inpatient care and medical supervision of nursing stations, communications and medical records. I am no longer employed with Grenfell organization. . . . [In] September 1976 I resigned.

In the context of doing the survey, from November 1976 to January 1977, he visited all the coastal Labrador communities and talked with a sample of people in their homes, with or without a translator, in whatever language they chose, and asking only the most general questions about their assessment of health care. Among the major points he makes in his summation is the following:

> The situation in Labrador today finds three cultural groups with very different histories now faced with very similar problems. On the most basic level the problem is obvious and complete; control of their lives is out of their hands. None of the major institutions or services of Labrador is controlled by the people of Labrador. Healthcare is obviously only one area of concern. Without changes in patterns of land ownership and use, and the control of industry and employment which that implies, as well as control of local government, education, communications and transportation, the health of the people is not going to radically alter. (Sarsfield 1977, 11)[13]

This names one of the central features of modern Labrador Native history: the struggle over controlling Native lives. At the center of this struggle, surprisingly in some ways, is health, for it has turned out to be impossible to stop suicide, substance abuse, domestic violence, and all the attendant consequences no matter what those supposedly in control do. And it seems that the central feature of this struggle over control, far broader than health even if that is one of its major terrains, is that no one has won this struggle for control, and in its present form probably no one can win.

Nor does the simple continuation of struggles bring any rewards to anyone. Our task here thus goes beyond describing the *what* of these struggles, to reach toward the how and the why and, most of all, to use old words, the whence and the whereto—from whence the struggle comes, and where it seems to be leading, or taking, all the "sides" in struggle. But complicated struggles do not really have anything as simple as sides, and we cannot use the too superficial term *parties*—as in the phrase "all the parties in this struggle"— or even the current seemingly inclusive but fraudulent pretense "all the stakeholders."

Corporations and states rarely have anything actually at stake when they impose their goals on Native peoples, for they arrange things so they get what they need. Thus, their presence in these hearings as one of an equal meeting of "stakeholders" is, to put it kindly, deceptive. The best we can do is stick with the somewhat simplifying term *struggle*, and all that it implies, for at least that term suggests the ultimately inescapable.

The Reasons of Civilization and Struggle

La lucha continua—"the struggle continues"—is a wonderful and cheering rallying cry. I have used it myself in various demonstrations, and have been pleased to do so, for it advertises the fact that the victims are not giving up, not letting the dominant live in the peace of domination. But when struggle becomes endless, an utter stalemate, it can often turn into something else. We have a lot to look at and think about in the attempts of the state, and more recently Native governments, to make a controlled and managed population, for doing so will help us not only discard such notions as "governmentality" but get a bit of a handle on the continuing failure of control and the positive and negative consequences of this for the well-being of ordinary Native people.

The Newfoundland government used its developing Canadian license to do as it wished with and to Native peoples to move the Naskapi from their summer homes, still in the mainland community of Davis Inlet, farther north to the Inuit community of Nutak. Nutak was a former Moravian mission community, where most of the fifty-seven Eskimo survivors of the 1918 pandemic in Okak were relocated, being joined by others, and the Newfoundland government by 1948 was servicing Nutak after the Moravians and HBC left. As a former mission community, most of the Inuit were living in houses, and when the Innu were moved there, they were living in tents. The idea of the government was that the Naskapi-Innu could support themselves by fishing for cod in the summer and cutting wood in the sheltered valleys behind Nutak to sell to the Inuit in Hebron; thus, they could be the servants of those who were, just barely at the end of the fur and sealskin trades, themselves the servants.

In 1948 Father O'Brien got a letter from an Innu he knew from Davis Inlet, an elderly leader of the Innu community there, whom O'Brien had made a leader, and who was being relocated to Nutak:

> Nutak August 31, 1948 Dear Father O'Brien we have left Davis Inlet and are going to live in Nutak, we don't know yet whether it will be better or not for us. . . . [Unclear] we are sorry to leave the church [in Davis Inlet] and we are sorry because we haven't seen the priest. Last year we had a hard winter, three children starved because we were too far in the country and bad weather stopped us before we could go to Davis Inlet. We ask your blessing, we don't forget you and we ask you to pray for all of us. Everyone very well now. We ask you to . . . [unclear] if you can't come yourself to send a priest to see us. Some of our babies are not baptized and some young people want to be married. I buried the children who starved we had to leave them in the country. We have no books now prayer books and wish you would send some. Good by, [unclear, but an Innu version of the author's name] Joe Rich. (dictated letter, FOB Papers)

This makes it clear why the Innu, when they were told that there would be work and food and a life for them in Nutak, went, confined in the hold of the freight boat/ferry that brought them there. When they realized that this was not so, they simply left, walking, showing up back in Davis Inlet five months after they left Nutak, with the hardships of the journey and the time in Nutak pressed into them.

In 1956, eight years after this forced attempt to expand Nutak, the government store there was closed, and the remaining Inuit population mostly moved to Nain, which was becoming the major Inuit community. As they were forced out of their home communities by imposed closure of crucial services and moved into Nain, they were housed in distinct sections of the community, separate from the older inhabitants—marking them as newcomers, still not fully and equally integrated into the social and political life of the community, decades later. The Innu, as we shall see in some more detail, were told to go here, go there. The Inuit just had their communities, including some very fine and prosperous places, closed out from under them by withdrawal of what had become crucial government services, and they were offered a few possibilities of where they might go. In both cases it was at the Newfoundland government's convenience, with no effective consultation with Native people.

One of the more devastating closures of an Inuit community occurred in Hebron, an old Moravian mission settlement where the Inuit had built very satisfying and productive lives, in what was by the 1950s a prosperous and fine community. Its economy was primarily rooted in a small-boat cod fishery, and throughout Newfoundland and Labrador this family-based fishery and the people who worked it were being muscled aside for the huge, and destructive, factory trawlers (the prologue of Sider [2003b] describes this process). On Easter Monday, 1959, the Inuit at Hebron were gathered into the church, rather than the community hall, and told by the missionaries and government spokesmen that their community would be closed, and they must move to Nain or elsewhere. The Moravian missionary had convinced the Newfoundland government that TB in the community could be solved by relocation. After Inuit were told they must move, about half the Inuit moved on their own; in the fall when the government store and the nursing station were closed, the remainder had no choice but to leave as well. As Carol Brice-Bennett perceptively argues, in the church they had been taught not to question. Had this move been announced in the community hall, things might have been different. So the Inuit were largely silent in the face of this imposed control of their lives and their well-being. This closure of their home community was a heartbreak, still hurting forty years later. And their arranged silence, using the Church to both initiate and impose relocation upon them, has been a further source of hurt (Brice-Bennett 2000).

One of the high-status Eskimo positions in the Moravian mission communities was the position of "chapel servant." This was part of a long-standing attempt by the missionaries to get the Inuit to listen to and accept what they were told—to serve their lords and their lords' Lord. As Carol Brice-Bennett (1981) has shown, the training to just listen and do—to behave as the missionaries desired—was very far from effective in the nineteenth and early twentieth centuries, when the Eskimos not only often went their own ways but protested loudly, clearly, and effectively, in words and in actions. Their protests do not seem nearly as confrontational for most of the twentieth century, although the land claims process reinvigorated assertiveness in the 1990s. Protest in the twentieth century was not at all absent; it just became significantly diminished, particularly in the mid-twentieth century, when the relocations were being imposed.

It is hard to know why. Several possibilities are likely, including the brutal mortality rate of the 1918 Spanish Flu and smallpox pandemics, which are likely to have both practically and emotionally diminished the capacity and the willingness for struggle. In addition, the Newfoundland government routinely and intensely misrepresented what Inuit (and also Innu) would be given in the context of relocation. The government lied, and it was difficult or impossible for the Inuit to know that in advance, or to have many options when the store and the health services were closed, even if they knew. So the bullying of the Inuit by the state was suffered in silence—a profoundly different kind of silence than those that created and sustained collective dignity. This was the silence of the psalm quoted as the epigraph to this chapter. Walter Rockwood, director of the Division of Northern Labrador Affairs, wrote in 1957, "One fact seems clear—civilization is on the northward march, and for the Eskimo and Indian there is no escape. The last bridges of isolation were destroyed with the coming of the airplane and the radio. The only course now open, for there can be no turning back, is to fit him as soon as may be to take his full place as a citizen of our society" (Samson 2003, 18).

That is one part of the story: the inescapable northward march of the state, wearing the self-deceiving mask of "civilization." The other part of the story is how civilization and the state acted when it got there. In looking at this we can also see a further pressure for concentrating Native peoples.

Voice
Dr. Sarsfield continued his discussion of the failure of health and health services in northern Labrador, with a special focus on Native communities, where the health crises were the most severe. In this quote we can begin to see how the issue is becoming voice, rather than voices:

> The decisions regarding possible expenditures [on health care] were made almost entirely by the Grenfell Association and one or two departments of the provincial government, often with a cautious eye to political and religious "realities". The coastal people did not have a significant voice in such issues as the placement and function of nursing stations. An example of the consequences of this is the health-care history of Davis Inlet, a town of 225 people. The clinic there was built in 1973 with the nurse being hired by the Grenfell Association late that year. Prior to 1973 the medical needs of Davis Inlet were mainly met by priest and nun volunteer work. The presence in Labrador of Davis Inlet Indians, then, helped attract federal aid to Labrador and therefore helped finance the nursing stations in Nain, Hopedale and Makkovik [all primarily Inuit communities] with very little benefit to Davis Inlet until 1973. The communities of Rigolet and Postville . . . are designated communities [communities where the federal government is supposed to substantially contribute to the cost of services to native people] leading to a portion of the financial contribution [for the costs of services] from Ottawa to St. John's, but there is an almost total absence of health services or facilities in these villages.

It is worth emphasizing that the provinces capital expenditures for Indians and Inuit the years 1959–64 total $280,564 [this equals $56,113 per year for all services to native peoples along the entire northern Labrador coast]. (Sarsfield 1977, 44)

Two separate issues are emerging here: the first is how scant were the services provided to Native peoples, despite the intensity of their needs. And while Innu health needs were so intense that the Canadian government provided some meager funds to address them, this money was primarily spent in Inuit and Euro-Canadian communities. The second issue, to which we shall come very shortly, is the way it was arranged that when services were provided, supposedly to Natives, a large proportion of the beneficiaries were Canadians, not the Native peoples—who were only considered Canadians as it suited the government's policies, plans, and expenditures.

Sarsfield discusses how provincial budgetary constraints shaped health care. He starts with a comparison of Labrador to what is available in northern and northern Native communities elsewhere in Canada. In this context he notes the paucity of nurses and doctors in Labrador Native villages; the shortage of medical information, with nurses in Labrador often buying their own medical manuals; the dangerously low quantities of basic medical supplies and oxygen tanks in Labrador village clinics and nursing stations; the absence of X-ray machines, microscopes, and nurses trained in their use; and the complete absence of incubators for premature babies, along with any substantial training in midwifery for Labrador nurses. Medicine in northern Labrador was only minimally financed and supported by the meager resources of the International Grenfell Association (Sarsfield 1977, 44–53).

He provides two summations of this situation, one about how Canadians are being favored in the attempt to remedy this, the other about how Natives are excluded:

There has recently been informal discussion of the satellite-relay television link between Saint Anthony [in northern Newfoundland, where there was a small cottage hospital serving both Newfoundland fisher families and Labrador inhabitants] and . . . Memorial University Department of Northern Medicine. The politics of health that lead to such decisions are totally separate from the realities of health needs. Telemedicine is extremely expensive and provides a very limited service for the huge majority of the population. It is, however, a very attractive plaything for many scientific professionals. The resources used by this endeavor could be so much better utilized in the Labrador communities for basic needs which would affect the health of most of the people, such as water supply, sewerage, housing and airstrips. . . . The obvious link in the discrepancy between planned-satellites and needed-water is the lack of involvement of the Labrador people in the setting of priorities and policies. . . .

The federal government has encouraged formation of community health councils in the Northwest Territories for years. However, it seems that in practice the federal response is often one of resisting placement of any *real* control in local hands, with most of the health councils being of a purely advisory nature. As a result health councils often seemed confused as to their role, and lethargic in response to their lack of direction and authority. A frequently heard comment is that a meeting of the Council is not needed as "we don't have any problems". A council's potential role in positive planning will only become apparent if the Council has executive powers. (Sarsfield 1977, 58–59; emphasis in the original)

People who themselves do not have any "real" control, as Dr. Sarsfield so perceptively put it, must one way or another confront the opposite: they live within and against the effort to control them either directly by pressing them to do something or by leaving them alone to suffer and die:

1982 APRIL 11: JUDICIAL INQUIRY INTO THE DEATH OF
ZACHARIAS TOWNLEY, [ESKIMO] NAIN, JAN 1, 1982
Mr. Townley was a passenger of a sled or komatik which was being towed by a snowmobile in the Nain area on December 30, 1981. Another passenger was in possession of a harpoon which struck the ground and accidentally flew back and hit the deceased in the abdomen. The deceased received prompt treatment at the nursing station in Nain on December 30, 1981 and was advised by the nurse who treated him to return at the slightest sign of pain or discomfort. The deceased had told the staff at the nursing station that the injury was caused by the broken or wooden part of a harpoon handle and not the metal part. On the following day Mr. Townley returned to the nursing station complaining of severe pain. He was seen by one nurse, Ann Footit, at the nursing station who advised him to take All Bran cereal for the pain in his stomach. On January 1, 1982 he returned to the nursing station and passed away.

His honor recommended that consideration be given to regulations under the "all-terrain and motorized snow vehicle act" which would require hunting instruments and weaponry to be securely fastened to both machine and drawn sled and that consideration be given to employment of full-time interpreters at medical facilities with native populations.

His honor also recommended that police investigation be conducted into the area of negligence as raised by the inquiry and that pending the final outcome the party concerned mainly nurse Footit be restricted from practice.

witnesses unable to be subpoenaed

Ann Footit, Nurse—in England

Dr K Watton, Coastal Doctor, in Uganda

Dr Shah in Iran[14]

Zacharias Townley was not left completely untreated to die in his suffering: he was advised by the nurse at Nain to eat All-Bran cereal. And the death of one more Inuit was certainly not sufficient grounds to ask the British government to return her to Newfoundland for further action.

As painful as was his death, it is also painful for his relatives and friends (and perhaps us) to helplessly contemplate situations where nothing people say really matters, even when their lives are at stake. This is a special kind of imposed silence: nothing you or yours say matters at all to how you will be treated. It makes no difference if or what you speak; "they" or "s/he" will not listen. This is also, we might note, the situation with domestic violence; we will address that later. That kind of imposed silence, radiating from the death of Zacharias Townley, has been completely generalized to the Native peoples of Labrador. It is what makes their villages concentration villages, for no one in charge cares what concentration camp inmates say about their situation—perhaps, in some ways, not even many of their fellow inmates, too preoccupied with their own problems and unmet needs to be able to listen, particularly when there is so little they can do.

The Bully Pulpit

This imposed silence lies at the core of what can best be understood as the bullying of Native peoples by the Canadian and Newfoundland governments. It has been the worst kind of bullying—pervasive, inescapable, and for decades without any remedy whatsoever. Organized Native protest in the 1980s helped in significant ways, and in the 1990s, as Native peoples started to get substantial legal rights, the overt bullying subsided a bit. It soon reemerged, in the guise of the imposed conditions for Native land claims. This new bullying was in the shockingly deceptive context of "recognizing" and "giving" Native people their legal rights—under Canadian law and very much under Canadian conditions. Chapter 7 addresses that and its surprising consequences, for despite all the bullying, Native rights has made many things better for Native peoples, while seemingly making life even more stressful for some Native peoples.

The bullying of Native peoples was so pervasive, so intense, and mostly so various that it is difficult to pick just a few characteristic instances that reveal its significant dimensions. Three somewhat arbitrary choices have been made here, to show dimensions of the engagement of government and Native peoples. The first entails the bullying of a comparatively small group of Native people. Here the point is that what is done to such a small group of Innu people could scarcely affect development one way or another—but it did help to establish how Native people were, and were going to be, treated. The second example is a large-scale one: the seizure of vast areas of the best Innu hunting lands in the interior of Labrador to make the reservoir for a hydroelectric dam—a reservoir that soon became the third largest government-made lake in the world. Innu who left their traps, snowshoes, and other equipment in their small trapping shelters and cabins in the spring of one year came back the next fall to find everything gone under water, for they were not even told where the reservoir would be, much less compensated or included in the planning. The third example is from the Inuit and concerns the high-handed and simultaneously deep lack of effective concern by the state for their health and well-being.

Shortly after confederation, Newfoundland became much more engaged with Labrador than it ever had been. Premier Smallwood, who engineered Newfoundland's confederation, called Labrador a "gift" to Newfoundland— a place whose seemingly limitless resources in water power, timber, and, in the mid-twentieth century, only *probably* mineral wealth would rescue Newfoundland from generations of poverty. In that context not only were Natives not going to be "given" (or allowed) any possibly interfering rights that might come with recognition of their aboriginal status—much less allowed to partner in any resource development project—but Native peoples, particularly the Innu, no longer wanted as fur trappers, began to be severely bullied. Some were literally driven from pillar to post, from Fort Chimo to Schefferville. Fort Chimo was the HBC fur-trading post in far northern Québec, near the northern tip of Labrador; Schefferville, just after World War II, was becoming a major iron-mining center, with a substantial demand for various kinds of labor. It is located in the middle of Labrador, near the western border with Québec.

It is not clear what drove the Innu from Fort Chimo to Schefferville—the government, their inability to survive the particularly harsh environs of Fort Chimo without supplies from a substantial fur trade (which, as we discussed in chapter 4, HBC itself said was too barren and too harsh for an effective fur trade), or some combination of these and other factors.

The Naskapi Nation website discusses the moves from place to place from the late nineteenth through the twentieth century.[15]

> In the early 1950s, the Naskapis made a partially successful effort to re-establish themselves at Fort McKenzie, where they had already lived between 1916 and 1948, and to return to an economy based substantially on hunting, fishing, and commercial trapping. They could no longer be entirely self-sufficient, however, and the high cost of resupplying them, combined with the continuing high incidence of tuberculosis and other factors, obliged them to return to Fort Chimo after only two years.

> For reasons that are not entirely clear, virtually all of the Naskapis moved from Fort Chimo to the recently founded iron-ore mining community of Schefferville in 1956. Two principal schools of thought about this move exist. One of them holds that the Naskapis were induced, if not ordered, to move by officials of Indian and Northern Affairs, while the other believes that the Naskapis themselves decided to move in the hope of finding employment, housing, medical assistance, and educational facilities for their children.

> Although officials of Indian and Northern Affairs were certainly aware of the intention of the Naskapis to move from Fort Chimo to Schefferville and may even have instigated that move, they appear to have done little or nothing to prepare for their arrival there, not even by warning the representatives of the Iron Ore Company of Canada or the municipality of Schefferville.

> The Naskapis left Fort Chimo on foot to make the 400-mile journey to Schefferville overland. By the time they reached Wakuach Lake, some 70 miles north of Schefferville, most of them were in a pitiable state, exhausted, ill, and close to starvation. A successful rescue effort was mounted, but the only homes that awaited the Naskapis were the shacks that they built for themselves on the edge of Knob Lake, near the railroad station, with scavenged and donated materials. A short time later, in 1957, under the pretext that the water at Knob Lake was contaminated, the municipal authorities moved them to a site adjacent to John Lake, some four miles north-north-east of Schefferville, where they lived without benefit of water, sewage, or electricity, and where, despite their hopes in coming to Schefferville, there was no school for their children and no medical facility. (Innu Nation/Armitage 1991)

The Naskapi shared the site at John Lake with a group of Montagnais, who had moved voluntarily from Sept-Iles to Schefferville with the completion of the railroad in the early 1950s.

The Iron mines in Schefferville began in 1954, and it is very likely that the Innu were encouraged to come there to help with exploration parties and the construction of a railroad through Québec to the St. Lawrence River. Then the mines were closed in 1982, leaving the people in the vicinity hung out to dry, although episodically there have been some brief flurries of resumption. Two further developments have occurred: a substantial portion of the Innu population moved away from their settlements near the mines, and in 2008 the Innu Nation, including especially the Innu of Sheshatshiu and Utshimas-sits, concluded an Impact Benefits Agreement with the remaining corporate owners of the reopened mines, which gives them a share of any current and future benefits.[16]

AS OLDER INNU HAVE seen it, the new kinds of problems they face began in 1949, with the focus being not on confederation with Canada but on New-foundland's newly intensified interest in Labrador. A variety of earlier issues, such as the Labrador boundary dispute between Québec and Newfound-land, resolved in 1927, are recounted as if they happened in 1949, because that is when they became real in the lives of Native peoples. In this perspective the relocation of Innu, low-level flying, and the building of what became the Smallwood reservoir, which flooded their best hunting lands, all spring from Newfoundland's intensifying focus on, and control over, Labrador.

In 2005 the Innu Nation put up on their website the transcript of a re-corded conversation that took place in 1984: "Assimilation of the Innu: A Dis-cussion between Sylvestre Andrew and Pien Gregoir, August 1984."[17] Both men were Innu, living at Sheshatshiu. Sylvestre Andrew was born in 1938. At the time of this conversation he was forty-six years old. Pien Gregoir was born in 1910; he was seventy-four.

> SYLVESTRE: The government never told us in advance what it was planning. It drew a map and marked the places that supposedly belonged to it. It's not very long ago that the Government of Newfoundland first came here. I think it was in 1949 that it first arrived. That's when Newfoundland joined Canada and a line was drawn on the map to separate us from the French [Québec]. Then the government of Newfoundland wrote on paper that they were re-

sponsible for us; for the Innu north of the line on that map. But it's all Innu land. . . .

After they have drawn the lines on the map, dividing the land among them, they do whatever they want. They don't even stop to think that this is Innu land. All the land that has been divided up is land that has been stolen from us. And if the government had told us in advance of their plans, of the things they wanted to do, we could have stopped them little by little. If we remain unable to stop them, they will completely finish up on our land. . . .

PIEN: And then we will be completely changed—we will be like French and English people. Before they had divided up our land they should have told us first. And they should have listened to us when we didn't approve of what they wanted to do. And today they still don't listen.

SYLVESTRE: No, they don't listen. And now what do you think made us comply with the government? How did the Whites trick us?

PIEN: That's it . . . the priest that went into the country to gather up the people in one place.

SYLVESTRE: . . . I too blame the Whites. The blame rests firstly with the priests who went from place to place in the country gathering the people to come into one place [this is about relocation]. And then the government came and tied the rope on us. We still can't untie ourselves today.

SYLVESTRE: Today, the date is the 14th of August, the year 1984. The Innu have been here for 7,000 years. . . . It was the year 1949 that Mr. Smallwood formed a government and took control over Labrador. And now it's the year 1984, today the date is the 14th. It was on the 13th of August that we heard that the Germans were going to practice on our land. It's the same land where we hunted, where they will practice how they intend to fight in a war. And that is our land. It's like what Mr. Smallwood did to the Mitshikamau area [the Innu name for their territory that was flooded by the hydroelectric dam at Churchill Falls] where they dammed and flooded the land. Mitshikamau was the most extensively used area for hunting. . . . It was the government in Ottawa that gave them permission to play games on our land. . . . The jets practice flying very low over the land; really close. . . . They will do a lot of damage to our land and kill a lot of animals.

PIEN: I think we will have no alternative in the future but to live the way they want us to live. Really, that's how they want us to live, just like them. They want us to buy our food only from stores, the way they do. They want to deprive us of our traditional foods from the country so that we will have to buy store-bought food. . . .

PIEN: Maybe we will all die. . . .

SYLVESTRE: You know, if we had known we could have stopped all this. We knew about it but we couldn't speak or understand the English people. . . . We knew our land well and knew how to survive in the country. But we didn't understand the Whites. That's why we didn't know what was planned for us and our land. [Now] they want to hide their plans from us, but they can no longer fool us as they did many times in the past.

PIEN: I don't think we can overturn every thing right away. . . .

SYLVESTRE: Thus there were once two groups of Innu that hunted in the barren grounds before they were permanently settled in villages. One group is now living in Schefferville [where the iron ore mines are]. They, too, were tricked by the government so that jobs could be given to them. The government is now trying to trick us as well by offering us jobs.

Not too long ago, then, we controlled our own lives. When we were in the country we made decisions ourselves not the government. . . . We could hunt wherever we wanted without fear of the government.

The text ends, after this crucial invocation of fear, for creating fear is crucial to how bullying works. It is important to realize how much of Innu and Inuit autonomy now is a triumph over this imposed "lesson" of fear, and seeing through the trickery. But there is the problem of what to do then: "I'm telling the truth—it's truly an Innu story . . . it's really an Innu land."

Women's Rights and the 5 Percent Solution

With Inuit relocation from their home communities several crucial dimensions of their situation deteriorated. In their new communities they were marked as outsiders, as people who did not fully belong, even though both the old-time residents and the newcomers were Inuit. And the neighborhoods were noticeably worse places to live than the older sections of the community. In the context of this disruption and decline, plus all the stresses in the communities to which they were sent, which had few or no facilities to deal with a substantial influx, indicators of social stress, including substance abuse and domestic violence, intensified significantly.

Women bore a very substantial portion of the brunt of this situation. The Newfoundland government, which was so active in centralizing the population, did very little to help deal with the consequences. They did, and still do, finance a lot of conferences and studies to describe and discuss this situation. A few brief quotes from one such study outline the situation. This study was sponsored by the Newfoundland and Labrador Victim Services Branch, Department of Justice (1996).[18]

The report focuses on the Northern Labrador Inuit communities of Rigolet, Makkovik, Postville, Hopedale, and Nain. The area has a total population, as reported in this study, of approximately three thousand people. Postville is the smallest community, with a population of approximately 270. Nain is the largest, with a population of approximately thirteen hundred. The report starts with sections on background and on history.

BACKGROUND

Each of the communities with the exception of Rigolet had Inuit who were resettled from Nutak, Okak, Hebron, and Killinik. Each of the communities, with the exception of Rigolet and Postville, are predominantly Moravian faith. Rigolet's population is mostly of Anglican faith, and Postville is mostly Pentecostal faith. . . .

There are two safe houses in the northern Labrador Inuit area, they are located in Nain and Hopedale. Each of the communities has a general store, electricity is provided by a diesel operated power plant, and with the exception of Postville each community has direct dialing telephone services, each community has a gravel airstrip and a dock. The communities have a nursing station and with the exception of Nain, a visiting dentist.

HISTORY OF THE NORTHERN LABRADOR SAFE HOUSES

The north coast of Labrador has only recently obtained two safe houses. [Both were in Inuit communities.] The first safe house was in Hopedale in 1995, this house was a rental unit. Then with the help of the Newfoundland and Labrador Housing Corporation, a new safe house was built in 1996. The same year Nain . . . was given Jupp Cottage from the Labrador Health Corp. Repairs were made to this unit and the safe house in Nain began. During its first year of operation, the Nain safe houses housed a total of 130 women and children, of these admittances only three were repeat users. The safe house in both Nain and Hopedale are run by volunteers. The volunteers for the most part are from the local women's group. The safe houses have relied on local charity for furniture and supplies. The Nain women's group holds bingo to raise money to pay the hydroelectric and telephone bills. This safe house and Hopedale have actually had to close due to no money to pay for the phone or Hydro bill. At the present time, 1998, the Nain shelter is closed due to needed repairs and the Hopedale shelter is operating when needed, run by volunteers.

The following is a sample from the discussions of the situation in specific communities:

Rigolet There is no safe house. There is an LIHC [Labrador Inuit Health Center] building [with] two community health workers. There is a traveling counselor who visits about every six weeks. Although the services of community health worker are available they are not used much in Rigolet for a number of reasons some of which are: the LIHC community health workers expertise is not always recognized; sometimes the workers are relatives of either the victim or the abuser; sometimes there are personality conflicts. Emergency help: There are no permanent police, they have to come from Goose Bay by airplane if the weather is good, they cannot respond if the weather is bad (which happens quite often in the spring, winter, and fall). The absolute minimum response time is two hours. When emergencies arise they are sometimes dealt with in the following ways: victims call family members; victims call the nursing stations. . . . Most people don't want to call the police because response from the police is slow. . . . When the police are called there is a long-distance telephone charge (which discourages women with low income) the calls are usually answered by someone in St. John's, Gander, or Corner Brook [all on the island of Newfoundland]. People are afraid to report crimes because they have to face the offender again and there is no police protection. Sometimes the police react as if they can't help when they encourage women not to press charges.

WHAT ARE THE PROBLEMS? [LOCAL WOMEN'S COMMENTS]
There is a lot of family violence, two women have been murdered in Rigolet.
. . . There is no safe house in our community, we don't know if it's safe to have one. Therefore, even though we know it is desperately needed, we have to say until the police are stationed here in Rigolet, having a safe house is out of the question. There is a lot of spousal abuse, two women were already murdered, one in late 1985 and one in early 1993. Most of the spouse abuse is known by the community, some of it is only known by family members. Spousal assault is becoming an accepted form of life, nobody pays attention to it anymore. Unspoken messages are being given to the victim (we don't care) into the abuser (it's okay). *That's what the silence is doing.* Since a beer license became available here last fall there is now more drinking, more children are being neglected. There is no social worker here, the help that is provided is provided by federal money, through LIHC, not from the Province. (emphasis added)

There are similar summary comments made by the residents of Makkovik and Postville:

Makkovik:
The bruises are not seen, no one says anything, everyone minds their own business. Children are suffering and witnessing. When the police visit they visit for only one day, there is no one in the community to handle extreme violence. . . . There are two residents of Makkovik on the police force but they are stationed elsewhere. Suicide attempts are kept confidential. When reports are made to the police, it is weeks before they come to check on it. If people do go to court to get off with a crime, there is nothing done.

Postville:
Sometimes the police won't respond because they have nowhere to put offenders. People see bruises and don't say any thing. There are no police, no social worker, there is no safe house. Sometimes women leave home to go to the clinic and we have a good nurse who lets them stay there until it is safe for them to go home. Some women leave their homes and go back again because there is nowhere to go, they walk around the community with the children. They are afraid to put other people in danger and they don't want to get families involved. There is elder abuse, youth taking advantage of them and taking their money. There are no budgeting skills. When we called the police we get St. John's, we have no direct dialing and it's hard to get through to police. We have no police presence, we are served from Hopedale, the police are too busy in Hopedale and Davis Inlet to help us. There is more teenage drinking, there is more child neglect due to drinking. The needs are there for a safe house, but without permanent police we would not be safe. There are not many planned police visits, they only come when they want to, not when they are needed.

I do not at all want to minimize the importance of people getting together to talk about their problems and to try to figure out solutions. And the Newfoundland government deserves praise for at least financing some of these meetings. But it is clear from these texts that a great many women are suffering very seriously—the domestic violence they experience can go very far beyond a black eye or some bruises—and it is equally clear that there is little, within what the government is willing to do or to finance, that they can achieve by way of stopping or altering this situation. As they so clearly and so heart-wrenchingly say, there is no such thing as a safe house without police to protect the house. In a small community everyone knows where the safe house is; nothing keeps an abused woman—and her children—from being followed there. That is why some women in trouble just take their children and walk around the community: they do not want to get their friends in danger by going there for sanctuary. And that is why the government's response to this situation is so appallingly inadequate. What percent of the $20 million the Germans paid to practice bombing on Native lands in Labrador would it have taken to effectively address this situation—if not to cure the impulse to effectively diminish the practice? Ten percent? Five percent? Five percent is $1 million.

Air and Land

During World War II, the United States, with Canadian assistance, built a large military air base at Goose Bay, at the inland edge of Hamilton Inlet, in central Labrador. During the war, the base was used for refueling supply aircraft on the journeys to and from Europe, and just after the war it was used for various relatively small-scale military and commercial purposes. In the 1970s NATO air forces realized that it was possible to send attack planes literally "under the radar." By flying at very low altitudes, one could sneak planes past radar defenses. But these flights supposedly take a substantial amount of pilot training. All of a sudden the Goose Bay air base had a new purpose in life, as Labrador's air space was rented, at substantial fees, to various NATO countries for training, with mostly Euro-Canadians getting the jobs for a quite massive endeavor, and mostly Innu and Inuit suffering—truly suffering—the effects. A large part of the controversy over the effects of these very low-level, often supersonic, flights focused on their impact on caribou and largely ignored their impact on people.

Peter Armitage, an expert on Innu culture history, began his discussion of the history of low-level flying over Innu country communities with a perceptive observation: "The paradox of our treatment of Native people is that we build museums to preserve and exhibit their cultural heritage, but through our actions and our attitudes we are party to their destruction as distinctive people" (1987, 3). He continues,

> In 1965, the Royal Air Force (RAF) [of Great Britain] began low level training with Vulcan Bombers. Since 1979, such training activities have grown year by year ... and expanding to include Luftwaffe F-4 Phantom II and Alpha jets, RAF Jaguars, and Tornado fighter-bombers. For the first time in the autumn of 1983, Luftwaffe Phantom II jets flew repeatedly over the camps of Innut from the community of La Romain. . . .

Lt Colonel Ross [of the Canadian Air Force said] . . . Canada will have the opportunity to contribute positively to the strengthening of the NATO alliance by providing an excellent training facility. Our prestige abroad will increase. . . . On December 7, 1983 the Canadian and West German government signed an agreement in Brussels whereby Canada agreed to a three-year extension of the Luftwaffe training activities in the Peninsula in return for $20 million. . . . Following this (July 1984) the federal and provincial (Newfoundland) governments approved a Luftwaffe request for two bombing ranges, despite Innu protests about the possible negative environmental impact of bombing activities and the violation of their collective rights to the territory which these training activities entail. (Armitage 1987, 4–5)

Starting in 1981 there were about fifteen hundred low-level flights a year (about six a day), which increased "to over 6,000 in 1988 and is projected to reach a maximum of 18,000 per year by 1996" (Harrington and Veitch 1991, 328). In the training areas the flights are designed to go thirty meters—a bit less than one hundred feet—above ground level; in the spaces between the training areas, which are more heavily used as hunting, trapping, and transport routes by Innu and Inuit, the planes are supposedly restricted to flying no lower than eighty meters—about 262 feet—above ground level. Six thousand flights a year, with a maximum of fifty usable weeks and five usable days per week, makes a minimum average of twenty-four flights a day somewhere in the practice zones—but no one in these zones knows where or when; eighteen thousand flights a year is triple that.

Much of the controversy surrounding these flights focused on their effects on caribou. The issue at stake is simple: deer and caribou, in the winter, usually have a very narrow margin of energy input/output, with most of the calories they get needed for warmth. If they run any distance, and spend their calories doing that, they often freeze to death. So the question became, did these flights run the caribou? Harrington and Veitch, in the article quoted above, claim not far enough to matter, as did the government hearings, with the non-Native population in central Labrador pushing hard to keep the flights and the associated support-services employment.

A supersonic flight one hundred or three hundred feet above the ground cannot be seen in advance. The realization that you have been overflown first comes with an extremely loud supersonic bang. I have spoken with Innu who told me that they were canoeing downriver, dropped their paddle in their startle, and had their canoe crash into the rocks or turn over. Women have often complained in the hearings that their children run or scream in terror, that they have spilled pots and burned themselves while cooking, and so forth. But Canada makes a lot of money from leasing Native lands to NATO, and Euro-Canadians—and a few Inuit—have gotten a lot of airport jobs.

One of the many upsets in researching the Native peoples' situations is the casual and cavalier ways that simplistic anthropological and psychological concepts have been used to justify the continuing devastation that is imposed on Native peoples. For a prime example I want to quote from one section of the *Canadian Public Health Association Task Force on the Health Effects of Increased Flying Activity in the Labrador area: the Interim Report*, July 1986.[19]

[SECTION] 6.2.2 STRESS

The effects of psychological stress brought about by rapid social and economic change is of particular concern to the native Indian people of the area. The amount of change that Indian people and Labrador have experienced in recent years has been well recognized and the population is demonstrating many of the ... commonly occurring effects of very rapid culture change. Research on social indicators shows that death by violence, including suicide, have increased dramatically within the Indian population in recent years. Similarly, alcoholism and alcohol-related disorders are often increased. For these people, culture change is not the slow, evolutionary process, rather it has been a rapid, revolutionary process.

The anticipated development of the air base ... will produce another stimulus for very rapid social, cultural and economic change that will affect the Indian population in the area. Rapid economic development in what is essentially a single industry community will increase stress level through the action of typical and predictable boomtown phenomena. ...

Native people can be expected to experience tensions related to value conflicts, changes in traditional lifestyle and changes within the population age structure. These tensions will produce an increase in the level of stress experienced by many of the native Indian people.

... The native populations will also experience stress related to the actual increase in jet aircraft flights over the territory. A certain amount of this stress will be directly attributable to the startle reactions experienced as aircraft pass overhead. A larger component of the stress will likely be attributable to people's increased levels of anxiety due to the entire issue of aircraft overflight. The task force has observed that this process is already operating. Many native people report that they are now nervous about going into the countryside because of the possibility of being overflown. The task force has also observed that there is a marked tendency for people to attribute a wide variety of physical and emotional symptoms to the present increase incidence of overflights. There is apparently a generalized anxiety about the overflights that is producing this phenomena.

There are those who would deal with this issue of psychological stress by eliminating the overflights entirely. If there are no overflights there would be no stress. Unfortunately this somewhat simple holistic solution will probably not be feasible. . . . A more realistic approach to the problem of stress would involve assisting native people to develop specific coping techniques in order to more successfully adapt to the presence of aircraft in the skies above them. It is often more feasible to assist people to learn specific techniques of coping with stress than it is to rely on the elimination of the cause of the stress. (16–17)

The title of this report is "Increased Flying Activity"—not low-level, supersonic bombing runs. The problem becomes the literally overwhelming arrogance and unconcern of the state and its hired agents—who are probably angling to be hired again to teach Native peoples "techniques of coping with stress." From the perspective of Native peoples the key issue is what can be done about this. It is an immensely difficult problem, more difficult than can be readily contemplated, by us or by the Native peoples, for people who have become, in the eyes and morality of the dominant, utterly disposable (particularly if it can be done quietly, and under the pretext of care) have few possibilities for successful opposition—not none, and that is absolutely crucial, but only few.

In September 1988 a number of Innu set up their tents and started living in the middle of a bombing range about sixty-five miles south of Goose Bay. A week after this about two hundred Innu set up their tents at the end of the runway. That brought a stop to the low-level practice bombing sorties, and it also brought a very assertive police force to arrest and jail the protestors. Seventy-five were charged with "public mischief." Eleven refused bail under the bail conditions by which they had to promise not to protest further, and they were still in jail a month later. The irony of this situation, where the Canadian government is insisting on promises from the Innu, when it has never kept any of theirs to them, seems to have escaped Canadian notice. In another wonderful note, one newspaper that carried this story was the *Sunday Times Colonist* of Victoria, British Columbia (October 9, 1988).

The Innu had no quick or decisive impact on the flights, but they made enough trouble for long enough that it helped to wind this practice down, eventually completely, as European governments came under popular pressure for destroying Indians. It also helped people to mobilize protest against the subsequent expansion of the hydroelectric dams that destroy Native lands. And whatever Innu protests both could and could not accomplish in terms of changing government policies and practices, it seems, with suggestive but scant evidence (beyond comments in passing), that the suicide, substance abuse, and domestic violence rates went significantly down during the protest years, from the early 1980s to the early 1990s.

Why not look for the statistics on this possible change in suicide rates? Because they are too unreliable. Almost all Innu children, including suicide victims, are buried in the churchyard, even though Catholic doctrine denies most suicides "Christian burial." A similar situation holds with the Moravians, where suicides are supposed, by hearsay at least, to be buried on the path to the graveyard, so that people step over them on the way to the cemetery. Hardly any, if any, suicides recently are so treated by Catholics or Moravians. My hunch is that this is a "deal" to suppress complaints about the various forms of abuse that drove children in that direction. Whether or not the protests diminished the suicides in ways that show up in the statistics is scarcely possible to determine in the context of statistics that have, at least until the recent past, minimized the practice. So on the basis of scant, mostly hearsay evidence, I tend to accept the possibility that collective self-destruction declined significantly in the years of active Innu protest. It raises a crucial possibility: that people do not have to actually take control of their lives to give themselves a healing, or a partially healing, dignity; an active and committed struggle toward that end of communal self-control suffices, at least somewhat. More protests might help to clarify this possibility.

Hunting the Hunters

In the early 1980s, just as the low-level flying protests were increasing, and the anger over the seizure of their best and most special hunting territory for the reservoir was also boiling up, the Newfoundland government decided to clamp down even harder on Native hunting:

> Tough new hunting laws that came into force in December will place unreasonable burdens on native hunters and Labrador and could adversely affect Inuit land claims, a native rights group said Monday. But the Newfoundland government said everyone will be treated fairly and that the laws are necessary to cut down on poaching.

Four Inuit hunters who were arrested after a helicopter raid on the hunting camp last November are the last to be charged under the old law, which provided for a $500 fine for a first offense and optional forfeiture of vehicles and firearms.

But the new law which carries a minimum $1000 fine, automatic forfeiture of any equipment used and a possible jail term is too much, says the Indian and Inuit Support Group of Newfoundland and Labrador. The volunteer association says the new law will put most of those charged with illegal hunting in jail and jeopardize native land claims in the north.

The issue with land claims is indeed crucial. Native rights were then primarily based on something called "aboriginal title." As Native people do not have the usual western title deed documents, aboriginal title was held to be based on continuity of traditional use. This perspective, limiting and unrealistic as it was,[20] was crucial to the victory of the Cree people in their fight against Hydro-Québec's development of the James Bay hydroelectric project, which appropriated vast regions of Cree lands. It probably seemed to the Newfoundland government, which was more careful than to put their intentions on paper, that they could foreclose this very serious possibility by making the usual Native hunting practices nearly impossible. The text continues:

> Newfoundland's natives are unique in Canada because they are not recognized as status Indians under the Indian act as they are in the rest of the country. That means their hunting rights and responsibilities are the same as those of any other Newfoundlander. Their non-status also seems to bear on native land claims in Labrador. Premier Brian Peckford has said their claims carry some merit, but no action has been taken towards settlement. And the question of status for Labrador Indians appear stalled. . . . Adrian Chanter, Vice President of the support group, said in an interview the new wildlife laws will drive more natives into towns in Labrador, further eroding their land claims and leading to more social problems in the native population. . . .
>
> Enforcement of the new laws he said includes helicopter borne raids on hunting camps and house to house searches in Inuit and Innu communities in search of illegally obtained caribou meat. . . .
>
> Biologists estimate the Labrador caribou herd to contain 250,000 animals. A wildlife officer admitted the main herd is in no danger from native hunters.[21]

It is reasonably clear here that Native people are being bullied and Native lives diminished to serve what the Newfoundland government regards as a higher purpose—the unfettered development of Labrador for what seems

Newfoundland's own interests. Two points are of special interest here: the contract written with Hydro-Québec was a massive giveaway from Newfoundland to Québec, so that the *entire* benefits of this development have gone to Québec. Newfoundland has since gone to court to try and reverse this total giveaway, but utterly without success. Had they included the Labrador Native people in the development process, this could not have happened, so there is the minuscule satisfaction that in diminishing Native people they diminished themselves even more. Not that this satisfaction does Native people any good; it just provides an iota of justice to a profoundly unjust situation, a potential lesson from which subsequent Newfoundland and Canadian governments have learned absolutely nothing at all.

This leads to the second point to be drawn from this miserable affair: the whole land claims process, where Canada and Newfoundland are supposed to "give" Native peoples their rights, or some of them, is organized to muscle Native peoples out of any real rights. Once again this is leading to both the diminishment of what could be a better and more respectful life for Native people and some real gains for Canadians as a whole. If Native lands are polluted by uranium mining on or adjacent to the few lands that are "given back" to Natives, under imposed conditions and without the information needed for protection, it will not be just Native people that suffer and die—small justice, if any, for the pollution is not at all likely to reach into the lives of the people that were ultimately responsible.[22]

At the core of what was happening in the period since Newfoundland joined Canada is this pervasive and destructive attempt to deny Native peoples their Native status, and to harness this denial, and the Native people themselves, to the unfettered use of Labrador by the state and commercial interests. Starting in the 1990s, the state was forced, by legal pressure, to recognize that Native peoples existed and had some enforceable rights. As we shall see in the next chapter, the task of the state was to try to use this recognition for the same ends as before. And the task of the Native peoples was to try to deal with this new situation, to struggle both against it and within it. This has turned out to be quite difficult to do well.

SEVEN

Today May Become Tomorrow

Our Culture and/or Our Children

In the 1980s the Canadian and Newfoundland governments, with some concern for future possible legal problems with their northern development plans, began to offer to "settle" land claims with Native peoples. In Labrador this did not become an active process until the mid-1990s. And in Labrador the Innu and the Inuit have had completely different kinds of participation in the land claims process. The Innu have yet (as of December 2011) to fully sign on to a land claims agreement, but the Inuit, in 2005, offered to pay every single adult enrolled member of their nation $5,000 if they would vote in the election required to approve the land claims settlement, as indeed the vast majority did.

This very substantial difference turns out to be driven by much the same reasons: land claims, as organized by the Canadian government, give Native peoples a lot of rights and take away a lot of rights. It thus puts Native peoples in a very difficult position—do they get what it seems can only be gotten from the state, or do they try not to give away much of what they know they are due?

The whole deeply contradictory process of making and accepting land claims with and against the Canadian state turns out to be just the introduction to a range of crucial issues, half-hidden beneath the surface of land claims. Land is itself neither rights nor recompense for imposed suffering, not even recompense for what the dominant society does not pretend to justify even to itself, and so now feels it should make recompense for, such as the rapes and beatings and violent suppression of Native languages that characterized life in residential schools. But rights to land, while making amends for none of this, are not trivial, not at all.

Two dynamics are at issue here. In the 1990s, while the land claims process was starting to be a real possibility, there was an intense collapse of the social relations of everyday life in Native communities—the kind of everyday life that reaches more or less effectively toward tomorrow. Then in the early 2000s, while things in general stayed difficult and destructive, there was a partial turnaround, the beginnings of a long reach toward tomorrow. The point of spending some time looking at the first issue—the collapse of the social relations of everyday life in the 1990s—is that it helps us understand the magnificence of the accomplishments that came in the early 2000s. Thus, the two dynamics that are at issue here are the land claims process, which was the passion of the political elite and the Native activists, whether they were for it or more cautious, and the changing dynamics of the daily lives of ordinary people. In each of these much was accomplished, and there were both substantial gains and important losses.[1]

To begin, it is important to consider the possibility that neither the efforts of the Canadian and Newfoundland governments to help Native people nor Native governments' own actions, while making some quite important contributions to Native well-being, have been very effective in forging this new partial turnaround. What has happened has largely happened at the level of the daily life of ordinary people. And this turns out to be much more difficult to understand or explain than the specific actions of political elites and organizations.

The Newfoundland and Canadian governments radiate an inability to act effectively when it comes to helping Native peoples, as hard as some workers may try and however much money the governments spend.[2] And more than being ineffective, government programs in many cases open up a gulf between the government agents and the people who need help, at times both helping and alienating many people. We start with a powerful example.

In January 2004, Colleen White, a recent social work graduate from Memorial University, St. John's, Newfoundland, returned to St. John's from seven months of social work in Sheshatshiu.[3] She circulated to members of Parliament a typescript paper she wrote, trying to identify and especially to remedy the problems with the organization of social work in Labrador that prevented actually helping Native peoples (White 2004).[4] A long description of the contents of this paper even made it into the front page of a St. John's Sunday newspaper (*Sunday Independent*, May 30, 2004).

Her essay begins, "Child, Youth, and Family Services in Sheshatshiu is at present a completely reactionary agency that fails miserably even in its ability to react." She starts her description of the problems with an example of a woman who left Sheshatshiu for Natuashish (the new Innu community on the mainland by Davis Island) to work and sent the child she had been given for foster care back to its parents, without even notifying the agency, which found out weeks later. It is hard to tell whether this is an evasion of responsibility on the part of the woman who gave the child back to its parents or an attempt by Native people to work things out for themselves. The agency is, however, responsible for that child once it has been given a foster care placement, and it is both surprising and significant, whatever the cause, that in a village this small none of the four social workers had any idea where the child was, or who was—or was not—caring for it. Nor was this an unusual example: Colleen White points out that in one only somewhat unusual week four children placed in foster care were turned over to another caregiver by their foster parent/s, with no one notifying the agency: "There is a complete lack of preparatory work done with caregivers and placements are found on a random basis, where the willingness of almost any community member to care for children qualifies them as a caregiver. Also, children are often placed with caregivers without a social worker having met with them, or having anything explained to them—other than when they will receive their first support payment. The result has been the haphazard placement of children." The essay continues, "Even more disturbing is the reality that social workers do not know the names of all their clients after four or five months on the job, let alone the struggles being experienced. If children and their families are not in the throes of crisis and despair they are ignored."

White claims that social workers who know children who are living in families with significant problems with alcohol, violence, and neglect usually make no response until the child gets into trouble, resorting to "gas-sniffing delinquency and sexual promiscuity to ease the pain. Rather than working with these families, to identify their needs and make the necessary referrals, the child or youth is targeted as the problem and is either incarcerated or is sent [out of the community] for treatment, sometimes three or four times, for months at a time, always placed back in the same family situation."

The concept here of "necessary referrals" assumed that there are, or at that time were, skilled child helpers available, which is a bit of a stretch. And Native people may or may not do better at arranging care among themselves, a point Ms. White does not raise. But the issue here is actually not that but the disconnect between government officials and what is actually happening in the villages. She points out that social workers in Sheshatshiu have more than double the caseload of social workers elsewhere in Newfoundland, and this is one factor that makes it difficult to do the job well.

This is 2004, in an Innu community, and a government agency that was known, in Colleen White's assessment, primarily for two activities: taking children away from parents, and issuing payments. It is clear that there has been a great deal of anger in the community against this agency. "On several occasions in the past files have been completely destroyed due to fire and vandalism.... [Social workers there told her] of coming to work one morning and finding files strewn around the parking lot and in the trees outside." This may be a very understandable reaction to a state agency that takes children from parents for foster placement—one more assault from a state that has perpetrated so many assaults—but children are ordinarily taken for reasons of severe neglect or abuse.

Unfortunately, the problems of Sheshatshiu are more widespread and have been long-lasting, partly—only partly—because no one seems to be effectively addressing them, sometimes including the political elite of the community.

To continue and to expand a story I started in chapter 4, in May of 2010 I was in Nain, just visiting. I went with the people I was visiting to the town bar, to see the scene, to have a beer, and just to relax. Characteristically outsiders go with a few five-dollar bills in their pocket. A local Inuit or two joins you at the table, you buy him or her or both a beer, and a half hour or so later, when they realize you will not buy another of these small twelve-ounce glasses, and the conversation also runs dry, they leave the table, to quickly be replaced by another person and another conversation. By 10:30 at night the place was getting potentially a bit rough, and as I am in my seventies and no longer up to dealing with that kind of turmoil, I left with my friends.

Just outside the bar was a young boy, about eight or nine years old, in only a short-sleeve shirt, shivering and tearful. Temperatures in May can drop 25 or 30 degrees Fahrenheit from day to night, and at this point in the evening it was a few degrees above freezing. The young boy asked us if his parents were in the bar; we got their names, went back inside, and asked the bartender. They were not there.

The boy had been locked out of his house. Some years earlier, in Davis Island, a house had burned down and six children died while their parents were out drinking. To avoid such a situation and the consequences that would be imposed by both the state and the community if something similar happened again, parents sometimes put their children out and lock the door when they go off drinking.

I held out my hand to the boy, who spoke English, and said, "Take my hand and I will walk you to your grandparents' house." He looked at me for a minute or so and replied, "I'm afraid of them. They hit me." I stayed with him while my friend went and talked with the people where he was living, and they found an elder woman who would take the child in for the night.

Now the story gets complicated, in part because of my upset, which kept me from seeing more productive ways of helping. The next morning I went to the Inuit government offices, a quite new, multimillion-dollar, very fine and well-furnished building, largely paid for by mining royalties. Upstairs I got to see an official, in charge of something relevant to this child, told the story, noted that it was very likely not unique, and urged opening a safe house for preteenagers (I know people can be a bit scared of the teenagers, who when they are high can be rather unpredictable). I suggested that all it would take is a room or two in the schoolhouse, some cots, blankets, milk, and cookies, and an elder or two or three, which, with all the unemployment and all the revenues from mining, should not be much of a problem.

Much to my surprise, I was quickly and decisively turned down: "What did you say your name was?" "Where did you say you were from?" "New York is an interesting place: I would like to visit it one day." Now with some time to reflect on this dismissal, I have a bit more perspective. I very much should not have just gone into an office saying what I thought might well be done about a long-standing problem—there were much slower, more cautious ways of opening a discussion on safe-house possibilities. At the moment I was too upset to realize this. Having grown up in an abusive family, my tolerance for incremental or slowly developing solutions was here, unfortunately, approximately zero. It gets worse, with misrepresentations—I like to think on both sides—piling one on top of the other.

On the way out I stopped to look at a very large picture that hung in the lobby, as the primary decoration of that space. It was a depiction of one version of the myth of Sedna, about four feet high. Sedna as portrayed in this picture is an Alaskan Inuit myth—three thousand miles away—about a young girl who goes ocean fishing with her father. They quarrel, and he throws her overboard. She tries to climb back into the boat, and he cuts her fingers off with his fishing knife, so she falls back in the ocean and drowns, becoming the goddess of ocean storms and ocean creatures. There was this huge image in the lobby of a young girl sliding back into the ocean with bloody stumps where her fingers once were, very large panicky eyes, and her mouth open as if in a silent scream. I went back upstairs, knowing it would do no good, to see another official and asked, "How do you think a little girl feels who comes here for help, because she is being beaten or raped by her stepfather or an uncle, or just because she needs an adult to talk with, and sees that picture on the wall?"

The answer I got, this time with a smile, was, "It is our culture." And having their own culture is indeed crucial to their effective land claims, a substantial part of how they can get the mining royalties that pay for such fancy tribal offices and the high salaries of the Inuit officials. But it is, or more precisely was, not their culture. The Inuit migrated to Labrador from Greenland, mostly in the fifteenth century. In Greenland the myth of Sedna is different than the version from Alaska: in the Greenland version, their history, she turns into a bird and flies away.

For my part I should have known better than to go back upstairs; for his, had he done something that more specifically addressed the problem, rather than making up claims about his supposed culture that became real by being nailed to a wall—as are the children—we both might have been more productive. For the issue, the absolute central issue on which I think we both failed, is doing something about the needs of children and other vulnerable people. We both were probably trying, each in our own way, but . . .

His idea of culture helped lift the Labrador Inuit out of poverty; mine at least kept me from the innocence that pervades the all-too-abstract concepts of anthropology: kinship, social structure, social organization, and, most of all, culture. There are many situations where these concepts prevent you from seeing the world as it is and as it is experienced in the daily lives of many. One cannot just throw these concepts out, because they have become part of the popular vocabulary and ideology of people, part of the lives that some live, and some must live both with and against.

Figure 7.1. Heather Igloliorte's wonderful and dramatic conte drawing *Sedna* (2001). Used by permission of the artist.

In this context, where anthropology is handed back to you—"It is our culture"—what is anthropology? What is a useful anthropology? I don't know how to completely answer this question, but, for a start, let me offer this: In 1973 the anthropologist Clifford Geertz published what became a very popular phrase in both anthropology and social history: "Believing, with Max Weber, that man is an animal suspended in webs of significance he himself has spun, I take culture to be those webs" (1973, chapter 1). All of a sudden culture became webs of significance, or more broadly, webs of meaning, with the sexism of this quote completely ignored. But webs are spun by spiders to catch and devour flies; webs are in no way just there between the beams or the branches, just neutrally and innocently present. Whatever else culture once was or now is, it is now always about inequality: transforming it, localizing it, creating it, trapping people within it, making it necessary to oppose or evade it—all this, simultaneously and sequentially, all this and much more. And meanwhile the children stand there, shivering and crying, left out in the cold. We must never make peace with that, or separate ourselves from that, whatever else we think and do about the issues such instances present us with.[5]

Children are so compelling a metaphor because they are not responsible for the world that does what it does to them. But they are only a metaphor for a much larger range of problems.

IN 1992, ON Valentine's Day, which local Innu said matters (Innu Nation and Mushuau Innu Band Council 1995, xiii), an Innu house burned down in Davis Island, in a community that had no fire protection, and six young children from one family burned to death. People did not know whether or not the children were in the house when it was on fire. This horrendous situation led to several community meetings that sought to deal with a range of problems, from parents who left their children alone while they went drinking to communities that had no water supply, fire hydrants, fire trucks, or systematic methods for dealing with house fires, as well as houses that were so poorly insulated that it took a lot of make-do heating to get some warmth. When Davis Island was built, in 1967, all this was promised to the Innu— water, sewerage, insulated and heated houses, houses with basements—but twenty-five years later is clearly not enough time for Canada to do what it promised.

The deteriorating situation in the village also led, just one year after this fire, to the Innu town constable, Simon Jacobish, videoing another six youths, ages eleven to fourteen, with plastic shopping bags in their hand, each with some gasoline in it, sniffing. One child screamed at the camera, "I want to die!" Others said they wanted to keep sniffing gasoline. The video was subsequently shown on the Canadian national news network, complete with commentary about how harsh life was *made to be* in that community, and both the Canadian government and the townspeople were pressured to do something.[6] We will shortly address what the townspeople did and tried to do, but we start with the Canadian government.

Before we can unravel some threads of this situation, we should note that eighteen years later, the Canadian news was full of stories about a similar incident in a Cree community in far northern Ontario, on the shores of James Bay, where once again people are wintering in tents and tarp-covered shacks with no sewerage and no insulation, while the Canadian government does nothing useful or effective.[7] The government does make a lot of speeches, and from time to time spends money—usually without asking the people for whom it is supposedly being spent how it might best be allocated. We might also usefully note, as background for understanding the depth of Canada's concern for Native peoples, that Australia, where the Aborigines have similar problems, has developed a gasoline called Pearl, from which one cannot get high, which is the only gas available on and near Native reserves. Canada has done nothing to implement this possibility: disposable people really are disposable, if only they would go quietly.

By the mid-1990s Canada was promising in speeches and press releases to get the Innu out of their impossible community, the one Canada persisted in calling Davis Inlet (referred to here as Davis Island), and to build a new community back on the mainland. Years later, years behind promise and schedule, it finally got built, and Innu moved in in the fall of 2002 and the spring of 2003. The community has been given an Innu name, Natuashish (see map 4, chapter 6); it was built at an announced cost of $52 million and was designed to be "Native" in its structure.[8] This did not for once mean no water, sewerage, or proper insulation, but a community with clusters of houses, so kin groups could live close to one another.

Even though Natuashish was actually a quite well built community, with solid houses that have piped water and sewerage, a community recreation and meeting place, and a sturdy and well-heated school, the problems have persisted. I don't know why; no voices from the community have effectively addressed this, and the government engages this problem like a fish engages a bicycle—it flops around a lot. Perhaps history is not easily made into the past by people who have been forced to live it.

In the spring of 2004, one year after Natuashish was fully settled and Davis Island closed, a thirteen-year-old girl was abducted by an eighteen-year-old youth, who lured her out past the edge of town with the promise of drugs or alcohol and held her forcefully in a tent just outside town for three weeks, until she escaped. During this time, he shot her several times with a BB gun, beat her intensely, and raped her repeatedly. No one in the town claimed to know anything, to have been aware of what was happening, or reported her as missing.

It feels like the end of the world, or the end of this world. But people keep going. And that, simultaneously, is the mystery, the triumph, and the loss.

When I asked, just earlier, what is anthropology? I think an answer has to start here.

The Chaos of Order

The utterly fictional and destructive name *Sheshatshit* now reveals its power, both in that village and in Davis Island. It names the package of imposed and inescapable social order that is, simultaneously, imposed and inescapable chaos. This context, which more specifically is a denial of both a livable today and a viable tomorrow, often seems to lead to a profound diminishment of caring among the people who suffer its consequences. Here it is crucial to be specific. People do not at all stop caring. Indeed, that is the problem. Caring becomes more difficult, nearly impossible to do effectively, and so it calls forth substitutes.

Most of all this is not due to people becoming nasty or aggressive but, to emphasize, because effective caring becomes impossible. For a father or a mother in this situation, your children or your spouse across the table from you, in the room with you, in your face with their needs, present you with what you cannot do, obligations you cannot fulfill, needs you cannot meet. Many children have skin diseases from the lack of water in the house; many times the breakfast food is frozen when the family wakes up—the house is that cold. In that sense—the sense that they confront you with what the state has made it impossible for you to do for them and with them—they are, or they seem to be, your antagonist. I need a drink to ease my pain, my anger at this situation, and maybe also my anger at them for confronting me with what I cannot do. With a drink I can at least take care of myself; with a sniff of gasoline at least some of my needs get met. Or maybe this is too neat a formulation about lives lived in imposed chaos.

We need to return to the point that history, for people who live it, can be very difficult to put in the past. We know this from the so-called post-traumatic stress disorders, the continuing stress injuries, of veterans who have experienced, and themselves perpetrated, horrors. They do not shake off the problems or their history by coming back home; to the contrary. We do not yet know the equivalence for people who live their everyday lives in the midst of imposed destruction.

Colin Samson and his colleagues gave a wonderfully sensitive description of the brutalization of the Innu at Utshimassits (as the Innu call the community that Newfoundland calls Davis Inlet and I more specifically call Davis Island, although it is on an island with another map name; Samson et al. 1999). The booklet, which is now available online, starts with charts about infant mortality in Canada, Sheshatshiu, and Utshimassits.[9] Sheshatshiu's rate is vastly higher than the national rate, and Utshimassits's is double that of Sheshatshiu. The differences in how people are treated and how they are sustained have all-too-real and all-too-deplorable consequences. It is the treatment we need to focus on, to get a sense of what is happening.

Samson quotes an Innu: "One time, the priest [the new one, after Father O'Brien was removed] saw me and my grandfather returning from *nutshimut* [their hunting territory, now Smallwood Reservoir] in a canoe. He was really mad [because I was not in school]. He got hold of my ear and almost pulled it off. Then he took a paddle and beat my grandfather with it" (Samson et al. 1999, 19). It is impossible to tell what "lessons" this more direct schooling taught. It is more than likely that helplessness to protect people near and dear to you was one. The other may be that power and authority express themselves— or more, define themselves—by the capacity to exercise violence with impunity. Before we completely blame the community for not better protecting that thirteen-year-old girl, we need to consider this lesson about people's inability to protect one another. And it was more than one evil, sadistic priest. Another Innu told Samson, "The people never struck or threatened to strike their kids ... before we first made contact with the white man. ... Innu eventually learned these actions towards kids ... when the priests and nuns first taught Innu children they were very strict and enforced discipline when Innu children misbehaved. That was the beginning of the Innu change in behavior in disciplining their kids" (Samson et al. 1999, 20–21). The first part of this quote, about Innu never hitting or threatening to hit their kids, may or may not be a bit of a romanticization, but it is doubtful that people who are not in violently unequal relations ever treated their children the way this priest taught.

And there is one further nightmare possibility. Nympha Byrne and Camille Fouillard, in their excellent recounting of Innu women's life histories (2000), show, without singling it out for comment, that orphan girls were formerly often very badly treated in the so-called traditional hunting and trapping country life. We have seen that this was a very difficult life, for reasons that had more to do with domination than climate. But if a pattern was established then of pressing hard on orphans, with both work demanded and food and care rewarded, as seems the case on evidence of several life stories in their book, then it may be that when the priest beat the grandfather in front of the child, and the child was tortured with ear pulls, with the child not able to protect the grandfather, nor the grandfather the child, in some ways, with the removal of the grandfather as the loving protector, the child—children in general in this context—became an orphan.

This will sound unbelievably, foolishly harsh, and I am not at all advocating it, but definitely advocating the need to consider why it was not done: it is profoundly unclear why at this time or at the next possible opportunity the priest was not shot and buried in an unmarked forest grave by the Innu whom he so intensely mistreated and humiliated. People get lost and die in the woods all the time—or just forced out of the community by collective action. We have to consider that for a variety of reasons, from their own decency, to their Catholic religion, to the long history of a prior priest—Father O'Brien—protecting and nourishing them, when many would have otherwise starved to death, getting rid of this brutal priest was not an option. And then, with particular impact on the current situation, we must consider the long-term consequences of this not being seen as an option, and this is the point—including about what is called development.

Aboriginal Land Claims and Corporate Mining Claims

The context for land claims is as influential in shaping what happens as are the land claims themselves. This context is only partly described by the fact that a number of Canadian court cases, starting in the 1990s, have held that Native peoples had enforceable rights to their aboriginal territories. Unless and until this situation was clarified—it was made specific who had what rights—development might be followed by disruptive and very high cost lawsuits. The corporation that developed the huge Voisey's Bay nickle mines on Inuit and Innu lands, starting in the early 1990s, repeatedly told the Inuit people, at a meeting to discuss the beginning of operations, that the corporation had to have "predictability." (This meeting will be discussed subsequently.) This need for predictability shaped much of how Native rights developed, or were allowed to develop by the state and corporations.

Here a different and broader part of the whole process of Native rights is also very much at issue. The whole process of court-ordered granting of Native people some specific rights, particularly to land, necessarily required building up and stabilizing the Native governments that held these land rights. Native governments needed to enter into contracts with the state and corporations over the use of this land in return for recompense, particularly cash, jobs, and some subcontracting. In sum, Native governments had to be further developed, with office buildings, "consultants," large enough budgets so the council could fly off to meetings and "training sessions," and elections that could in some ways pass muster. These elections, however, have included very large shipments of what I call musical beer to Innu communities, to help orchestrate the electoral dance outcome, with no effective whistle-blowing possible, although the way elections have been conducted deeply and openly upset many Innu people. The Inuit have orchestrated their electoral dance by using cash not to buy votes but to buy voting. In that context people could themselves figure out how they should vote.

Building up Native governments, both by Native people and by the state, in the context of seeking more or less effectively to coordinate Native land rights with the needs of the state and corporations, became associated with elaborating the performance and display manifestations of what became called Native culture. This display of Native culture was effectively used as part of the rationale for Native claims against corporations and the state. There was very little in these displays that actually had any roots in daily life of the locale, although the fact that Innu or Inuit culture is on open display likely has quite positive associations.

Jeremy Beckett (2012), with insight gained from almost six decades of working with and for Australian Aborigines and Torres Straits Islanders, has labeled this whole process, which in Australia started in the 1970s, "re-indigenization." He has discussed it in ways that suggest its dual impact.

On the one hand, this re-indigenization gives, to some Native people at least, dignity, a contribution to positive identity formation and maintenance, and jobs, for the whole process has both direct bureaucratic and fiscal components and supports Native community programs and tourism. Yet ordinary Native people can, as Beckett shows, approach the whole subject, including their own history, with great care and caution—another manifestation of living history.

My sense is that Native people know that this current flamboyance of the displays of Native culture has little to do with their needs and feelings, and the fiscal flamboyance of Native governments built on mining royalties and state subsidies has only a brief tomorrow, for reasons that cannot be reduced to just the time span of the mine, although that is indeed short. The nickle mine that substantially underwrote a very fancy set of Inuit tribal offices when it opened in 1995 was scheduled to run out of ore and close in 2019. Those who still hunt and fish have a different sense of history, today, and tomorrow. In this context privatized values and beliefs may well be more secure than public displays, and the source of more of what little stability is possible.

Moreover, the flamboyant displays of government and especially of public culture—and beyond these specific arenas, the whole process of re-indigenization—are becoming associated with two kinds of losses. First, Inuit and Innu now have some rights, but these are mostly granted rights. So Native peoples collect royalties from mining, but they do not seem to be able to seriously control pollution. Royalties are today, for the money is quickly spent. Pollution is primarily about tomorrow.

Second, the whole flamboyance of government, with fancy offices, substantial salaries and expense accounts, and the often costly performance of culture, constructs a wedge in the community, for the majority of the ordinary people in Native communities neither can enjoy the fruits of office nor can afford to participate in what is displayed as "their culture." What Native people have now by way of rights is better than the absence of rights they had before. On this there is not a shred of doubt. All I am trying to show here is that within these irreplaceable gains there are significant problems, particularly for the nonelite Native peoples.

LAND CLAIMS BEGIN and end with three impositions. First, Native peoples will get specific rights but in return must, as the state says, renounce all their other rights and claims. Second, what they will get is a small portion of their original lands and in addition a cash payment for giving up, supposedly forever, everything else. Third, the entire cost of their land claim process—multiple years and vast numbers of hours each year of expensive Canadian lawyers, law firms, and researchers—will be deducted from this cash settlement. The process is arranged, once again, so that Euro-Canadians benefit greatly from what is "given to" or "done for" Native people. It might help quiet down a bit of the uproar that conservative Canadians usually make over how much of "their" tax monies are "given" to Native peoples if it were stated how much of this went straight into the pockets of Euro-Canadians.

Land claims require demonstrating "traditional use and occupancy" from colonial times onward, and this takes very substantial amounts of research to do. Canada brags that it is progressive because its courts accept oral history (Brody 1981), but it passes the entire charge for gathering this evidence by "experts" onto the Native people making their claim, as if Canada had no responsibility for putting Native people in this situation. Canada pays the fees of the lawyers and law firms, as well as the small army of academic "recognized experts" who do the research, and all of it comes off the settlement at the end. Canada only starts the settlement process—by formal appeal from Native peoples to do so, years before the actual process starts—with Native peoples it knows in advance will win, so Canada will not itself pay for the lawyers and researchers who do the work of demonstrating what Canada and the previous colonial regimes took. Many, probably most, of the lawyers and consultants work hard and well—that is not the point. The point is just to introduce the stacking of the deck, the difference between the announced settlement, when it is finally announced decades after the claim is made, and what Native people actually get. Would that the difference between what was given and what is gotten were only financial. It is overshadowed by the difference between rights and effective rights.

Canada has insisted, in the land claims process, on the Native people having a governmental entity—a fancy term for government—that would have the authority to commit their people to one settlement or another. But the government that was required for this land claims process had to meet Canadian ideas of what a Native government should be, elections and all, and this usually bore little if any relationship to Native practices of self-organizing or self-governing.

In 1994 an Inuit political organization, the Inuit Tapirisat of Canada, presented the document "Self-Government Discussion Paper: Western Legal Frameworks and the Self-Government Rights of Aboriginal Peoples" (Inuit Tapirisat 1994). It is a very thoughtful and well-developed analysis of the whole issue of self-government as it became embedded in the struggle for land rights.

The document points out that when the European colonists claimed land by discovery, by possession, by conquest, or for other reasons, they were simultaneously claiming full sovereignty over this land and the people/s on it. This sovereignty included, in the eyes of the Europeans, the right to make laws and to govern the people/s on the land according to these laws. These were principles and practices of discovery that the Europeans arranged with one another, so that however intensely they killed Native peoples in their struggles for land in the "New World," they would not routinely kill all that many of each other. These "agreements" between themselves supposedly kept mutual murderousness partly under control by clarifying which European nation had what land and sovereignty rights, and on what basis. Under these arrangements surviving Native peoples usually kept their rights of possession and occupancy, so their lands could be acquired by treaty and purchase when simple conquest or introduced diseases did not do their work at an affordable cost. In Labrador the Newfoundland government denied that there were Native peoples, so "modernity," as it were, started with the fiction that there were no peoples with rights. The fiction was too transparent to last.

Modern Innu land claims in Labrador were provoked by the consequences of seizing Innu lands for the Churchill Falls–Smallwood Reservoir hydroelectric project and were given further impetus by the success of other First Nations peoples in Canada in suing for their rights. By the 1990s Labrador Native land claims were bound up with the discovery of an extraordinarily rich and valuable deposit of heavy metal ores—particularly nickle, but also copper and cadmium—at a place on the Labrador coast called Voisey's Bay by the Inuit and Emish by the Innu. It had comparatively easy access by large freight boats, making it even more attractive as a potential mining site. Both Inuit and Innu had very clear claims to Voisey's Bay, for it was about twenty-two miles south of the Inuit settlement of Nain and about thirty-five miles north of the Mashua Innu settlement of Davis Inlet—the original Davis Inlet site on the mainland. Both peoples had long used it for hunting, fishing, trapping, and trading with a trader named Voisey, who the Innu called Emish. It was impossible to start mining there, at least in the twenty-first century, while totally ignoring Native rights and claims, for fear of what the courts might subsequently do, although Newfoundland came close to trying.

Shortly after realizing the potential value of these ores, the mining company—INCO, which was soon bought out by Vale, a company with an even worse reputation for trampling on Native and union rights—began very active exploratory and development work to determine the extent and quality of the find and to develop specific plans for excavating and transporting the ore. The Innu objected:

> Active development work began by 1994. When the Innu realized that the activities at the site were intensifying in February of 1995, the Innu Nation and the Mushuau Innu First Nation Council issued an eviction order to Diamond Fields Resources [the first holder of the claim]. We demanded that they stop drilling until they had prepared an environmental and cultural protection plan. We went on to the land to protest for 12 days. It was a peaceful protest. The threat to economic development was, however, too much of a concern for the Newfoundland government. The Premier of Newfoundland sent in 56 officers of the Royal Canadian Mounted Police. An attempt by the Labrador Inuit Association, which also has rights in the Emish area, and the Innu Nation to reach a negotiated agreement with the company ended abruptly when they made it clear that it would not recognize Aboriginal rights and resumed exploration activity.[10]

The University of Connecticut's Arctic Circle website sums up the developing situation in ways that reveal the Newfoundland government's contempt for Native rights—a contempt that fortunately turned out not to be legally sustainable, but did not disappear:

> In early 1997, the Innu Nation and Labrador Inuit took legal action by bringing their case to the provincial court demanding that the construction of a road and airstrip associated with the Voisey's Bay nickel mine stop until a full environmental assessment was undertaken—an assessment to include aboriginal representatives. The mining company's position was that present drilling and airport construction was limited to exploration [as opposed to mineral extraction] and thus a full environmental assessment was not required. In July, Newfoundland's Supreme Court Justice, Ray Halley, rejected the legal basis for the claims of the two aboriginal organizations. This led to the Innu-Inuit protest in August of 1997, a demonstration of special significance in that it was the first time the two indigenous groups actively collaborated in support of their claims on the land. As summarized by Katie Rich, president of the Innu Nation:

> > Our thinking on this matter is very clear. A project of this nature requires proper planning and a proper environmental assessment. It also requires aboriginal consent. The Innu cannot give approval to this project without a land rights agreement and an Impact Benefits Agreement in place. Inco, Ltd. [the parent company of Voisey's Bay nickel mine] is trying to proceed without any of this.

> On September 22nd [1997], much to the frustration of the provincial government of Newfoundland and the mining companies, the three judges of the Newfoundland Court of Appeals blocked the provincial government's order to allow a mining company to bypass environmental regulations and allow continuing exploration of nickel mining operations. Instead, they ruled that Voisey's Bay Nickel Company must go through a full environmental assessment for its proposed 12 kilometre road and 1 kilometre airstrip. In their 33 page statement, they further remarked:

> > Reconciling the use of the Earth's resources with the protection and preservation of the environment is recognized as one of the major challenges of our time.

> And while recognizing the legitimate interests of investors and the substantial numbers of Newfoundlanders and Labradorians "... who have legitimate expectations of badly needed employment," the three judges stated:

After all, indiscriminate development without regard to environmental impact translates eventually into agonizing problems for generations yet unborn from every corner of the province, whether it be the depleted fishery; forestry harvesting in the absence of silvaculture; uncontrolled effluent and emissions from plants; or, the tragedies of fluorspar or asbestos mines. . . . We are sure that all parties involved would not want to have the mining development at Voisey's Bay to be placed in the same category.

As to the aboriginal land claims, the Court was far less specific. Acknowledging the immediate concerns of the two indigenous populations and the land to which they have been linked for generations, the judges nevertheless stated that general issues must transcend those related to land claims. The Court of Appeal did award legal costs to the Labrador Inuit Association and the Innu Nation.[11]

This puts the whole issue for Native people in the early 2000s as clearly as possible: while the courts see reasons to protect the environment, despite the willingness of Newfoundland to do anything in return for a few jobs and some tax revenue, they do not see any reason to protect Native rights. This kind of attitude puts Native peoples in an extraordinarily difficult situation, for it seems that to protect their rights and their well-being they will need to frame the issues in ways that minimize or ignore their rights.

The required environmental assessment of course did not change much at all, nor did Native rights. What slowed things down a bit was Newfoundland's insistence that the ore be refined on the island of Newfoundland—at a place called Long Harbour, where there was a failed oil refinery but a decent deepwater port built at government expense. Opposing this were the unionized mill workers in Ontario, who did not want to lose their jobs to Newfoundland, and they engaged in a variety of job actions to reinforce their claims. In January 2000 the project completely stalled over this controversy, but the ore was far too valuable for this to last very long.

By 2002 all this and more was coming to a head. In July of 2002 a "Voisey's Bay Interim Measures Agreement" was drawn up with the Labrador Inuit Association, which was officially formed in 1973 to pursue land claims and self-governance. Almost simultaneously, a "Memorandum of Agreement with the Innu Nation and the Province of Newfoundland" was also signed, so that the development of the mines could proceed without effective legal challenge. These were soon followed by "Impact Benefits Agreements" that set forth some precautions that will be taken in the development and working of the mine, as well as some benefits, from levels of employment and subcontracting to cash payments that Native communities will receive. As the mining company always requires, the conditions that are specified in the Impact Benefits Agreements are confidential, so there is no way for anyone but those who signed the documents and their successors to know what they contain.

It is surprising that Native governing groups, whose land it was, agreed to this, for it keeps them from learning from each other's agreements. Once again there is an inability to say "What part of no don't you understand?" as the women's movement taught. It is the mining companies that have the most to lose from delays.

In 2004, as the work to start actual mining in Voisey's Bay was intensifying, I joined the audience for a meeting between Vale mining company officials and Inuit leaders, in the central Labrador administrative town of Goose Bay. The Innu seem to have been excluded from this meeting.

The mining officials over and over again repeated how they wanted both "predictability" and "traditional ecological knowledge" (TEK) for their mine that was just about to start operations. They wanted to hire Native "consultants," who they said would provide "advice" to the mining company based on their TEK. The mining company officials also said, several times, that they would be going to the leaders of the Inuit to tell them whom to hire, and they wanted to do this in a way that "respected elders" and "respected native culture"—both phrases repeated multiple times.

There was no mention of any way Native peoples could enforce their advice—could use their TEK to stop pollution, or destruction of key wildlife habitats, or to deal with any other problem. Native people were to be paid for their "advice," and the company was going to make sure that this advice did not interfere with the necessary predictability, although of course they did not say this directly. Nor was there any mention at this meeting of the scale of the mining operations, or how in the context of this scale TEK could be relevant.

The mine started production in 2005. The environmental impact statements that can be found online end for the year 2005. Moreover, I have only been able to locate Vale's (the mining company) statements of environmental impact; I can find no Canadian or Newfoundland assessments, although there are several online statements, dating mostly from the 1990s, that assert that the assessments will be done to very high standards. If any actual data exist for environmental impacts after mining started, other than Vale's public relations statements, they are very well hidden from public view.

The mining complex at Voisey's Bay, as described on the company's on-line site, in addition to five major diesel generating plants (which when the mine was in full production burned 24 million liters of diesel fuel a year), warehouses, barracks for at least 250 workers, maintenance facilities, an air-strip, and a port, has at its core the open-pit mine, which generates 1.3 tons of overburden waste for every ton of ore taken [the measure used is long tons, 2,200 pounds, or 1,000 kilos).[12] The ore is taken to a crusher, which the com-pany site says is built to crush fifteen hundred tons of ore an hour. It goes then to a course-ore storage facility, which stores a day and a half's production of crushed ore. From there it is fed into a concentrator, which is "designed to process [produce] 6,800 tonnes of ore [concentrate] per day." These figures, as we shall see, conceal more than they reveal.

The concentrated ore is trucked—ninety tons per load—eleven kilome-ters to a port, where it is stored until it can be loaded onto a freight boat to be taken for processing. There are huge "sedimentation ponds" on this mining site, right across the road to the port from the workers' barracks: "water (in the form of rain or snow) that falls on the mine site is collected here and treated before being released into the environment," as the company website puts it. They also explain that the pond, or the channel to the pond, had a bit of a leak in 2005, but they are actively revegetating eleven hectares (27.2 acres) of land, beginning with covering this land with dyed-green mulch. The "water" turns out to be a killer.

It is impossible to figure out, from accessible information, how much waste is being dumped from the overburden of the mine, and from the dif-ference between the concentrated ore that is taken out of the site and the crushed ore that the mine produces. The figures do not make sense, or if they do, then something very serious is happening. The company says its crusher can potentially produce fifteen hundred tons of ore an hour, which is, by guess, about thirty thousand tons per twenty-hour day, allowing time for maintenance. It is very doubtful that more than five hundred tons of ore can be delivered per hour (for that is 1,100,000 pounds), and the figure is probably more like 360 tons. The point is that if the crusher is producing, as a guess, about eight thousand to twelve thousand tons of crushed ore a day, and the concentrator is reducing this to, say, six thousand tons of concentrate (leaving some time for servicing the concentrator), then there are several tons of waste being generated each day. What is happening to it, and with what consequences, if the water that runs off the mine pit kills vegetation? The company says that dangerous waste is dumped in the sedimentation pond, but it is doubtful that this is just a pond, in the usual sense of the term, and as the mine when started was given a useful life of fourteen years, which ends in 2019, what happens to the pond then? Putting this all together, we can just note that if the concentrator is working at its rated capacity, 6,800 tons a day, that is 14,960,000 pounds of ore concentrate. We can allow for some slack and make a guess: we are talking about, say, 10 million pounds of ore concentrate a day, or half that, or a fourth of that—the actual figure does not matter at all, only some very rough approximation of the scale of mining, to address the relevance of TEK in this context. There are two obvious points: offering to pay for TEK advice is clearly a bribe, not just in jobs and cash but to make people think that they are useful and wanted; and Native people will probably have a very good sense of the ecological consequences of this mining after the consequences happen, and even more after the mining company has pulled up stakes and gone elsewhere.

The mine at Voisey's Bay employs about fifteen people (approximately 1 percent of the current population) from Nain as heavy equipment operators or the equivalent. They earn about $60,000 to $80,000 Canadian per year. A further forty or so people from Nain (about 2.6 percent of the population) are hired as security guards, cafeteria workers, cleaning crew, etc., for between $30,000 and $40,000 per year. And this is done through a Native-owned mine services company, which makes a significant markup on these salaries. Another Inuit-owned "environmental" company provides four or five environmental observers, some local managers, and a few secretaries. The money is big-time; the people are few when measured against the needs.

In recent years the Nunatsiavut (Labrador Inuit) government has gotten very serious about environmental consequences of the new developments. They can do little if anything about what is already going on, but they have become significantly engaged in the planned future developments. In 2010–2011 they used a high-tech consulting firm, not TEK, to show that a planned hydroelectric project on the lower Churchill River, contrary to the claims of the corporation that was to do this development, was likely to produce significant mercury and other kinds of life-destroying pollution. At the same time the Nunatsiavut government imposed a moratorium on uranium mining on their lands, until the consequences can be reviewed.

Innu protests have a completely different trajectory. The Innu, who have yet to sign a land claims agreement (as of 2011), recognize that these imposed agreements reserve very far more to the state than to Native people. When they do not sign off on these agreements, they have different possibilities for protecting their rights, and different experiences from these struggles. They demonstrated on the Voisey's Bay site very seriously, destroying some drilling equipment when the region was being tested and again later. Voisey's Bay is their land too, being jointly part of Innu and Inuit territory. They recognize, however, that they cannot effectively confront the police power of the Newfoundland government, which put a very forceful police presence against the demonstrations as a great deal of potential revenue for the state is at stake, and small and irrelevant matters like justice and morality, and few and irrelevant peoples like Indians, are not going to stand in the way.

All the talk about respecting Native culture and respecting Native elders—another abstraction, for nothing concrete or specific was ever named—pushed a crucial issue into the background. The point here is that a privately owned, profit-making major corporation, whose major criterion of judgment has to be the profits to be made, for the corporate managers are responsible to the shareholders, was in the process of taking something that belonged to Native peoples, and doing so almost entirely on the corporations' terms. Despite the fact that before the first decade of the twenty-first century was out the mining company was paying some royalties to the Innu, this taking was a full-scale dispossession of Native peoples and the material basis of their modern lives.

This point now is crucial: to talk about respecting Native culture, Native elders, and TEK is, just barely under the surface of this all-too-respectful air, a way of defining Native people as primitives, as yesterday—you have tradition, you have culture; we have progress, development, technology, and thus we deserve your ore as we live in the present. We have, in sum, your ore and your future, and we are taking both on our terms.

And Native people are supposed to be grateful that the modern world looks back over its shoulder to respect Native cultures and traditions? It certainly sounds better than the usual humiliations and slanders, but actually it turns out to be cut from the same cloth. It is very different from respecting Native rights, Native ownership of the ores and the rivers, Native sovereignty. You do that, and Natives can perhaps learn to respect Canadian, U.S., and corporate culture. For a change, this might even give Native peoples something to respect, rather than to only envy.

It is a pity that all the academics given huge grants to study TEK never stopped to think about why they were getting these grants, nor their role in the dispossession of Native peoples from their rightful place in the modern world. Anyone who lives collectively by using the flora and fauna of course knows a great deal about their resource base, its context, and its fluctuations, but TEK as it is invoked by states and corporations is not about this. What's at stake with mining and hydroelectricity and the massive erosion that follows industrial clear-cutting of timber are the profits, the taxes, and the political gains from increased Euro-Canadian jobs that are produced when people literally have the ground cut out from under them—both their land base and their tomorrows. As with HBC, and now even vastly more, there is a lot of money to be made from fatally impoverishing Native peoples, even while they get very substantial royalties at this particular moment.

The Problem of Tomorrow Today

At the beginning of this book I wrote about people having the ground cut out from under them. Now, near the end, we have a situation where once again it is actually happening.

And it is happening in more ways than one, and more ways than can easily be described, for now it is both material and symbolic, and the contempt and sidelining of real Native concerns are concealed beneath an extremely thick layer of deference to "culture" and "elders," plus substantial payments to Native political entities. There are also multiple signed agreements between states, corporations, and their Native "partners" in modernity, except for the fact that only one partner has to renounce forever the bulk of its rights and claims.

We are back at the center of the social world: the problem of tomorrow.

It seems to many that Native youth can be "given" a tomorrow when the state invests large sums of money in schools and sports facilities and finances Native gatherings and conferences to discuss domestic violence and sub-stance abuse. None of these engagements with the problem of tomorrow as it exists in the everyday lives of ordinary Native people, Innu or Inuit, can pos-sibly have any real effect—nor have they. As one schoolteacher, after teaching with real caring for his students for several years in Sheshatshiu and then leaving, told me, schools cannot do much if the community is devastated—a school cannot be an island, separated from imposed and often inescapable social chaos.

Sports wear off energy and give youth "something to do." But the hockey rinks the government builds are far more for boys than girls, teaching the lesson of winners and losers; in a context where many children routinely get battered by parents and others, hockey also encourages a sport where victory is in part based on success in battering your opponents. It may be a popular

Canadian pastime, but it still also is what it is.[13] Sports such as basketball and swimming would more likely be an asset in the lives of girls and middle-aged and older men and women.

The conferences on domestic violence and substance abuse rarely if ever go beyond talk. I have read years of their transcripts; the sadness is compounded by the fact that they say the same things year after year, over and over, with the fly-in, fly-out government officials making the same nice noises, year after year, over and over.[14]

Meanwhile, the youth have their own ways of dealing with tomorrow: they kill themselves, and even more intensely, they attempt to kill themselves, perhaps hoping that someone will notice and care.

One year after the house fire in Davis Island that killed six children, six more children barricaded themselves in an unheated shack to sniff gasoline, when they were discovered and videotaped by the constable—who was also trying to get people in Canada to notice and care what was happening, so that something could be done. Following that incident, the Davis Island band chief, Katie Rich, said that suicide attempts in the village nearly tripled, from an average of four and a half a month to a bit more than twelve a month (*Newfoundland Express*, November 3, 1993, A3). No one seems to know what to do about this in ways that find and address causes. In 2010, after the third Inuit youth in Nain jumped off the new radio tower to his death, the local Inuit government put up a chain-link fence, topped by barbed wire, around the radio tower: not at all useless, and not at all fundamental.

In the period when the Impact Benefits Agreements with the mines were being negotiated and signed, and the payments to Native political entities started, in 2002–2003, the population of Davis Island was moved to the new village of Natuashish, on the mainland. But the problems of alcoholism, domestic violence, and suicide did not subside much, if at all. During the same time period, plans to develop another hydroelectric facility below Churchill Falls were intensifying dramatically—the so-called Lower Churchill or Muskrat Falls project. The plans were for a massive project—including changing or reversing the course of three rivers, with another huge dam and reservoir. Native peoples, both Innu and Inuit, had to be included in the negotiations for this. They have rightly been very cautious and have so far managed to delay development—or more precisely to contribute a further factor to the technological, financial, and interprovincial transmission and investment problems that have delayed development. Native peoples' concerns have caused significant attempts by the Newfoundland government to get the cooperation of the Native governments, but so far the digging has not started, and the state's lies about the ecological consequences have not stopped. But a lot of money and pressure are being pumped into and onto Native governments to help assure assent, which seems by 2012 to be taken for granted.

My sense of what is happening is that a profound split is developing in Native communities, both Innu and Inuit. On the one hand, you have an elite segment that rides the benefits wagon in all these developments and has the dignity of both being asked to negotiate and access to the funds and the allocation of at least part of the employment this development makes possible, for themselves and for those they include. Meanwhile, on the less green side of the fence are the larger body of ordinary people who see their futures and their dignity even further eroded, as their ways of life disappear with no replacement but a welfare check.

Whatever happens next depends on how this split, which is not fixed but partly fluid, is addressed, and who gets to say no to what. This I think will ultimately turn on how much local democracy is developed, which is not about voting but developing ways that ordinary people have their needs and their rights respected. Learning how to say no and mean it, and hear it when it is said, which entails first a new and a deeper respect for Native women's rights, also would confront both the state and corporations with the unavoidable necessity of respecting the rights and claims of Native peoples.

Native peoples are not in the slightest way to blame for the appalling ways they are treated by the state, corporations, and more generally by the dominant society. But since none of these entities can be expected to change unless they have to, primarily by pressure from Native societies (with some assistance from allies in the dominant society), it turns out that in very deep ways Native womens' rights are fully and completely the pathway to Native rights: the basis of one is the basis of the other.

What the Porcupine Chief Knew

On the north Pacific coast, including the province of Canada now called British Columbia and the Alaska Panhandle, there is a cool-weather rainforest, one of the few in the world. The region is extremely rich in valuable fur-bearing animals. In the nineteenth century it was the locale of a brutal fur trade, with a lot of Native deaths from war and disease, and a lot of Native wealth, made manifest in flamboyant inequalities. When you look past the fuss that has been made in appreciation of the potlatch, totem poles, and the extraordinarily symbol-dense art, it was a hard place and a hard time for a great many Native people to live a peaceful, everyday life. The wealth behind that spectacular art was concentrated by two facts: four major European trading enterprises were trying to get their hands on the furs, and so prices stayed relatively high, and Native people in this region died more rapidly from disease and war than did the fur-bearing animals they hunted and trapped—a very unusual situation in the North American fur trade. With increasingly fewer people chasing the proliferation of high-priced furs, it was possible for the survivors to put on rather spectacular displays.

In this context one people, called the Tsimshian, told a wonderfully insightful story. Some anthropologists have called such stories myths, which tries to make the story timeless and general when the wisdom of this story lies in its historical and social specificity—its critique of the ways of the fur trade, and its depiction of the ways that people were being butchered in it and for it.

The printed text of this story is called "The Porcupine Hunter." Porcupines are very easy to catch, because they do not run when attacked, but curl up in a ball. And they have a meat that is rich in calorie-dense fat, which makes porcupines a particularly good cold-weather food, especially for fur trappers who spend most of their day on the move along their trap lines, rather than hunting food. It is the same situation on the north Pacific coast as in the interior forests of Labrador.

This story was widely broadcast among anthropologists by Franz Boas, who worked on the northwest coast in the early twentieth century. Instead of using Boas's Europeanized version of the tale, we will go to the original texts that were sent to Boas by his partly bilingual Native informant, Henry W. Tate. The originals are stored at Columbia University's Rare Book Room, at Butler Library, and the texts presented here come from these originals. I owe my realization of this possibility, and my introduction to the wonders of the actual text, to the transcriptions that have been made and published, with annotations, in Ralph Maud's exceptionally useful book *The Porcupine Hunter and Other Stories* (1993). Anyone interested in understanding Native fables, myths, and tales from a range of new perspectives would be well repaid by a serious engagement with Maud's book.

Henry Tate's first language and the forms of his thinking and presentation were that of the Tsimshian at the time that he started writing to Boas. From 1903 to his death in 1913, he sent Boas about two thousand pages of interlinear Tsimshian and English text, and he was paid by the page, which probably made the texts rather full. Here is what he sent:

> There was a great Porcupine hunter in one of the native Village. every year he went in the early Fall to hunt some Porcupine, it because they are rich food in those days among the natives. every Fall he has slain so many and dried their meats and fats, and in Winter time some stranges people from different Villages come to him and buy the dried meats from him and he became a very rich man. He has many Valleys for his hunting grown, and he has build a huts in each Valley to dried meats and tallow. . . . He has four valleys as his hunt-

ing grown. Every year he went to his first camp., and when he slew all the porcupines. Then he went to the next camp . . . and so on . . . He made a good
club . . . , very hart wood. to clubbed the Porcupine. After he made smoke in the
den of the Porcupine and when the porcupine ran out that he clubbed them to
slain. Then all the Porcupine regretful and distress for this man. Therefore on
these last year of this Hunter stard very early in than [than in] other fall. . . . And
this time he has gain a great number of Porcupine slains. . . . he went alone to
looked over the large rock a little further above his huts, and when he reached
there, Then he saw a large Porcupine a brown fur. Just went round at the foot of
a large Spruce tree. . . . he ran after it [the large brown Porcupine] and he behold
a large door was already opened before him a large fire burned in the center
of a large house who invited him in. so he enter there and they spread a mats on
one side of the fire. and a great chief seated at the real of his house, Then . . . [the
chief] order to his young man and said, ran around the village and invite all them
women in my house so that I might dance to welcome my guest. . . .

And he stood the Porcupine to dance, then the leader of the singing begun
to singing, and this is their singing

Pronounce my name, Pronounce my name, strike, strike. This is the words
of this tune. Repeat many.

The Porcupine ran around his own large fire and when this singing rest a while
that he stood at the frount of his guest (a Hunter) and he said to his guest the
hunter Pronounce my name my brother who is my name says he While he stop
and stood before. Then the Hunter said thy name is little porcupine, yes, my
name is that, says, the chief Porcupine while he striked the Hunter's face with his
pinnes tail, They began to sing again, and the Chief Porcupine began to dance
once more. while the hunter's face was full with the Porcupine pins. And at the
end of their singing that he stopped before the hunter and said. now whose my
name my brother said he. thy name was little (is) ugly Porcupine he striked his
face again with his pinne tail and said I that his my name. Then they sing again,
the Chief Porcupine ran around the fire while his attendants keep singing, and
he stoped again before him who is my name my brother? The man said thy
name is (little) Scorch. He striked him again with his pinne-tail. yes, that is my
name, and the Hunter's face full with the pins of Porcupine. Then his face was
swollen, its very hartly to see his eyes. . . . [and once again with another wrong
name, "Little Leaning Fellow" and the porcupine again agrees and slaps him
again in the face. Then:]

That a soft touched by his side. It was a mouse woman who asked him, Did you know these who punished you? The poor blind hunter said no. It is the porcupine Chief said the Mouse woman. because you slew them every years passed. . . . Now you may be last time at the end of their singing then all these Porcupine will be strike all over your body . . . if your not (right) answer to the chief's name. is name was sea otter of green side mountain. . . . . then all those Porcupines are ready rush on him. Then the chief at the frount of him said, now who is my name dear Man? then the poor man that was blind . . . answered with his low voice and said thy name is Sea-otter at green side of a mountain.

Then the Chief Porcupine order his people to wash the face of the poor man. Then all of the Porcupine working at this man's face and they took out the new green excrement from the stomach [and, Maud points out from his familiarity with the context, also the bladder] of the first wife of the chief Porcupine, and they rubbed on the face where his pins was. Then some pins are come out again by itself. Then they took the second wife of the chief excrement they rubbed on his face, and some of the pins came out again, and man's face was become less pins that was before. Then the thirth wife's excrement they rubbed, and the swell on his face became less, the pins loose and fell off from his face. The fourth wife of the chief excrement are rubbed on his face, and all those pins are all come out, and not one single pins are remain in the face of this Hunter. . . .

Then the chief Porcupine order his attendants to give him food. . . . And when the hunter . . . ate the food in the house then the chief have said to him I will become to your friends together, he said, My people are much regretfully for you have slew great number of them. so I took you in to my house to slay your right there. But because you are right to pronounce my chief name, therefore I'll save your life, wherefore I ask you kind don't make smoke in the Den of Porcupines in any places. If you need Porcupines meat don't kill so many of them. And soon as you kill one or more than that dried their meats in good fire, and finished to eat them soon before winter so that my people would not had any sickness in the Winter, and cast the Porcupine's bones into fire and let not your young people ate the head of the young Porcupine lest they forgot everything. . . . Then the hunter went out from there to his own huts. while his wife sitting there and weeping, because her husband lost [for] many days.[1]

Influenced by the characteristic innocence of early and mid-twentieth-century anthropology, many of us who read such tales have missed much of what they were saying. We did this particularly by making these tales mythic, not real, and using them, under the influence of Lévi-Strauss, to illuminate imaginary—overly neat and overly unified—social structures rather than actual history, discordant realities, and peoples' visions of an impending future.

In this particular story what is being revealed is, to begin, a very widespread history of the relations between Native peoples and fur traders, a history that stretches with some modification from Labrador on the Atlantic coast through Hudson's Bay in northern Canada and across into the northwest Pacific coast. With more modification the same history reaches down across the Great Lakes and on into the southeastern United States and the Great Plains. By looking closely at some very specific pointers in this story, we can start to see that history in useful ways.

Two general points need to be made, before we begin with the details of the story. First and obviously, the porcupines both stand in for the Native peoples in the fur trade and simultaneously are what they are—a key element of supply in this trade. It is in general very hard to both hunt for commercially valuable pelts and at the same time get enough food, for these are different kinds of activities, and many of the fur-bearing animals do not by themselves provide adequate food. Porcupines, relatively easy to procure, and relatively abundant, were indeed a major food source for the Native workers in the northern fur trade. Most of all, porcupines, like the people called Indians, were a necessary element of the trade, and both Indians and porcupines died in large numbers to keep it going.

Second, the hunter has an even more ambivalent position in the story than does the porcupine, being at the same time and in the same person a representative for, and a symbol of, the alien intruder, the fur trader, and probably also a local Native, profiting greatly from his insertion in the trade as a supplier of food for the producers—a supplier who, like Native people, had a different set of relations with his own village than with other Native people, for the story notes that the porcupine hunter sold the meat to people from strange—that is, different—villages.

Note also, at the outset of the story, that the Porcupine Hunter was killing every porcupine in the four valleys he worked, year after year, and becoming rich by selling the smoked meat. When you kill animals for your own use, your need to kill is limited by the amount you can use, but when you kill to sell, there is scarcely any limit, so long as there is a market. Getting rich in this way is a new kind of inequality. The story of the Porcupine Hunter opens up as a story of relationships that form at the origin of the fur trade.

At the core of the confrontation between the Porcupine Chief and the Hunter is not knowing Porcupine's—the Native people's—real name, not bothering to learn it before all the use and all the death of animals and of Native peoples began. The Hunter was beating porcupines to death without even caring about their names. So this killer of porcupines for profit has to make up names, has to guess, because he really does not know their right name. Indeed, in the United States, and in Canada until recently, not a single Native people are called what they call themselves. Not one. And anthropologists and others call such stories as these myths?

The Hunter's arrogance and his anger at being put in the position of having to know the name of his victims, of those he uses so destructively, is revealed in the names he offers. The first name the Hunter calls out is a simple diminutive, the diminutive as a name for the other that domination always uses, here "Little Porcupine." When he is slapped and stuck for this arrogance and this mistake, the second name the Hunter calls the Chief is "Little Ugly Porcupine." He is still trying to assert and to rub in his domination, although it is his face that will be rubbed by the end of the story. The third try, as his face is swollen and stuck full of pins, is to call the Porcupine "Little Scorch." This is a complex gambit on the part of the Hunter, for as Maud points out, it refers to another Tsimshian story where a porcupine is tormented by a bear and tossed repeatedly into a fire. The Hunter knows a bit of the porcupine's past and is flaunting this knowledge along with his arrogance. Stuck again, the "the poor grief hunter" becomes confused in his pain and by now his blindness, and then he tries the name "Little Leaning Fellow"—a name that, along with the familiar diminutive, either has a different kind of meaning, is just nonsense, or references something we do not know.

At each wrong name the Porcupine Chief agrees: "Yes, that is my name," he says, calling the Hunter brother, and then he slaps the Hunter in the face with his barbed tail. Porcupine is both admitting I am what you call me— Indian, Savage, Tsimshian, ugly, wild, diminished—and forcefully demonstrating that the Hunter is wrong to call him that, and deserving of assault, of punishment. This is a historically sensitive and insightful perception, for Native people really were made into what they were and are wrongly called. "Indian" is not just a name; as we have seen, it imposed ways of life that people had to live within and against. Those who gave such names and sought to shape such lives deserve what they get in return, although the return can be far more indirect, or taken out on other Natives or other family members. Perhaps that is why, in this stunningly sensitive story, the Hunter is called brother.

When mouse woman—the smallest and most vulnerable of all the characters in the story—helps the Hunter with Porcupine's real name, the assault on the Hunter stops. It is likely a matter of insisting upon respect, upon one's collective dignity, one's proper name, and an intense desire to be who one really is, not what one is called. But at the same time as this insistence on his own name the Porcupine Chief has been admitting to being what he is called, which indeed happens, along with resistance, often simultaneously, when you are far enough down the hierarchies of domination to have little other choice.

Brother Hunter, in the midst of his attempted denial and forced acceptance of the inescapable by Porcupine, in the midst of the arrogant domination he still tried to impose, but no longer can, still has the quills in his face. Pronouncing Porcupine Chief's real name did not make the quills fall off.

These quills are removed by rubbing the Hunter's face in the excrement of all four of the Chief's wives. Much as I enjoy the image of the Hunter's face being rubbed in shit, and would just like to leave the story with this wonderful image in mind, it is even more heartening to be more exact about what is happening.

What is rubbed in the Hunter's face, as Ralph Maud points out, is the green, partly digested contents of the chief's wives' stomachs, intestines, and (as Maud adds, from his knowledge of Tsimshian ways) bladders. In sum, the Hunter's face is rubbed with material that at the moment it was taken for use has a double future, a double presence: as nourishment and as excrement, as food and as feces. It is probably this double future that holds the possibility of both alleviating (nourishing, healing) the suffering of the afflicted and yet at the same time not completely erasing the memory, the reality, the history, of what has been experienced: it is both life and shit, tomorrow and shit, rubbed in the Hunter's face to bring him back to life, to give him another tomorrow. This is how the remedy works: its effectiveness lies in the fact that it is a substance with a crucial double future. In the most fundamental formulation, this dual presence within the healing substance is not just food and feces but life and death, simultaneously. This is the best that Native people in the fur trade, or more generally any of us, can hope for: to live and to die, not just to die.

For understanding the current situation of Native peoples, including especially Labrador Native peoples, the two most poignant and revealing parts of the story come at the end. First, the Porcupine Chief, in return for saving the Hunter's life, and feeding and treating him like an honored guest, does not ask the Hunter to stop killing porcupines but only to limit how many he kills, to treat those that are killed with respect, and to use them in ways (*and finished to eat them soon before winter so that my people would not had any sickness in the Winter*) that keep porcupines more free of the dreaded and deadly diseases that strike most severely in winter. Native people have long known their situation is, at bottom, unavoidably deadly, that many will unavoidably die from the hunter/trader/Native elite intrusions, but they are trying, as this story shows, to limit the extent of their deaths. It is a story about the impending future, not the mythic past.

Second, there is Porcupine's heart-wrenching request to the Hunter, at the end, not to let your young people eat the head of our young. Native people, invoking their own and the intruders' young, fully understood that what is at stake in all this are two futures—the future of the dominant intruders and their own future. The story tells more: that these two futures are linked. To feed the young of the dominant from the vision, the knowledge, the senses and the sensibilities—in sum, the heads—of the Natives' young is for *both* to forget where they came from, what they once did, and how they got and will get to where they are, or where they should be, going. That both are losers from feeding the heads of Native young to the intruders' young is most powerfully summed up in the exquisitely ambiguous phrase at the final part of the story: *And [after you eat the Porcupine] cast the Porcupine's bones into the fire [a mark of respect] and let not your young people ate the head of the young Porcupine lest they forgot everything.* There is, at the end, after all the recognition of the brutality that "Indians" must deal with, one extraordinarily decent recognition of the Hunter's humanity and of the ways that women pay the price for their husband's (shall we say) arrogance, or lack of decency: *Then the hunter went out from there to his own huts. while his wife sitting there and weeping, because her husband lost [for] many days.*

Indeed, it is the Native youth that are now paying the highest price for our disrespect, as we hunt for new ways to appropriate their lands, their resources, their livelihoods, and their lives, and for the fundamentally disrespectful ways the dominant discard Natives when they are finished using them. The point here is simple but crucial: in the midst of all this, Native youth must keep their heads for there to be a future. The key to how this might happen is very far from simple.

The most subtle part of the story occurs when the Hunter finally gives Porcupine Chief his real name. The Hunter does not get it quite right. Mouse woman said that Porcupine Chief's name was "sea otter of green side mountain." The Hunter says, in a far more Europeanized construction, with less local specificity, "Sea-otter at green side of a mountain." "Green Side Mountain" is the name of a specific mountain; "green side of a mountain" is the side of any mountain facing the coastal rains.

I take this to suggest that if the porcupine youth are to keep their heads, they must know and insist upon their real name, which is not what they were called and to some extent not what they became in the context of the fur trade. Porcupine Chief and his singers knew, at the outset, that the Hunter had no idea what their real name was, for the song that began to call the Hunter out already contained his punishment: *Pronounce my name, pronounce my name, strike, strike. Many times.* Porcupine Chief then accepts the Hunter's Europeanized version of his real name—it is the best the Hunter can do—but Porcupine Chief must also know, exactly, his own name and his own specific locality.

Accepting as real that subtle but serious difference, that inability to give Native people exactly what is their due, is how Native people negotiate, build, and continually must rebuild their own future in the midst of a continuing, inescapably destructive domination. They try to know what is the best that can be had from their murderous intruders, and seeking and accepting that is how they have their own future after domination is finished with them— used up what domination uses and moves on, leaving discarded mine tailings, polluted and empty waters, clear-cut hillsides, and discarded people. But if the youth can keep their heads, if they can recognize what they both can and cannot get through persistent, repeated, full-scale counterattack, and if they do not forget, they still have a future.

Or so the story tells us.

Warriors against Violence

The story of the Porcupine Chief is wise, grim, and hopeful. Its wisdom lies in the realization that against a powerful and destructive outside force, bent on making money beyond any other standard or moral value, all that can be done is to limit and contain the destruction, so that most people can continue to live their lives with some respect and dignity.

Its grimness lies in the realization that against a powerful and destructive outside force, bent on making money beyond any other standard or moral value, all that can be done is to limit and contain the destruction, so that many, but not all, people can continue to live their lives with some respect and dignity.

The hope lies in the power that emerges from Native ways, the hard-sticking barbs that can be deployed (look up Oka; look up Wounded Knee 1973)—all that it takes to make the destructiveness limited, to make the outside force treat you with some dignity and respect, not in the empty words of mining corporations and governments, but in their actions.

At the core of the power to do this is the expressiveness and power of Native creativity. Only so much can actually be done to reshape domination, but what can be and is done is to reshape how people live within and against this domination—the ways they make their own world among themselves, for themselves. The ways that struggle against domination by ordinary people helps to transform, positively, their relations to one another are crucial.

To help see and think this, consider three special and useful stories from more recent Native struggles. The first is painful, but that pain is an important start, for struggle very often begins in pain.

Let me begin with a bit of background to situate the stories:

In the 1970s I did some support work with two "Red Power" movements. The first was the American Indian Movement (AIM) and their engagement with the 1973 occupation of the village of Wounded Knee—the same nameplace as the Hotchkiss Revolving Canon machine-gun massacre of unarmed Native people in 1890. The occupation of Wounded Knee in 1973 was a wonderful struggle against a very brutal opposition: wonderful for its intelligence, its bravery, and its accomplishments.

But it was a very tense time, because the U.S. Marshals and the FBI brought a lot of firepower against the 1973 occupation. Two of the approximately two hundred Sioux who were part of the occupation were killed, and one sympathizer, who disappeared, probably was as well. In the midst of all this tension some relaxation became important. The AIM people, some of whom were using trails past the FBI blockade to go in and out of the occupation, carrying supplies and news, told jokes to break the tension and to deal with the very real danger. Here are two of them, which are very far from just jokes.

The first one is about a White man who beats up a Native American's children, abuses his wife, kills his horse and his dog, and then runs away. The "Indian" starts to track him down, follows his trail across several states, hears he has moved to Alaska, follows him there, and after several years of looking finds him. He confronts the man who caused him and his family so many and such serious injuries:

"You the man who beat up my kids? You the man who abused my wife? You the man who killed my horse and dog?"

"Yes."

"Watch out."

Then the Indian turns around and starts back to what remains of his home.

It is a standard notion that only Jews can tell jokes that make fun of Jews, so I must start by reminding the reader that this was a fantasy-story I heard from politically committed Native Americans, deeply engaged in a powerful, dangerous, and helpful struggle. It is both a very poignant and a very compelling fantasy-story, for it brings to the forefront the fact that overwhelming domination can teach passivity, and often (but not always) does. States routinely do this, especially to particularly vulnerable peoples. Domestic violence often does it as well. But there are always, at least episodically, times when people break out of this passivity and become committed to struggle, including confrontational struggle.

It is easy to say that this transcendence of passivity, which has regularly occurred for both Innu and Inuit, needs to flourish. But first, in general, how? And second, more specifically, there is the question of how this is possible for children, who are particularly vulnerable, with vulnerabilities that in many wonderful and appropriate ways make them weak and fragile. Moreover, many wounded children become deeply immersed in a mixture of utter passivity and utter defiance of their situation, with actions such as sniffing gasoline which, I think, make and express both passivity and defiance simultaneously.[2] This mixture can be particularly hard to transcend. We will return to this after the second AIM joke-story, and then one from the "Mohawk," or more properly the Kanien'keh'às:ka, occupation of Ganienkah.

The second AIM story concerns the dogs, all then creatures of the forest before domestication, who decided that they needed a chief to deal with what was happening to them:

> The dogs gathered in a large circle in a clearing in the middle of the forest to pick their chief. One dog, a very large and very powerful dog, said that the strongest dog should be chief, as he could better deal with all the attacks upon dogs, and all the dissension among the dogs. Several other dogs agreed, but there was a lot of opposition from some who said that all this would do was to lead to fighting and assaults between the dogs, and they had enough of that. The quarreling got very intense, until another dog, gray in muzzle, said that the wisest dog should be chief, for then the dogs would be more likely to know what to do. More agree, but once again there was much dissent by those who claimed that wisdom without strength is useless. Several more suggestions were made, and the opposition

and the anger over their differences was increasing until dogs were growling at each other, showing their fangs, and things started to look dangerous. Then one young dog spoke up, "I have an idea about how to pick a good chief. The chief should be the one who smells best under the tail." And ever since then that is what dogs do when they meet: they are looking for their chief.

There is much that we can learn from this, in addition to the flamboyant critique of chiefs and chiefly forms of organization. For chiefs were and are— in Labrador and elsewhere throughout North America—an imposition of the state from its need to have someone that can be dealt with, someone who can sign treaties, land sales, mining leases, and other alliances and concessions. When the Bureau of Indian Affairs in the United States required the Navajo to have a tribal council in 1922, it was specifically to sign oil exploration and mining leases, and an "official" Hopi government was created in 1951 to sign a mining lease with Peabody coal, which subsequently strip-mined, polluted air and water, used up vast quantities of the limited underground water, and paid royalties on the coal that were a small fraction of customary royalties. In the eyes of the state and corporations, that is what chiefs and "Indian governments" were all about, and Native political organizations, and their "chiefs," many of whom try intensely to do something positive for their people, must necessarily begin in the struggle against this imposed view of what chiefs are and what they are supposed to do.

In addition, the required "elections" for chiefs, like elections almost everywhere in so-called democracies, are fundamentally undemocratic. Money both talks and votes, over and over and over again, and incumbents, with their hands on the reins of power, can often easily steer elections. If the United States and Canada themselves have nothing more than the fantasy pretense of being democracies, can the Native Americans and First Nations do any better? How? The major difference seems to me that in the United States and Canada a substantial number of people still think they live in democracies. Native and First Nations peoples often know better.

I think there is no way out of this but for Native people to change their political organization. The state will always insist on having a chief by one name or another—president is getting popular, I think unfortunately—and it is difficult if not impossible to keep elections from being corrupted by money and patronage: the favors, including jobs, that incumbents can dispense in these communities that characteristically have very few sources of employment.

But a council of elders, who would have to grant assent to all acts and regulations, and who would have powers of introducing acts and regulations, would provide not just control but a doorway to democracy. To begin, they would have to be chosen by acclamation—by unanimous consent. Those who oppose one candidate or another for the council would have to be negotiated with until consent was reached.

Those who are familiar with the requirement for unanimous consent in the political organization and mobilization of Native communities, for example, among the Cherokee of the eighteenth century—Fred Gearing (1962) is brilliant on this—note that it never worked by reaching complete agreement, but by a give-and-take that moved toward either expressed or silent assent, as part of a long process that ensured that almost everyone got some of what they wanted, for no decision was made in isolation from this long process.

And the beauty and power of a council of elders so constituted is that it is utterly democratic: everyone has a chance to grow into the role—men, women, the wise, the strong, even those who smell like they ate the money of states and corporations, or know how to do this. Unlike "chiefs," who tend to be young, fluent in the language and the ways of the dominant, and usually all too comfortable both with and around power—which may or may not be helpful to the needs of ordinary Native people—the status of elder is a reward for a substantial part of a lifetime well lived, and lived increasingly and usefully for others.

Both the state and corporations make a lot of noise about "elders" and about respecting elders. It is almost always either empty or fraudulent—a pretense of respect for Native ways—because it is *never* the case that the people they pretend to listen to, or speak to (and very rarely to speak with), are given any power whatsoever. There is no way to be an actual elder unless one can shape events, at least partially. The state and corporations, when they say they are doing something for and with unspecified "elders" who have no specific rights or powers, are often simply trying to do something that caution would modify or prevent. When, for just one example, the state talks about fixing the poor conditions in Native communities, the expressed deference to elders is usually a framework for doing nothing effective whatsoever, but with a lot of respect.

Real elders have effective influence in their communities, from the respect they have earned from living a substantial portion of their lives well. People, as we have seen, watch them in silence for cues, for the examples they set, and listen to what they occasionally say. But now, to live this status in ways that matter to the community, and to break open the forms of government that the dominant state has imposed, elders must be an integral part of communal self-governance. And this council of elders must be balanced between men and women—because before the missionaries got their hands on Native societies this equality was fundamental (Anderson 1991), and in recent years women have been crucial makers of important struggles.

One more story brings this to both a close and a beginning.

In 1974–1975 Native people in northern New York State, on the U.S./Canadian border, primarily from a reserve called Akwesasne, occupied an area of state forest land in the Adirondack Mountains that they called Ganienkah—the land of flint. They wanted a place that was theirs, with no permission from the state of New York or from the United States, with no appealing to state laws, which they asserted would be demeaning and unjust, for the United States does not appeal to their laws and ways to do what they want. As members of a sovereign nation, which had never relinquished one drop of their sovereignty, they were going to live on this land that had always been theirs, that had always been important to them.

The land they repossessed to live on was part of the Adirondack State Forest. It was not settled or used by the state, save an occasional hunter or hiker. But both New York State and neighboring "White" people freaked. The state tried to evict them, and the local Whites engaged in a variety of their usual "cowboys and Indians" violence, including especially nighttime drive-by shootings from moving cars—the epitome of bravery.

So especially in the first year or so of the occupation, while all this violence was being brought to them, armed Native Americans patrolled the borders of their land, particularly at night. Several were army war veterans, had very good rifles, and were very good shots—not the kinds of people that you would want to attack, when they could retaliate, even with a few bravery-inducing beers sloshing about between your stomach and your brain.

I worked with one Native American man, from a community called Mohawk, a people now calling themselves Kanien'keh'às:ka, who was part of this occupation, and part of the people that helped maintain the perimeter—the border between Ganienkah and external assault. We were giving talks at colleges and high schools—one "Indian" and one "White" New Yorker—seeking to explain and to get support for what was happening, seeking to generate enough protest against New York State for allowing or not pursuing local Whites who were shooting at Indians.

The man I worked with, the wonderfully wise and gentle person who went by the English name Tom Porter, who was very active in the armed defense of the border of Ganienkah, at some point in his talk to the students would say, "I am a warrior: I cut and carry wood and carry water for the old people, I make sure they are safe and warm and well. I help the children. I teach the children our language and our ways and make sure they are safe and well fed. I am a Mohawk warrior—my people, their well-being, are my responsibility." He made no mention whatsoever, ever, of his very effective work in the armed defense of the border, night after night. That was only incidental to what being a warrior was about.

What an extraordinary, special, vital worldview. Thirty-six years later, in 2011, Ganienkah is still there, and I am still overwhelmingly impressed with what I learned from Tom Porter while trying to be of some help to his people's cause, his people's struggle.

There are substantial numbers of Innu and Inuit people who share and who live this vision—all the women and men who in their daily actions reach out to each other and to the children of their communities. The point of this story is to underline the fact that what Tom Porter talked about were not moments or gifts of kindness and concern but a vision of a better future.

Much as I respect the risks people take in their more spectacular confrontations, and much as I think they are crucial for getting certain things done, it is in daily life that tomorrow is formed. This is a tribute to all those many Native people who, in the midst of multiple kinds of assaults, make tomorrow in their caring about and for each other today.

That is the note on which I end this work. What is needed in Labrador are warriors against violence—truly warriors because it will be a sometimes confrontational struggle, both within the community and against the state and corporations. The warriors, like the elders, will be both men and women, older and younger, who are committed to two simultaneous struggles: first and foremost to enhancing, with their actions, the well-being of the people of their community, and only then, only as necessary after this primary task, to the confrontational struggle against the assaults of the state and the dominant society. A nation with elders with real power and warriors with real commitments to their community and to each other is a nation with a tomorrow. There are few if any other possibilities.

CHAPTER ONE. **Historical Violence**

1. Armen Keteyian, "Suicide Epidemic among Veterans," *CBS News* (February 11, 2009), cbsnews.com/stories/2007/11/13/cbsnews_investigates/main3496471.shtml.

2. An important book on different kinds of maps is Hugh Brody's *Maps and Dreams* (1981). Our maps will be quite different from the kinds of First Nations maps he so well described, but his book remains thought provoking about the social construction of maps.

3. Coffee is a complex substance in its own right: people do seem to get somewhat dependent on it, as it reduces headaches by opening the blood vessels in the frontal part of the brain and also seems to facilitate bowel movements. In nineteenth-century Greenland we are dealing with not just a desire for coffee, but a craving that led people to the point of starvation and exposure.

4. This is a rejection of Foucault's fantasies of the orderliness at the core of domination. In his book *Discipline and Punish* (1978), which opens with a central metaphor derived from the design of a nineteenth-century prison in Pennsylvania that was organized as a panopticon—with spokes of corridors radiating from a central observation point—he makes the point that those in control could see all and control all. I went to visit this prison. The spokes are far from straight, nor are they level, so that it is not easy to see very far down most of them. Furthermore, the cells, being set back from the corridors, were out of sight. On paper it looks like coherent and complete domination; in fact, it is something much more complicated and messy.

5. The point here is analogous to Freud's writings on what he termed "introspection"—looking within oneself—as a way to understand. Introspection as an analytical technique is based on looking within yourself to sense your similarity with the person you are trying to helpfully understand, for without this you cannot help, and yet at the very same time to sense the difference, for without this you cannot get enough separation for

perspective. This doubled sensibility is also crucial to anthropology, particularly when it is rooted in enough familiarity to listen for the silences. This perspective rejects the fad called "reflexive anthropology," which is overly rooted in "looking within" the anthropologist's self. It has always impressed me as the conceptual equivalent of tourism.

6. For one exceptionally insightful instance of the continuing onslaught in Labrador, see Samson (2003). For an analysis of the formative processes that emerge in this context in Native societies, see esp. chapters 10 and 11 of my *Living Indian Histories* (Sider 2003b).

7. Carol Brice-Bennett (2000) has given an extraordinarily moving description of a return visit of Inuit to Hebron, from which they had been tricked into leaving years earlier. The title itself, *Reconciling with Memories*, suggests what was at stake in this return visit, long after the trauma.

8. Amartya Sen's (1981) work on famines pointed the way to this crucial realization. Sen showed, for famines in India and Africa, that a decline in available food, for example, of 10 percent, ordinarily led to almost doubled mortality rates: closer to 20 percent than 10 percent. Mortality from famines is almost impossible to count well, partly because of the social chaos that follows, and partly because it is difficult to assign numbers to people who, weakened by hunger, die later from disease and equally hard to count those who flee, many of whom die en route. But the point is still crucial: in famines many eat as usual and others die of want, with far more dying than can be explained by the decline in available food. This is one widespread aspect of the social construction of famines, and this situation, although extreme, has become the type case for the concept of "partial solutions" used here. I don't intend to generalize these proportions, but only the idea of the inequalities and the biases of disasters. "Partiality" suggests the incompleteness of the ways tragedy strikes—in many cases some continue to live as usual, while some die—and this difference is not at all random.

9. To help modern urbanites understand what follows: Milk that comes directly from a cow separates. The cream, which is oily, rises to the top, floating on the more dense milk. Milk that is now offered for sale is mostly "homogenized"—the molecules broken apart from one another with pressure or "grinding," so that the fatty, high-cholesterol cream stays mixed into a now artificially uniform substance we also call milk. To talk about, and then to deal with, "the Cherokee" or "the Navajo" or "the Inuit" or "the Innu" is to artificially homogenize, with pressure and grinding, into an artificially uniform entity with mostly unhealthy consequences.

10. The fact that no Native strategy for dealing with domination can work well for very long often leads to severe factional struggles among indigenous peoples. Competing factions advocate alternative strategies, which some understand will not work either. This situation is discussed in depth in my *Living Indian Histories* (Sider 2003b).

11. Linda Green (1999) offers a fine study of gender in the context of what she calls structural and political violence.

12. The "Indian coat hanger"—widespread in the northeast at least, and in the houses of poorer peoples of all ethnicities—is discussed for First Nations very insightfully and poignantly by Anne McGillivray and Brenda Comaskey in their excellent book *Black Eyes All of the Time: Intimate Violence, Aboriginal Women, and the Justice System* (1999).

"All of the time" in the title points toward the failures of the justice system as much as a continuing problem within Native communities.

13. Some might well say that this discussion of dependence, hostility, and separation takes little or no account of "cultural difference." Yes, I am sure that in "different cultures" women get hit in different ways for different reasons, with different excuses. But hit is hit. I also know there is a literature that argues that in some "different cultures" women have come to regard this as "normal." If you want to start there and rethink the issues here, you are welcome to do so, but recognize that doing this is about perpetuation. I start from the point that violence by men against women, for one example, or by the state against Native peoples, however different in surface form, are each opposable, within and against their continuities and their differences. To not just recognize but overly emphasize "cultural differences" is to minimize the possibilities of oppositional movements learning from one another.

14. Nicolas Argenti, in his wonderful book *The Intestines of the State* (2007), called my attention to this key quote.

15. I wrote about this in the first and second editions of my book on rural Newfoundland (Sider [1986] 2003). The point that local people knew what was happening was perhaps the most hotly contested point of this contentious book, particularly by the Newfoundland elite. It is a revealing and sad fact for both the left, with their fantasies about vanguard parties enlightening the masses, and the liberals and the right, with their fantasies about industrial capitalist societies being democracies (so the problems lie with the voters), that both share the notion that the masses do not know and must be taught.

CHAPTER TWO. Owning Death and Life

1. York (1992) is an excellent general study of dispossession. The most powerful case study is still by Anastasia Shkilnyk (1985). Her book has an extraordinary logic to it: you first read about Native people destroying themselves and each other, with very serious alcohol abuse, page after page of this seemingly self-imposed tragedy, and then you find out that they have been relocated to a horribly constructed place and that they are suffering intensifying neurological damage from mercury poisoning because the government did not bother to regulate the discharge from a mill or tell the Native people not to eat the fish from their lake, which once was a major food source. Frank J. Tester and Peter Kulchyski (1994) document the extent to which knowingly murderous displacement, maintained with lies and false promises, has been a Canadian government practice, and Colin Samson (2003) and Carol Brice-Bennett (2000) document this in recent Labrador Innu and Inuit history.

2. This may be one of the many reasons why the diminutive—including terms such as *boy* and the use of first names for adults in subordinate positions—is used. It marks both adult dependency and subordination and perhaps also goes beyond contempt to pretend that this dependency is both necessary and productive, as it is with children.

3. Indeed, a general history of the Innu and Inuit remains to be written. And it would be an exceptionally difficult task, because I doubt it could productively take a narrative format, but would reside in the incomplete and unbalanced contradictions that have

shaped events. Indeed, it seems to me that a good history of Native peoples would require new ways of understanding contradictions. Hegel, who taught us to think in terms of contradictions, was far too neat and orderly to be useful for this task, as were Max Weber and Michel Foucault. Foucault's central concept of "governmentality," in a situation where 30 to 40 percent of children born have FASD because their mothers were often, and knowingly, drunk during their pregnancy, is very far from a useful perspective, for FASD makes people simultaneously both more and very much less governable. Nicolas Argenti's (2007) perspective on the history of the African grasslands in the Cameroons holds some important suggestions for what is needed, as does Jeremy Beckett's (2012) work on re-indigenization. The point here is that we need to do the conceptual work for a general history of Innu and Inuit before we can further develop the history itself.

4. See, for a start, MacDonald (2008), Beckett (2000), Austin-Broos (2009), and Cowlishaw (2004). The parallels between Labrador Innu and Inuit and Australian Aborigines will likely well repay substantial thought.

5. Cape Chidley is actually in the province of Québec, being a few miles north of the Labrador political boundary, which is on a small and rocky island. But in common parlance Cape Chidley is spoken of as the northern end of Labrador.

6. For an overview of the transformations of Newfoundland from colony to country, back to colony, and then to a province of Canada, see chapter 8, "A Political Holiday," in Sider (2003a), or the more available first edition (1986).

7. Patrick McGrath (1927) has a very solid article on the whole boundary controversy, how the Privy Council's Judicial Committee decided on the height of land, and the difficulty of specifying its location. The entire record of the evidence submitted by both Québec and Newfoundland for the court to consider has been published (Great Britain, Privy Council 1927), and almost all of it is available online, courtesy of the Maritime History Archives at Memorial University. It is an extraordinary resource for Labrador and Arctic history, as the vast majority of the data are reprints of primary sources.

8. For an in-depth consideration of current perspectives on the issues for understanding long-term Arctic history, see esp. Maschner, Mason, and McGhee (2009), from which much of this section is taken; and for the controversy that focused on the earlier and less developed interpretations, see McGhee (1994).

9. "Thule" is both a place name and the name for a historically specific Arctic people. From ancient Greek usage Thule refers to the far North Atlantic, primarily east of the northern Scottish Islands, variously Iceland or Greenland. More recently it came to refer to Greenland, and then to a specific place in Greenland. Thule-Inuit, named after an archaeological site in Greenland, refers to a people whose descendants are now known as Inuit.

10. This is an almost standard process in the history of science. When Copernicus in the early sixteenth century claimed that the earth and the planets circled the sun, as against the long-standing Ptolemaic view that the earth was the center of the universe, with everything turning around it, he could not muster adequate evidence to conclusively "prove" this theory. Indeed, for almost a century the Ptolemaic astronomers could predict eclipses, using their immensely complex epicycles, as effectively as those who followed Copernicus and Kepler. What the new interpretation had on its side was Oc-

cam's razor: shave away unnecessarily complex interpretations. Now the Dorset-Thule debate is nowhere near as momentous, even for Arctic historians, but it is important for understanding the history of the north, and why things unfolded as they did, and the Copernican example makes a nice illustration of why I side with the more modern, straightforward, and to my mind more logical interpretation, whose primary advocates are Robert McGhee, Herbert Maschner, and Patricia Sutherland.

11. Maschner, Mason, and McGhee (2009) are the center of this interpretation, which is getting both more popular and more contested.

12. Typhus may have been a New World disease contribution to the Norse, and beyond them to other Europeans.

13. This is a complex point. Carol Brice-Bennett (1981) has shown that in the early nineteenth century Labrador Eskimo women became allies of the Moravian missionaries, seeking to use their assistance to diminish ill treatment by their husbands. Inequality, then as now, produces some surprising inversions as people look for ways to deal with their situation. Here victims of inequality become allies of the dominant.

14. Columbus's early engagement with the Caribbean is analyzed in detail in my essay on the long-lasting simultaneous incorporation and exclusion of Native peoples (Sider 1987).

15. The full document is now quite accessible, being part of the evidence republished in 1927 by Great Britain in the boundary dispute over Labrador between Québec and Newfoundland (Great Britain, Privy Council 1927). The first four volumes of the document have been put online, in searchable format, in part by the Maritime History Archives of Memorial University, with more volumes to come in the future. See http://www.heritage.nf.ca/books.html.

16. The term *mener* in medieval and early modern French means "to lead, to guide, to persuade, to subdue." In Cotgrave's 1611 French/English Dictionary: http://www.pbm .com/~lindahl/cotgrave/621small.html.

17. Evelyn Plaice (1990) has a useful brief history of the origin of the first Davis Inlet settlement with a Métis/Inuit/Cree interweaving. The point here is the volatility of identities, which continues with Métis becoming Labrador Inuit Association members and also asserting a Métis identity. More recently some began calling themselves "Southern Inuit." Plaice's point about locality-focused identities is helpful, to go beyond the ways the politics of Native claims interweaves with identity claims.

18. This section on the Dutch activities in coastal Labrador is drawn from Braat (1984) and Kupp and Hart (1976).

19. Proclamation of Hugh Palliser, To Bring about Friendly Intercourse with Esquimaux Indians. 1 Sept. 1764 By His Excellency Hugh Palliser, Governor and Commander in Chief in and over the Island of Newfoundland. See www.heritage.nf.ca/law/lab3 /labvol3_930.html.

20. Caribou have their own very extreme demographic cycles, which ecological historians estimate are in twenty-year cycles between peak and trough. In 1990 the George River herd, the largest of three main herds in northern and central Labrador, was estimated at about 800,000 animals. By 2010 it was estimated at about 74,000 (http://www.desdemonadespair.net/2010/12/caribou-herd-down-90-percent-in.html;

reprinted December 25, 2010, from the *Globe and Mail*, Toronto, December 23, 2010).
This may be a somewhat larger than usual herd collapse, due to contemporary interventions and disruptions, from logging and hydroelectric dam flooding (of an area larger
than Rhode Island), plus hunting with snowmobiles and high-powered rifles.

21. I use the spelling Nascopie or Naskapi depending on which was used at the time or
by the person I am discussing or quoting.

CHAPTER THREE. Living within and against Tradition

1. In Australia there is a very controversial book, Peter Sutton's *The Politics of Suffering*
(2009), which claims that Aboriginal peoples were better off under the repressive and
domineering control of the missionaries and the government, before "liberals" gave
them substantial autonomy. Under conditions of control there was less violence within
native communities, although Sutton skips over the fact that during an earlier period
there were also substantial amounts of waged work, whereas now the center of native
economies is the dole and royalties. Sutton argues that what is needed now is a return
to that pervasive control, and the Australian government has embraced this perspective.
Initially it may seem that I am arguing something similar to Sutton, when in fact my
whole book makes fundamentally opposing points.

2. Putting a specific date to the "decline of traditional life" is close to impossible,
because that would require specifying what was "tradition." For purposes here the
closure of the Moravian trading posts in Eskimo communities and their sale to the HBC,
and then the termination of the HBC trade with both Indians and Eskimos, will serve to
point toward the end of prior major components of native lives. Both will be discussed
in subsequent chapters.

3. The Moravian mission journals for several of their mission stations in Labrador are
published as the Periodical Accounts Relating to the Foreign Missions of the Church of
the United Brethren, 1890–1961. Reading through these accounts, particularly for crisis
years, helps to clarify general policies and procedures, as well as how they changed or
did not at times of crises.

4. Ommer (1990) has several articles that are very helpful for an initial analysis of
credit. Of particular importance are the articles by James Hiller, Steven Antler, Arthur
Ray, Patricia Thornton, and Carol Brice-Bennett. Chapter 3 of Sider ([1986] 2003a) is
a focused analysis of the logic of merchant capital as the context for truck and specific
forms of credit.

5. In both cases there was some "leakage," or "trespass," as native peoples traded a
portion of their production to other than their supplier, but the bulk of the trade went to
the supplier.

6. There are other versions of this fable, where the goose, or hen, or even the swan, is
pressured to lay two golden eggs a day, rather than one, and dies from the strain. These
are fables about both greed and fatal inequalities, not just greed.

7. Other authors, such as Strong (1929), suggest that the figure was 150, or 150 the first
winter and more the second. There is no way of being precise, as Naskapi communities
were far from stable in location and in who lived where.

8. See http://www.hbc.com/hbcheritage/history/people/builders/simpson.asp, accessed August 2010.

9. See especially Brice-Bennett's Memorial University MA thesis (1981). Memorial University did not then give doctorates in anthropology; this thesis is clearly at or beyond that usual level.

10. Lassalle was following Malthus, who thought that population would grow and resources would not. While it is conceivable that there could be more people than a resource base could sustain, Malthus did not grasp the point that technological developments can massively expand the available supplies of goods, nor did Malthus grasp any of the implications of inequality: in the social construction of famines some people are fatally scanted even though, as Sen (1981) has shown, there would be enough for everyone were it divided equally, and while a substantial portion of the population nourish themselves quite well.

11. There is a significant current analogy. A star U.S. football player, who left a very high paying team position to enlist in the U.S. Army, was sent to Afghanistan, and there he was killed by his fellow U.S. soldiers—it is called "friendly fire." The U.S. Army for quite a while tried to deny this, until the truth was uncovered by his angry family. Senator John McCain, pandering to the right wing of U.S. politics, said in a public meeting that this soldier's soul was with God. The soldier's brother, in the audience, shouted back: "No, . . . he is fucking dead." See http://www.guardian.co.uk/science/punctuated-equilibrium/2010/sep/27/bill-maher-richard-tillman.

12. For a more well-developed understanding of the issues, see Lea (2008) on the problems and inadequacies of helping, and Shkilnyk (1985) or especially White (2004) for the social construction of both native suffering and its appalling consequences precisely in the context of the state's "helping" and "assistance."

13. On the difference between relations with native peoples in areas where the hunger for land or for furs predominated, see Trigger (1976). On how crucial the fur trade was in the formation of Canada, see Innis ([1955] 1999).

14. There is no consistent spelling of Naskapi—there are many variations, and none have any further meaning. Beyond the point that the so-called Naskapi and the so-called Montagnais are northern and southern manifestations of the same people, and that it was easier for HBC to starve the people they called Montagnais into submission than the Naskapi, thus partially making different peoples in ways that still have some persistence, there is no need to pay attention to the different spellings of the name.

15. Caribou herds, as we have noted, are subject to extreme demographic cycles. For a contemporary example of these cycles, which is useful because it is based on herd-size estimates that were made in part by helicopter, the size of the caribou herd centered on George River, in the north central interior of Labrador, approximated almost 800,000 animals in the mid-1980s and collapsed to an estimated 74,000 animals by 2010—a 90 percent reduction. There are guesstimates of a similarly proportioned demographic herd collapse at the beginning of the twentieth century, followed by severe Naskapi famine. After each of these collapses, it takes decades for the herd to recover (Moore 2010).

16. When the caribou herd collapsed, the Naskapi were severely stricken with famine,

as they did not even have the small backup possibilities that other native people did, save to go and beg from the Moravians, for those who could make it to a mission station.

17. This history of the French term *Huron* is informed by the Access Genealogy site. See http://www.accessgenealogy.com/native/tribes/huron/huronhist.htm, accessed February 28, 2011.

18. A long-lasting reading through Jesuit, HBC, and Moravian records makes that instance very far from unique. The HBC traders often attributed such inconclusive acts as due to their own macho power, but most, in their writing, were scarcely known for their capacity to understand much beyond their own self-interest.

19. Linda Green's forthcoming book on TB among Alaskan native peoples makes this point with exceptional power. Helge Kleivan (1966) has a very useful appendix detailing Eskimo mortality, community by community, for the entire duration of the Moravian community records until the 1960s. The Father O'Brien Papers, although covering only the period from 1923 to 1946, provide a remarkably detailed account of endemic problems. These papers are quoted and discussed extensively in chapter 4.

20. Hind also notes, with regard to these fires,

that the Nasquapees were once very numerous in the Labrador Peninsula there is every reason to believe; and famine (not wars, as with many other Indian tribes) has been the cause of their decrease in numbers. [Hind had cited Gaspar Cortreal on the large population of natives in this area in the early 1500s.] In many parts of the Peninsula the wild animals which formerly abounded have almost disappeared, and consequently the means of subsistence of the native races have been withdrawn. Rabbits were once quite common on the mainland as far east and north as the Atlantic coast of the Labrador Peninsula. The porcupine was everywhere abundant on the Gulf coast, and reindeer covered the country. The destruction of mosses, lichens, and forests by fires has been the most potent cause in converting Labrador into a desert. (1863, 2:111)

21. Nancy Scheper-Hughes's *Death without Weeping: The Violence of Everyday Life in Brazil* (1992) makes the claim that very poor people in Brazil don't cry when their children die, because they are accustomed to it. It is a very similar declaration to that made by Henry Kissinger, a key architect of the napalm bombing that burned families of Vietnamese villagers alive, who claimed that "they" don't mind as much when their children are killed as "we" would.

22. From 1926 to 1948 Diamond Jenness was the chief of anthropology at the National Museum of Canada.

23. Anthropology is a very peculiar discipline in this perspective. The founders of the social and cultural anthropology that dominated the twentieth century—Franz Boas, Bronisław Malinowski, Alfred Radcliffe-Brown, E. E. Evans-Pritchard, and some others—all treated the native people among whom they lived rather badly, and all had a very limited, if any, sense of either social history or current broader context. The importance of this is that we have to realize that it was from that crowd that anthropology inherited its fundamental concepts—culture, social organization, kinship systems, etc. If you still want to hang on to the *primacy* of these concepts, think of going to a native person whose mother died in an imposed famine and asking what, in his traditional

culture, were their ceremonial foods, or what he would call his mother's brother, who easily survived. Anthropologists did this all the time, perhaps not right after the death, but not all that much later. To do anthropology, still important despite its peculiar past, means to change its concepts—the tools that shape our sense of what to look for and how to listen.

24. Professor Jeanne Briggs, of Memorial University of Newfoundland, who is fluent in Inuktitut, kindly verified these published translations.

25. I have discussed this quote at length, as well as the text from which it is taken, in Sider (1987).

26. From the online Newfoundland and Labrador Heritage Site, primarily done as a teaching aid. See http://www.heritage.nf.ca/law/flu.html, accessed January 24, 2011.

27. See http://en.wikipedia.org/wiki/1918_flu_pandemic, accessed January 24, 2011.

28. See http://en.wikipedia.org/wiki/Black_Death for a very good general history, better than its related page "The Bubonic Plague." Its sense of the causal forces is conceptually cautious, blaming a homogenized "population increase" rather than inequality and impoverishment.

29. The population increase was real; it is the supposedly causal relation of this increase to declining per capita output that is quite speculative. Malthus, the eighteenth-century founder of this elitist ideology, has almost always been shown to be wrong when concrete cases are examined.

30. There are excellent general histories, presented in the bibliography, that go deeply into the Inuit and Innu worldview, and this work is designed not to compete with them but to focus on the formation of current issues and problems. A suggestion for students: the primary sources, the HBC and Moravian records in particular, still repay exploring before too much reading in the secondary sources.

31. The mortality rates among the Indians in the interior are currently close to impossible to estimate with any degree of confidence. Their lives and deaths were so far "beyond the pale," so far beyond the palisades that "civilization" constructs against demands to care about others, that they could die almost unnoticed.

32. The West Indies were a major locale for the sale of Labrador salted and sun-dried cod. While the better grades went to Europe, the lowest grades were shipped to the Caribbean, originally as slave food, later as food for the poor. In return the vessels in that trade brought back large quantities of lowest-grade rum. Sider ([1986] 2003a) discusses this trade in detail.

33. A different set of figures is given by S. Hutton (1912), who ran a small hospital (for the Grenfell medical mission) at Okak: "The most severe pandemic [of influenza] . . . was in August 1904. . . . 324 cases came under my notice. . . . Death occurred in 47. . . . All . . . were Eskimos." Note here again that none of the Euro-Canadians living in Okak died. History matters.

CHAPTER FOUR. **The Peoples without a Country**
1. Keep in mind that Du Bois had the first PhD from Harvard granted to an African American, and his knowledge of English grammar and vocabulary was superb. He chose to put the two words, *dark* and *water*, together into one.

2. This is also the central lie of most elections, especially the superexpensive recent elections in so-called democracies. This is particularly so in those places like the United States and Canada where elections largely turn on the amount of money that can be raised. This is not to say simply that the candidate with the most money wins, but candidates get enough money, and enough obligations to their sponsors, that their promises to lessen the problems of their electorate are exactly like the promises of people who abuse their spouses, children, and elderly parents: we won't do it again, we are better now, we love you, we promise. What else can we *yet* do but try to believe one pack of liars or the other—is it possible to think we have many other realistic options?

3. A personal but crucial note is warranted. I grew up in a family that was psychologically and physically abusive, episodically violent, deeply crazy, with parents who were not very good as either parents or people. When I was quite young, I realized my parents were crazy, and I knew that more than anything I did not want to grow up to be like them. At one point in my work in Labrador I told this to a medical doctor who had worked with Native people for more than a decade, and I asked her, with real intensity, why the Native youth could or did not do what I did, look at their parents and say, to themselves at least, when I grow up I absolutely do not want to be like that. She told me that when I went out on the street to play with my friends, or visited them in their homes, I could see something different, but the problems of domestic violence and the related issues are so widespread in Labrador that the children think of them as normal.

I have recently started doubting the totalizing or overwhelming normalization of domestic violence and its related ills, both thinking and hoping that there might be other reservoirs from which people can draw sustenance. That is the subject of my next National Science Foundation Grant (ARC 1140707), just about to start, and will be the subject of my next publications.

4. Stewart Tolnay and E. M. Beck's *Festivals of Violence* (1995) is excellent on this. In addition to *Festivals of Violence*, Leon Litwak's *Trouble in Mind* (1998) is crucial to understanding impunity, a central if widely ignored feature of all modern states. To understand how much is at stake, we must realize that the popular term *lynch mob* used to describe acts of impunity against African Americans is, in almost all cases, a lie. *Lynching party* is by far the more accurate term, for many lynchings were announced in advance by poster, to draw a large crowd, and in several cases excursion trains were rented to bring the crowds out to watch, while food and postcards were sold to celebrate the event. The point here is that when the state decides to use impunity to assault, as destructively as possible, a class or category of victims, large sectors of the population support, and in some ways even enjoy, making the task of mobilizing support from other sectors of the dominant society a limited option in most historical moments. See Litwak (1998) for a brilliant and crucial exploration.

5. Max Weber's popular fantasy, repeated in countless introductory textbooks, that "the state has a monopoly on the legitimate use of violence" was written by someone who never knew anyone who was lynched or murdered by a paramilitary with utter impunity. The petty bourgeoisie, and all those who benefit from the state's squeeze on the vulnerable, need to believe Weber, and that violence against people socially present as vulnerable "others" can be categorized as either legitimate or illegitimate. Would that

the world were so neatly organized. There is an excellent bumper sticker these days that strikes to the heart of the legitimacy issue, with the U.S. Supreme Court deciding that corporations are persons, legitimately entitled to any person's rights to free speech: "I'll believe that corporations are people when Texas executes one." The state, in ways that vast numbers of its inhabitants know are illegitimate, grants legitimacy and the right to defy both law and democracy as it pleases.

6. Chapter 6 will take up issues of the so-called weapons of the weak that supposedly engage and limit domination.

7. What governments do and do not constrain is often revealing. It seems the U.S. government, for example, seeks to constrain openly fascist groups like Aryan Nation, perhaps to keep from being identified as similar to Nazi Germany, but scarcely lifts a little finger against armed groups on the Mexican border that hunt Latin American citizens coming to the United States to work as if they were wild animals not even protected by a regulated hunting season. Such examples make it important to think about the relationship between what anthropologists call culture and the state.

8. The ears are the organ of both hearing and balance. Without ears we could scarcely stand upright. If anything defines the posture of the state in its dealings with Native peoples, it is its absolute unwillingness to act in an upright fashion. In chapters 7 and especially 8, we see the state not listening—not listening so intensely and so profoundly that the suffering it made has endured for decades. This is a focused deafness, a very focused imbalance that lets the state show less concern for Native peoples than for corporations. Northern Native peoples are currently freezing and starving due to the actions of the Canadian government. As the current conservative (Harper) government in Canada daily illustrates, the lack of ears to hear (or eyes to see) Native needs leaves the state rolling around uncontrollably in the mess it has made, and continues to make, wallowing and splashing in the muck of its own lies. Even when the state pretends to do something decent, like recognize some Native rights and some Native land claims, mostly when the courts have forced the issue, it does so in such a limited and destructive way that it is usually almost better for Native peoples to walk away from the negotiating table before signing (assuming they are even at the table, and not just their extremely expensive but necessary hired consultants). Far more is at stake than a bit of wordplay to say that the state is not just deaf but has no ears and so can neither hear nor stand upright.

9. The ambivalence of the word *parties* here is intentional. Litwak (1998, chapter 6) is crucial on this. In every case, in the U.S. South, in the Canadian northlands, in Australia, the angry or—even more scary—cheerful popular and official racism that underwrites government mistreatment of its vulnerable "others" is crucial.

10. This comment on gesture is taken from Judith Butler's wonderful review "Who Owns Kafka?" (2011).

11. This notion of "fuzzy-wuzzies" refers to a point that I will elaborate in my forthcoming collected essays. A friend of mine, as a ten-year-old child after World War II, went with his father to Guam, a Pacific Island. His father, an engineer, had been sent to help rebuild the island. While there my friend stepped on a land mine. Two or three hours later, someone came and told his father that his son was in the naval hospital. His father ran there and found his son lying on the floor of the waiting room, with a ban-

daged arm—which is now still not fully working. When the father tried to find out why his son was left on the floor, the hospital staff said, "We thought he was a fuzzie-wuzzie." That was what the navy called the Chamorro, the native people of Guam. My friend as a small boy had very curly black hair and was then darkly tanned.

That, to honor both my friend and the abused people he was mistaken for, is what I mean by an anthropology, somewhat more popular in the twentieth century than now, that is about what I call "the quaint customs of the fuzzie-wuzzies." What "they" do is a matter of wonderful curiosity that may even help us "understand ourselves," as so many introductory textbooks still put it, but somehow they do not quite have the same feelings or needs as "we" do, and we do not need to pay full attention to their injuries, beyond the symbolic and literal bandages that we so generously provide. When fisher-men put a hook through a worm or a live minnow, they almost all tell their youth, whom they are teaching to fish, that it doesn't hurt the worm or the minnow. And the most upsetting thing about this is that, watching the frantic struggles of the living creature they are holding in their hand while they impale it, they all probably know better. For too long the role of anthropology was both to help us know and simultaneously to help us not know.

12. Many of the quotes that follow come from the archived correspondence to, and in a few cases from, Father Edward O'Brien. While much of the correspondence to him spells his name O'Brian, his actual name was O'Brien, and so the papers are cataloged. The collection is held at Archives and Special Collections at The Queen Elizabeth II Library, Memorial University of Newfoundland. See O'Brien (1923–1947). My citation to this collection will be abbreviated FOB.

13. Jack (John) Kemp is unusual: rather than say "the Indians," he talks about them as individual people. In some of his correspondence he translates from the Innu language to write a letter dictated by a local Innu. Kemp comes across as one of the most decent and caring of the HBC agents. Thus, what he does is particularly revealing, such as when he says he can only give "a little flour," or when his suggestions for alleviating native suffering never even consider constraining White encroachments on Innu territory.

14. We might usefully ask ourselves how the HBC post managers implementing this policy could not have realized that strategies that lower costs by also diminishing the producers cannot possibly work in the long run. We can then note that currently U.S. businesses continue to downsize their work force and their wage bill, move manufacturing overseas, etc., without realizing that they are simultaneously massively diminishing the consumption of their own goods. Did they think that an explosive expansion of consumer credit, as a temporary patch over this problem, could go on forever? Self-interested domination usually turns out to be extraordinarily shortsighted, which in the long run may be either a pathway to the collapse of current forms of exploitation or the introduction to even more oppression.

15. A similar issue, the dependence of the Eskimos on the Moravian missionaries, formed in the early nineteenth century, was discussed at some length, and with much insight, by Carol Brice-Bennett in her "Two Opinions" (1981). Of special importance is her gender-focused analysis, showing that women particularly benefitted from their alliance with the missionaries.

16. L. Jane McMillan is excellent on this in her work with the Mi'kmaw. See, for a start, McMillan (2011).

17. A similar point was made by Paul Willis in his *Learning to Labour* (1977), explaining how British working-class youth, knowing that the school system is set up against their interests, defy it by being "bad," and by so doing reproduce as their future the working-class lives of their parents, against whom and whose lifestyle they had rebelled. But this book was written at a time when one could continue to earn a living from a working-class position.

18. See Sider ([1986] 2003a), esp. the chapter entitled "A Political Holiday," for a fuller explanation of the changing status of Newfoundland before it joined Canada. Schematically the situation is this: Newfoundland was directly governed from Great Britain by naval governors sent out to the island until 1824, when it was reorganized as a colony. In 1855 the colony was granted "Responsible Government" status, meaning that the legislature, rather than the royal governor, usually controlled the situation. This is the basis for dominion status. In 1934 Newfoundland was bankrupt, unable to borrow or to pay its bills, and the legislature voted to give up its dominion status and revert to being a directly governed colony of Great Britain. It kept this status until confederation with Canada in 1949.

19. The term seems to have been invented by Edward Tompkins, a consultant, who wrote a report (1988) for Jack Harris, a member of the Newfoundland Parliament with a particularly decent record as a spokesperson for native causes. The report, entitled "Pencilled Out," is an exceptionally well-done document, and a model for good legislative research, but it ends long before all the consequences of being penciled out had emerged or developed.

20. See http://www.ammsa.com/publications/windspeaker/residential-school -students-left-out-agreement and especially the text of Associate Chief Justice Murray Sinclair's presentation to the Aboriginal Justice Learning Network, April 16–18, 1997. Justice Sinclair was the head of the Truth and Reconciliation Commission. This presentation to the Learning Network is at http://www.ammsa.com/content/historical -relationship-between-canadian-justice-system-and-aboriginal-people. L. Jane McMillan alerted me to these documents.

21. The governments of Newfoundland and occasionally Canada finance gatherings of native women to air their grievances and explain their problems, and government officials routinely put in an appearance and make a brief speech. These speeches are full of platitudes of concern and cliché statements about respect for elders and concern for gender equality. I find it difficult to even read these government speeches year after year, with the same platitudes, the same total lack of effective action, and the same promises to finance another conference, while the same high rates of youth suicide, domestic violence, and substance abuse continue unabated.

22. One of my sons had a T-shirt with a somewhat realistic drawing of the human digestive system from mouth through stomach and intestines, ending in the colon. Around this drawing were the words "*shit doesn't just happen.*" We can usefully take this as a precise, if rather gentle, critique of Newfoundland's treatment of Labrador.

23. Upper Canada and Lower Canada get their designation from the flow of the St.

Lawrence River from the Great Lakes to the Atlantic Ocean. Upper Canada, including primarily Ontario, is upriver, against the current; Lower Canada, primarily Québec, is downriver. As the river runs from southwest to northeast, and as we are accustomed to the convention of calling north "up," the way Canadian regions are named takes a moment to grasp.

24. Baudelaire's title for his poem was *Les Fleurs du Mal*. I prefer to use my translation, the flowers of hurt, rather than the usual "Flowers of Evil." Evil focuses on what is being done to the vulnerable; hurt centers the issues on how the vulnerable must, in this context, live. The poems address both.

CHAPTER FIVE. **Mapping Dignity**

1. With our competitive educational system, full of grades and rankings, and with our increasingly unequal societies, we are often centered on the production of self. Perhaps we can leave that training long enough to see what has been different in these societies.

2. The ability of men to hunt successfully, and to return alive from their hunts, is also of course part of the relations between men and women and not just the relations between men and men. For both men and women the relation between adults and children is also relevant here. Goudie (1973) and Byrne and Fouillard (2000) are excellent sources for a broader range of examples. The examples here will suffice to introduce a larger range of issues.

3. The blank area on the Native map, on the southern coast of Labrador, is the locale of early and continuing more intense Euro-Canadian settlement and use.

CHAPTER SIX. **Life in a Concentration Village**

1. This centralization program is described and analyzed in my essay "The Ties That Bind" (Sider 1980) and in Sider (2003a).

2. In the 1950s and 1960s Newfoundland fish merchants, who controlled the trade, were paying fisher-families two and a half cents a pound for cod fish, headed and gutted—about a third of the weight of the fish thrown back in the sea. At the same time Norwegian fisher-families were getting seven cents a pound for cod fish, and two and a half cents a pound for the heads and guts to feed farmed mink. This created a very substantial difference in quality of life.

3. In the 1960s Newfoundland subsidized the development of a factory on the west coast of the island to make "linerboard"—basically wood chips and glue—from timber imported from Labrador. They could not get enough labor for the factory until wages were raised significantly above what was planned; for this and other reasons the factory soon went bankrupt and the province lost tens of millions of dollars. In the 1970s, after centralization of the island's population was quite far along, the province subsidized building an oil refinery, and the line of cars of people looking for construction work on the day hiring was announced to begin was over four miles long. Even politicians can learn lessons this dramatic.

4. Population numbers matter to what kinds of choices become available. It might well be easier for several million people to have an "Arab Spring" than for a few hundred Native activists drawn from a total population of a few thousand Native people to do

something as effectively defiant. It is not clear if what the Arab activists so perceptively call "the North American autumn" makes it easier or harder for Native people to develop and achieve their alternatives. It's not impossible for relatively few activists to make a large and effective dent in the body politic, but their struggles often unfold on a more symbolic terrain, which enables superficial and short-term "solutions" to be imposed.

5. Kirk Dombrowski (2001), who did field research in southeast Alaska, provided this example.

6. "So passes the glories of the world." The full phrase, from which this more usual version is derived, is even more of an indictment of the world that does this to people. It comes from Thomas à Kempis, *The Imitation of Christ*, written in 1418: *O quam cito transit gloria mundi* ("How quickly the glory of the world passes away") (see *Wikipedia*).

7. As this situation intensifies and people see their future increasingly diminished and their partially viable yesterdays increasingly unlikely to continue, something can snap, and people turn on those who dominate them, whatever the cost. Severity and pervasiveness of oppression fortunately cannot constrain opposition with any certainty.

8. The crucial case establishing Native collective rights—but only one case among many moving the Canadian state in this direction—is *Delgamuukw v. British Columbia* (1997) 3 S.C.R. 1010, also known as "Delgamuukw vs. the Queen."

9. This was followed by Colin Samson's deeply perceptive analysis (2003) of how the Innu people were being squeezed by state and capital, so that they were trapped between an unlivable yesterday and a destructive tomorrow. This book attracted the wrath of some classic ethnographers on grounds that had little to do with the issues his book sought so usefully to develop. Indeed, part of my anger against traditional anthropology, quite visible here, has to do with its frequent inability to go beyond the all-so-rewarding current intellectual fads—from the nonsense of "hybridity" (as if there were anything pure) to postmodern textual analysis—to engage with what is actually happening to people.

10. This is a tribute to an extraordinary book by Zygmunt Bauman, *Modernity and the Holocaust* (2000), in which he argues that the holocaust, far from just being a specifically German phenomenon, was both a central and a more general moment in the continuing formation of modernity.

11. The Norwegian Refugee Council, Internal Displacement Monitoring Center, has an online study: Development-Induced Displacement. See http://www.internal -displacement.org.

12. December 1987, Government of Newfoundland and Labrador, Policy regarding Aboriginal Land Claims, Intergovernmental Affairs Secretariat, Native Policy Unit. The document is signed, with a cover letter, by Newfoundland and Labrador's provincial premier, Brian Peckford. The typescript is on file in the Newfoundland and Labrador Legislative Library.

13. Sarsfield's wonderful clarity brought only small and not very deep changes. Certainly the actual material control of lands and the economy that he so perceptively regarded as the essence of a healthier future was very decisively sidelined.

14. The quote is from the press release of the judicial inquiry, in the Newfoundland and Labrador Provincial Archives.

15. See http://www.naskapi.ca/en/History#journey. The historical anthropologist Peter Armitage was the author.

16. It may also include compensation for the vast amount of pollution, particularly lake pollution, caused by the mining and mine tailings. I have been unable to access this Impact Benefits Agreement, which is almost certainly restricted, so that other Native peoples cannot see what they might get.

17. See www.innu.ca. The conversation was also published in *Native Issues* 4, no. 1 (1984): 25–33.

18. *Providing safe housing to abused women and children: an exploration of the safe house model in Newfoundland and Labrador. Appendix: Safe houses in Northern Labrador.* Presented to Victim Services, NL Dept. of Justice, by Charlotte Wolfrey, President, Tongamiut Inuit Annait and Melanie Gear, Acting Coordinator, Tongamiut Inuit Annait. On file at the Legislative Library, Newfoundland and Labrador Provincial Legislature, St. John's. I thank Trinne Sciolden for finding this document for me. I transcribed this document in an extreme rush, so there may be some small elisions. I can, however, vouch for the general fidelity of the text.

19. On file at the Newfoundland and Labrador Legislative Library.

20. What made this request for continuity of traditional use unrealistic is that it required Native peoples to live unchanged lives, which was impossible, and it defined as "traditional" work for fur-trading companies, which by the late mid-twentieth century was no longer available. The Canadian state could not define pre-contact land use as "traditional," although of course it was, as this would give surviving Native peoples grounds to claim very much more.

21. "Native Rights Group Charges New Hunting Laws Were Too Rigid," *Telegraph Journal*, February 8, 1983, St. John, New Brunswick.

22. Indeed, the Inuit of Labrador have just (December 2011) voted, in council, to end their moratorium on uranium mining, effective when they have in place a set of environmental regulations. Producing such regulations is immensely difficult to do well, and there is ordinarily a lot of lobbying by corporations to make sure it is not done all that well.

CHAPTER SEVEN. **Today May Become Tomorrow**

1. Note that the phrase used almost entirely throughout is "the Newfoundland government." Technically and legally it is the Newfoundland and Labrador government. Labrador does indeed send representatives to the provincial parliament, and the government in St. John's even has bureaucracies and ministries concerned with Labrador affairs. It used to be what Canada has called "northern development and native affairs," which tells you right in the name what comes first. As Native rights became an issue for development planners, who can no longer just do as they wish, at least not right away, Native well-being has become a more prominent issue for the government. But—and this is crucial—Labrador is still governed and administered very much for the convenience and benefit of Newfoundland, so to call the government Newfoundland and

Labrador, rather than Newfoundland, is to participate in an important misrepresentation, particularly when the focus is on Native peoples.

2. Tess Lea's 2008 study of a similar situation with Australian Aborigines, where a substantial portion of the bureaucrats who deal with Aboriginal peoples seem to mean well but are nonetheless very ineffective, is an instructive example of a general problem. It is particularly interesting that after multiple cases of this situation the book just stops: no conclusions, no recommendations, nothing to point even to the possibility of change or improvement. That may be the unstated conclusion: within the present general organization of government's engagement with Native peoples there is no realistic way forward. The whole system needs change.

3. In 2001 the name was changed from Sheshatshit. Would that this change represented a new level of governmental sensitivity. This will soon be discussed.

4. White's critique is quite harsh and does not take into account either what social workers try to do or the obstacles they face in offering help from a government that has done a lot of harm. Nonetheless, one can get a sense from her paper of the breakdown of a system.

5. This sentence ends with a preposition, which is grammatically incorrect. It is a poke at the compulsion to always play by the rules, even in the face of such sorrow. For anything much to change we may have to stop playing by the rules.

6. See http://archives.cbc.ca/emissions/emission.asp?page=42&ID.

7. "In October, the Attawapiskat First Nation declared an emergency. And no one came to help" (see http://www.guardian.co.uk/commentisfree/2011/dec/11/canada-third-world-first-nation-attawapiskat?newsfeed=true). The community, situated in far northern Ontario and made up of eighteen hundred citizens, mostly Cree, has announced that its situation is dire, due to a "severe housing shortage." The community has been visited by an opposition MP and filmed. The images relayed back are horrifying. There are generations of families living in flimsy tents or shacks built from mismatched plywood and covered with tarpaulins. Mould seeps through insulation and runs down the walls. Pails of excrement are being thrown in ditches. Children have chronic skin diseases brought on by poor living conditions; others have third-degree burns caused by cheap stoves. A hundred people live in a prefab trailer, crammed into rooms with just four bathrooms for all. The temperature drops a few more degrees below zero every day. It gets as low as −40 degrees Celsius in the winter—without the wind chill. Mothers say baby shampoo freezes sitting on the shelf.

Most citizens of Attawapiskat have endured these desperate conditions since a sewage overflow drove them from their homes in 2009. Some have lived this way for longer. Now, with most temporary accommodations deteriorating, the situation has become critical. But despite repeated calls to the Department of Indian and Northern Affairs, their issues have been ignored.

There are more problems. Schooling takes place in temporary constructions, erected after a diesel fuel leak took the main building in 2000, and even after an energetic campaign by students, no plans to build a new one have been made. Unemployment, alcoholism, and crime are rife. Disaster officials are now working at the scene. To add to the irony, a few miles away (and on Attawapiskat land), the DeBeers diamond mine extracts hundreds of millions of dollars in resources, delivering valuable tax dollars to governments—but, while it employs a small part of the community, the riches, for a variety of reasons, remain in the hands of others. It's a scene one frequently sees in the developing world. But here it is, in Canada. . . . Meanwhile, Attawapiskat, and so many communities like it, calls for help and hopes for change.

This is worth quoting at length because the last line makes manifest what I call the all-too-popular "yoohoo" strategy for how serious social change can happen: "Here I am state, come and be nice to me." As if the state did not know, year after year. As if the state could be talked into playing nice. Give candy to the bully and maybe he or she will be my friend. Far more usually change—and also at first more oppression—comes in the context of a very serious, in-your-face confrontation, such as when the Innu physically put an abusive magistrate on an outbound plane and then scattered oil drums on the airfield to keep the police from flying back in.

8. There are actually two sets of figures tossed about. One, widespread in Newfoundland, says $52 million; another says that Canada subsidized the move to the tune of $153 million. This may be a typographical error, or Canadians paying each other.

9. See assets.survivalinternational.org/static/files/books/InnuReport.pdf, accessed December 2011.

10. See http://arcticcircle.uconn.edu/SEEJ/voisey/intro.html.

11. See "The Future of Voisey's Bay: Introduction," Arctic Circle, http://arcticcircle .uconn.edu/SEEJ/voisey/intro.html.

12. See Vale's company website, http://www.vbnc.com/ProjectOverview.asp. The diesel fuel figure was computed by Jenny Higgens and can be found at http://www .heritage.nf.ca/society/voiseys_bay_environment.html.

13. In the 1960s, when I was working as a civil rights organizer with the Lumbee Indian people, in the southeastern United States, they started a "Homecoming Festival" that included a beauty contest for young Lumbee women, organized just like U.S. beauty contests, with a swimsuit competition for gawping at bodies, and a talent show for finding out which one person was the best at one thing or another. The idea that there should be some public acknowledgment of respect for many, not one, elderly women and men who helped to raise children and grandchildren did not seem to occur to those who organized the Homecoming Festival, nor was there any protest to copying the individualist, competitive, and sexualized values of the dominant society as part of a new assertion of Indian lives. Hockey, an essentially violent and deeply aggressive sport, in northern Indian communities is just another manifestation of this broader issue of separate and distinct lives lived both against the put-downs of native people and within the values that have put them down. It is a heart-wrenchingly difficult task for native people to give birth to different ways.

14. It hurts to put a comma between fly-in and fly-out, as it suggests a space, which might be a space of listening. There is no evidence for that in what happens subsequently.

CHAPTER EIGHT. **Warriors of Wisdom**

1. Columbia University, Butler Library, Rare Book Room. Tate Manuscripts, Tale No. 41, Story of the Porcupine Hunter, pp. 1816–1831. Manuscript Collections, Henry W. Tate Collection, American Indian Tales, Box 2. Call no. x898c42/t18.

2. The historian Alf Ludtke (1995) writes of "confrontational disengagement" among German industrial workers in the early twentieth century. This concept is similar to what is being proposed here, particularly in that both his perspective and mine transcend a simple opposition between resistance to and cooperation with domination.

REFERENCES

Adorno, Theodor, and Max Horkheimer. 2010. "Towards a New Manifesto." *New Left Review* 65:33–62.

Aldridge, D., and K. St. John. 1991. "Adolescent and Pre-adolescent Suicide in Newfoundland and Labrador." *Canadian Journal of Psychiatry* 36:432–436.

Anderson, Karen L. 1991. *Chain Her by One Foot: The Subjugation of Native Women in Seventeenth-Century New France*. London: Routledge.

Archibald, Linda, and Mary Crnkovich. 1999. *If Gender Mattered: A Case Study of Inuit Women, Land Claims, and the Voisy's Bay Nickel Project*. Electronic document. http://publications.gc.ca/collections/Collection/SW21-39-1999E.pdf.

Argenti, Nicolas. 2007. *The Intestines of the State*. Chicago: University of Chicago Press.

Armitage, Peter. 1987. "Why Can't They Accept a Moratorium on Low-Level Flying?" *Peace Magazine* 3 (5): 15–16.

Assembly of First Nations. 2005. "Federal Government Funding to First Nations: Critique and Explanation." July 22. http://64.26.129.156/cmslib/general/Federal-Government-Funding-to-First-Nations.pdf.

Auger, Réginald. 1991. *Labrador Inuit and Europeans in the Strait of Belle Isle: From the Written Sources to the Archæological Evidence*. Quebec: Université Laval, Centre d'études nordiques no. 55.

Austin-Broos, Diane. 2009. *Arrernte Present, Arrernte Past: Invasion, Violence, and Imagination in Indigenous Central Australia*. Chicago: University of Chicago Press.

Baker, Jamie. 2005. "Naskapi Future Rests on Plan." *St. John's Telegram*, July 20, A1.

Bakewell, Charles M. 1939. *Source Book in Ancient Philosophy*. Rev. ed. New York: Charles Scribners Sons.

Barkham, Selma. 1980. "A Note on the Strait of Belle Isle during the Period of Basque Contact with Indians and Inuit." *Études/Inuit/Studies* 4 (1–2): 51–58.

———. 1982. "Documentary Evidence for 16th Century Basque Whaling Ships in the

Straits of Belle Isle." In *Early European Settlement and Exploration in Atlantic Canada: Selected Papers*, edited by George M. Story, 53–95. St. John's: Memorial University of Newfoundland.

Bauman, Zygmunt. 2000. *Modernity and the Holocaust.* Ithaca: Cornell University Press.

Beckett, Jeremy. 2000. *Wherever I Go: Myles Lalor's "Oral History."* Melbourne: Melbourne University Press.

———. 2012. "Returned to Sender: Some Predicaments of Re-indigenization." *Oceania* 82 (1–2): 104–112.

Berger, John. (1983) 2011. "The Time of the Cosmonauts." In *Once in Europa.* New York: Vintage.

Birket-Smith, Kaj. 1959. *The Eskimos.* London: Methuen.

Black-Rogers, Mary. 1986. "Varieties of 'Starving': Semantics and Survival in the Subarctic Fur Trade, 1750–1850." *Ethnohistory* 33 (4): 353–383.

Boas, Franz. 1926. "Two Eskimo Riddles from Labrador." *Journal of American Folklore* 39:486.

Braat, J. 1984. "Dutch Activities in the North and the Arctic during the Sixteenth and Seventeenth Centuries." *Arctic Anthropology* 37 (4): 473–480.

Brice-Bennett, Carol. 1976. "Inuit Land Use in the East-Central Canadian Arctic." In *Inuit Land Use and Occupancy Project*, vol. 1, edited by Milton R. Freeman. Ottawa: Department of Indian and Northern Affairs.

———. 1981. "Two Opinions: Inuit and Moravian Missionaries in Labrador, 1804–1860." MA thesis, Memorial University of Newfoundland.

———. 1986. *Renewable Resource Use and Wage Employment in the Economy of Northern Labrador.* Ottawa: Royal Commission on Employment and Unemployment, Newfoundland and Labrador.

———. 1990. "Missionaries as Traders: Moravians and Labrador Inuit, 1771–1860." In *Merchant Credit and Labour Strategies in Historical Perspective*, edited by Rosemary E. Ommer, 223–254. Fredericton, NB: Acadiensis.

———. 1994. Dispossessed: The Eviction of Inuit from Hebron, Labrador. Happy Valley: Labrador Institute of Northern Studies.

———, ed. 1999. *Remembering the Years of My Life: Journeys of a Labrador Inuit Hunter.* Recounted by Paulus Maggo. Social and Economic Studies, no. 63. St. John's, NL: ISER.

———. 2000. *Ikkaumajânnik Piusivinnik = Reconciling with Memories: Titigattausimajut Katiutisimaningit Hebronimi 40 Jâret Kingungani Nottitausimalidlutik = A Record of the Reunion at Hebron 40 Years after Relocation.* Nain, NL: Labrador Inuit Association.

———. 2003. *Hopedale: Three Ages of a Community in Northern Labrador.* St. John's, NL: Historic Sites Association of Newfoundland and Labrador.

Brody, Hugh. 1981. *Maps and Dreams: Indians and the British Columbia Frontier.* Vancouver: Douglas and McIntyre.

Budgel, Richard. 1984. "Canada, Newfoundland, and the Labrador Indians, 1949–69." *Native Issues* 4 (October 1).

Butler, Judith. 2011. "Who Owns Kafka?" *London Review of Books* 33 (5): 3–8.

Byrne, Nympha, and Camille Fouillard, eds. 2000. *It's Like the Legend: Innu Women's Voices*. Charlottetown, PE: Gynergy Books.

Canada. 1994. *Suicide in Canada*. Ottawa: Health Canada.

Canada, Indian and Northern Affairs. 1996. *Innu Nation Claim May 1996*. Electronic document. http://arcticcircle.uconn.edu/SEEJ/voisey/innu.html.

Canada, Royal Commission on Aboriginal Affairs. 2004. *Royal Commission on Aboriginal Affairs, Report*. Electronic document. http://www.ainc-inac.gc.ca/.

Canada, Royal Commission on Aboriginal Peoples [Rene Dussault, Georges Erasmus]. 1995. *Choosing Life—Special Report on Suicide among Aboriginal Peoples*. Ottawa: Royal Commission on Aboriginal Peoples. http://www.ainc-inac.gc.ca/.

Canada Supreme Court Reports. 1939. *In the Matter of a Reference as to Whether "Indians" in S.91 (24) of the British North American Act Includes Eskimo Inhabitants of the Province of Quebec*. Ottawa: Queens Printer.

Carmichael, Ann G. 1983. "Infections, Hidden Hunger, and History." In *Hunger and History: The Impact of Changing Food Production and Consumption Patterns on Society*, edited by Robert I. Rotberg and Theodore K. Rabb. Cambridge: Cambridge University Press.

Cartwright, George (Capt.). (1792) 1980. *A Journal of Transactions and Events, During a Residence of Nearly Sixteen Years on the Coast of Labrador; Containing Many Interesting Particulars, Both of the Country and Its Inhabitants, not Hitherto Known*. 3 vols. Newark, UK: Alin and Ridge.

Chappell, Edward. 1818. *Voyage of His Majesty's Ship Rosamond to Newfoundland and the Southern Coast of Labrador, of Which Countries No Account Has Been Published by any British Traveller Since the Reign of Queen Elizabeth*. London: Printed for J. Mawman.

Cowlishaw, Gillian. 2004. *Blackfellas, Whitefellas, and the Hidden Injuries of Race*. Oxford: Blackwell.

Damas, David. 1969. *Contributions to Anthropology: Band Societies: Proceedings of the Conference on Band Organization, Ottawa, August 30 to September 2, 1965*. Ottawa: National Museums of Canada.

———. 1984. *Handbook of North American Indians*. Vol. 5, *Arctic*. Washington, DC: Smithsonian Institute Press.

———. 2002. *Arctic Migrants / Arctic Villagers*. Montreal: McGill-Queen's University Press.

Das, Veena, Arthur Kleinman, Margaret Lock, Mamphela Ramphele, and Pamela Reynolds. 2001. *Remaking a World: Violence, Social Suffering, and Recovery*. Berkeley: University of California Press.

Davies, K. G. 1963. *Northern Quebec and Labrador Journals and Correspondence, 1819–35*. Introduction by Glyndwr Williams. London: Hudson's Bay Record Society.

Diubaldo, Richard J. 1989. "You Can't Keep the Native Native." In *For Purposes of Dominion: Essays in Honour of Morris Zaslow*, edited by Kenneth Coates and William Morrison. North York, ON: Captus University Press.

Dombrowski, Kirk. 2001. *Against Culture: Development, Politics, and Religion in Indian Alaska*. Lincoln: University of Nebraska Press.

———. 2010. "The White Hand of Capitalism and the End of Indigenism as We Know It." *Australian Journal of Anthropology* 21 (1): 129–140.

Dreaddy, Kimberly (for the provincial association against family violence). 2002. *Moving toward Safety: Responding to Family Violence in Aboriginal and Northern Communities of Labrador.* Women's Policy Office, NL House of Assembly.

Duhaime, Gerard. 2000. "Introduction: For a Better Understanding of Present-Day Economy." *Études/Inuit/Studies* 24 (1): 5–8.

Dumond, Don E. 1979. "Eskimo-Indian Relationships: A View from Prehistory." *Arctic Anthropology* 16 (2): 3–22.

Evano, Stephanie. 2003. *Le Suicide et la Mort Chez Lez Mamit-Innuat.* Paris: L'Harmattan.

Farmer, Paul. 2003. *Pathologies of Power: Health, Human Rights, and the New War on the Poor.* Berkeley: University of California Press.

Feit, Harvey A. 1991. "The Construction of Algonquin Hunting Territories: Private Property as Moral Lesson, Policy Advocacy, and Ethnographic Error." In *Colonial Situations: Essays on the Contextualization of Ethnographic Knowledge* (*History of Anthropology*, vol. 7), edited by George W. Stocking, 109–134. Madison: University of Wisconsin Press.

Fitzhugh, William W. 1972. *Environmental Archeology and Cultural Systems in Hamilton Inlet, Labrador: A Survey of the Central Labrador Coast from 3000 BC to the Present.* Smithsonian Contributions to Anthropology, no. 16. Washington, DC: Smithsonian Institution Press.

———. 1985. "Introduction." In *Cultures in Contact: The Impact of European Contacts on Native American Cultural Institutions, A.D. 1000–1800,* edited by William W. Fitzhugh, 1–18. Washington, DC: Smithsonian Institution Press.

Fornel, Louis. (1743) 1927. "Relation du voyage du Sieur Louis Fornel a la Baye des Esquimaux, 16 Mai au 27 aout 1743." Great Britain, Privy Council, Documents Relating to the Labrador Boundary Dispute, 3280–3303.

Foucault, Michel. 1978. *Discipline and Punish: The Birth of the Prison.* New York: Random House.

Fouillard, Camille, and Katie Rich. 1995. *Gathering Voices: Finding Strength to Help Our Children.* Vancouver: Douglas and McIntyre.

Frankl, Viktor E. 1959. *Man's Search for Meaning: An Introduction to Logotherapy.* Boston: Beacon.

Gearing, Fred. 1962. *Priests and Warriors: Social Structures for Cherokee Politics in the 18th Century.* American Anthropological Association Memoir 93. Menasha, WI: American Anthropological Association.

Geertz, Clifford. 1973. *The Interpretation of Cultures: Selected Essays.* New York: Basic Books.

Giles, Winona, and Jennifer Hyndman, eds. 2004. *Sites of Violence: Gender and Conflict Zones.* Los Angeles: University of California Press.

Gosling, W. G. 1910. *Labrador: Its Discovery, Exploration, and Development.* Toronto: Musson.

Goss Gilroy, Inc., Institute for Human Resource Development, Bobbie Boland, and Don Gallant and Associates. 2004. *Formative Evaluation of the Violence Prevention Initiative, Final Report.* Electronic document. http://gov.nl.ca/vpi/.

Goudie, Elizabeth. 1973. *Woman of Labrador*. Edited and with an introduction by David Zimmerly. Toronto: P. Martin Associates.

Great Britain, Parliament, House of Commons. 1857. Select Committee on the Hudson's Bay Company, 1857. 1 microfiche; 3 pages. CIHM 49182. Queen Elizabeth II Library, Memorial University of Newfoundland.

Great Britain, Parliament, House of Commons. Select Committee on the Hudson's Bay Company. 1857. Report from the Select Committee on the Hudson's Bay Company [microform]; together with the proceedings of the committee, minutes of evidence, appendix and index. 7 microfiches, filmed from National Library of Canada. CNS/Microform.

Great Britain, Privy Council, Judicial Committee. 1927. In the matter of the Boundary between the Dominion of Canada and the Colony of Newfoundland in the Labrador Peninsula. Documents filed for case. London.

Green, Linda. 1999. *Fear as a Way of Life: Mayan Widows in Rural Guatemala*. New York: Columbia University Press.

———. N.d. "To Die in the Silence of History: Yupik People and Tuberculosis in Southwestern Alaska." Unpublished manuscript.

Grenfell, Wilfred T. 1934. *The Romance of Labrador*. New York: Macmillan.

Hale, Charles R. 2002. "Does Multiculturalism Menace? Governance, Cultural Rights and the Politics of Identity in Guatemala." *Journal of Latin American Studies* 34:485–524.

Harper, Francis. 1964. *The Friendly Montagnais and Their Neighbors in the Ungava Peninsula*. Lawrence, KS: Allen Press.

Harrington, Fred H., and Alasdair M. Veitch. 1991. "Short-Term Impacts of Low-Level Jet Fighter Training on Caribou in Labrador." *Arctic* 44 (4): 318–327.

Henriksen, Georg. 1973. *Hunters in the Barrens: The Naskapi on the Edge of the White Man's World*. St. John's, NL: ISER.

———. 1993a. "Life and Death among the Mushuau Innu of Northern Labrador." ISER Research and Policy Paper no. 17. St. John's, NL: ISER.

———. 1993b. *Report on the Social and Economic Development of the Innu Community of Davis Inlet, to the Economic Recovery Commission*. Newfoundland Legislative Library.

Hiller, James K. 1967. "The Foundation and the Early Years of the Moravian Mission in Labrador, 1752–1805." MA thesis, Memorial University of Newfoundland.

Hilton, G. W. 1958. "The Truck Act of 1831." *Economic History Review* 10, New Series (3): 470–479. Accessed February 24, 2010. http://www.jstor.org/stable/2591266.

Hind, Henry Youle. 1863. *Explorations in the Interior of Labrador*. 2 vols. London: Longman, Green.

Hubbard, Mina. 1909. *A Woman's Way through Unknown Labrador: An Account of the Exploration of the Nascoupee and George Rivers*. New York: Doubleday Page.

Hutton, S. K. 1912. *Among the Eskimos of Labrador: A Record of Five Years' Close Intercourse with the Eskimo Tribes of Labrador*. Philadelphia: J. B. Lippencott.

Innis, Harold Adams. (1955) 1999. *The Fur Trade in Canada: An Introduction to Canadian Economic History*. With a New Introductory Essay by Arthur J. Ray. Toronto: University of Toronto Press.

Innu Nation. (1984) 2005. *Assimilation of the Innu: A Discussion between Sylvestre Andrew and Pien Gregoir, August 1984.* Electronic document. http://www.innu.ca/index.php ?option=com_content&view=article.

Innu Nation and Mushuau Innu Band Council. 1995. *Gathering Voices: Finding Strength to Help Our Children.* Vancouver: Douglas and McIntyre.

Inuit Tapirisat of Canada. 1994. *Submission of the Inuit Tapirisat of Canada to the Royal Commission on Aboriginal Peoples.* Inuit Tapirisat of Canada.

Jenness, Diamond. 1965. "Eskimo Administration: III. Labrador." Arctic Institute of North America, Technical Paper no. 16. St. John's: Memorial University of Newfoundland, Labrador Institute.

Kaplan, Susan. 1985. "European Goods and Socio-economic Change in Early Labrador Inuit Society." In *Cultures in Contact: The Impact of European Contacts on Native American Cultural Institutions, 1000–1800,* edited by William W. Fitzhugh, 45–69. Washington, DC: Smithsonian Institution Press.

Kennedy, John C. 1982. *Holding the Line: Ethnic Boundaries in a Northern Labrador Community.* Social and Economic Studies, no. 27. St. John's, NL: ISER.

Kettl, P. A., and E. O. Bixler. 1991. "Suicide in Alaska Natives, 1979–1984." *Psychiatry* 54:55–63.

Klein, Naomi. 2005. "Lookout: Terror's Greatest Recruitment Tool." *Nation,* August 29.

Kleivan, Helge. 1966. *The Eskimos of Northeast Labrador: A History of Eskimo-White Relations, 1771–1955.* Oslo: Norsk Polarinstitutt, Skrifter nr. 139.

Krech, Shepard, III. 1984. *The Subarctic Fur Trade: Native Social and Economic Adaptations.* Vancouver: University of British Columbia Press.

Kupp, Jan, and Simon Hart. 1976. "The Dutch in the Strait of Davis and Labrador during the 17th and 18th Centuries." *Man in the Northeast* 11:3–20.

Labrador and Aboriginal Affairs, Newfoundland and Labrador. 2005. *Labrador Inuit Land Claims.* Electronic document. http://www.exec.gov.nl.ca/exec/igas/land _claims/agreement.html.

Labrador Inuit Association. 1983. Legislative Library. Brief to the Commission Parlementaire de la Presidence Du Conceil et de la Constitution. December. Newfoundland and Labrador, Province of Indian Affairs and Northern Development.

Labrador Inuit Land Claims Agreement. 2004. Labrador Inuit Land Claims Area. http://www.exec.gov.nl.ca/exec/igas/land_claims/agreement.html.

Lea, Tess. 2008. *Bureaucrats and Bleeding Hearts: Indigenous Health in Northern Australia.* UNSW Press.

Leacock, Eleanor. 1954. *The Montagnais "Hunting Territory" and the Fur Trade.* American Anthropological Association. Memoir no. 78. Menasha, WI: American Anthropological Association.

Leacock, Eleanor, and Nan Rothschild, eds. 1994. *Labrador Winter: The Ethnographic Journals of William Duncan Strong, 1927–1928.* Washington, DC: Smithsonian Institution Press.

Lester, David. 1997. *Suicide in American Indians.* New York: Nova Science Publishers.

Litwack, Leon F. 1998. *Trouble in Mind: Black Southerners in the Age of Jim Crow.* New York: Knopf.

Loring, Stephen G. 1992. "Princes and Princesses of Ragged Fame: Innu Archaeology and Ethnohistory in Labrador." PhD diss., University of Massachusetts.

Loring, Stephen, and Daniel Ashini. 2000. "Past and Future Pathways: Innu Cultural Heritage in the Twenty-First Century." In *Indigenous Cultures in an Interconnected World*, edited by Claire Smith and Graeme Ward, 167–189. Sydney, Australia: Allen & Unwin.

Low, Albert P. 1896. *Report on Explorations in the Labrador Peninsula along the East Main, Koksoak, Hamilton, Manicuagan and Portions of Other Rivers in 1892–93–94–95.* Ottawa: Geological Survey of Canada. Annual report. Vol. VIII.

Ludtke, Alf, ed. 1995. *The History of Everyday Life: Reconstructing Historical Experiences and Ways of Life.* Trans. William Templer. Princeton: Princeton University Press.

Lysaght, A. M. (Averil M.), ed. 1971. *Joseph Banks in Newfoundland and Labrador, 1766: His Diary, Manuscripts, and Collections.* Berkeley: University of California Press.

Macdonald, Gaynor. 2008. "Difference or Disappearance: The Politics of Indigenous Inclusion in the Liberal State." *Anthropologica* 50 (2): 341–358.

MacGregor, William. 1907. Correspondence. Maritime History Archives, Newfoundland Governors 1904–1909. File: File 2.050. Keith Matthews, Series 3. 04/10. Memorial University of Newfoundland.

Mailhot, J., J.-P. Simard, and S. Vincent. 1980. "On Est Toujours l'Esquimau de Quelqu'un" [One Is Always the Eskimo of Someone]. *Études/Inuit/Studies* 4 (1–2).

Mailhot, José. 1986. "Beyond Everyone's Horizon Stand the Naskapi." *Ethnohistory* 33 (4): 384–418.

———. 1997. *The People of Sheshatshiu: In the Land of the Innu.* Social and Economic Studies, no. 58. St. John's, NL: ISER.

Marcos, Subcomandante Insurgente. 2001. *Our Word Is Our Weapon: Selected Writings.* Edited by Juana Ponce de Leon. New York: Seven Stories.

Marquardt, Ole. 1999. "A Critique of the Common Interpretation of the Great Socio-Economic Crisis in Greenland, 1850–1880: The Case of Nuuk and Qeqertarsuatsiaat." *Études/Inuit/Studies* 23 (1–2): 9–34.

Martijn, C. A. 1980. "The 'Esquimaux' in the 17th and 18th Century Cartography of the Gulf of St. Lawrence: A Preliminary Discussion." *Études/Inuit/Studies* 4 (1–2).

Martijn, Charles A., and Norman Clermont, eds. 1980. *The Inuit of Southern Quebec—Labrador.* Special Issue, *Études/Inuit/Studies* 4 (1–2).

Maschner, Herbert, Owen Mason, and Robert McGhee. 2009. *The Northern World AD 900–1400.* Salt Lake City: University of Utah Press.

Maschner, Herbert, and Robert McGhee. 2009. "Prologue and Introduction." In *The Northern World AD 900–1400*, edited by Herbert Maschner, Owen Mason, and Robert McGhee, 1–6. Salt Lake City: University of Utah Press.

Mason, Arthur. 2002. "The Rise of an Alaskan Native Bourgeoisie." *Études/Inuit/Studies* 26 (2): 5–22.

Maud, Ralph, and Henry W. Tate. 1993. *The Porcupine Hunter and Other Stories: The Original Tsimshian Texts of Henry W. Tate.* Vancouver: Talonbooks.

McGee, John T. 1961. "Cultural Stability and Change among the Montagnais Indians of the Lake Melville Region of Labrador." PhD diss., Catholic University, Washington, DC.

McGhee, Robert. 1994. "Disease and the Development of Inuit Culture." *Current Anthropology* 35 (5): 565–594.

McGillivray, Anne, and Brenda Comaskey. 1999. *Black Eyes All of the Time: Intimate Violence, Aboriginal Women, and the Justice System*. Toronto: University of Toronto Press.

McGrath, Patrick. 1927. "The Labrador Boundary Dispute." *Geographical Review [Canada]* 17 (4): 643–660.

McLean, John. (1849) 1932. *John McLean's Notes of a Twenty-Five Year's Service in the Hudson's Bay Territory*. Edited by William S. Wallace. Toronto: Champlain Society.

McMillan, L. Jane. 2011. "Colonial Traditions, Co-Optations, and Mi'kmaq Legal Consciousness." *Law and Social Inquiry* 36 (1): 171–200.

Medick, Hans. 1981. "The Protoindustrial Family Economy." In *Industrialization before Industrialization: Rural Industry in the Genesis of Capitalism*, edited by Peter Kriedte, Hans Medick, and Jürgen Schlumbohm; translated by Beate Schempp, 38–73. Cambridge: Cambridge University Press.

Merk, Frederick, ed. (1931) 1968. *Fur Trade and Empire; George Simpson's Journal Entitled Remarks Connected with the Fur Trade in the Course of a Voyage from York Factory to Fort George and Back to York Factory 1824–25, with Related Documents*. Cambridge, MA: Harvard University Press.

Minde, Henry. 2003. "The Challenge of Indiginism: The Struggle for Sami Land Rights and Self-Government in Norway, 1960–1990." In *Indigenous Peoples: Resource Management and Global Rights*, edited by Svein Jentoft, Henry Minde, and Ragnar Nilsen, 75–105. Delft, Netherlands: Eburon.

Moore, Oliver. 2010. "Caribou Crisis in Labrador." *Globe and Mail [Toronto]*, December 23, 2010. http://www.theglobeandmail.com/news/national/caribou-crisis-in -labrador/article1321061/.

Naskapi Indian Band [Quebec]. 2005. *Agreements Database James Bay and Northern Quebec Agreement 1975, 1984, 1990*. Electronic document. http://www.aadnc-aandc.gc.ca /DAM/DAM-INTER-HQ/STAGING/texte-text/jb0507_1100100030831_eng.pdf.

Newfoundland and Labrador. 2002. Memorandum of Agreement concerning the Voisy's Bay Project. July 22. Jane Helleur & Associates Inc.

———. 2005. Final Report, Violence Prevention Initiative: Results and Recommendations of Community Consultations and Provincial Forum: Status of Women, Violence Prevention Initiative, Newfoundland and Labrador House of Assembly. March 21.

Newfoundland and Labrador, Government of. 1974. *Summary of the Report of the Royal Commission on Labrador*. St. John's: Unlisted [Newfoundland Government] [copies in Legislative Library].

———. 1991. *Community Profiles: Aboriginal Communities of Hopedale, Sheshashit, Rigolet, Postville, Nain (Town), Makkovik*. Statistics.

———. 1995. *Toward the Year 2000: The Provincial Strategy against Violence: An Action Plan. Executive Summary*.

———. 2002. *Voisey's Bay Development Agreement. Includes industrial and employment benefits agreement*.

———. 2003. *2002–2003 Annual Report*. Newfoundland and Labrador, Voisey's Bay

Nickel Company Ltd., and INCO Ltd. 2004. Bill 44 An act to ratify and give force of law to the Labrador Inuit Land Claims Agreement. First session, 45th General Assembly, 53 Eliz. II, 2004 Cong., 329. St. John's, NL: Earl Tucker, Queen's Printer.

Newfoundland, Dominion. 1910. *Fishery Report*, Enclosure 3, Medical Report. CO 880-21.

O'Brien, E. J. (Edward Joseph). 1923–1947. Papers [12cm], Photocopy Acquired from Nigel Markham, St. John's, Nfld., 1985, Calendar of the collection by Nigel Markham including biography of O'Brien. Letters and Papers during His Service as Priest to the Indians and Monsignor, Roman Catholic Church of Carbonear. Archival Collections, Centre for Newfoundland Studies, Queen Elizabeth II Library, Memorial University of Newfoundland.

Ommer, Rosemary. 1990. *Merchant Credit and Labour Strategies in Historical Perspective*. Fredericton, NB: Acadiensis.

Pasteen, Tshishenish. [2002?]. *Hard to Say Goodbye to Emish [Voisey's Bay]*. Electronic document. Innu Nation Website. http://www.innu.ca.

Pauktuutit—Inuit Women's Association. 2004. *Nuluaq Project: National Inuit Strategy for Abuse Prevention. Analysis Report: Inuit Healing in Contemporary Inuit Society*. Ottawa Aboriginal Healing Foundation.

————. 2005. *Applying Inuit Cultural Approaches in the Prevention of Family Violence and Abuse. Nuluaq Project: National Inuit Strategy for Abuse Prevention*. Ottawa, Aboriginal Programs Directorate, Department of Canadian Heritage.

Piglia, Robert. 2011. "Theses on the Short Story." *New Left Review* 70:63–66.

Plaice, Evelyn. 1990. *The Native Game: Settler Perceptions of Indian/Settler Relations in Central Labrador*. Social and Economic Studies, no. 40. St. John's, NL: ISER.

————. 2005. "Leemos! Land, Identity, and the Case of the Labrador Metis." Unpublished typescript.

Price, Jacob. 1990. "Conclusion." In *Merchant Credit and Labour Strategies in Historical Perspective*, edited by Rosemary Ommer, 360–373. Fredericton, NB: Acadiensis.

Prichard, H. Hesketh. 1911. *Through Trackless Labrador*. London: William Heinemann.

Ray, Arthur J. 1984. "Periodic Shortages, Native Welfare, and the Hudson's Bay Company, 1670–1930." In *Subarctic Fur Trade*, edited by Shepard Krech III, 1–20. Vancouver: University of British Columbia Press.

Richling, Barnett. 1989. "'Very Serious Reflections': Inuit Dreams about Salvation and Loss in Eighteenth-Century Labrador." *Ethnohistory* 36 (2): 148–169.

Rogers, Edward S. 1973. *The Quest for Food and Furs: The Mistassini Cree, 1953–54*. Publications in Ethnology, no. 5. Ottawa: National Museum of Man.

Ross, C. A., and B. Davis. 1986. "Suicide and Parasuicide in a Northern Canada Native Community." *Canadian Journal of Psychiatry* 31:331–334.

Rowe, Frederick. 1980. *A History of Newfoundland and Labrador*. Toronto: McGraw-Hill Ryerson.

Rowsell, E. R. 1957. Correspondence to E. L. Andrews, Deputy Minister of Public Welfare. May 23. Maritime History Archives, File PF 317 196. Dept. of Public Welfare, Cartwright, Labrador. Stacey Collection, Archives and Manuscripts Division, Queen Elizabeth II Library, Memorial University of Newfoundland.

Ryan, James J. 1988. Economic Development and Innu Settlement: The Establishment of Sheshatshit. Typescript, 22 leaves. Newfoundland Centre, Queen Elizabeth II Library, Memorial University of Newfoundland.

Samson, Colin. 2003. *A Way of Life That Does Not Exist: Canada and the Extinguishment of the Innu.* St. John's, NL: ISER.

Samson, Colin, and Survival International. 1999. *Canada's Tibet—the Killing of the Innu.* London: Survival.

Sarsfield, Peter. 1977. *Report to the Naskapi Montagnais Innu Association and the Labrador Inuit Association regarding the Health Care Delivery System in Northern Labrador.* January 31. Typescript. Newfoundland and Labrador Legislative Library.

Scheffel, David. 1981. "The Demographic Consequences of European Contact with Labrador Inuit, 1800–1919." PhD diss., Memorial University of Newfoundland.

Scheper-Hughes, Nancy. 1992. *Death without Weeping: The Violence of Everyday Life in Brazil.* Berkeley: University of California Press.

Scott, Colin H. 2001. *Aboriginal Autonomy and Development in Northern Quebec and Labrador.* Vancouver: University of British Columbia Press.

Scott, James C. 1985. *Weapons of the Weak: Everyday Forms of Peasant Resistance.* New Haven: Yale University Press.

Sen, Amartya. 1981. *Poverty and Famines: An Essay on Entitlement and Deprivation.* New York: Oxford University Press.

Shkilnyk, Anastasia M. 1985. *A Poison Stronger Than Love: The Destruction of an Ojibwa Community.* New Haven, CT: Yale University Press.

Sider, Gerald M. 1980. "The Ties That Bind: Culture and Agriculture, Property and Propriety in the Newfoundland Village Fishery." *Social History* 5 (1).

———. 1987. "When Parrots Learn to Talk, and Why They Can't." *Comparative Studies in Society and History* 29 (1).

———. 1989. "A Delicate People and Their Dogs: The Cultural Economy of Subsistence Production. A Critique of Chayanov and Meillassoux." *Journal of Historical Sociology* 1 (2).

———. 1993. *Lumbee Indian Histories: Race, Ethnicity and Indian Identity in the Southern United States.* Cambridge: Cambridge University Press.

———. 1996. "The Making of Peculiar Local Cultures." In *Was Bleibt von Marxistischen Perspektiven in der Geschichtsforschung?*, edited by Alf Luedtke. Goettingen, Germany: Vandenhoeck und Ruprecht.

———. (1986) 2003a. *Between History and Tomorrow: Making and Breaking Everyday Life in Rural Newfoundland.* 2nd ed., revised and expanded. Toronto: University of Toronto Press.

———. 2003b. *Living Indian Histories: Lumbee and Tuscarora People in North Carolina.* 2nd ed., revised and expanded. Chapel Hill: University of North Carolina Press.

Smith, Gavin. 2010. "Through a Class, Darkly; but Then Face to Face: Assessing the Potential for Praxis through the Lens of Class." Paper.

Smith, James G. E. 1979. "Indian-Eskimo Relations: An Introduction." *Arctic Anthropology* 16 (2): 1–2.

Speck, Frank G. 1935. *Naskapi: The Savage Hunters of the Labrador Peninsula.* Norman: University of Oklahoma Press.

Status of Women Canada. 2005. *Aboriginal Women's Roundtable on Gender Equality.* Electronic document. http://www.swc-cfc.gc.ca.

Stopp, Marianne P. 2002. "Reconsidering Inuit Presence in Southern Labrador." *Études/Inuit/Studies* 26 (2): 71–106.

———, ed. 2008. *The New Labrador Papers of Captain George Cartwright.* Montreal: McGill-Queen's University Press.

Strong, William D. 1929. "Cross-Cousin Marriage and the Culture of the Northeastern Algonquin." *American Anthropologist* 31 (2): 277–288.

———. 1930. "A Stone Culture from Northern Labrador and Its Relation to the Eskimo-Like Cultures of the Northeast." *American Anthropologist* 32 (1): 126–144.

Sutton, Peter. 2009. *The Politics of Suffering: Indigenous Australia and the End of the Liberal Consensus.* Carleton, Victoria: Melbourne University Publishing.

Tanner, Adrian. 2004. "Aboriginal Social Pathology and the Quebec Cree Healing Movement." Paper. Department of Anthropology, Memorial University of Newfoundland. Published in Lawrence J. Kirmayer, 2009. *Healing Traditions: The Mental Health of Aboriginal Peoples in Canada.* Vancouver: University of British Columbia Press.

Tanner, Adrian, Robin McGrath, and Carol Brice-Bennett. 1997. *"Spirituality" among the Inuit and Innu of Labrador: A Background Report for the Environmental Impact Assessment of the Voisey's Bay Mine and Mill Project.* Electronic document. In *Community Resource Services Ltd., St. John's, NL, on Innu Nation / Mamit Innuat Index.* http://vinl.valeinco.com/eis/chap20/chap20a.htm.

Tanner, Väinö. 1947. *Outlines of the Geography, Life & Customs of Newfoundland-Labrador (the Eastern Part of the Labrador Peninsula) Based Upon Observations Made During the Finland-Labrador Expedition in 1939, and Upon Information Available in the Literature and Cartography.* Cambridge: Cambridge University Press.

Taylor, J. Garth. 1977. "Moravian Mission Influence on Labrador Inuit Subsistence, 1776–1830." In *Approaches to Native History: Papers of a Conference Held at the National Museum of Man, Oct. 1975,* edited by D. A. Muse, 16–29. Ottawa: National Museums of Canada.

———. 1979. "Indian-Inuit Relations in Eastern Labrador, 1600–1976." *Arctic Anthropology* 16 (2): 49–75.

———. 1980. "The Inuit of Southern Quebec-Labrador: Reviewing the Evidence." *Études/Inuit/Studies* 4 (1–2).

Tester, Frank James, and Peter Kulchyski. 1994. *Tammarniit (Mistakes): Inuit Relocation in the Eastern Arctic.* Vancouver: University of British Columbia Press.

Thornton, Patricia. 1990. "The Transition from the Migratory to the Resident Fishery in the Strait of Belle Isle." In *Merchant Credit and Labour Strategies in Historical Perspective,* edited by Rosemary E. Ommer. Fredericton, NB: Acadiensis.

Thwaites, Reuben Gold. 1896. *The Jesuit Relations and Allied Documents.* Vol. 2, *Acadia: 1612–1614.* Cleveland: Burrows Brothers.

———. 1897. *The Jesuit Relations and Allied Documents: Travels and Explorations of the Jesuit Missionaries in New France, 1610–1791.* Cleveland: Burrows Brothers.

Tolnay, Stewart, and E. M. Beck. 1995. *A Festival of Violence: An Analysis of Southern Lynchings, 1882–1930.* Urbana: University of Illinois Press.

Tompkins, Edward. 1988. *Pencilled Out: A Report Prepared for Jack Harris, MP, on the Impact of the Exclusion of Newfoundland and Labrador's Native People from the Terms of Union in 1949.* March 31. Copy on file in the Newfoundland and Labrador Legislative Library, House of Commons, Ottawa.

Toulmin, Stephen. 1958. *The Uses of Argument.* Cambridge: University of Cambridge Press.

Townsend, Charles Wendell. 1910. *A Labrador Spring.* Boston: D. Estes and Co.

Traube, Elizabeth G. 1986. *Cosmology and Social Life: Ritual Exchange among the Mambai of East Timor.* Chicago: University of Chicago Press.

Tremblay, Normand. 1981. *Natalité et Mortalité Chez les Inuit de la Baie d'Ungava (Nouveau-Québec).* Québec: Centre d'études nordiques, Université Laval Collection Nordicana, no. 44.

Trigger, Bruce. 1976. *The Children of Aataentsic: A History of the Huron People to 1660.* Montreal: McGill-Queen's University Press.

———. 1990. *The Huron, Farmers of the North.* 2nd ed. San Francisco: Holt, Rinehart and Winston.

Tuck, James A. 1989. *Red Bay, Labrador: World Whaling Capital A.D. 1550–1600.* St John's, NL: Atlantic Archaeology Limited.

Tucker, Ephraim W. 1839. *Five Months in Labrador and Newfoundland, during the Summer of 1838.* Concord: I. S. Boyd and W. White.

Turgeon, Laurier. 1998. "French Fishers, Fur Traders and Amerindians during the 16th Century." *William and Mary Quarterly 3d Series* 55 (4): 585–610.

Turner, Lucien. 1894. *Ethnology of the Ungava District, Hudson Bay Territory.* Washington, DC: Bureau of American Ethnology. Annual Report, 11, 159–350.

Tyrrell, Joseph B. 1931. *Documents Relating to the Early History of Hudson Bay.* Toronto: Champlain Society.

Vanast, Walter J. 1991. "'Hastening the Day of Extinction': Canada, Quebec, and the Medical Care of Ungava's Inuit, 1867–1967." *Études/Inuit/Studies* 15 (2): 55–84.

White, Colleen A. 2004. *Social Work in Sheshatshiu: A Unique Helping Landscape.* Copy on File in the Newfoundland and Labrador Legislative Library, St. John's, NL.

Whiteley, W. H. 1964. "The Establishment of the Moravian Mission in Labrador and British Policy, 1763–83." *Canadian Historical Review* 45 (1): 29–50.

Widdowson, Frances, and Albert Howard. 2008. *Disrobing the Aboriginal Industry: The Deception behind Indigenous Cultural Preservation.* Montreal: McGill-Queen's University Press.

Williams, G., ed. 1969. *Andrew Graham's Observations on Hudson's Bay. 1767–1794.* London: Hudson's Bay Record Society, Publication 27.

Willis, Paul. 1977. *Learning to Labour.* Farnborough, U.K.: Saxon House.

York, Geoffrey. 1992. *The Dispossessed: Life and Death in Native Canada.* Toronto: Little, Brown (Canada).

INDEX

aboriginal communities, 29; aboriginal status, 107, 195; aboriginal title, 184, 206; aboriginal use and occupancy, 184; aboriginal autonomy, 57; self-government rights, 223

abuse, xii–xiii, 9–10, 15, 17–18, 28, 53, 60, 62, 93, 110, 111, 114, 136, 163, 199, 244, 260n2, 261–62n11; elder abuse, 200, 227, 230, 231. *See also* substance abuse

alcohol, alcoholism, ii, 2, 4–6, 9–10, 56, 67, 80, 85, 126, 203, 211, 217, 232, 253n1, 267n7; and autonomy, 71. *See also* fetal alcohol spectrum disorder

Anderson, Karen, 39, 248

Andrew, Sylvestre, 195

anger, 85, 91, 159, 205, 218; against social work agency, 212; against anthropology, 265

anthropological concepts, xiv, 215, 217, 258–59n23, 261n7, 261–62n11

Argenti, Nicolas, 253n14, 254n3

Armitage, Peter, 194, 201, 202, 266n15

assimilation, 140, 195

Australia, xix, 8, 9, 28–29, 115, 217, 221, 254n4, 256n1, 261n9, 267n2

autonomy, 12, 24, 28–29, 56–66, 71, 86–87, 90, 197, 256n1; productive autonomy, 125–26

Bakie, Maureen, 60

baptized, 77, 187

Barkham, Selma, 40

Barren Ground, barrens, 32–33, 55, 59, 67, 74, 99, 102, 104, 121–22, 146, 156, 194, 197. *See also* Mashua Innu; Naskapi, Nascopie

Basque fishers and whalers, 34–40, 42–43, 50, 79

Baudelaire, Charles, 143

beaver, beaver wars, 63, 73–76, 82–83

Beckett, Jeremy, 221, 254nn3–4

beer, musical beer, 199, 212, 220, 248

Belle Isle, Strait of, 29, 30, 31, 34, 36, 41, 51, 79, 88, 101

Berger, John, xiii, xiv, 108

Black Plague, Black Death, 77, 80, 96–97, 259n28

Boas, Franz, 92–95, 236, 258n23

boy, 11, 119, 128, 149–50, 212–13, 231, 253n2, 262n11. *See also* child, children

Brice-Bennett, Carol, 17, 47, 49, 62, 68, 90, 91, 105, 118, 120, 122–23, 128–29, 148–50, 181, 188, 252n7, 253n1, 255n13, 257n9, 262n15

Briggs, Jeanne, 259n24

British North America Act, 139

bubonic plague. *See* Black Plague, Black Death

bullying, 189, 192–93, 197, 268n7

Byrne, Nympha, 219, 264n2

Canada: and promises, 113, 216, 267–68n7; Upper and Lower, 263–64n23 canoe, canoe travel, 32, 43–45, 48, 78, 101, 118, 119, 202, 219

caribou, 49, 54–56, 63–64, 67, 84, 87, 92, 95, 99, 101–2, 104–5, 118–19, 121–22, 127–28, 146–47, 173, 178, 194; demographic cycles, 255n20, 257nn15–16; laws against hunting, 137, 206. *See also* Barren Ground, barrens

Cartwright, Captain George, 51, 88

cemetery, 161, 205

chaos, xiii, 3–6, 18, 80, 110, 145, 183, 153, 218, 231, 251n8

"chief," 122, 171, 246–47

child, children, xi, xii, 12, 23, 44, 46, 68, 69, 81, 92–96, 102, 130, 160, 163, 166, 175, 179, 209, 245, 249, 258n21; impossibility of protecting, 71, 78, 84, 119, 142, 169, 178, 187, 218, 219; locked out, 213–16; missionary children, 87. *See also* youth

cod, 34, 47, 91, 99, 101, 122, 123, 128, 132, 137, 146, 186–87, 259n32, 264n2

coffee addiction, 5–6, 256n3

coherent, 5, 6, 251n4

colonial, 9, 22, 23, 38, 44, 69, 73–74, 76, 79, 131, 136, 165, 169

Columbus, 40, 93, 255n14

Commission of Government, 138

concentration villages, xii, 107, 148, 166, 181, 192

Confederation of Canada with Newfoundland, 30, 107–8, 133–41, 177, 195, 203, 206, 217, 257n13, 260n2, 261n8, 263n21

Confederation of Newfoundland with Canada, 108, 134–35, 139–40, 184, 193, 263n8; Innu view of, 195–97

confrontation, xix, 3, 8, 9, 13, 40, 93, 181, 191, 244–45, 249, 269n2; Inuit-European, 31, 42, 51–52; Inuit-Moravian, 91, 181; with government policies and practices, 173–78, 230, 233, 268n7; with one's own family, 218–19

contradiction, 17, 22, 42, 47, 48, 51, 140, 176, 184, 253n3; disposable and useful peoples, 170; HBC relations to Eskimos, 126; land-claims process, 183; Moravian trading posts, 88–89

control, uncontrollable, 1, 18, 24, 56, 57, 66, 87, 110, 118, 135, 136; getting "high," 27, 173; HBC, 59–60, 63, 67, 82–83, 100, 123–25,

129–30; Innu and Inuit collective self-control, 70–71, 74–75, 116, 185–86, 205–7, 247, 265n13; Moravian, 28, 46, 49, 67, 89; state, 29, 141, 164, 169–70, 179, 183–84, 191, 196–97, 223, 251n4, 256n1, 261

cope, coping, xii, 13–14, 54, 72, 204

copper, 224

costs and returns of fur trade, 82

credit, 59–65, 81, 256n4, 261n14; HBC, 105, 123, 126, 129–30; Moravian, 102–3, 105, 120–22

Cree, xi, 99, 206, 216, 235n17, 267n7

culture, xiv, 13, 14, 26, 39, 61; and political organization, 221–22; webs of significance, 215, 253n13, 258n23

curious custom, 117

daily life, xii, 56, 61–62, 65–66, 83, 134–35, 137, 145, 210, 218, 221, 231, 235, 249

dangerous, 26, 41, 61, 77, 78, 167, 190, 228, 245

Davis Inlet, 31 (map 1), 104, 118–20, 122, 127–29, 142, 146–47, 173–76, 178, 186–87, 189, 200, 217–18, 224, 255n17

Davis Island Village, 174

Davis Strait, 48

death, 1, 3, 25–26, 28, 66, 68, 69, 70, 72, 81, 88, 97–98, 102, 103–6, 119, 121–22, 130, 161, 166, 168, 191–92, 203, 213, 216, 220, 235, 240–42; for Jesuits, 77–78

democracy, 107, 183, 233, 247, 261n5

dependency, 18, 24, 25, 28, 52, 125, 253n2

Descartes, René, 151

development, 41, 56, 61, 96, 108, 126–27, 134–35, 182–83, 193, 206–7, 209, 220, 224, 226, 257n10, 264n3, 266n1; divergent, 164–65, 203, 230, 265n11; environmental issues, 229, 232; political organization of, 172, 233

dignity, 12, 22, 24, 77, 115, 126, 142–43, 145–53, 166, 189, 205, 221, 233, 241, 243–44

discontinuity, 17, 18

disease and housing, 218, 267n7

displacement, 26–29, 34, 42, 52–53, 57, 165, 253n1, 265n11

disposable, 3, 13, 163, 166–73, 182, 204, 217

dispossession, 26, 230, 253n1

dogs, 33, 49, 87, 98, 102, 106, 113, 116, 122, 129, 146, 149, 245–46

Dombrowski, 14, 72, 170, 172, 265n5

domestic violence, xi, 2, 6, 9–10, 16–19, 60, 85, 111, 125–26, 181, 185, 197, 199–201, 231, 245, 253, 260nn2–3

domination, inconclusive/incoherent, xiii, 5, 6–10, 13–14, 18, 22–24, 27–29, 39, 49, 57, 60, 65–66, 85, 99, 109–10, 114, 129, 143, 165, 173, 179, 181, 183, 240

Dorset, 35–38, 255n10

Du Bois, W. E. B., 108, 109

Dutch fishers, 34, 42, 48, 75, 79, 255n18

elder abuse, 200, 227, 230, 231

elders, 61, 66, 69, 71, 84, 97, 116, 149, 151, 173, 175, 187, 213, 246, 247–49

enthusiasm, 47, 90

environmental assessment, environmental impact, 171, 202, 224–29, 266n21, 268n12

epidemics, xi, xii, 10–12, 39, 50, 54, 60, 66, 70, 76–77, 79–80, 83, 85, 96–98, 101–5, 116, 118, 121–22, 176, 179, 184, 251n1

"Eskimo," making and self-making of, 10, 12, 18, 21–24, 25–57, 60–66, 69–70, 84, 86–98, 101–5, 118–20, 122–26, 130–31, 134, 139–42, 156, 164–65, 171, 183, 186, 188–92, 255n13, 256n2, 258n18, 259n3, 262n15

"Esquimaux Indians," 22, 51; separation of, 38–39, 43–46

everyday life. See daily life

expendable, 163–69

famine, 12–13, 15, 52, 56, 60, 64, 67, 70–71, 80, 83–84, 99, 104, 128, 166, 169, 252n8, 257n10, 257nn15–16, 258n20; and disease, 97–98, 102, 105. See also starvation

fatalism, 70

fetal alcohol spectrum disorder (FASD), 6, 60, 126, 254n3

fieldwork methods, xiii–xv, 92, 112–13, 177, 182–83; and silences in field research, xiv, xv, 15, 19, 20, 21, 109, 182, 252n6; and surprises, xiv–xv, 14–15, 22, 178, 213

fires: forest, 82, 101; home and buildings, 212, 216, 232

fixing, 178–79, 247

flooding, 115, 135, 195–96, 256n20

flour, lard, sugar, tea, 56, 64, 82, 95, 120, 123, 128–29, 262n13

forced relocation, xi, xii, 11, 12, 26, 28, 50, 57, 60, 66, 81, 85, 98, 99, 104, 111, 121, 141, 148,

163, 166, 173–74, 176, 187; and epidemics, xii, 122

Fornel, Sieur Louis, 42–46

Fort Chimo, 31 (map 1), 33, 82–83, 102, 117, 193–94

foster care, 211–12

Fouillard, Camille, 219, 264n2

French treatment of Innu, 76–79

fur, fur trade, xiii, 11, 12, 19, 26, 33, 34; early history, 36, 38, 39

gasoline, xi, 4–5, 10–11, 16, 71, 125, 211, 216–18, 232, 245

Geertz, Clifford, 215

girl. See child, children

governmentality, 183, 186, 254n3

government store, 178, 187–88

Green, Linda, xv, 258n19

Greenland, xiv, 5–6, 35–37, 214, 251n3, 254n9

Gregoir, Pien, 195–97

Grenfell, 103, 129, 181, 185, 189–90, 259n33

Hamilton Inlet, 42, 51, 53, 87–88, 92–94, 132–33, 180, 201

Happy Valley–Goose Bay, xiv, xviii, 133, 155, 161, 179, 199, 201–4, 227

Hebron, 89, 97, 120, 123, 130–32, 186; closed, 166, 187–89, 198, 252n7; epidemics, 102, 104–6

Henriksen, Georg, 67, 104, 122, 146–47

high (from gasoline or alcohol), 4, 7, 10, 27, 217, 235

Hiller, James, 62, 105

historical violence, 1–24

history (as concept), xiii, 25–28, 57, 84–85, 126, 134–35, 137, 150, 165, 215, 217–18, 221

holocaust, 19, 75, 116, 265n10

honey bucket, 173–77

hope, 18, 22, 47, 108–9, 115, 117, 194, 241, 243–44

Hopedale, 70, 99, 102, 104–6, 121–22, 189, 198

houses, housing, xii, 11, 50, 85, 112, 122, 141, 165, 168–69, 174–77, 181

hunting laws, 205, 266n21

Huron, 73, 75–79, 258n1

hydroelectricity, 72, 128, 231

Igloliorte, Heather, xix, 215

Impact Benefits Agreement, 195, 225–27, 232, 266n16

impunity, 114

incoherent. *See* coherent

inconclusive, 19–20, 27, 78, 258n18

"Indian coat hanger," 16, 252n12

inequality, 15, 40, 51, 69, 97, 169–70, 172, 216, 239, 255n13

infant mortality, 69, 218

influenza, 54, 67, 71, 79, 101, 103–4, 121, 184, 259n33

Innis, Harold, 19–20, 257n13

innocence, innocents, 13, 37–38, 97, 180, 214, 238

Innu become "Indians," 25–57, 98–101

Innu Nation, 195, 216, 224–26

Inuit. *See individual topics*

iron, 35–38, 42, 51

iron law of wages, 68–70

Jenness, Diamond, 88, 98, 99, 101, 103, 257n22

Jesuit, 37, 39, 46, 55, 76–79

Killiniq, 30

kindness, 89, 127, 249

Kleivan, Helge, 49, 106, 131

knowing, knowledge, 4, 16, 17, 19–21, 67, 71, 96, 113, 125, 149, 151, 175, 197, 214, 217, 223

Labrador boundary, 30, 137–38; ecology, 29, 31–34, 73

Labrador Inuit Association, 224, 226, 255n1

land claims, 114, 118, 184, 207, 220, 222–26, 265n12

Lassalle, Ferdinand, 68, 257n10

Leacock, Eleanor, 151–52

legal rights (including denial of), 23, 28, 72, 141, 192, 206, 207, 209, 223, 225–26

legitimacy, 114

Levi-Strauss, C., 238–39

life expectancy, 69, 169

longhouses, 53

Low, A. P., 102, 117

low-intensity warfare, 46–47

low-level supersonic flights, 114, 127, 195, 201–5

lying, 11, 113, 177, 188

MacDonald, Gaynor, 28

Maggo, Paulus, 148–50

Mailhot, José, 180

Makkovik, 189, 198–200

manhandling, 130–31

Mashua Innu (current name for Naskapi Innu), 67, 224

Maud, Ralph, 236, 238, 240, 241

McLean, John, 33–34, 83, 99

measles, 54, 67, 71, 79, 97, 102, 104–5, 121

medical services, 67, 185, 190–92

Medikabo, Mathieu, 151–52

memory, memories, 13, 19, 21, 108, 110–12, 116–17, 128, 241

mental health, 155

Metis, 23, 47, 98, 136–37, 180, 255n17

Mingan, 76, 79, 88, 101

mining, 18, 40, 62, 72, 124, 170, 193–94, 207, 213, 220–31, 246, 266n16

modern, modernity, 3, 29, 48, 133, 164–66, 173, 176, 182, 184, 223, 230–31

Mongol expansion, 36

Montagnais, 55–56, 74–77, 82, 101–3, 151, 165, 179, 195, 257n14

Moravian, 2, 12, 18, 26, 28, 46–50, 52–53, 56–57, 60–66, 69–70, 81–92, 94, 96–99, 107, 120, 130, 171, 187–88, 255n13

mortality, 9, 12, 60, 68, 73, 75, 77, 81, 84, 88, 91, 98, 188, 218, 252n8, 259n31

mosquitos, 32, 54

muskeg, 32

Nain, 46, 86, 88, 90, 99, 102–6, 121–22, 129, 131, 148, 155–58, 187–192, 198, 212, 224, 229, 232

names for native peoples, 22

Naskapi, Nascopie, 55–56, 67, 74, 79, 82, 92, 99–100, 102, 104, 111–12, 121, 128, 146–48, 165, 178, 186, 194–97, 256n21. *See also* Mashua Innu

Natuashish, 211, 217, 232

needs, unmet and unmeetable, 7, 14, 17, 20, 26, 47, 49, 55–56, 63–64, 72, 82, 84, 85, 90, 98, 103, 110, 113, 116, 119, 120, 123–25, 128, 169, 172, 190, 192, 199, 207, 214, 218, 233, 239

normal, normalized, 17, 121, 253n13

Norse, 34–38

North West River, 118–19, 120, 127, 133, 142, 176, 179–81

not-yet-past, 25–29, 84

Nutak, 123, 132, 166, 174, 186–87, 198

O'Brien, Father E. J., 118–22, 127–33, 142, 171, 186–87, 219–20, 258n20

Okak, 47, 88, 97–98, 103–6, 122, 186, 198, 259n33
orphans, 219
ought and is, 84

Palliser, Hugh, 52, 54, 255
partial (coping, solutions, violence, understandings), xv, 4, 7, 13–15, 21–22, 27, 47, 108, 130, 194, 205, 210, 247, 252n8, 265n7
passivity, 245
Pearl gasoline, 217
pencilled out, 133–36, 139, 141–42, 263n19
Piglia, Robert, xiii–xiv
political elites, 14, 39, 40, 69, 72, 109, 114, 159, 164, 170–72, 179, 210, 212, 222, 233
pollution, 72, 171, 207, 222, 227, 229, 266n16
porcupine, 55, 101, 128
predictability, 6, 19, 147–48, 203, 213, 220, 227
Price, Jacob, 62, 64
Prichard, Hesketh, 102
priest, 37, 54–56, 76, 77–79, 81, 142, 174–81, 187, 189, 196, 219–20
"primitive," 9, 35, 48, 164–66, 230
promises, 12, 110–13, 116, 167, 169, 174, 176, 178, 204, 216–17, 253n1, 260n2, 263n21
protest, 67, 102, 188, 192, 202, 204–5, 212, 224–25, 229
Psalm 32, 182, 189
posttraumatic stress disorder (PTSD), 110–11, 116, 218

"quaint customs," 117, 261–62n11
Québec, 30, 32, 39, 87, 135, 137–39, 165, 193, 195, 206–7

Red Bay, 34, 41
re-indigenization, 221–22, 253–54n3
relief, 115, 120–23, 128–32, 137–38
relocation, xi, xii, 11–12, 50, 57, 60–61, 66, 85, 98, 111, 113, 126, 140–41, 171, 179, 188, 195–97
reproduction, social reproduction, 17, 36, 68, 70, 72, 153
resettlement, 174, 176, 179
residential schools, 111, 136–37, 178, 210, 263n20
"respect," 124, 145–46, 149, 153, 170, 227, 230–31, 233, 241–44, 247, 263n21
Rich, Joe, 187
Rich, Katie, 225, 232

"riddles," 92–94
rights, 23, 28, 84, 90, 107, 124, 126, 134–36, 139–41, 170, 172–73, 177, 183–84, 192–93, 202, 206–7, 210, 220–26, 230–31, 261n8, 265n8
Rigolet, 189, 198–99
"rod of iron," 59, 67, 83, 100
Royal Commission on Aboriginal Peoples, 148

safe house, 198–200, 213
salmon, 93, 103, 137
Samson, Colin, 218–19, 252n6, 265n9
Sarsfield, Peter, 184–91, 265n13
"savage," 22, 77–78, 86, 240
Schefferville, 193–95, 197
Scheper-Hughes, Nancy, 258n21
schools, residential and village, 6, 81, 89, 111, 136–37, 141–42, 159, 176, 178–79, 194, 210, 217, 219, 231
seals, 5, 26, 33, 35, 37, 44, 47–49, 56, 61–63, 65, 87, 91, 98, 103, 106, 122–24, 127, 129–31, 137, 141, 150, 170
seasonal round, 54
Sedna, xix, 214–15
self-destruction, xii, 2, 9–11, 22, 60–61, 71, 84, 179, 184, 205
Sen, Amartya, 15, 169, 252n8
Seven Years' War (French and Indian War), 76, 87
sewerage, xii, 174–77, 191, 216–17
Sheshatshit, 176, 180–81, 218, 267n3
Sheshatshui, 159–61, 176, 195, 211–12, 218–19, 231
Shkilnyk, Anastasia, 253n1
silence, xv, 15, 19–21, 109–10, 145, 148–51, 153, 182, 188–89, 192, 199–200, 247, 251–52n5
silent violence, 19, 20
Simpson, George G., 59, 67–69, 81, 83, 100
sled dogs, 33, 49, 87, 102, 113, 116, 118, 122, 127, 146, 191
smallpox, 54, 67, 79, 88, 97, 104, 121, 188
Smallwood, J., 135, 193, 195, 196, 219, 224
snowmobiles, 33, 178, 191, 256n20
sociability, 71
social construction, 143, 165, 251n1
social organization, social structure. See anthropological concepts

social reproduction, 70, 83, 124, 145, 157, 164, 167, 175, 178, 181, 201, 209, 214, 215

social work, 172, 174, 177, 199–200, 210–12

Society for the Furtherance of the Gospel, 89

SOS, 20–21

Spanish Flu, 96, 98, 104–5, 107, 109, 113, 116, 121, 133, 188

Speck, Frank, 103

squeeze, 67, 83–84, 103, 121, 130, 140, 260n5, 265n9

stakeholders, 186

starvation, 50, 67–68, 83, 100, 128–29. See also famine

stress, xii, 2, 5, 77, 83, 90–91, 98, 104, 110, 120, 137, 193, 197, 203–4, 218

stroll, 86

Strong, William Duncan, 121, 128

structural violence, 15

struggle, inconclusive struggle, 10, 17, 19–21, 25, 29, 109, 168, 173, 183, 185–86, 188, 207, 211, 223, 230, 244–46, 248–49, 252n10

subsistence, 35, 49, 68, 87, 91, 101, 122, 125, 146, 178, 258n20

substance abuse, 2, 4, 5, 6, 10, 16, 60, 232, 254n3, 264–65n4

suffering, xii, xiii, xix, 1–8, 11–12, 15, 18, 20, 26–28, 60–61, 68, 72, 77–78, 98, 100, 103–4, 109–10, 113, 115, 117, 168–69, 181–82, 192, 200–201, 210, 241, 253n1, 257n12, 261n8, 262n13

suicide, xi, xiii, xix, 2, 9–10, 12, 23, 60, 72, 80, 85, 126, 181, 185, 200, 203, 205, 232, 263n22

survival, 2, 50, 57, 74, 81, 121, 165, 178

syphilis, 50, 80, 103

Taylor, J. Garth, 38

telemedicine, 190

terminal inequalities, 15, 169

Thule, 35–37, 254n9, 254–55n10

Timor, 93–94

tomorrow, 2, 9, 14–17, 47, 59, 66, 68, 70, 95, 108, 125, 132, 151, 153, 168–70, 209–33, 241, 249, 265n9

Tompkins, Edward, 140–41, 263n19

Townley, Zacharias, 191–92

trade, organization of, 65–66

trading posts, 28, 33, 48, 50, 55–56, 63–64, 67,

69, 81–84, 86, 93, 99, 102, 118–23, 126, 128, 132–33, 138, 256n2

tradition, traditional, xi, 11, 50, 57, 59–106, 111, 118, 133, 164, 167, 169, 180, 196, 203, 206, 219, 222; forming and dying simultaneously, 67, 164

traditional ecological knowledge (TEK), 227, 229–31

trapping, 55–56, 61–64, 66–67, 76, 93–96, 122–25, 127, 132, 166, 194; trapping territories and encroachment, 118–20, 127, 130, 133, 135, 141, 174–75, 193, 202, 224

Traube, Elizabeth, 93

trauma (and PTSD), 230

"truck," Truck Act of 1831, 29, 59–60, 62–65

Truth and Reconciliation, 107, 136, 263n20

tuberculosis (TB), xii, 12, 50, 54, 80–81, 105, 119, 141, 176, 184, 188, 258n19

typhoid, 102

unbefriended, 122

Ungava, 30, 32–34, 69, 74, 76, 79, 81–83, 99, 103, 137

Utshimassits, 195, 218

Valery, Paul, 19

veterans, 2–3, 19, 110, 218, 248

Viking, 35, 131

Voisey's Bay, 104, 121, 220, 224–30

vulnerable, vulnerability, 3, 8, 12, 20, 27, 29, 37, 39, 56, 75, 103, 113, 122, 125, 170, 179, 214, 245, 260–61n5, 261n9, 264n24

warrior, 36, 235–49

welfare, 72, 119, 123, 133–34, 139–41, 178–79, 233; welfare state, 8

whales, whaling, 31, 34–44, 47–56, 62, 79, 81, 86, 88, 90–91

White, Colleen, 210–12

White Plague, 96, 98, 104

women, women's rights, 6, 39, 44, 47, 66, 69, 71, 90, 99, 102, 104, 111, 117, 119, 125, 128, 132, 150, 156, 197–201, 203, 219, 227, 232–33, 240–42, 247–49

wrong, 17, 19, 71, 85, 114, 125, 137, 173, 237, 240

youth, xi, xii, xix, 2, 4, 10, 23, 60, 85, 116, 136, 150, 155, 160, 166, 172, 173, 200, 211–12, 216–17, 231–32, 242–43, 260n3, 263n21. See also boy; child, children